D1010667

Encounter with Books

a guide to Christian reading
edited by Harish D. Merchant

Inter-Varsity Press
Downers Grove, Illinois 60515

Second printing, November 1971

*Inter-Varsity Press
is the book publishing division
of Inter-Varsity Christian Fellowship.*

ISBN 0-87784-862-9

Library of Congress Catalog Card Number: 74-98503

Printed in the United States of America

Now may this little book a blessing be
To those who love this little book and me
And may its buyer have no cause to say
His money is but lost and thrown away.
John Bunyan, *Pilgrim's Progress,* Part Two

contents

section number	section title	contributors	page number
	Table of Contents		vii
	List of Contributors		xi
	List of Abbreviations		xvii
	Preface	Harish D. Merchant	xxiii
1	**Bible**		
	Introduction	Keith Crim	1
1A	Texts and Translations	F. F. Bruce	1
1BA	Commentaries, Dictionaries and Reference Books: Old Testament	Samuel J. Schultz	6
1BB	Commentaries, Dictionaries and Reference Books: New Testament	Merrill C. Tenney and Harish D. Merchant	15
1C	Study Guides	Harish D. Merchant	22
1D	Interpretation	A. Berkeley Mickelsen	25
1EA	Archaeology and Geography: Old Testament	Charles F. Pfeiffer	28
1EB	Archaeology and Geography: New Testament	W. J. Martin	31
1F	Inspiration and Authority	Bernard Ramm	33
2	**Christian Doctrine**		
	Introduction	Clark H. Pinnock	39
2A	General	Philip E. Hughes	40
2B	God and Creation	Harold B. Kuhn	44
2C	Man and Sin	Fred H. Klooster	46
2D	Person and Work of Christ	G. W. Grogan	48
2E	Salvation and Sanctification	M. Eugene Osterhaven	52
2F	Holy Spirit	John F. Walvoord	56
2G	Christ and Fellowship	William C. Robinson and Robert P. Roth	57

2H	Last Things	William M. Arnett	59
3	**Christian Witness**		
	Introduction	C. Stacey Woods	67
3A	History of Church	Joel L. Samuels	67
3B	Creeds and Denominations	John H. Gerstner	71
3C*	Evangelism	Harish D. Merchant	
3D	Missions	H. Wilbert Norton	72
3E	Non-Christian Religions	James W. Reapsome	76
4	**Christian Life**		
	Introduction	Calvin Malefyt	83
4A	Biography, Journals and Autobiography	Joseph Bayly	83
4B	Family and Marriage	Dwight H. Small	87
4C	Christian Classics	Paul M. Bechtel, Joseph C. Holbrook, Jr., Harish D. Merchant	92
4D	Hymns and Psalms	J. B. MacMillan	97
5	**Christian Ethics**		
	Introduction	J. Oliver Buswell, Jr.	103
5A	Sex, Morality and Conduct	Robert K. Bower	103
5B	Social Responsibility	David O. Moberg	107
5C	Urban Society	David S. Schuller	111
5D	Poverty and Hunger	James W. Reapsome	113
5E	Racial Conflict and War	Jaymes P. Morgan, Jr.	115
5F	Fellowship and Group Dynamics	Ivan J. Fahs	117
6	**Defense of the Faith**		
	Introduction	Harold Lindsell	123
6A	General	Gordon R. Lewis	123
6B	Philosophy	Arthur F. Holmes	127
6C	Liberalism	Kenneth Hamilton	131
6D	Nature of Physical Universe	David L. Dye	136
6E	Science and Technology	Richard H. Bube	139
6F	Education	J. Marion Snapper	141
6G	Psychiatry and Medicine	E. Mansell Pattison	145
6H	Psychology and Counseling	Harold I. Haas	150
6I	Journalism	McCandlish Phillips	153
6J	Political Science	Samuel Richey Kamm	155
6K	Economics	David O. Moberg	161
6L	Roman Catholicism	Herbert M. Carson	164
6M	Modern Cults and Sects	Anthony A. Hoekema	167
7	**Humanities and the Arts**		
	Introduction	Frank E. Gaebelein	173
7A	Fiction	Charles Huttar	173
7B1	Non-Fiction (Twentieth-Century)	S. Barton Babbage	180

7B2	Non-Fiction (Early)	Daryl Adrian	186
7C	Poetry	Clyde S. Kilby	189
7D	History	C. Gregg Singer	191
7E	Culture	Gwyn Walters	194
7F1	Drama	Nancy M. Tischler	196
7F2	Theater	George Ralph	199
7F3	Films	S. Summers and Harish D. Merchant	201
7F4	Television	Haddon W. Robinson	206
7F5	Dance	Katherine Iverson	207
7F6	Cartoons	Robert L. Short	210
7G1	Christianity in the Arts: Painting and Related Media	Harish D. Merchant and Ellen Clinkenbeard	212
7G2	Christianity in the Arts: Architecture	Donald J. Bruggink	220
7H	Church Architecture	Donald J. Bruggink and Stephen S. Smalley	223
7I	Music	J. Buchanan MacMillan	227
7J	Composers	J. Buchanan MacMillan	231
7K	Jazz and Pop	William Robert	235
7L*	Recorded Classics	Harish D. Merchant	
8*	Library of Children's Books	Gladys Hunt	
	Author Index		241

*Appears in the Supplement (see p. xxv) as a list of references without annotations.

contributors

name	affiliation	subsection(s)
Daryl Adrian	Assistant Professor of English, Ball State University	7B2
William M. Arnett	Professor of Christian Doctrine, Asbury Theological Seminary	2H
S. Barton Babbage	Vice-President, Gordon Conwell School of Theology	7B1
Joseph Bayly	Managing Editor, David C. Cook Publishing Company	4A
Paul M. Bechtel	Professor of English, Wheaton College	4C
Robert K. Bower	Professor of Practical Theology and Pastoral Counseling, Fuller Theological Seminary	5A
F. F. Bruce	Rylands Professor of Biblical Criticism and Exegesis, University of Manchester	1A
Donald J. Bruggink	Associate Professor of Historical Theology, Western Theological Seminary	7G2, 7H
Richard H. Bube	Professor of Materials Science and Electrical Engineering, Stanford University	6E

J. Oliver Buswell, Jr.	Professor of Systematic Theology, Covenant Theological Seminary	5
Herbert M. Carson	Minister, Bangor Baptist Church, Bangor, Ireland	6L
Ellen Clinkenbeard	Artist, Freeland, Michigan	7G1
Keith Crim	Book Editor, John Knox Press	1
David L. Dye	Chief Scientist, Trees Facility, Air Force Special Weapons Center, Kirtland A.F.B., New Mexico	6D
Ivan J. Fahs	Director, Vision and Visual Manpower Survey, University of Minnesota	5F
Frank E. Gaebelein	Headmaster Emeritus, The Stony Brook School	7
John H. Gerstner	Professor of Theology, Pittsburgh Theological Seminary	3B
G. W. Grogan	Lecturer in Dogmatic Theology, London Bible College, England	2D
Harold I. Haas	Professor of Psychology, Concordia Senior College	6H
Kenneth Hamilton	Associate Professor of Systematic Theology, University of Winnipeg	6C
Anthony A. Hoekema	Professor of Systematic Theology, Calvin Theological Seminary	6M
Joseph C. Holbrook	Minister, Denver, Colorado	4C
Arthur F. Holmes	Professor of Philosophy, Wheaton College	6B
Philip E. Hughes	Professor of Historical Theology, Gordon Conwell School of Theology	2A

Gladys Hunt	Writer, Ann Arbor, Michigan	8
Charles Huttar	Professor of English, Hope College	7A
Katherine Iverson	Instructor in Physical Education and Dance, University of Redlands	7F5
Samuel Richey Kamm	Professor of History and Social Science, Wheaton College	6J
Clyde S. Kilby	Professor of English, Wheaton College	7C
Fred H. Klooster	Professor of Systematic Theology, Calvin Theological Seminary	2C
Harold B. Kuhn	Professor of Philosophy of Religion, Asbury Theological Seminary	2B
Gordon R. Lewis	Professor of Systematic Theology and Christian Philosophy, Conservative Baptist Theological Seminary	6A
Harold Lindsell	Editor, *Christianity Today*	6
J. Buchanan MacMillan	Professor of Music History and Theory, Nyack Missionary College	4D, 7I, 7J
Calvin Malefyt	Minister, University Reformed Church, Ann Arbor, Michigan	4
W. J. Martin	Professor of Hebrew and Ancient Semitic Languages, University of Liverpool	1EB
Harish D. Merchant	Associate Professor of Materials Science, University of Toledo	1BB, 1C, 3C, 4A, 4C, 7F3, 7G1, 7L

A. Berkeley Mickelsen	Professor of New Testament Interpretation, Bethel Theological Seminary	1D
William Robert Miller	Editor, Cambria Press, New York, New York	7K
David O. Moberg	Professor of Sociology, Marquette University	5B, 6K
Jaymes P. Morgan, Jr.	Instructor in Systematic Theology, Fuller Theological Seminary	5E
H. Wilbert Norton	Professor of Missions, Wheaton College	3D
M. Eugene Osterhaven	Albert C. Van Raalte Professor of Theology, Western Theological Seminary	2E
E. Mansell Pattison	Assistant Professor and Coordinator for Social and Community Psychiatry, University of Washington	6G
Charles F. Pfeiffer	Professor of Ancient Literatures, Central Michigan University	1EA
McCandlish Phillips	Reporter, *The New York Times*	6I
Clark H. Pinnock	Professor of Systematic Theology, Trinity Evangelical Divinity School	2
George Ralph	Assistant Professor and Associate Director of Theater, Hope College	7F2
Bernard Ramm	Professor of Systematic Theology, California Baptist Theological Seminary	1F
James W. Reapsome	Journalist, East Petersburg, Pennsylvania	3E, 5D

Haddon W. Robinson	Associate Professor of Practical Theology, Dallas Theological Seminary	7F4
William C. Robinson	Professor of Historical Theology, Columbia Theological Seminary	2G
Robert P. Roth	Dean of the Graduate School, Northwestern Lutheran Theological Seminary	2G
Joel L. Samuels	Librarian, Trinity Evangelical Divinity School	3A
David S. Schuller	Associate Director, American Association of Theological Schools	5C
Samuel J. Schultz	Professor of Bible and Theology, Wheaton College	1BA
Robert L. Short	Writer, Evanston, Illinois	7F6
C. Gregg Singer	Professor of History, Catawba College	7D
Dwight H. Small	Minister, Peninsula Covenant Church, Redwood City, California	4B
Stephen S. Smalley	Senior Lecturer in New Testament, University of Ibadan, Nigeria	7H
J. Marion Snapper	Professor of Education, Calvin College	6F
S. Summers	Director, The St. Clement's Film Association	7F3
Merrill C. Tenney	Dean of the Graduate School, Wheaton College	1BB
Nancy M. Tischler	Associate Professor of English and Humanities, Pennsylvania State University	7F1

Gwyn Walters	Professor of Ministry, Gordon Conwell Theological Seminary	7E
John F. Walvoord	President, Dallas Theological Seminary	2F
C. Stacey Woods	General Secretary, International Fellowship of Evangelical Students	3

abbreviations

AAB	Ann Arbor Books		BAB	Bantam Books
AAK	Alfred A. Knopf		BAG	Bagster
AB	Acme Books		BAIB	Bailey Brothers
ABMJ	American Board of Mission to Jews		BAR	Barrie and Rockliffe
			BAT	Batsford
ABP	Abingdon Press		BB	Basic Books
ABS	American Bible Society		BBC	British Books Center
AC	Abingdon-Cokesbury		BBH	Baker Book House
ACB	A. and C. Black		BEF	Bethany Fellowship
ACC	Appleton-Century-Crofts		BENB	Benziger Brothers
AFIP	Audio Films-Ideal Pictures, 10 Fisk Place, Mt. Vernon, New York 10550		BEP	Bedminster Press
			BETP	Bethany Press
			BFBS	British and Foreign Bible Society
AHPC	American Heritage Publishing Society		BH	Bodley Head
AIC	Art Institute of Chicago		BHC	B. Herder and Company
AL	Allenson		BHP	Beacon Hill Press
ALBA	Alba		BICA	Bible Institute Colportage
ALP	Aldine Publishing		BK	Black
ALTA	Alec Tiranti		BKIE	Blackie
AMEL	American Elsevier		BL	Blackwell
AMSP	AMS Press		BLES	Bles
ANB	Anchor Books		BM	Bobbs-Merrill
AP	Penguin Books		BN	Barnes and Noble
APH	Augsburg Publishing House		BO	Burns and Oates
ARCH	Archon		BP	Beacon Press
ARM	A. R. Mowbray		BPC	Block Publishing Company
ARMH	Academy of Religion and Mental Health		BR	Broadman
			BRAN	Brandon, 221 West 57 St., New York 10019
ARP	Archabbey Press			
AS	Assemblies		BRL	Brill Leoden
ASP	Association Press		BRO	Brokie
ATH	Atheneum		BRP	Brockhampston P.
ATL	Atlantic-Little		BRUP	Bruce Publishing
AU	Allen and Unwin		BT	Bible Truth
AUP	Augsberg Press		BTB	Back to the Bible

BTT	Banner of Truth Trust	CYC	Christian Youth Cinema, 277 Keswick Ave., Glenside, Pennsylvania 19038
B.W.P.	Black and White Plates		
CA	Capricorn		
CAL	John Calder	d	Pence
CAPE	Cape	DASP	Dallas Seminary Press
CAS	Cassel	DC	Doubleday and Company
CAUP	Cambridge University Press	DE	Dell
CBRP	Church Book Room Press	DEC	Denison and Company
CC	Chilton Company	DEL	Delisle
CENT	Centenary	DES	Dean and Son
CET	Charles E. Tuttle	DEU	Deutsch
CHAP	Channel Press	DGG	Deutsch Grammophon Gesselschaft
CHP	Collins and Harvill Press		
CHP	Church Pastoral	DI	Dial
CHPU	Christian Publishing	DLT	Darton, Longman and Tod
CI	China Inland	DO	Dover
CK	Carey Kingsgate	DOB	Dobson
CL	Christian Literature	DODD	Dodd-Mead
Cl	Cloth	DOR	Doron
CLA	Clarke	DS	Deveon S.
CLC	Christian Literature Crusade	DSP	Duell, Sloan and Pearce
		DUC	Duckworth and Company
CLCP	Covenant Life Curriculum Press	DUF	Dufour
		DUP	Duke University Press
CLP	Claredon Press	EB	Edward Brothers
CM	Collier-Macmillan	EB	Ernest Bonn
CMS	Christian Medical Society	ED	Edition
CNP	Clarkson N. Potter	(ed.)	editor
CO	Collins	EDEN	Eden
COAL	Continental 16, 241 East 34 St., New York 10016	EP	Epworth Press
		EPD	E. P. Dutton
COL	Collier	ES	Eyre and Spottiswoode
COLP	Columbia University Press	ET	English Translation
COM	Coward-McCann	et al.	and others
CON	Concordia	EUP	English University Press
CONT	Contemporary Film, 267 West 25 St., New York 10001	EV	Evanston
		EVL	Everyone's Library
		EVP	Evangelical Press
COUS	Cousino, 1941 Franklin Ave., Toledo, Ohio 43624		
C.P.	Color Plates	FA	Folklore Association
CP	Craig Press	FAT	F. A. Thorpe
CPC	Chandler Publishing Company	FAW	Fawcett
		FAWI	Faith at Work Inc.
CR	Crusade	FB	Falcon Books
CRE	Cresset	FER	Fertig
CRIB	Criterion Books	FF	Faber and Faber
CRO	Crown	FO	Fontana
CS	Constable	FOB	Foundation Books
CSS	Charles Scribner's Sons	FP	Fortress Press
CSY	Constable Young	FR	Friendship
CUP	Cornell University Press	FRP	Free Press
CW	Chatto and Windus	FSB	Four Square Books

FSG	Farrar, Stauss and Giroux		IVP	Inter-Varsity Press
FW	Funk and Wagnalls			
			JC	James Clarke
GAL	Gallancy		JEN	Jenkins
GALX	Galaxy		JH	John Hopkins
GB	George Braziller		JKP	John Knox Press
GC	Garden City		JM	J. Murray
GC	Geoffrey Chapman		JMD	J. M. Dent
GL	Gospel Light		JP	Judson Press
GOL	Gollancz		JPSA	Jewish Publishing Society
GP	Grove Press			of America
GPP	G. P. Putnam		JTS	Jewish Theological
GRO	Grosset			Seminary
GRS	Graphic Society		JUP	Julian Press
GS	G. Schirmer		JW	John Wiley
HA	Harcourt, Brace and World		KCP	King's Crown Press
HAI	Harry Abrams Inc.		KJV	King James Version
HALE	Hale		KR	Kregel
HAR	Harrap			
HARV	Harvill		LA	Living Age
HAS	Harrison Trust		LAK	Lakeland
HAS	Hastings		LB	Little, Brown
HAW	Hawthorn Books		LC	Lippincott Company
Hb	Hardback		LITP	Liturgical Press
HCTI	Hebrew Christian		LO	Longmans
	Testimony to Israel		LOB	Loizeaux Brothers
HE	Herald		LOG	Longmans, Green
HEE	Heinemann Education		LP	Library Publishers
HEW	H. E. Walters		LSUP	Louisiana State University
HH	Herder and Herder			Press
HHA	H. Hamilton		LU	Lutterworth
HHP	Hillary House Publishing			
HM	Houghton-Mifflin		MACD	MacDonald
HO	Hogarth		MAG	MacGibbon
HOM	Horace Marshall		MAGN	Magnas
HP	Humanities Press		MAY	Mayflower
HR	Henry Regnery		MB	Mercury Books
HRP	Harper and Brothers		MC	McMillan
HRW	Holt, Rinehart and Winston		MCL	McLeod
HS	Hodder and Stoughton		ME	Methuen
HU	Hutchinson		MEB	Meridian Books
HUM	Humphries		MENT	Mentor Books
HUP	Harvard University Press		MER	Mercier
HWD	Hill and Wang Dramabook		MG	Morehouse-Gorham
			MH	McGraw Hill
Illus.	Illustration		mins.	Minutes
IND	Indiana		MIS	Moody Institute of Science,
IP	Independent Press			12000 E. Washington Blvd.,
IR	Irvin			Whittier, California
ISUP	Iowa State University Press		MJ	M. Joseph
IUP	International Universities		ML	Modern Library
	Press			

MMM	Mass Media Ministries, 2116 N. Charles St. Baltimore, Maryland 21218
MMS	Marshall, Morgan and Scott
MO	Mowbray
MOR	Morrow
MP	Moody Press
MSCP	Michigan State University Press
MU	Murray
MUP	Muhlenberg Press
MUS	Musson
NAL	New American Library
NBS	Neighborhood Bible Studies
NCC	National Council of Churches
ND	New Direction
NE	Nelson
NEL	New English Library
NGS	National Geography Society
NI	Nisbet
NICNT	New International Commentary on New Testament
NOP	Nonesuch Press
NP	Newman Press
NYGS	New York Graphic Society
NYUP	New York University Press
OB	Oliver and Boyd
ODP	Odessey Press
OL	Oliphants
OM	Overseas Mission
(OoP)	Out of Print
OPC	Orthodox Presbyterian Church
OUP	Oxford University Press
OW	Owen
P.	Plates
PAB	Pantheon Books
PAH	Paul Hamlyn
PAP	Patern Press
PAUP	Paulist Press
Pb	Paperback
PB	Phoenix Books
PBH	Paper Book House
PD	P. Davies
PE	Penguin
PEBS	Protestant Episcopal Book Society

PEL	Pelican
PEP	Peter Pauper
PGPC	Presbyterian Guardian Publishing Corporation
PH	Prentice-Hall
PHAP	Phaiden Press
PHI	Prentice-Hall International
PI	Pickering and Inglis
PIS	Piper S.
PJ	Parry, Jackman
PJK	P. J. Kennedy
PL	Philosophical Library
POB	Pocket Books
pp.	pages
PP	Paternoster Press
PRA	Praeger
PRC	P. Reilly Company
PRPC	Presbyterian and Reformed Publishing Company
PS	Peter, Smith
PSUP	Pennsylvania State University Press
PTS	Protestant Truth Society
PUP	Princeton University Press
PUT	Putnam
RAIN	Rainbird G.
RE	Revised Edition
REG	Regnery
REGE	Regel Books
REI	Reiner
REV	Revell
RH	Random House
Ri	Reissued
RIV	Rivington
RM	Rand McNally
RO	Routledge
RP	Ronald Press
RR	Russell and Russell
RSV	Revised Standard Version
RTS	Religious Tract Society
RV	Revised Version
RY	Rylee
s	Shilling
SAGP	St. Anthony Guild Press
SAP	St. Andrew Press
SBL	Society of Bible Literature
SCH	Schocken
SCMP	Student Christian Movement Press
SCP	Sutton Courtenay Press
SEYP	Seymour Press

SGM	Scripture Gift Mission
SH	Shaw
SHE	Sheed
SHP	Shakespeare Head Press
SHOE	Shoe
SKI	Skira
SM	St. Martins
SO	Soron
SP	Seabury Press
SPCK	Student Propagation for Christian Knowledge
SPP	Scripture Press Publishing
SS	Simon, Schuster
SU	Scripture Union
SUP	Syracuse University Press
SV	Studio Vista
SW	Secker and Warburg
SWP	Southwestern Publishing
TA	Tavistock
TAP	Talbott Press
TAPR	The Architectural Press
TFP	The Faith Press
TH	Thames and Hudson
THS	The Hymn Society
TIME	Time
TN	Thomas Nelson
TNS	Thomas Nelson Sons
TNTC	Tyndale New Testament Commentary
TP	Tyndale Press and Inter-Varsity Fellowship
TPL	The Philosophical Library
TRA	Translantic
TTC	T. T. Clark
TUD	Tudor
TW	Transworld
TWPC	The World Publishing Company
TYC	Thomas Y. Crowell
UB	University Books
UCP	University of Chicago Press
UCPH	United Church Publishing House
UFP	University of Florida Press
UL	University of London
UMIP	University of Michigan Press
UMP	University of Minnesota Press
UNCP	University of North Carolina Press
UND	University of Notre Dame

UOCP	University of California Press
V.	Volume
(VE)	Various Editions
VI	Vintage
VIN	Vingatens
VIP	Viking Press
VKP	Van Kampen Press
VP	Victory Press
(VT)	Various Translations
WA	Walck
WAR	Warne
WAR	Wartburg
WAT	Watts
WAWC	W. A. Wilde Company
WB	Ward, Lock
WB	Word Books
WBE	William B. Eerdmans
WC	Westminster Commentary
WDP	World Dominion Press
WH	William Hunt
WICK	Wycliffe Press
WN	Weidenfeld
WP	Westminster Press
WPC	World Publishing Company
WS	Woodfield and S.
WSP	Washington Square Press
WUL	World University Library
WW	World Works
WWN	W. W. Norton
WYB	Wyvern Books
YUP	Yale University Press
ZPH	Zondervan Publishing House
ZW	Zwemmer

preface

The aim of this book is simple: to aid in finding a profitable path through the endlessly growing jungle of books. I hope it will acquaint Christians with the range of published literature and help them build sound reading habits. Its primary appeal is to secular college and theological students, ministers, and laymen. Although scholars may use it occasionally for advanced research, they are likely to feel its limited scope.

I hesitate to call the book a bibliography, because it is not an exhaustive and indiscriminate listing of references prepared by those trained only in library science. From a virtually inexhaustible maze of books, a few representative ones are selected and discussed by those who are acquainted with them. The comments are written in a spirit of freedom: "here are some books I have enjoyed." Hence, I prefer to call it a "guide."

The Guide has been written within the framework of the historic evangelical Protestant tradition rooted in wholehearted obedience to the authority of the Scriptures. This does not mean, however, that all the books discussed are "safe" or "sound." Even though some works may appear radical or may have unacceptable theological presuppositions, they often contain a wealth of factual data or much needed provocative intellectual stimuli. Their inclusion is not intended to lead some astray but to make their reading experience flexible and well-rounded.

A quick glance at the Table of Contents gives an indication of the scope of the project. It was arrived at only after prolonged discussions with several friends and others whom I esteem "to be in the know" as far as books are concerned. It will be noticed that the term "books" is used in the broadest sense, for films and records are also included.

A British publication, *A Guide to Christian Reading* (edited by A. F. Wallis and published by Inter-Varsity Fellowship, 1961, 157 pp., 6s 6d), was of much help. In some areas, such as science or inspiration of the Scriptures, considerable evangelical literature exists. In other areas, such as journalism or dance, one has difficulty finding even a single book written from the evangelical point of view. The inclusion of these latter sections is intentional; perhaps some Christians will pioneer in formulating a unified point of view for these areas.

The Guide is divided into eight sections. A short introduction to the subject opens each section. All sections, except the eighth, are further divided into subsections. Each subsection introduces a specific subject and discusses, one at a time, ten or more books.

The annotation of each book indicates its content, literary style, significance to the broader field, audience (beginners or advanced readers), and doctrinal viewpoint (evangelical or shades of liberal). The entries within each section or subsection are arranged either chronologically or in order of increasingly difficult subject matter. This allows the reader to *encounter the books* within the specific area in continuously flowing commentary. Where neither of the above two arrangements is possible, the entries are arranged alphabetically by the author's last name.

This is essentially an American book. However, an attempt has been made to make it useful to those in the sterling areas. If the book referred to is published on either side of the Atlantic, the entry indicates both U.S. and British publishers. The referred book may be hardbound or paperback, but is readily available through U.S. or British booksellers. In exceptional cases significant out-of-print publications are included, but are so indicated. In the event that much of the published material on a subject is in the form of magazine or journal articles, they are included sparingly.

In the interest of saving space, most of the book references are abbreviated. Those who intend to use the Guide extensively should try to understand the abbreviation procedure. The use of the Table of Abbreviations which follows this preface will clarify each entry. For example:

Hughes, H. P., ed., *The Moffats* (ET), 2 V., HRP, RE, 1968, 439 pp.,
Hb $5.50, Pb $1.75; SCMP, 1960, Hb 16s; PE, 1966, Pb 5s (VE).

This means that the book, *The Moffats* edited (ed.) by H. P. Hughes, is available in English translation (ET) in two volumes (2 V.) in a revised edition (RE) published by Harper and Row (HRP) in 1968. The 439-page work may be bought in hardback format (Hb) at $5.50 and in paperback format (Pb) at $1.75 for both volumes. The book was published in Great Britain by Student Christian Movement Press (SCMP) in 1960 in the hardback format at 16s and by Penguin Books (PE) in 1966 in paperback format at 5s. Various other editions (VE) of the book are also available.

Putting together the Guide has been essentially a cooperative project, my job being limited to planning and coordinating. I must confess, however, that even so the job turned out to be much more than I bargained for when I volunteered initially. I suspect this has been the experience of most contributors who, with very little reward, agreed to help. To quote a letter which accompanied a completed manuscript, "You are a fine friend, but you surely make me work hard. Sing Hallelujah when you receive this manuscript, will you? It represents about 100 hours of labor, sweat and tears!"

My great concern has been to keep the Guide from becoming a mere list. A useful by-product of this project is, however, a list of booklets and records published separately as a supplement to the present book (*Bibliography on Booklets, Paperbacks and Records* by Inter-Varsity Press $1.00). The Table of Contents and the Author Index which appear in this volume are common to the major work as well as the supplement.

The present volume is not a mere list. I have tried to impart cohesiveness and structural unity to the contributions of sixty-seven persons so that it will become an "encounter" for those who use it. To do this, I have occasionally invoked my editorial prerogatives in adding to or deleting from some contributions or in combining or splitting from others. The drastic changes, however, have been few.

I have added one or more book references at the end of some annotations as "see also." The editor's hand has also been at work in the subsections 1BB, 4A, 4C, 7F3, and 7G1, which explains the appearance of my name along with that of the contributor. The asterisk (*) after the entry number indicates a book especially recommended by the editor.

Needless to say, I like to read and do so extensively. Here are some books that have made a significant impact on my own thought and life. Most of them may be found discussed in the Guide through the Author

Index. They do not, of course, constitute a suggested reading program.

J.S. Bach, *Passion According to St. Matthew* (Recording)
John Baillie, *Our Knowledge of God*
R. H. Bainton, *Here I Stand—A Life of Luther*
Ludwig von Beethoven, *Quartets for Strings, Nos. 1-16* (Recordings)
G. C. Berkouwer, *Man: The Image of God*
Dietrich Bonhoeffer, *Life Together*
K. G. Boon, *Rembrandt, the Complete Etchings*
Peter Bura, *Van Gogh*
E. J. Carnell, *The Kingdom of Love and the Pride of Life*
Oscar Cullmann, *Christ and Time*
Francois deFenelon, *Christian Perfection*
Elizabeth Elliot, *Shadow of the Almighty*
M. K. Gandhi, *An Autobiography*
O. Hallesby, *Prayer*
Dag Hammarskjöld, *Markings*
T.C. Hammond, *In Understanding Be Men*
Olov Hartman, *Holy Masquerade*
C. S. Lewis, *Christian Reflections*
C. S. Lewis, *A Grief Observed*
Paul Little, *How to Give Away Your Faith*
J. G. Machen, *What is Faith?*
D. O. Moberg, *Inasmuch*
Leon Morris, *Cross in the New Testament*
John Owen, *The Glory of Christ*
Michael Polanyi, *Personal Knowledge*
Francis Poulenc, *Gloria* (Recording)
Michael Quoist, *Prayers*
J. A. T. Robinson, *Honest to God*
J. C. Ryle, *Holiness*
Charles Schultz, *Peanuts* (Several paperbacks in continuing series)
Irving Stone, *Agony and Ecstacy*
J. R. W. Stott, *The Baptism and Fullness of the Holy Spirit*
Paul Tournier, *The Meaning of Persons*
A. W. Tozer, *Knowledge of the Holy*
A. W. Tozer, *Pursuit of God*

Four women have borne the major burden of secretarial and clerical details and more or less have carried the heat of the day. Without their dedication and gracious care this book could not have been brought to completion. Mrs. Barbara Smoll, my past student, typed what appeared to be an endless flow of manuscripts while attending to a family of five. Miss Jeanne Barnard, also my student, spent day and night researching bibliographic information in the library while preparing to graduate and to leave for a summer in Europe. Miss Pat Laughlin attended to the cataloging, proofreading, and indexing problems associated with the book. The Author Index at the end of the book is largely her work. Mrs. Georgia Wright, on the University secretarial staff, typed correspondence with the contributors. Finally, I would like to acknowledge direction and encouragement provided by Mr. James Nyquist, Director of Inter-Varsity Press, from very early stages of the project.

H. D. Merchant
University of Toledo

section 1
BIBLE

1. BIBLE: INTRODUCTION
Keith Crim

The Bible has always been the supreme book for Christians, because here, and only here, we have God's revelation of what he is like and what he requires us to do. The Bible is a book of great variety, containing many kinds of writings, but in all parts of the Bible, from beginning to end, are the words and the events in which God is revealed.

Like every other book from the ancient world, the Bible needs explanation because it was written in other languages by men of other cultures. Since God chose to reveal himself through the Hebrew, Aramaic, and Greek languages at certain definite times in specific human cultures, everyone who takes the Bible seriously welcomes all the information he can get about the Bible in its original form and time. Many books are available which explain in terms of ancient history, archaeology, geography, and linguistics the times chosen by God for his revelation.

But we cannot be satisfied with studying the Bible just as an ancient book. After we have learned as best we can what meaning the Bible had for people in Bible times, we want to know what meaning it has for us and for our contemporaries. Here again there are many books that can help us, of which the most valuable are the ones that try to show us the total meaning of the Bible, seen in the light of the person and work of Christ.

Because of the great variety of types of writings in the Bible—legal codes, genealogies, stories, prayers, proverbial sayings, poems, sermons, prophecies, to name only a few—it is misleading to try to find God's will for us in any of the parts unless we have a clear idea of the scope and purpose of the whole Bible. But when these parts in all their variety are seen in relation to God's saving purpose for mankind, the way is open for us to find the message of the Bible for our lives.

A word of caution. Books about the Bible cannot take the place of the Bible itself. Such books can be put to best use by the person who is regularly and systematically reading the Bible and trying to live by what it teaches. Test each book about the Bible by what the Bible itself says. Look up the passages referred to. Question and evaluate what the writer is saying about the Bible. This will help you in two ways: you will get a better knowledge of the Bible, and you will develop more skill in finding what is of real value in books and in rejecting what is not valuable.

After we have learned all we can from reading and studying about the Bible, we still are dependent on the Holy Spirit for the conviction that the Bible is God's Word to us. As we read the Bible prayerfully and expectantly, the Spirit bears witness by and through the words of the Bible, and speaks to each one of us in a constantly new way each day of our lives, meeting our needs and building us up in faith and in grace.

1A. TEXTS AND TRANSLATIONS
F.F. Bruce

There was a time when one translation of the Bible in English served most people for all purposes—for use in church, for theological study, for personal devotion. That day has long since disappeared. We are in the happy position of having a great variety of English versions of the Bible and still more of the New Testament—some, like the Revised Standard Version, retaining the recognizable cadences of traditional "Bible English" and lending themselves to liturgical use; some endeavoring to reproduce for the student the finer nuances of the original languages, even if English idiom has to suffer in the process; some aiming at direct communication of the Bible message to readers with a minimum of biblical or any other literary culture. The "beat" generation and the dwellers in the cotton patch have had their special needs catered for—and rightly so, for Bible translation into their idioms is as necessary as Bible translation into the remoter dialects of the Amazon Valley or New Guinea.

The list of versions given below is selective and has in view the type of reader for whom this book has been compiled. Further aid in putting the listed versions in their context will be found in the companion list of books telling how the Bible came to us. A seventeenth-century Confession of Faith ascribes the preservation of the biblical text in substantial purity throughout the centuries to "the singular providence of God"; a survey of the record and of the situation in our day will confirm the validity of this ascription.

Editions of the Original Texts:
Old Testament
1. KITTEL, R., ed., *Biblia Hebraica*, Stuttgart, Wurttembergische Bibelanstalt, 1961, 1434 pp., $6.80; BAIB, RE, 1962, 90s. The principal critical edition of the Hebrew Bible. The Masoretic text was edited for the third edition (1937) by P. Kahle; the seventh edition represents a revision of the third by A. Alt and O. Eissfeldt.

2. SNAITH, N. H., ed., *The Hebrew Bible*, BFBS, 1958, 1366 pp., 20s. The handiest readily available pointed text of the Hebrew Scriptures.

Editions of the Original Texts:
New Testament
3. ALAND, K., ed., *Novum Testamentum Graece*, Stuttgart, Wurttembergische Bibelanstalt, ED 24, 1960, 470 pp., $1.35. This is the current edition of the famous Nestle text, used by scholars throughout the world. A thorough revision is shortly to appear.

4. ALAND, K., et al., ed., *The Greek New Testament*, ABS, 1966, 920 pp., Pb $1.95; BFBS, 21s. A new edition of the Greek text, prepared by K. Aland, M. Black, B. M. Metzger, and A. Wikgren with the collaboration of forty other scholars, sponsored by five Bible Societies and designed with special reference to the needs of Bible translations.

5. KILPATRICK, G. D., ed., *The Greek New Testament*, BFBS, 1958, 816 pp., 9s. This is one of the most useful editions, with a good select critical apparatus. Available in pocket size or with wide margins.

Translations
6. *The Amplified Bible*, ZPH, 1965, 1485 pp., Hb $17.95, Pb $9.95; OL, 1536 pp., 70s. The New Testament appeared in 1958 and was followed by the Old Testament in two stages. The "amplification" consists mainly in providing the reader with all the meanings which the original word or phrase can bear; unfortunately, it does not always indicate which is the precise meaning in any single context.

7. *The Anchor Bible*, DC, 1964. An interconfessional enterprise in which Protestant, Catholic and Jewish scholars collaborate to produce a new translation of the Bible with introduction and commentary on each book. It is edited by W. F. Albright and D. N. Freedman and is to comprise 38 volumes, of which about one-third have appeared.

8. BECK, W. F., *The New Testament in the Language of Today*, CON, 1963, 470 pp., $4.75; CON, 35s. A scholarly and idiomatic version by an American Lutheran.

9. *The Berkeley Version of the Holy Bible*, ZPH, 1959, 1233 pp., $7.95; OL, 1148 pp., 40s. The New Testament was translated by Gerrit

Verkuyl and was published separately in 1945; the Old Testament was translated under his editorship by twenty American scholars, and is the better part of the version. A masterpiece of conservative scholarship.

10. BRATCHER, R. G., *Good News for Modern Man: The New Testament in Today's English Version,* ABS, 1966, 600 pp.; CO, 1967, Pb 75¢; CO, Pb 5s. A runaway best-seller in simple contemporary English, illustrated by line-drawings.

11. *The Confraternity Version of the Holy Bible,* SAGP, 1941. This work, sponsored by the Episcopal Committee of the Confraternity of Christian Doctrine, is a new American Catholic version. The New Testament (1941) was a thorough revision of the Douay-Rheims version; the Old Testament (to be completed in four volumes) is a new translation from the original texts.

12. GOODSPEED, E. J., et al., *The Complete Bible: An American Translation,* UCP, 1939, 1332 pp., Hb $6.00; $6.75 with Apocrypha; OUP, 50s. The New Testament (1923) and Apocrypha (1938) of this version were translated by Edgar J. Goodspeed; the Old Testament (1927) was translated by J. M. Powis Smith with the collaboration of three other scholars and revised (1935) by Theophile J. Meek. The translators aimed at a version in American English, avoiding "expressions which, however familiar in England or Scotland, are strange to American ears."

13. HOOKE, S. H., *The Bible in Basic English,* CAUP, 1949, 910 pp., $4.95; (N.T. only) $1.95; CAUP, 15s. For this version the basic English vocabulary of eight hundred fifty words was augmented by fifty special "Bible words" and one hundred "listed as giving most help in the reading of English verse." Within these limits,

this is a scholarly translation from the Hebrew and Greek texts. The prefatory note ascribes the translation to "a Committee under the direction of Professor S. H. Hooke"; actually, it was the unaided work of Professor and Mrs. Hooke.

14. *The Jerusalem Bible,* DC, 1966, 2045 pp., $16.95; DLT, 84s. Adapted from *La Bible de Jerusalem* (an annotated French version by members of the Dominican Biblical and Archaeological School in Jerusalem) under the editorship of Alexander Jones. The translation is based on the Hebrew and Greek texts, the idiom is vigorous and modern; the introductions and notes are scholarly and up-to-date. This must be the first English Bible for general use in which the form Yahweh, familiar to scholars, is printed regularly as the name of the God of Israel.

15. KNOX, R. A., *The Holy Bible,* BO, 1954, 1200 pp., 16s. This is accurately described on the title page as "a translation from the Latin Vulgate in the light of the Hebrew and Greek originals." The translation was undertaken at the commission of the Cardinal Archbishop of Westminster; its secondary character detracts from its value, but against that must be set the fact that the translator was one of the ablest English stylists of his day, and in this regard his work achieved high distinction.

16. MOFFATT, J., *A New Translation of the Bible,* HS, 340 pp., $7.00; HS, 25s. A version which for many years enjoyed great popularity because of its free and colloquial idiom, at times was more Scots than English. Its main defect lay in the undue liberties which it took with the text.

17. *The New English Bible: New Testament,* OUP, 1961; CAUP. The first installment of a new version sponsored by the principal non-

Roman churches of Great Britain and Ireland; the publication of the Old Testament is expected about 1970. This version breaks with the tradition extending from William Tyndale (1525-35) to the Revised Standard Version; it is not a revision of previous versions but an entirely new translation into "timeless English."

18. *PHILLIPS, J. B., *The New Testament in Modern English,* MC, Pb $1.45; BLES, 1958, 576 pp., Pb 10s 6d. This is the most popular of recent private translations of the New Testament. It first appeared in a series of separate volumes: *Letters to Young Churches* (1947), *The Gospels in Modern English* (1952), *The Young Church in Action* (1955), *The Book of Revelation* (1957). The rendering is designedly paraphrastic; it brings out the meaning in fresh and readable fashion, especially in the epistles.

19. PHILLIPS, J. B., *Four Prophets,* MC, 1963, 161 pp., $3.95; BLES, Hb 45s, Pb 15s. A translation into modern English of Amos, Hosea, Isaiah 1-39, and Micah.

20. *Revised Standard Version of the Holy Bible,* NE, 1952. This is the English version most widely used today. It represents a revision of the King James Version (1611) and American Standard Version (1901) executed by a committee set up by the International Council of Religious Education. The New Testament was published in 1946, the whole Bible (apart from the Apocrypha) in 1952, the Apocrypha in 1957. In reprints of 1962 some eighty-five emendations were incorporated in the text. This is the latest English Bible in the tradition which stems from William Tyndale's work of 1525-35.

21. *Revised Standard Version of the Holy Bible: Catholic,* NE, 1966, 1276 pp., 25s. In this edition a few alterations have been made in the RSV text of the New Testament in the light of Catholic tradition. The books of the Apocrypha, instead of coming as an appendix to the Old Testament, are incorporated within it in the positions which they occupy in the Latin Vulgate.

22. RIEU, C. H., *The Acts of the Apostles: A New Translation,* PE, 1957, 176 pp., Pb 3s 6d. This volume in the Penguin Classics is contributed by the son of the editor of that series. a classical scholar like his father. The value of his translation of Acts, in the best tradition of English classical learning, is enhanced by the thirty pages of introduction which precede it and sixty pages of notes which follow it; these are of historical rather than theological relevance.

23. RIEU, E. V., *The Four Gospels: A New Translation,* PE, 1952, 246 pp., Pb 95¢; PE, Pb 3s 6d. This volume in the Penguin Classics, by the editor of that series, is the work of a distinguished scholar with considerable experience in translating Greek literature into English for the general reader. The translation is not only accurate but reflects deep and sympathetic insight into the purpose of the evangelists.

24. SCHONFIELD, H. J., *The Authentic New Testament,* MENT, 1958, 478 pp., Pb 50¢ (OoP); DOB, 1955, 568 pp., 25s. An independent translation by a Jewish scholar who believes in Jesus as the Messiah of Israel but stands outside the Christian Church.

25. *The Torah: The Five Books of Moses,* JPSA, 1963, 393 pp., $5.00. This is the first installment of *A New Translation of the Holy Scriptures According to the Masoretic Text,* produced by a committee of American Jewish scholars under the chairmanship of H. M. Orlinsky. In textual matters it is very conservative; in

idiom it is contemporary, thus breaking loose from the pattern set by *The Holy Scriptures According to the Masoretic Text,* JPSA, 650 pp., $12.00, which was strongly influenced by the diction of the King James Version.

26. *The Twentieth Century New Testament,* MP, 1961, 449 pp., Hb $3.50, Pb $1.29; HOM, 1902. (OoP) This excellent version, based on Westcott and Hort's Greek text, was produced by an anonymous group of non-specialists, whose identity was not divulged until 1955 (see K. W. Clark, "The Making of the Twentieth Century New Testament," *Bulletin of the John Rylands Library,* 38, 1955-56, pp. 58-81). The 1961 edition unfortunately obscures some of the distinctive features of the original.

27. WEYMOUTH, R. F., *The New Testament in Modern Speech,* HRP, 1938, 474 pp., $3.75; JC, 7s 6d. This version, first published in 1902 and revised in 1924, achieves a high level of accuracy, especially in the rendering of Greek tenses.

28. WILLIAMS, C. B., *The New Testament in the Language of the People,* MP, 1966, 572 pp., $3.95; SPCK, 10s 6d. This version, first published in 1937, attempts to reproduce in English the finer nuances of Greek usage, some of which are better expressed by such gestures as the raising of an eyebrow. The effect thus tends in places to be heavily and pedantically prosaic. It may have been designed as a more conservative counterpart to Goodspeed's *American Translation.*

29. WILLIAMS, C. K., *The New Testament: A New Translation in Plain English,* LOG, 1952, 574 pp., 8s 6d. (OoP) "Plain English" in the title is based on a list of fifteen hundred "fundamental and common

words that make up ordinary English speech," drawn up as part of the *Interim Report on Vocabulary Selection* (1936). Like "Plain English" itself, this version is specially designed for people whose native tongue is not English but who have to learn English as their medium of higher education and communication with the outside world.

How the Bible Came to Us
30. BEEGLE, D. M., *God's Word into English,* WBE, 1965, 230 pp., Pb $2.25. The first chapter asks the question, "Why revise God's Word?" and the book as a whole answers it with reference to the main English versions of the Bible.

31. BRUCE, F. F., *The Books and the Parchments,* REV, RE, 1963, 286 pp., $4.50; REV, RE 3, 25s. An account of the original scripts and languages, the canon, text, and versions of the Bible from the beginnings of alphabetic writing to the New English Bible.

32. *BRUCE, F. F., *The English Bible,* OUP, 1961, 234 pp., $3.75; LU, 1963, 255 pp., 25s; ME, Pb 12s 6d. Published at the same time as the New English Bible (New Testament), outlining the history of English translations of the Bible from Anglo-Saxon times.

33. BURROWS, M., *Diligently Compared,* NE, 1964, 278 pp., $6.50. A comparison of the Revised Standard Version and the King James Version, showing how the later version differs from the earlier one, and why.

34. DENNETT, H., *A Guide to Modern Versions of the New Testament,* MP, 1966, 142 pp., $2.75; BAG, 1965. A useful handbook which not only fulfills the promise of its title but includes notes on several published helps to Bible study.

35. GOODSPEED, E. J., *Problems of New Testament Translation,* UCP, 1945, 215 pp., $2.50. (OoP) Popular discussions of one hundred passages which present problems to the New Testament translator.

36. GRANT, F. C., *Translating the Bible,* NE, 1961, 183 pp., 15s. Chapters on the principles, problems, and history of Bible translation, celebrating the three-hundred-fiftieth anniversary of the King James Version.

37. KENYON, F. G., *Our Bible and the Ancient Manuscripts,* HRP, 1958, 352 pp., $5.00; ES, RE 5, 42s. This is a posthumous edition (including some account of the relevance of the Dead Sea Scrolls) of a classic work by a leading world-authority on biblical manuscripts, first published in 1895. The last edition prepared by the author himself (who died in 1952) appeared in 1939.

38. KENYON, F. G., *The Story of the Bible,* WBE, 1967, 150 pp., Pb $1.95. Although this is a popular work, its first edition (1936) contained the first public announcement of an important manuscript discovery. This posthumous edition includes an additional chapter on "The Last Thirty Years" by F. F. Bruce.

39. KNOX, R. A., *On Englishing the Bible,* BO, 1949, 101 pp. (OoP) Eight delightfully written essays arising out of the author's experiences as a Bible translator.

40. MacGREGOR, Geddes, *The Bible in the Making,* LC, 1949, 447 pp., $6.00; JM, 1960, 310 pp., 30s. A survey of the history of the Bible, concentrating mainly on the English Bible.

41. POPE, H., *English Versions of the Bible,* HH, 1952, 787 pp., 80s. This is specially valuable for its account of Catholic versions. In dealing with Protestant versions Pope is apt to be tendentious; Bullough's contributions are completely impartial and objective.

42. REUMANN, J. H. P., *The Romance of Bible Scripts and Scholars,* PH, 1965, 248 pp., $6.95. Some fascinating chapters in the story of Bible transmission and translation, from the Septuagint translators to Ronald Knox.

43. ROBINSON, H. W., ed., *The Bible in Its Ancient and English Versions,* OUP, 1954, 350 pp., 21s. (OoP) A symposium in which a team of specialists deal with the original texts, the Greek, Latin, Syriac, and other early versions and the principal phases of the English Bible.

44. VAUGHAN, Curtis, ed., *The New Testament from 26 Translations,* ZPH, 1967, 1237 pp., $12.50. Here the main variations in rendering from the King James Version are noted verse by verse throughout the New Testament.

45. WEGENER, G. S., *6000 Years of the Bible,* HRP, 1963, 352 pp., 427 illus., $7.95; HS, 1963, 35s. An attractively told and lavishly illustrated account of the Bible from Noah and the Ark to Willard Libby and the Carbon-14 test.

1BA. COMMENTARIES, DICTIONARIES AND REFERENCE BOOKS: OLD TESTAMENT
Samuel J. Schultz

The Old Testament together with the New Testament constitutes the literature identified as God's written revelation or Holy Scripture. Jesus in his earthly ministry frequently quoted, interpreted, and appealed to the Old Testament as authoritative and trustworthy. To the one who regards the person and work of Jesus Christ as the foundation of the Christian faith and acknowledges Jesus as God the

Son, *worthy of worship and adora-
tion, the Old Testament ultimately is
as vital as the New.*

*Biblical literature currently re-
flects two basic viewpoints concerning the Old Testament. A large
segment of modern scholarship as
developed during the last two centuries reconstructs the Old Testament
in the light of currently prevailing
theories of authorship. The authors
reflect primarily their own insights
and understanding of the events as
they occurred. A basic presupposi-
tion in this view is that revelation did
not consist in the communication of
revealed truths and that the Bible is
primarily a human product.*

*The other basic viewpoint held by
modern scholars is the recognition of
the Old Testament literature as reliable and trustworthy in its unreconstructed form. The principles of revelation and inspiration claimed and
assumed in the Bible are regarded as
essential presuppositions for interpretation. Beyond the native ability of
the authors the Spirit of God guided
them so that what they wrote was
entirely reliable and constituted a
divine-human product. Consequently
the distinctive feature of the Old
Testament which raises it above the
level of secular literature and history
is the disclosure of God in its historical events and messages.*

*Interpretation of the Old Testa-
ment is directly affected by the viewpoint that the modern scholar uses in
his approach in any extensive consideration of its contents. By way of
example this would be readily apparent in dating Deuteronomy as
Mosaic literature or as a document
written in the sixth century B.C. The
book of Daniel is interpreted as history by those who date it in the Mac-
abean era of the second century
while those scholars who recognize
the validity of predictive prophecy
recognize it in its unreconstructed
form as a sixth-century document by
Daniel. In the literature listed below*

*both basic viewpoints are suggested
to introduce the reader to some of
the interpretations available by modern scholars.*

Dictionaries and Encyclopedias

1. *DOUGLAS, J. D., ed., *The New
Bible Dictionary,* WBE, 1960, 1424
pp., $12.95; TP, 1960, 1376 pp. plus
plates and maps, 45s. This volume
projects the evangelical biblical scholarship of the Tyndale Fellowship for
Biblical Research with the coopera-
tion of colleagues in America, Europe, the Commonwealth and other
lands. The articles reflect a spirit of
loyalty to the Holy Scriptures and
provide a better understanding of
God's Word to man.

2. TENNEY, Merrill, ed., *The Pic-
torial Bible Dictionary,* ZPH, 1963,
1000 pp., $9.95; MMS, 70s. This
fully illustrated volume contains over
5,000 entries. Over 700 illustrations
are used to acquaint the reader with
various subjects discussed in their setting in biblical times. Articles are
concise and adapted to aid the layman in his understanding of the
Scriptures.

3. BUTTRICK, G. A., ed., *Interpreter's Bible Dictionary,* 4 V., ABP,
1962, $45.00. The articles in this dic-
tionary would largely reflect the
viewpoint projected in the *Interpreter's Bible Commentary* which is
liberal but mediating at various
points. Frequently the views expressed would represent a contrast to
those presented in the two Bible dictionaries noted above.

4. ORR, James, *International Standard Bible Encyclopedia,* WBE, 1939,
3500 pp., $37.00; OL, 294s. This
five-volume work was first published
in 1920. The articles are reasonably
conservative. Helpful are the numerous biblical references throughout
each article facilitating the study of
related passages in the Bible.

Introductions to Content, History and Background

5. SCHULTZ, S. J., *The Old Testament Speaks*, HRP, 1960, 436 pp., $6.00; HRP, 45s. True to its title this book introduces the reader to a consideration of the Old Testament without the modern reconstruction and reshuffling of the text. The message of the Old Testament is delineated in the context of history, archaeology and biblical theology making the reader aware of the living God himself rather than of what the Hebrews supposedly thought. Dr. E. J. Young's appraisal of this volume was that this book was "written with the full awareness of what the modern 'critical' school has to say yet with complete loyalty to the Scriptures." The text of this book appeals to the layman as well as the scholar, providing the basis for further study through footnotes, selected bibliography, charts, and maps. See also, R. K. Harrison, *A History of Old Testament Times*, MMS, 1957, 256 pp., 17s 6d.

6. ANDERSON, B. W., *Understanding the Old Testament*, PH, 1957, 552 pp., $8.75. This handbook for the student of the Old Testament offers an interesting survey based on the reconstruction of the biblical text according to theories of modern scholarship. Within the framework of the drama of Israel from Abraham to the eve of the Christian era he traces the literary and theological development of Israel primarily from the naturalistic perspective. See also, H. J. Kraus, *The People of God in the Old Testament*, LU, 1958, 92 pp., 2s 6d.

7. SCHWANTES, S. J., *A Short History of the Ancient Near East*, BBH, 1965, 192 pp., $4.95. This book provides interesting reading for anyone who wants to become familiar with the people and the culture related to the Old Testament. With this illumi-

nating background, the reading of the Scriptures offers a new perspective and added insight. It contains helpful maps and illustrations. For interesting sidelights from archeology, see C. H. Gordon, *The World of the Old Testament*, PB, 1960, 312 pp., 30s.

8. BRIGHT, John, *A History of Israel*, WP, 1959, 550 pp.; SCMP, 1960, 512 pp., 50s. In these pages the author offers a mediating position in his interpretation of Israel's history. Although he rejects the theory of the evolution of Israel's religion as held by Wellhausen, the author views favorably the reconstruction of the Old Testament text according to current literary criticism. See also, W. F. Albright, *The Biblical Period*, HRP, 1950, 60 pp., Pb $1.45; BL, 11s 6d; and W. F. Albright, *From the Stone Age to Christianity*, DC, 1957, 444 pp., Hb $7.00, Pb $1.45; JH, 40s.

9. deVAUX, R., *Ancient Israel: Its Life and Institutions*, MH, 1961, 592 pp., $10.95; DLT, RE 2, 1965, 608 pp., 55s. Written by a Catholic scholar, this book has gained a fine rating for its approach to the nation of Israel as it existed during Old Testament times. It offers the reader a better understanding of the world in which the Israelites lived. See also, for a conservative history by a Roman Catholic scholar of great learning, P. Heinisch, *History of the Old Testament*, LITP, 1952, 492 pp., $6.50.

10. GEISLER, L. and W. E. Nix, *A General Introduction to the Bible*, MP, 1968, 448 pp. This resource book is a *must* in the library of the inquisitive student concerned with the transmission, canonicity, and accuracy of the biblical text. Should the Apocrypha be included in the Bible? If you want a scholarly answer to this question you should read this book. See also, B. M. Metzger, *An In-*

troduction to Apocrypha, OUP, 1957, 286 pp., $4.00; OUP, 30s.

11. *MANLEY, G. T., ed., *The New Bible Handbook,* IVP, 1949, 477 pp., $4.95; TP, 15s. This book offers the reader an introduction to a wide range of subjects related to Old Testament study. These encyclopedic articles on inspiration, authority, the canon, modern criticism, history, and geography provide guidance for further study. Each book of the Old Testament is considered separately.

12. *ARCHER, G. A., *A Survey of Old Testament Introduction,* MP, 1964, 508 pp., $6.95. For a thoroughly conservative and scholarly analysis of the authorship of the Old Testament books this book offers the most up-to-date and incisive analysis of twentieth-century criticism. Abreast of linguistic and archaeological evidence, the author provides a reasonable biblical basis for the Mosaic authorship of the Pentateuch. Although it gives consideration to all of the Old Testament books two chapters each are allotted to the books of Isaiah and Daniel which next to Deuteronomy provide crucial areas for Old Testament interpretation.

13. EISSFELDT, Otto, *The Old Testament,* HRP, 1965, 862 pp., $11.00; OUP, 70s. This introduction, including the Apocrypha and Pseudepigrapha, and works of similar type from Qumran, traces the history of the formation of the Old Testament on the basis of the theories of modern critical scholarship. Latest developments in Old Testament studies are related to the principal schools and trends in biblical research and are amply documented and supported by an extensive bibliography. It reflects the most up-to-date reconstruction of the Old Testament but does not take seriously the biblical view of inspira-

tion, revelation, and authority of Scripture.

14. UNGER, M. F., *Introductory Guide to the Old Testament,* ZPH, 1951, 420 pp., $5.95. For an initial introduction to the problems of authorship of the books of the Old Testament this book is excellent. It will acquaint the layman with the basic problems and difficulties and offers a constructive and biblical perspective.

15. YOUNG, E. J., *An Introduction to the Old Testament,* WBE, 1949, 414 pp., $5.00; Ri, TP, 1958, 456 pp., 19s 6d. This author offers an intensive scholarly analysis of the critical problems concerning the authorship of Old Testament books. Through footnotes and bibliographical references the student is guided into a careful appraisal of the basic presuppositions held by modern scholarship. See also, *The Study of Old Testament Theology Today,* CLA, 1958, 112 pp., 10s 6d.

16. AALDERS, G. C., *A Short Introduction to the Pentateuch,* TP, 1949, 173 pp. (OoP) For a brief analysis of the Graf-Wellhausen theory on the authorship of the Pentateuch this book provides an introductory orientation. The author favors Mosaic authorship but allows for post-Mosaic material in the Pentateuch.

17. HARRIS, R. L., *Inspiration and Canonicity of the Bible,* ZPH, 1957, 304 pp. (OoP) Questions pertaining to the canonicity of the Bible are given serious and scholarly consideration in these pages. Any one concerned with the arrangement of the Old Testament books or the division of the Old Testament into two or three parts should read this book.

18. WRIGHT, G. E., ed., *The Bible and the Ancient Near East,* DC, 1961, 410 pp., Hb $7.50, Pb $1.95;

RO, 50s. This book was published in honor of William Poxwell Albright with essays contributed by some of his former students who respect him as a great scholar, teacher, and friend. For an appraisal of modern Old Testament scholarship from a mediating position the first chapter entitled "Modern Study of Old Testament Literature" (pp. 13-31) by John Bright is basically significant.

19. OEHLER, G. F., *Theology of the Old Testament,* FW, 1883, 593 pp. (OoP); Ri, ZPH. This standard work on Old Testament theology is regarded an acceptable evangelical emphasis. Although it is a re-issue, it provides a valuable guide in the study of theology. Some Old Testament scholars consider its value so significant that they regard it as absolutely essential for an evangelical library. See also, H. H. Howley, *The Faith of Israel,* WP, 1957, 220 pp., $3.95; SCMP, 1956, 18s.

20. HENGSTENBERG, E. W., *Christology of the Old Testament and a Commentary on the Messianic Predictions,* Ri, KR, 1956. (OoP) Although this was originally published in 1863 it is considered essential for twentieth-century theology. It is especially helpful and reliable from an evangelical perspective. For the student of the New Testament it provides an enriching background. See also, Erich Sauer, *The Dawn of World Redemption,* Ri, WBE, 208 pp., Pb $1.95; PP, 1951, Hb 10s 6d, Pb 5s.

21. SCHULTZ, S. J., *The Prophets Speak,* HRP, 1968. In keeping with the subtitle "The Law of Love—The Essence of Israel's Religion," this book projects the idea that the core of the prophetic message in the Old Testament was the same as that in the New Testament, namely, that man should love God with all his heart and his neighbor as himself. Beginning with Moses as the first proph-

et, under whom this relationship of mutual love between God and Israel was established, the author points out that this law of love was the primary message of each of the Old Testament prophets. Jesus as the last of the prophets not only endorsed their message but fulfilled it as the God-man.

22. ELLISON, H. L., *Men Spake from God,* WBE, 1958, 160 pp., $3.25; PP, 1966, Pb 5s. A brief study of each prophet, an outline and analysis of each book, and a consideration of the main questions of criticism and exegesis—these features make this an interesting book to read.

23. BEECHER, W. J., *The Prophets and the Promise,* Ri, BBH, 1963, 427 pp., $13.95. Based on the unreconstructed text of the Old Testament this book acquaints the reader with the biblical conception of a prophet and his message. It is essential to a fuller understanding of the Messianic message as given in Old Testament times. Important is the emphasis the author gives to the relationship of the prophets to the revelation given through Moses as represented in the Pentateuch. The prophets supported the law and supplemented it through their divinely-given messages.

24. ELLISON, H. L., *The Centrality of the Messianic Idea for the Old Testament,* TP, 1957, 23 pp., 1s 6d. This author guides his reader in a helpful consideration of the central theme of the Old Testament so that the New Testament becomes more meaningful.

25. WRIGHT, G. E., *The Old Testament against Its Environment,* REG, 1950, 116 pp., 10s 6d. Although this book is not written from the evangelical perspective it can be profitably used by an evangelical who has had seminary training. It provides

helpful information presented from a mediating position.

26. *YOUNG, E. J., *My Servants the Prophets,* WBE, 1952, 231 pp., $4.00. For an excellent biblical approach to the study of the prophets this book is invaluable. Prophets are recognized as spokesmen for God from whom they received their message.

Commentaries

27. *DAVIDSON, F., ed., *The New Bible Commentary,* WBE, 1953, 1199 pp., $8.95; TP, ED 2, 1954, 1200 pp., 40s. This is an excellent one-volume commentary from an evangelical point of view. It provides a general coverage of each book.

28. ALLEMAN, H. C. and E. E. Flack, *Old Testament Commentary,* MUP, 1948, 893 pp., $5.00. Although not evangelical this volume can be used with great profit by the discerning student.

29. PFEIFFER, C. F. and E. F. Harrison, ed., *The Wycliffe Bible Commentary,* MP, 1962, 1525 pp., $11.95; OL, 1963, 1526 pp., 65s. Each book of the Bible is given a careful analysis and exegesis from an evangelical point of view. This should be a very helpful volume for the average student of the Scriptures.

30. HARPER, A. F., ed., *Beacon Bible Commentary,* BHP, 1964. An evangelical commentary written by scholars who approach the Scriptures from the viewpoint of Wesleyan-Arminian theology.

31. BUTTRICK, G. A., ed., *The Interpreter's Bible,* 12 V., ABP, 1951, $89.50. These volumes are written from the liberal perspective. Interpretation of the Old Testament is based on the reconstruction of the text according to the theories of literary criticism.

32. KEIL, C. F. and F. Delitzsch, ed., *Biblical Commentary on the Old Testament,* 25 V., Ri, WBE, 1950, $82.50. These volumes introduce the reader to excellent scholarship in his exegetical study of the Old Testament. Since they were written during the nineteenth century they lack the supplement of current studies. They are especially helpful for the scholar interested in the Hebrew text, and are essential for an evangelical library.

33. *Laymen's Handy Commentary Series,* Ri, ZPH, 1960. These handy, pocket-size volumes provide excellent interpretative helps for the layman in his study of the Old Testament. Ellicott's writings are recognized for their devotion to Scripture and their concise and lucid expositions.

Pentateuch

34. ALLIS, O. T., *The Five Books of Moses,* PRPC, 1943, 320 pp., $3.75.

35. HEIDEL, Alexander, *The Babylonian Genesis,* UCP, 1942, 153 pp., Pb $1.50; UCP, ED 2, 1951, 10s 6d; and *The Gilgamesh Epic and Old Testament Parallels,* UCP, 1949, 296 pp., Pb $1.95; UCP, ED 2, 14s. These two studies have been greatly appreciated by Old Testament students. The former offers an analysis of the cuneiform creation accounts while the latter provides a translation and analysis of the Babylonian flood stories. Helpful in this study of comparing the Babylonian and biblical accounts of creation and the flood are chapters 3-5 (pp. 26-71); See also, M. F. Unger, *Archaeology and the Old Testament,* ZPH, 1954, 339 pp., $5.95; PI, 1965, 248 pp., 30s.

36. PFEIFFER, C. F., *The Book of Leviticus,* BBH, 1957, 60 pp., Pb $1.25; and *The Book of Genesis,* BBH, 1958, 108 pp., Pb $1.50. Approaching the Bible as inspired history the author provides helpful aids

in outlines and explanations to the content of the text. Another book by the same author is available, entitled *The Patriarchal Age,* BBH, 1961, 128 pp., $2.95; PI, 1965, 13s 6d.

37. *KIDNER, Derek, *Genesis,* IVP, 1967, 224 pp., $3.95; TP, 11s 6d. This is another helpful volume in the Tyndale Old Testament commentary series under the general editorship of D. J. Wiseman.

38. PIETERS, Albertus, *Notes on Genesis,* WBE, 1943, 196 pp., $2.00. (OoP) Addressed to ministers and serious Bible students, this author discusses in one hundred and eighteen notes numerous topics, questions, and problems throughout the book of Genesis.

39. LEUPOLD, H. C., *Exposition of Genesis,* 2 V., BBH, 1949, 1220 pp., $3.95 each. This is a modern Lutheran exegesis of the Hebrew text. The author carefully examines the grammatical statements as well as the historical circumstances.

40. WHITCOMB, John C., Jr. and H. M. Morris, *The Genesis Flood,* PRPC, 1960, 518 pp., $6.95. A helpful book in attempting to correlate scientific data and earth's early history. Serious evaluation is given to the inadequacies of uniformitarianism and evolutionism as unifying principles. The authors propose a system of creationism and catastrophism based on the Bible.

41. GOODING, D. W., *The Account of the Tabernacle,* CAUP, 1959, 116 pp., $4.00; CAUP, 22s 6d. A brilliant study of the problems of Hebrew and Greek texts.

42. MEYER, F. B., *Exodus,* 2 V., Ri, MMS, 1952, 17s. (OoP)

43. KELLOGG, S. H., *The Book of Leviticus,* WBE, 1960, 566 pp. (OoP)

A very helpful commentary providing helpful insight and understanding concerning the details of the religion of Israel as given in Leviticus. The author attempts to point out the significance of this book for the modern reader.

44. GREENSTONE, J. H., *The Holy Scripture with Commentary: Numbers,* JPSA, 1939, 374 pp., $2.50. (OoP) This conservative Jewish commentary provides helps and suggestions in the reading and interpretation of the Hebrew text.

45. JENSEN, I. L., *Numbers: journey to God's rest-land.* MP, 1964, Pb 39¢. Although brief this book written from an evangelical perspective provides interesting reading and stimulation toward a rereading of the book of Numbers.

46. MANLEY, G. T., *The Book of the Law,* WBE, 1957, 162 pp., $3.00. (OoP); TP, 192 pp., 15s. The author shares with his reader a study of the sources of the book of Deuteronomy taking into account modern scholarship. This study deserves serious consideration for extensive investigation into the literary structure of Deuteronomy.

47. REIDER, J., *The Holy Scripture with Commentary: Deuteronomy.* JPSA, 1937, 356 pp., $2.50. (OoP) For a better understanding of the text of Deuteronomy this commentary has considerable merit. It represents a conservative Jewish perspective.

Historical Books
48. GETTYS, Joseph, *Surveying the Historical Books,* JKP, 1963, 163 pp., $2.00. After surveying the views on authorship from liberal to conservative this author favors the viewpoint projected by John Bright. Using the outline and study guide approach the author highlights the main

divisions of each book and offers a bibliography for further study. Included also are provocative questions for thought and discussion.

49. AHARONI, Y., *The Land of the Bible*, WP, 1967, 409 pp., $7.95; BO, 63s. For an up-to-date background of the historical books this author offers the best available at present. Biblical evidence is taken seriously and related to other evidence. Sources for historical geography are also discussed critically.

50. PINK, Arthur, *Gleanings in Joshua*, MP, 1964, 430 pp., $4.95. This book is recommended for the reader who prefers the devotional and typological approach. It provides interesting outlines of the text.

51. GARSTANG, John, *Joshua-Judges*, HRP, 1931, 424 pp., $5.00. (OoP); CSY, 20s. (OoP) Although partially dated this commentary offers archaeological interpretation that is still valuable. For supplemental information see also, *The Story of Jericho*, MMS, RE, 1948.

52. *CUNDALL, A. E. and Leon Morris, *Judges and Ruth*, IVP, 1968, 318 pp., $4.00; TP, 15s 6d. Scholarly without being too technical, practical, and brief.

53. JENSEN, I. L., *Joshua: restland won*, MP, 1966. This brief evangelical treatment of Joshua may be helpful to make this historical account of Joshua's conquest more meaningful for the modern reader.

54. KAUFMAN, Jecheskel, *The Biblical Account of the Conquest of Canaan*, MAGN, 1953, 98 pp., $1.25. (OoP); OUP, 106 pp., 8s. Although this is not evangelical it can be profitably used by a conservative with seminary training.

55. COX, S., *The Book of Ruth*, RTS, 1922. (OoP) This is a popular exposition of the book of Ruth. It is regarded by many as a good evangelical interpretation.

56. CROCKETT, W. D., *A Harmony of the Books of Samuel, Kings and Chronicles*, Ri, BBH, 1951, 365 pp., $3.95. This is a valuable book for the student who is interested in correlating the parallel and supplementary accounts within these historical records of Israel.

57. PFEIFFER, C. F., *The Divided Kingdom, Israel and Judah*, BBH, 1957, 117 pp., $2.95. For tracing the developments in Israel and Judah in a chronological order this popular summary can be very helpful for studying this period in Israel's history in which two kingdoms existed. Among the prophets, Jonah and Daniel are strangely missing during the Divided Kingdom period.

58. THIELE, E. R., *The Mysterious Numbers of the Hebrew Kings*, UCP, 1951; WBE, RE, 1965, 232 pp., $6.00; PP, 1966, 352 pp., 30s. For the serious student of the historical account of the Divided Kingdom period, this volume is essential. Many of the numbers which appear contradictory to the average reader make sense when understood in terms of the system of keeping records in ancient times. The revised edition has an excellent chapter on the composition of the books of Kings. For theological studies from Kings, see R. S. Wallace, *Elijah and Elisha*, OB, 1957, 164 pp., 7s 6d.

59. WRIGHT, J. S., *The Date of Ezra's Coming to Jerusalem*, TP, 1947, 32 pp., 1s 6d. From the biblical perspective the author provides a scholarly approach to some of the problems modern scholars have raised concerning Ezra and his effective ministry during Nehemiah's times.

60. ANDERSON, S. E., *Nehemiah the Executive,* VKP, 1954, 168 pp., $2.50. (OoP) This popular treatment may be helpful to the average reader. It is written from an evangelical viewpoint.

Poetical Books
61. BLACKWOOD, A. W., Jr., *A Devotional Introduction to Job,* BBH, 1959, 166 pp., $2.95. This book is recognized as an evangelical approach to the text of Job. It is excellent for devotional study.

62. *ELLISON, H. L., *From Tragedy to Triumph: The Message of the Book of Job,* WBE, 1958, 127 pp., $2.50. (OoP); PP, 1958, 10s 6d. (OoP) The reader will find this very helpful for understanding the message of the book of Job. It is excellent for guiding the student to a meaningful application of Scripture to life.

63. *ALEXANDER, J. A., *The Psalms Translated and Explained,* Ri, ZPH, 568 pp., $5.95; OL, 1955, 32s. This is regarded as absolutely basic to the library of an evangelical student of the book of Psalms. This author's study is recommended for the layman as well as the scholar.

64. HENGSTENBERG, E. W., *Commentary on the Psalms,* TTC, 1876. (OoP) Evangelical and scholarly in emphasis this commentary is regarded as very reliable and helpful.

65. LEUPHOLD, H. C., *Exposition of the Psalms,* WAR, 1959, 1010 pp., $9.95. Written by a Lutheran scholar, this commentary offers excellent help for a devotional study of the Psalms.

66. *KIDNER, D., *The Proverbs,* IVP, 1964, 192 pp., $3.00; TP, 8s 6d. This verse by verse study of Proverbs provides interesting and stimulating reading. Varied subjects such as child

discipline, the price of chastity, the tongue, and others are considered topically. For a conservative Jewish commentary, see J. H. Greenstone, *Proverbs with Commentary,* JPSA, 1950, 354 pp., $3.50. (OoP)

67. GORDIS, Robert, *Koheleth— The Man and His World,* JTS, 1955, 404 pp., $2.45. This is an excellent commentary on the text of Ecclesiastes from the Jewish viewpoint. It is scholarly and stimulating for the advanced student as well as the layman. For an evangelical viewpoint, see C. Bridges, *Ecclesiastes,* Ri, BTT, 1960, 324 pp., 10s 6d.

68. BURROWES, G., *A Commentary on the Song of Solomon,* BTT, 1958, 458 pp. (OoP) Although this book is weak on exegesis and considered by many as extreme in typology, it is evangelical and stimulating for the average reader. Some scholars recommend it highly.

69. GORDIS, Robert, *The Song of Songs,* JTS, 1954, 108 pp. (OoP) Written by a Jewish scholar this commentary offers aid in understanding the Hebrew text. It is stimulating and provocative.

Major Prophets
70. ALEXANDER, J. A., *Commentary on the Prophesies of Isaiah,* 2 V., ZPH, 1953, 990 pp. (OoP); CLA, 1846. (OoP) This is regarded as one of the finest commentaries by some Old Testament scholars. It reflects sound biblical scholarship. See also, John Calvin, *Sermons on Isaiah's Prophecy of the Death and Passion of Christ,* CLA, 1956, 162 pp., 12s 6d.

71. COPASS, B. Z., *Isaiah, Prince of Old Testament Prophets,* BR, 1944, 191 pp. (OoP) This volume is essential to an evangelical student's library. The layman as well as the advanced scholar will find this book extremely helpful in understanding the

significance of the message of Isaiah.

72. *YOUNG, E. J., *The Book of Isaiah,* 2 V., WBE, 1964 and 1966, 534 pp. each, $7.95 each. This author offers a very helpful and evangelical exegesis of Isaiah from the amillennial perspective. The book of Isaiah is recognized as a single literary unit containing predictive prophecy concerning Cyrus as well as Jesus Christ. For background to the book of Isaiah, see also, *Studies in Isaiah,* TP, 1954, 208 pp., 12s 6d; and O. T. Allis, *The Unity of Isaiah,* PRPC, 1952, 144 pp., Pb $1.50; TP, 1951, 12s 6d.

73. LAETSCH, T., *Jeremiah,* CON, 1953, 412 pp., $4.50; CON, 1952, 46s. Laetsch regards the Hebrew text as a trustworthy and reliable basis for his exegesis of Jeremiah's message. He also includes the book of Lamentations in this volume.

74. BRIGHT, John, *Jeremiah,* DC, 1965, 372 pp., $7.00. A scholarly interpretation of Jeremiah. Bright gives more recognition to the authenticity of the text of Jeremiah than many modern scholars.

75. *ELLISON, H. L., *Ezekiel: The Man and His Message,* WBE, 1964, 144 pp., Pb $1.75; PP, 1956, 10s 6d. This volume offers very helpful explanations concerning numerous questions and problems that the reader of Ezekiel asks in reading the biblical text. Highly recommended.

76. FAIRBAIRN, P., *An Exposition of Ezekiel,* ZPH, 1960, 504 pp., $5.95; OL, 512 pp., 48s. Generally regarded as a good commentary.

77. HOWIE, C. G., *The Date and Composition of Ezekiel,* SBL, 1950, 122 pp., $1.50; SCMP, 1962, 142 pp., 6s 6d.

78. CULVER, R. D., *Daniel and the Latter Days,* REV, 1954; MP, 1964, 991 pp., $3.95. This volume offers an interpretation of the eschatalogical passages in the book of Daniel from the premillennial point of view. The author's bibliography provides a helpful guide for further study.

79. *YOUNG, E. J., *The Prophecy of Daniel,* WBE, 1949, 330 pp., $4.50. This commentary projects the exegesis of the book of Daniel from the amillennial perspective. It is very helpful in explaining the original text.

80. WHITCOMB, J. C., *Darius the Mede,* PRPC, 1959, 84 pp., Pb $1.50. Especially helpful and reliable for the evangelical is this volume in offering a study in historical identification.

Minor Prophets
81. LAETSCH, Theodore, *The Minor Prophets,* CON, 1956, 566 pp., $8.50; CON, 46s. The layman can use this commentary with the confidence that the author regards the biblical text as trustworthy and reliable. It is excellent for the study of each prophet individually in his historical context.

82. LEWIS, J. P., *The Minor Prophets,* BBH, 1966, 105 pp., Pb 75¢. This volume offers an adequate introduction to the prophets and their messages.

1BB. COMMENTARIES, DICTIONARIES AND REFERENCE BOOKS: NEW TESTAMENT
Merrill C. Tenney
Harish D. Merchant

Concordances
1. *CRUDEN, Alexander, *Complete Concordance to the Holy Scriptures,* HRW, 1949, 792 pp., $4.00; HRW, 1930, 32s. (Based on KJV); for abridged portable edition, see *Pocket Concordance and Bible Guide,* CL,

1958, 230 pp., $12.00; PI, 1958, Hb
7s 6d, Pb 5s.

2. ELLISON, J. W., ed., *Nelson's
Concordance to the Holy Bible*, NE,
1957, 2157 pp., $20.00. (Based on
RSV.)

3. *JOY, C. R., *Harper's Topical
Concordance*, HRP, RE, 1962, 628
pp., $8.95.

4. MOULTON, W. F. and A. A. Ged-
en, *Concordance to the Greek New
Testament*, Ri, KR, 1957, $17.50;
TTC, 70s.

5. *YOUNG, Robert, *Analytical
Concordance to the Bible*, WBE, RE,
1955, 1051 pp., $15.50; LU, 1879,
75s-88s. Over 300,000 references
with the literal meaning and pronunciation of the original Hebrew and
Greek words.

Dictionaries
6. *BRUCE, F. F., et al., ed., *The
New Bible Dictionary*, WBE, 1962,
$12.95; TP, 50s. Probably the best
modern dictionary.

7. BUTTRICK, G. A., et al., ed., *The
Interpreter's Dictionary of the Bible*,
4 V., ABP, 1962, $45.00.

8. HASTINGS, J. H., *Dictionary of
the Bible*. CSS, RE, 1963, 1080 pp.,
$15.00; TTC, RE 2, 100s.

9. ORR, James, ed., *The International Standard Bible Encyclopedia*, 5 V.,
WBE, RE, 1930, 3500 pp., $37.50;
WBE, 294s. Outstanding older dictionary.

10. *TENNEY, M. C., ed., *The Pic-
torial Bible Dictionary*, ZPH, 1963,
1000 pp., $9.95; MMS, 70s. Well
written with excellent pictures.

Vocabulary and Word Studies:
11. KITTEL, G. and G. Friedrich,
eds., *Theological Dictionary of the
New Testament*, 4 V., WBE, 1964-67,
$22.50 each. Useful for detailed re-
search.

12. TRENCH, R. C., *Synonyms of
the New Testament*, Ri, WBE, 1950,
416 pp., $4.50; JC, 1963, 18s. Much
richly suggestive material, although
partly outdated.

Grammars and Lexicons:
13. *ARNDT, W. F. and F. W. Ging-
rich, *A Greek-English Lexicon of the
New Testament*, ZPH, 1963, 910 pp.,
$14.00; UCP, 1957, 130s. A standard
work.

14. DEISSMANN, G. A., *Light from
the Ancient East* (ET), BBH, 1966,
535 pp., $7.95.

15. MACHEN, J. G., *New Testament
Greek for Beginners*, MC, 1923,
$5.25; CM, 38s. An excellent per-
ceptive grammar.

16. MOULE, C. F., *An Idiom Book
of New Testament Greek*, CAUP, ED
2, 1959, 246 pp., Hb $6.00, Pb
$2.95; CAUP, Hb 35s, Pb 18s 6d.
Valuable for students.

Introductions:
17. BARRETT, C. K., ed., *The New
Testament Background: Selected
Documents*, SP, 1957, 316 pp.,
$4.50; SPCK, 21s.

18. BLAIKLOCK, E. M., *Rome in
the New Testament*, TP, 1956, 36
pp., 1s 6d. Excellent short study.

19. BRUCE, F. F., *The Books and
the Parchments*, PI, RE, 1950, 260
pp., $4.50; PI, RE 3, 288 pp., 25s.

20. *BRUCE, F. F., *The New Testament Documents: Are They Reliable?*, IVP, 1965, 120 pp., Pb $1.25;
TP, RE 5, 1960, 128 pp., 3s 6d.
Scholarly presentation of historical
trustworthiness.

21. FLACK, E. E., et al., *The Text, Canon and Principal Versions of the New Testament,* BBH, 1956, 64 pp., $1.50.

22. *GUTHRIE, Donald, *The Gospels and Acts,* IVP, 1964, 360 pp., $5.95; TP, 1965, 21s. Background and critical questions are lucidly discussed; recommended.

23. *GUTHRIE, Donald, *Hebrews to Revelation,* IVP, 1962, 320 pp., $4.95; TP, 1964, 18s 6d. Very thorough treatment of critical questions.

24. *HARRISON, Everett, *Introduction to the New Testament,* WBE, 1964, 496 pp., $5.95; PI, 1966, 37s 6d. Excellent concise introduction; conservative.

25. *MANLEY, G. T., ed., *The New Bible Handbook,* IVP, 1947, 465 pp., $4.95; TP, ED 3, 1950, 380 pp., 15s. A very useful introduction for the student.

26. METZGER, B. M., *The Text of the New Testament,* OUP, 1964, 280 pp., $7.00; OUP, 42s.

27. SOUTER, A., *The Text and Canon of the New Testament,* AL, ED, 1954, 236 pp., $2.75; DUC, 9s 6d.

28. STONEHOUSE, N. B., *Paul Before Areopagus,* WBE, 1957, 204 pp., $3.50; TP, 15s. Essays on New Testament subjects.

29. STOTT, J. R. W., *Basic Introduction to the New Testament,* WBE, 1964, 179 pp., Hb $3.75, Pb $1.45. Good survey for beginners.

30. *TENNEY, Merrill C., *New Testament Survey,* Ri, WBE, 1961, 484 pp., $5.95; TP, RE 2, 25s. Well illustrated and written survey.

31. *TENNEY, Merrill C., *New Testament Times,* WBE, 1965, 396 pp.,

$5.95; TP, 25s. Well illustrated and written cultural background.

General Literature

32. *DAVIDSON, F., A. M. Stibbs, E. F. Kevan, eds., *New Bible Commentary,* WBE, 1954, 1200 pp., $8.95; TP, ED 2, 1954, 1199 pp., 40s. Probably the best one-volume commentary.

33. HENRY, Matthew, *Exposition of the Old and New Testaments,* 6 V., Ri, REV, 1953, 2000 pp., $7.00 per V. (OoP); PI, 22s per V.; MMS, 1 V., 1960, 2000 pp., 75s.

34. JAMIESON, R., A. R. Fausset and D. A. Brown, *Commentary, Experimental and Practical, on the Old and New Testaments,* WBE, 1444 pp., $35.00; OL, 1934, 60s. (OoP)

35. LANGE, L. P., ed., *A Commentary on the Holy Scriptures,* 25 V. (VE) Critical, doctrinal, and homiletical; learned, detailed, and practical.

36. *NICOLL, W. R., ed., *The Expositor's Greek Testament,* 5 V., WBE, 1952, $25.00. Over 2,000 expositions; uneven but useful for study of the Greek text.

37. ROBERTSON, A. T., *Word Pictures in the New Testament,* 6 V., BR, 1943, $22.50. These word studies can be used by those who are unacquainted with Greek.

38. VINCENT, M. R., *Word Studies in the New Testament,* 4 V., WBE, ED 2, 1957, $25.00. Combination of lexical study and exegetical commentary.

Gospels: General Works

39. ANDREWS, S. J., *The Life of Our Lord on Earth,* ZPH, 1954, 543 pp., $5.95. (OoP) Good treatment of chronological problems.

40. EDERSHEIM, Alfred, *The Life and Times of Jesus the Messiah,* 2 V., Ri, WBE, 1953, 1523 pp., $8.95; PI, 1959, 63s. Old but never superseded. Excellent for Jewish background. For an abridged edition see *Jesus the Messiah,* WBE, 1954, 646 pp., $4.95.

41. STONEHOUSE, N. B., *Origins of the Synoptic Gospels,* WBE, 1963, 198 pp., $4.50; TP, 1964, 208 pp., 12s 6d. Authorship, order and independence, apostolic tradition, and ultimate origin are discussed.

New Testament Commentaries

Matthew

42. MORRIS, Leon, *The Story of the Cross,* WBE, 1957, 128 pp., $2.00; MMS, 10s 6d. A devotional study on chapters 26-28.

43. RIDDERBOS, H. N., *Commentary on Matthew* (NICNT), WBE (in preparation).

44. STONEHOUSE, N. B., *The Witness of Matthew and Mark to Christ,* TP, RE 2, 1958, 288 pp., 12s 6d. (OoP) A first-rate theological study.

45. *TASKER, R. V., *The Gospel According to St. Matthew* (TNTC), WBE, 1962, 285 pp., $3.50; TP, 1961, 12s 6d. Reverent and thorough exegesis.

Mark

46. *COLE, Alan, *The Gospel According to St. Mark* (TNTC), WBE, 1962, 264 pp., $3.95; TP, 11s 6d. Succinct and helpful.

47. LANE, W. L., *Commentary on Mark* (NICNT), WBE; TP (in preparation).

48. SWETE, H. B., *The Gospel According to St. Mark,* Ri, WBE, 1951, 434 pp., $6.00. (OoP) A commentary of solid worth on the Greek text.

Luke

49. *GELDENHUYS, J. N., *Commentary on the Gospel of St. Luke* (NICNT), WBE, 1951, 688 pp., $6.00; MMS, 35s. Work of massive scholarship.

50. PLUMMER, Alfred, *St. Luke,* CLA, ED 5, 1956, 592 pp., $8.00; TTC, 28s. An excellent commentary on the Greek text.

51. RAMSAY, Sir W. M., *Luke the Physician,* Ri, BBH, 1956, 432 pp., $4.50. (OoP) Absorbing historical treatment.

52. WALLS, Andrew, *The Gospel According to St. Luke* (TNTC), WBE; TP (in preparation).

John

53. HENDRICKSEN, William, *Gospel of John,* 2 V., BBH 1953-54, 768 pp., $6.95; BTT, 1959, 25s.

54. MORRIS, Leon, *Commentary on the Gospel of John* (NICNT), WBE (in preparation).

55. *TASKER, R. V., ed., *The Gospel According to St. John* (TNTC), WBE, 1960, 240 pp., $3.95; TP, 10s 6d. Best shorter commentary.

56. TENNEY, Merrill C., *John: The Gospel of Belief,* WBE, 1948, 321 pp., $4.00. An analytic survey.

57. WESTCOTT, B. F., *The Gospel According to St. John,* WBE, 1950, 426 pp., $5.00; CLA, 1958, 18s 6d. Excellent and indispensable.

Acts

58. *BLAIKLOCK, E. M., *The Acts of the Apostles* (TNTC), WBE, 1959, 198 pp., $3.50; TP, 200 pp., 10s 6d. Strong in historical material.

59. *BRUCE, F. F., *Commentary on the Book of Acts* (NICNT), WBE, 1954, 566 pp., $6.00; MMS, 35s.

Probably the best commentary available today.

60. BRUCE, F. F., *Commentary on the Acts of the Apostles*, WBE, 1953, 152 pp., $6.00; TP, ED 2, 1952, 25s. Greek text. Deals mainly with technical, critical, and linguistic matters.

61. RACKHAM, R. B., *The Acts of the Apostles* (WC), BBH, ED 15, 1964, 642 pp., $6.95; ME, ED 14, 1901, 30s.

62. RAMSAY, Sir W. M., *Pictures of the Apostolic Church*, Ri, BBH, 1959, 367 pp., $3.50. (OoP) Useful historical commentary.

The Pauline Epistles

63. CONYBEARE, W. J. and J. S. Howson, *The Life and Epistles of St. Paul*, Ri, WBE, 1949, 850 pp., $5.50. Old, but thorough, and still useful.

64. ELLIS, E. E., *Paul's Use of the Old Testament*, OB, 1957, 216 pp., 21s. (OoP) A fine and erudite study of Paul's exegesis.

65. *GUTHRIE, D., *New Testament Introduction: The Pauline Epistles*, IVP, 1963, 320 pp., $4.95; TP, 1963, 18s 6d. Recommended.

66. *MACHEN, J. G., *The Origin of Paul's Religion*, Ri, WBE, 1967, 329 pp., Pb $1.95. Seeks to show that Paul has not "developed" his doctrine beyond what is present, in form at least, in Christ's teaching.

67. *RAMSAY, Sir W. M., *St. Paul the Traveller and the Roman Citizen*, Ri, BBH, 1960, 402 pp., Pb $2.95. Especially valuable for historical and archaeological background. See also, Sir W. M. Ramsay, *The Cities of St. Paul*, Ri, BBH, 1960, 452 pp., $2.95.

Romans

68. *BRUCE, F. F., *Commentary on Epistle to the Romans* (TNTC), WBE,

1963, 288 pp., $3.95; TP, 12s 6d. One of the finest, combining scholarly acumen with simplicity.

69. HODGE, Charles, *The Epistle to the Romans*, Ri, WBE, 1950, $5.50. Informative although somewhat dated.

70. LIDDON, H. P., *Explanatory Analysis of St. Paul's Epistle to the Romans*, LO, 1893, 308 pp. (OoP) The only commentary of its kind on Romans. Extremely valuable for students.

71. MOULE, H. C., *The Epistle to the Romans*, PI, 1928, 488 pp., 22s 6d. A most valuable commentary. For a shorter version, see the same title, CAUP, 1952, 270 pp., $2.75; CAUP, 15s.

72. *MURRAY, John, *The Epistle to the Romans* (NICNT), 2 V., WBE, 1960, 408 pp. and 286 pp., $5.00 each; MMS, 25s each. A sustained modern commentary in the reformed tradition.

I and II Corinthians

73. *GROSHEIDE, F. W., *The First Epistle to the Corinthians* (NICNT), WBE, 1953, 416 pp., $5.00; MMS, 30s. Valuable, takes account of the modern scholarship.

74. *HUGHES, Philip, *Commentary on the Second Epistle to the Corinthians* (NICNT), WBE, 1960, 544 pp., $6.50; MMS, 30s. Probably the best modern commentary.

75. *MORRIS, Leon, *The First Epistle of Paul to the Corinthians* (TNTC), WBE, 1958, 250 pp., $3.95; TP, 12s 6d. Clear and useful for beginners.

76. *TASKER, R. V., *The Second Epistle of Paul to the Corinthians* (TNTC), WBE, 1958, 192 pp., $3.95;

TP, 9s 6d. Useful short commentary for beginners.

Galatians

77. *COLE, Alan, *The Epistle of Paul to Galatians* (TNTC), WBE, 1965, 192 pp., $3.50; TP, 10s 6d. Best modern short commentary.

78. LIGHTFOOT, J. B., *Galatians,* Ri, ZPH, 1957, 384 pp., $5.95; OL, 36s. An outstanding commentary.

79. RAMSAY, Sir W. M., *A Historical Commentary on St. Paul's Epistle to the Galatians,* Ri, BBH, 478 pp., $6.95. Contrasts with Lightfoot above.

80. *RIDDERBOS, H. N., *The Epistle of Paul to the Churches of Galatia* (NICNT), WBE, 1953, 240 pp., $4.00; MMS, 25s. Excellent and recommended.

Ephesians

81. BRUCE, F. F., *Epistle to the Ephesians,* REV, 1962, 144 pp., $3.00; PI, 13s 6d. Useful for the beginner, lucid and clear.

82. *FOULKES, Francis, *The Epistle of Paul to Ephesians* (TNTC), WBE, 1963, 176 pp., $3.50; TP, 9s 6d. Perceptive and convincing.

83. MOULE, H. C., *Ephesians Studies,* ZPH, 352 pp., $3.95; PI, 1937, 17s 6d. Profound commentary.

84. ROBINSON, J. A., *The Epistle of Paul to the Ephesians,* MC, 1909, 328 pp. (OoP); Ri, JC, 1961, 18s 6d. Based on Greek text. One of the most useful works on Ephesians.

85. *SIMPSON, E. K. and F. F. Bruce, *Commentary on the Epistle to the Ephesians and the Colossians* (NICNT), WBE, 1958, 328 pp., $4.50; MMS, 25s. Some of the most edifying expositions.

Philippians, Colossians and Philemon

86. *CARSON, H. M., *Epistle of Paul to the Colossians and to Philemon* (TNTC), WBE, 112 pp., $3.00; TP, 7s 6d. Recommended short commentary for the beginner.

87. HENDRICKSEN, William, *Epistles to Colossians and Philemon,* BBH, 1965, 243 pp., $6.95.

88. HENDRICKSEN, William, *Epistle to the Philippians,* BBH, 1963, 224 pp., $5.95; BTT, 218 pp., 15s.

89. LIGHTFOOT, J. B., *The Epistle of St. Paul to the Philippians,* Ri, ZPH, 1957, 350 pp., $4.95; Ri, OL, 1953, 40s. Probably the best commentary available.

90. LIGHTFOOT, J. B., *St. Paul's Epistles to the Colossians and Philemon,* Ri, ZPH, 1957, 430 pp., $5.95; OL, 36s. A classic among Greek text commentaries.

91. *MARTIN, R. P., *The Epistle of Paul to the Philippians* (TNTC), WBE, 1959, 186 pp., $3.50; TP, 9s 6d. Useful short treatment.

92. *MOTYER, J. A., *Philippians Studies: The Richness of Christ,* IVP, 1966, 188 pp., $3.50; TP, 15s. Brings home the message with force and urgency.

93. MOULE, H. C., *Colossian and Philemon Studies,* Ri, PI, 1947, 328 pp. (OoP); PI, 17s 6d. Rewarding and glowing commentary.

94. MOULE, H. C., *Philippian Studies,* Ri, PI, 1928, 264 pp., 17s 6d. Precipitates beauty and light of the Scriptures.

95. *MULLER, J. J., *The Epistle of Paul to the Philippians and to Philemon* (NICNT), WBE, 1955, $3.50; MMS, 25s. Penetrating and useful.

96. ROBERTSON, A. T., *Paul and the Intellectuals,* Ri, BR, 1959, 134 pp., $2.50; (OoP) Studies in the theology of the Colossians.

I and II Thessalonians
97. HENDRICKSEN, William, *I and II Thessalonians,* BBH, 1953, $4.50.

98. *MORRIS, Leon, *The Epistles of Paul to the Thessalonians* (TNTC), WBE, 1957, 152 pp., $2.75; TP, 8s 6d. Useful brief commentary.

99. *MORRIS, Leon, *The Epistles to the Thessalonians* (NICNT), WBE, 1959, 274 pp., $4.00; MMS, 25s. Full and judicious.

The Pastoral Epistles
100. *GUTHRIE, Donald, *The Pastoral Epistles* (TNTC), WBE, 1957, 228 pp., $3.75; TP, 10s 6d. Valuable in criticism and exegesis.

101. HENDRICKSEN, William, *I and II Timothy and Titus,* BBH, 1957, 404 pp., $6.00; BTT, 1960, 21s.

102. PARRY, R., *The Pastoral Epistles,* CAUP, 1920. (OoP) Commentary on Greek text. Full discussion of Pauline authorship.

103. VAN ELDEREN, B., *Commentary on the Epistles to Timothy and Titus* (NICNT), WBE (in preparation).

Hebrews
104. *BRUCE, F. F., *Commentary on the Epistle to the Hebrews* (NICNT), WBE, 1964, 448 pp., $6.50; MMS, 30s. Presents a new dimension of the work of Christ.

105. DAVIDSON, A. B., *Hebrews,* TTC, 260 pp., 9s. A magisterial statement of the argument.

106. *HEWITT, Thomas, *The Epistle to the Hebrews* (TNTC), WBE,

1961, 218 pp., $3.75; TP, 1960, 10s 6d. A short commentary which achieves new clarity.

107. WESTCOTT, B. F., *The Epistle to the Hebrews,* WBE, 1950, 504 pp., $6.00. Excellent grammatical commentary based on Greek text.

General Epistles:

James
108. MAYOR, J. B., *The Epistle of St. James,* MC, 1892 (OoP); OL, 622 pp., 56s. An excellent commentary based on Greek text.

109. *ROSS, Alexander, *The Epistles of James and John* (NICNT), WBE, 1954, 250 pp., $4.50; MMS, 30s. Valuable commentary taking into account the latest critical research.

110. *TASKER, R. V., *The General Epistle of James* (TNTC), WBE, 1957, 144 pp., $3.00; TP, 7s 6d. Concise and compelling.

Peter and Jude
111. CRANFIELD, C. E., *I and II Peter and Jude,* AL, 1960, 128 pp., $3.00; SCMP, 6s. Short and geared toward students.

112. *FINDLAY, G. G., *Fellowship in the Life Eternal,* Ri, WBE, 1955, 431 pp., $5.00. (OoP) A rich exposition of the three Epistles.

113. *GREEN, M., *II Peter and Jude* (TNTC), WBE, 1968, $4.50; TP, 12s 6d. Helpful beginners' commentary.

114. MAYOR, J. B., *The Second Epistle of Peter and the Epistle of St. Jude,* BBH, 1965, 239 pp., $6.95. Based on Greek text, very thorough.

115. SELWYN, E. G., *The First Epistle of St. Peter,* SM, 1946, 534 pp., $6.00; MC, ED 2, 1947, 518 pp.,

35s. Based on Greek text, learned and judicious.

116. SKILTON, J. H., *Commentary on Peter and Jude* (NICNT), WBE (in preparation).

117. *STIBBS, A. M. and A. F. Wallis, *The First Epistle of Peter* (TNTC), WBE, 1959, 192 pp., $3.50; TP, 9s 6d. Rich and thought-provoking.

118. *STOTT, John R., *The Johannine Epistles* (TNTC), WBE, 1964, 230 pp., $3.75; TP, 10s 6d. Illuminating and helpful for students.

119. WALLS, Andrew, *II Peter and Jude* (TNTC), WBE; TP (in preparation).

120. WESTCOTT, B. F., *The Epistles of John*, MC, ED 3, 1966, 321 pp., 30s. The best available commentary on the Greek text.

Revelation
121. BECKWITH, I. T., *Apocalypse of John*, BBH, 1967, $8.95. One of the best of the commentaries on the Greek text.

122. BLAIKLOCK, E. M., *The Seven Churches*, MMS, 1950. (OoP) Up-to-date historical background.

123. *HENDRIKSEN, William, *More Than Conquerors*, BBH, 1947, 216 pp., Hb $3.95, Pb $1.00; TP, 1962, 17s 6d. An exposition on synchronous-historical lines; recommended.

124. MORRIS, Leon, *Revelation* (TNTC), WBE; TP (in preparation).

125. MOUNCE, R. H., *Commentary on Revelation* (NICNT), WBE (in preparation).

126. RAMSAY, Sir W. M., *The Seven Churches*, BBH, 1963, 446 pp.,

$4.95. (OoP) Vivid historical and topographical studies.

127. STOTT, John R., *What Christ Thinks of the Church*, LU, 1958, 128 pp., Hb 6s 6d, Pb 5s 5d. (OoP) Exposition of chapters 1-3.

128. *TENNEY, Merrill C., *Interpreting Revelation*, WBE, 1957, 220 pp., $3.50. Excellent analytical commentary.

129. WALVOORD, John F., *The Revelation of Jesus Christ*, MP, 1966, 352 pp., $5.95; MMS, 37s 6d.

1C. STUDY GUIDES
Harish D. Merchant
Studying the Bible is a Christian's privilege. It is unfortunate that although most listen to sermons, not many read the Bible regularly and only a few study the Word of God systematically. Even a cursory research of the Gospels, for example, can bear surprisingly exciting rewards in furthering a Christian's knowledge as well as his maturity. A majority of the principles of Christian life are scattered throughout the Bible; they only need to be crystallized, ordered, and absorbed.

Often the Christians are staggered by the vastness of the Bible, complexity of the doctrines, and fatness of the voluminous commentaries, dictionaries and reference books. They lack discipline to research the Bible on their own and incentive to do so in fellowship with others. For them the Bible study guides are just the answer. They are simple, related to either books in the Bible or to pertinent subjects of Christian concern, and inexpensive.

1. *Some Basic Texts*, IVP, RE 4, 1955, 32 pp., Pb 15¢; TP, Pb 6d. To know Bible passages accurately by heart and to be able to find them immediately is of tremendous value

to one's own spiritual life and in Christian service. Selected Bible texts are given on the basis of Christian life and of Christian doctrine.

2. CARSON, H. M., *Light on the Way,* IVP, 39 pp., Pb 15¢; TP, Pb 6d. A month's course of readings from the Bible with comments and inductive questions. It is designed as a devotional aid for the beginner.

3. *QUIET TIME,* IVP, 1945, 30 pp., Pb 30¢; TP, ED 5, 1957, 48 pp., Pb 1s. Growth in the Christian life originates in daily communion with God. This guide discusses meaning and purpose of devotions and suggests several practical methods.

4. DERHAM, A. M., *A Christian's Guide to Bible Study,* HS, 1963, 63 pp., Pb 3s 6d. Attitude, basic principles, methods, and tools for personal Bible study. Very simple and practical for young Christians.

5. *TRAINA, R. A., *Methodical Bible Study,* New York Biblical Seminary, 1952. A comprehensive, analytical approach to Bible study which defines and illustrates the three types of questions: observation, interpretation, and application. Recommended. See also, *Methods of Bible Study,* SCMP, 4s.

6. WOOD, S. N. and J. R. Hill, *Bible Class Teaching and Leadership,* SU, 1964, 153 pp., Pb 6s. A practical book which discusses the methods and problems of planning, communicating, and illustrating the biblical truth in the Sunday School class.

7. *STIBBS, A. M., *Understanding God's Word,* IVP, 1950, 64 pp., Pb 75¢; TP, Pb 4s; *Obeying God's Word,* IVP, 1955, 79 pp., Pb 75¢; TP, Pb 4s; *Expounding God's Word,* TP, 1960, 112 pp., Pb 6s. An indispensable trilogy for those who want to dig into and teach from the Bible. The first

volume discusses what the Bible actually says and what it means. The section on parable, allegory, and figurative language is particularly useful. The second volume considers the practical implications of the authority of Scripture and the analysis of what we believe and how we act in view of the biblical teaching. The third volume gives some of the principles and methods of biblical exposition to help the teacher get the message of the Word of God across in relevant, intelligible terms.

8. *ARCHIBALD, R. T., *The Spirit's Sword,* IVP, 1949, 42 pp., Pb 60¢. (OoP) An excellent guide for individual study or for two or three working together. It is meant for those who have earnest desire to grasp the biblical teachings, for it goes on to show through a large number of Scripture references that the Word of God is indeed a two-edged sword in the matter of Christian doctrine as well as of life.

9. STIBBS, Alan M., gen. ed., *Search the Scriptures,* IVP, RE, 1968, 544 pp., $4.95; TP, Hb 19s; 3 V., Pb 17s set. A systematic course of daily study, based on the question-and-answer method, designed to cover the whole Bible in three years. Instead of going through the Bible books in sequence, long books are broken into smaller sections giving a variety between Old and New Testament materials.

10. *Standing Orders,* IVP RE, 1969, Pb 75¢. A Bible study guide which helps those in the nursing profession study such subjects as their attitudes toward people, service, loneliness, and the problems of suffering, affections, and honesty.

11. *IVCF Guide to Campus Christian Life,* IVP, 1965, Pb $1.50; *Leader's Notes to IVCF Guide,* IVP, RE, 1969, 37 pp., Pb 95¢. The IVCF

Guide directs personal Bible study with a wide variety of topics pertaining to Christian life such as personal evangelism, sin, and growth, knowing God's will, and Christian marriage. There are twelve topics and eighty-four studies. *Leader's Notes* gives several outlines for using the Guide for group discussions.

12. *NYQUIST, James F., *Leading Bible Discussions,* IVP, 1967, 59 pp., Pb 75¢. A practical, field-tested guide for leaders in preparing, leading, and evaluating inductive discussion-type group Bible studies. Especially useful for student and young adult groups. See also, D. C. K. Watson, *Learning to Lead Group Bible Study,* FB, 1962, 18 pp., Pb 1s; *Know How to Lead Bible Study and Discussion Groups,* SU, Pb 1s 6d; *Chart for Adventure,* Methodist Youth Department, 2 Chester House, Pages Lane, Muswell Hill, London, N. 10, 1961, 63 pp., Pb 1s 6d.

13. KUNZ, Marilyn and Catherine Schell, *How to Start a Neighborhood Bible Study,* Neighborhood Bible Studies, Box 222, Dobbs Ferry, New York 10522, 1966, 24 pp., 50¢. A brief guide for initiating, promoting, and leading participation type Bible studies in the home or neighborhood.

14. ERB, Margaret, *Basic Christianity,* IVP, 1952, 88 pp., Pb 75¢. The Bible studies here are designed for non-Christians or young Christians on subjects such as what God is like, the effects of sin, and what belief is. Also included are the suggestions for the leaders.

15. *Hold the Faith,* IVP, 1956, 71 pp., Pb 60¢; TP, Pb 2s. An introductory Bible study course for six months of daily study covering the life of Christ, the early history of the Church, Genesis, selected Psalms, and doctrines from four epistles.

16. *KUNZ, Marilyn and Catherine Schell, *Conversations with Jesus Christ,* NBS, 1960, 70 pp., Pb $1.00. Thirteen discussions for inductive group Bible study from the Gospel of John. Emphasis is entering into the conversations of Jesus Christ and learning about his person.

17. *Discussions on the Life of Jesus Christ,* IVP, 1962, Pb 75¢. Another discussion guide with twelve studies for those who want to know more about the person and work of Jesus Christ, and the implications of his claims as recorded in the Bible.

18. STEEVES, P., *The Character and Work of Jesus Christ,* IVP, Pb 95¢. Questions for study and application, plus commentary in daily studies on Jesus' deity, lordship, love, death, and resurrection.

19. *Christ in You,* IVP, 1966, 16 pp., Pb 30¢. A personal study guide for young or new Christians to start studying the Bible for themselves. It deals with basic, practical issues which all Christians encounter as they mature. The six studies included are Jesus Christ—our living God, assurance of eternal life, abiding in Christ, living in fellowship, facing sin and temptation, and becoming fruitful disciples.

20. *KUNZ, Marilyn, *Patterns for Living With God,* IVP, 1961, 59 pp., Pb 75¢. Twelve Old Testament character studies for those interested in discovering God's hand in the lives of Caleb, Gideon, Samson, Ruth, Elijah, Jehoshaphat, Naaman, Jonah, Josiah, Daniel, Ezra, and Nehemiah.

21. HOLLINGSWORTH, Jane, *Discovering the Gospel of Mark,* IVP, 1950, 41 pp., Pb 75¢. This guide helps the student, through sixteen studies, discover the teachings in Mark through inductive Bible study

principles and gives directions for leading a group discussion on Mark.

22. *HUMMEL, C. E., *The Search,* IVP, 1966, Pb 75¢. The author uses thirty-one studies of Luke's Gospel to supply direction in an interested non-Christian's search for the purpose of existence.

23. *First Century Christians,* IVP, 30 pp., Pb 50¢. A group Bible study guide for the book of Acts of the Apostles.

24. HOLLINGSWORTH, Jane and Alice Reid, *Look at Life with the Apostle Peter,* IVP, 1945, 66 pp., Pb 75¢. The guide helps individuals and groups uncover spiritual treasures from Peter's life and letters with the aid of sixteen studies.

Note: The Neighborhood Bible Studies, Box 22, Dobbs Ferry, New York 10522, has excellent discussion guides available as follows: *Four Men of God—Abraham, Joseph, Moses, David; Psalms; Proverbs; Gospel of Mark; Gospel of John; Book of Acts; Romans; Ephesians;* and *John and James.* They are especially useful for small community groups and are recommended.

1D. INTERPRETATION
A. Berkeley Mickelson
Hermeneutics or interpretation is concerned with understanding. A good interpreter seeks to understand the meaning the original author(s) wanted to convey and how the original hearers or readers would have comprehended the utterance. He seeks further to state this meaning in such a way that modern men living in a far different culture and time can likewise grasp this meaning. Earlier endeavors to convey meaning, the role of history, culture and language, the attitude and approach of the interpreter—all of these elements are essential to being able to interpret with empathy and with authentic penetration into the thought being conveyed from person to person. Methods and procedures have only one purpose: to prevent the distortion of thought and to insure that thought will be transmitted with integrity and with clarity. The following works deal with important aspects of interpretation.

History
1. WOOD, D., *The Interpretation of the Bible,* AL, 1958, $2.75; DUC, 184 pp., 10s 6d. A brief history of interpretation from the New Testament to the present day. Touches all the main questions. Helpful for beginners. Evangelical in outlook. For a scholarly account of medieval exegesis, see B. Smalley, *The Study of the Bible in the Middle Ages,* UND, 1964, 406 pp., Pb $2.25; BL, ED 2, 1952, Hb 45s.

2. *NEIL, Stephen, *Interpretation of the New Testament,* OUP, 1964, 360 pp., Hb $7.00, Pb $2.25; OUP, 368 pp., Hb 45s, Pb 10s 6d. Careful and detailed treatment of the issues that have been debated in the last one hundred years and the individuals who were involved in these discussions. Essential for all students who want to understand present-day issues. Where we are is the effect of that through which we have come. For the historical approach to interpretation, see the old classic by M. S. Terry, *Biblical Hermeneutics,* Ri, ZPH, 1956, 782 pp., $9.75; Ri, OL, 1950, 50s.

Methods, Attitude, and Approach
3. FISHER, F. L., *How to Interpret the New Testament,* WP, 1964, 172 pp., $4.50. A primer on tools for the interpretation of the New Testament and steps to be followed. See also, L. Berkhof, *Principles of Biblical Interpretation,* BBH, ED 2, 1952, 170 pp., $2.95.

4. RAMM, Bernard, *Protestant Biblical Interpretation*, RE, 1956, WAWC, 272 pp. First presented in lecture form; carefully revised. Discusses key aspects of hermeneutics. First-rate systematic theologian looks at procedures of varieties of theological interpreters. Evangelical in outlook and perspective.

5. *MICKELSEN, A. B., *Interpreting the Bible*, WBE, 1963, 425 pp., $5.95. Comprehensive text which seeks to cover every aspect of hermeneutics in the light of contemporary issues. Seven chapters are devoted to various kinds of figurative language. Language, context, history, and culture underline the nature of literal language. Evangelical in outlook and perspective.

6. MINEAR, P. S., *Eyes of Faith*, Ri, BETP, 1966, 307 pp., Pb $3.45. This book purposes to set forth the biblical perspective which is often assumed but not explicitly stated. Since many aspects of this perspective are foreign to modern man, he cannot understand the message of the Bible because of his ignorance and hostility. As timely and relevant as when first written.

7. MARLÉ, René, *Introduction to Hermeneutics*, HH, 1967, 150 pp., $4.50. A product of the biblical renaissance in the Roman Catholic Church. Careful evaluation of Bultmann. Clearly sets forth a responsible Roman Catholic attitude towards principles of hermeneutics.

8. ALONSO-SCHOKEL, Louis, *The Inspired Word*, HH, 1965, 418 pp., $8.50. Comprehensive Roman Catholic treatment of the inspired Scriptures and how they must be interpreted as literature written in various kinds and forms of human language.

9. BLACKMAN, E. C., *Biblical Interpretation*, WP, 1957, 212 pp., $3.00; IP, 1959, 12s 6d. Discusses biblical interpretation in the light of the issues raised in the middle of the 20th century. Wrestles with the question of the nature of the Bible's authority. Looks at modern criticism of the Bible and examines the present-day task.

Approach to Parables

10. HUNTER, A. M., *Interpreting the Parables*, WP, 1961, 126 pp., $2.50; SCMP, RE, 1964, 128 pp., 6s 6d. Brief treatment of the main aspects of parables and how these are to be handled by the interpreter. Uses and evaluates the works of C. H. Dodd and Joachim Jeremias. Centers the parables in the framework of the proclamation of the Kingdom.

11. LINNEMANN, Eta, *Jesus of the Parables*, HRP, ET, 1966, 215 pp., $4.95; SPCK, 216 pp., 35s. Author divides the book into two parts: basic principles and specific parables. Thorough scholarship is evident on every page. Over one-third of the book involves carefully worked out footnotes. Selected parables are interpreted to illustrate the principles that the author has presented.

12. BRAATEN, C. E., *History and Hermeneutics*, WP, 1966, 205 pp., Hb $3.95, Pb $1.95. Braaten popularizes a great deal of technical data on history and its connection with revelation. He clarifies the differences between history and historicism. His chapter on the Historical Event of the Resurrection is solidly evangelical with full awareness of all the issues involved.

13. STENDAHL, Krister, "Biblical Theology, Contemporary," in *Interpreter's Dictionary of the Bible*, ABP, 1962, I, pp. 418-432. This article is more than a valid method for biblical theology (historical theology of the Old and New Testaments). It touches both upon biblical and systematic

theology. The first half of the article looks at the descriptive task—what *did* it mean. The second half raises the hermeneutic question—what *does* it mean.

14. LEVIE, Jean, *The Bible, Word of God in Words of Men*, PJK, ET, 1961, 323 pp., $7.50; DS, 1964, 336 pp., 21s. An Old Testament Roman Catholic scholar describes the impact on Roman Catholic biblical scholarship of historical, archaelogical, and exegetical developments from 1950 to 1960. He interprets the encyclical "Divino afflante Spiritu" (1943) as the Magna Carta of Roman Catholic biblical scholarship. The role of the Church as an interpreter is not a special charismatic gift in philology or history, but she has God's power to understand in the process of time and in the light of the Spirit.

15. SMART, J. D., *The Interpretation of Scripture*, WP, 1961, 317 pp., $6.00. Discusses all of the key issues as they affect the interpreter today. The interpretation of Scripture is set forth with a comprehensive awareness of past theological approaches as well as present possibilities. The book is oriented theologically. For Smart "revelation is *in the text itself,* in the words that confront us there in all their strangeness, and not in a history or a personal biography or an event that we reconstructed by means of the text" (pp. 195-196).

16. *NIDA, E. A., *Message and Mission, Importance of Language*, HRP, 1960, 253 pp., $5.00; HRP, 37s 6d. A superb treatment of what communication really involves. The subject is developed anthropologically and linguistically. Yet the psychology and theology of communication are not neglected. Those who have a message and mission must take seriously all that is involved in communicating. This is the burden of the book.

17. NIDA, E. A., *Religion Across Culture*, HRP, 1967, 150 pp. In this volume, Nida examines religious communication. He distinguishes between communication that involves the natural and the supernatural. He compares Hinduism, Buddhism, Islam, and Christianity to show the different kinds of communication involved. The differences in Christianity from the others underlines what Christianity has that is unique.

18. MOREAU, J. L., *Language and Religious Language*, WP, 1961, 207 pp. (OoP) An investigation of the philosophical aspects of language by a New Testament scholar. Philosophically, Moreau would favor the "translation" of the New Testament message into a system that combines existentialism and process theology.

Existentialist Approach

19. BULTMANN, Rudolf, "Is Exegesis with Presuppositions Possible?" in *Existence and Faith*, MEB, 1961, pp. 389-396, Pb $1.75; HS, 320 pp., Hb 21s; CO, 1964, 384 pp., Pb 8s 6d. This essay shows that there is no neutrality in exegesis. Certain liberal convictions of Bultmann are clearly evident in his approach to presuppositions. Yet it is a strong plea that exegesis be unprejudiced and there must be a growing understanding.

20. ROBINSON, J. M. and J. B. Cobb, eds., *The New Hermeneutic*, EV, 1964, 243 pp., Hb $5.00; HRP, 37s 6d. This volume is a series of essays in which the existentialist approach to hermeneutics is presented, critically evaluated, and reappraised. Although religious existentialism has claimed to be the heir of the liberal banner, it has come into difficulty because it has not addressed itself to the question of how we verify truth claims of theology which has its intermediate source in historical documents or kerygma. This book does

not deal adequately with this basic weakness.

21. FUNK, R. W., *Language, Hermeneutic, and Word of God,* EV, 1966, 317 pp., $7.50; HRP, 60s. This volume is for an advanced student in that it presupposes an extensive acquaintance with religious existentialism. From an existentialist point of view, Funk examines language as event, the language of theology, the role of language in parable and in letter.

Current Issues
22. KLASSEN, William, and G. F. Snyder, eds., *Current Issues in New Testament Interpretation,* HRP, 1962, 302 pp. (OoP) This is a collection of essays in honor of Otto Piper, and deals with many areas of New Testament studies. Interpretation is carried out rather than discussed methodologically. Questions dealing with the Gospels, Epistles, the Apocalypse, Canon, Gnosticism are all highlighted and presented in a succinct fashion.

23. HERZOG, Frederick, *Understanding God,* CSS, 1966, 191 pp., Hb $4.50, Pb $2.95. The main task of the book is to show how we come to understand God, but Herzog also provides an incisive critique of both the "Death of God" theology and the New Hermeneutic. This is a most refreshing book because it firmly pursues basic questions of how we know and the reality of being.

24. BARR, James, *Old and New Interpretation,* HRP, 1966, 215 pp., $5.50; SCMP, 216 pp., 30s. Barr grapples with the question as to how the Old and New Testaments are related. He examines favorite keys and points out what they lack. He looks as typology, allegory, and salvation and the roles played by each in both covenants. In addition to presenting his own conclusions, Barr has an ap-

pendix on Fundamentalism—how he feels it has been misunderstood and his own analysis of its approach.

25. WESTERMANN, Clauss, ed. & author, *Essays on Old Testament Hermeneutics,* JKP, ET, 1963, 363 pp., $7.50; SCMP, 1964, 45s. The crucial issues of Old Testament interpretation are discussed by various German Old Testament scholars. The questions are formulated in the manner they were presented in the decade 1950-1960. Nevertheless, these are pertinent questions that will always demand attention.

26. THASS-THIENEMANN, Theodore, *The Subconscious Language,* WSP, 1967, 437 pp., $6.95. The author, a rare combination of linguist, psychologist, and philosopher, explores the understanding of the language, including the language of the Bible, from the standpoint of psychoanalysis. In so doing, he draws from the vast variety of languages and throws light on a number of difficult biblical texts and words.

1EA. ARCHAEOLOGY AND GEOGRAPHY: OLD TESTAMENT
Charles F. Pfeiffer

Archaeology and geography are indispensable tools for Bible study. While interest in the sites where biblical events took place has never been lacking, it is only within the last century that scientific archaeological work has been carried on, and much of it has been done within the last few decades. For this reason it is necessary to use recent works by authorities who have kept abreast of the discoveries in the Near East since World War II.

The prime value of archaeology to the Bible student is its contribution to contemporary knowledge of the culture of the Israelites and their neighbors—Egyptians, Hittites, Babylonians, Assyrians, Persians, and a host of others. Excavations have

given us a knowledge of such elements of material culture as houses,
temples, tools, pottery, weapons, and
articles of personal clothing and
adornment. Texts discovered in the
Near East have been deciphered and
translated, providing thousands of
examples of law codes, court decisions, contracts, letters, royal annals,
epics, hymns—every type of written
material in a literate community. The
judicious use of such material enables
the modern biblical scholar to read
the Bible against its Near Eastern
background.

Since many biblical sites were
abandoned centuries ago, Bible students long had to rely on tradition to
assist them in locating places named
in the Bible. These traditions often
proved correct, but one service of
modern archaeology has been the
authentication or the correction of
ideas about geography held in earlier
years. Geography, like history and
archaeology, provides a tool for the
understanding of the setting of the
biblical narratives.

1. AHARONI, Jochanan, *The Land
of the Bible,* WP, ET, 1967, 409 pp.,
$7.95; BO, 63s. A historical geog-
raphy which includes both history
and a survey of the archaeological
data for history has been prepared by
a leading Israeli archeologist and
translated by an able American Semi-
tist. This is a serious work for serious
students.

2. *ALBRIGHT, W. F., *The Archaeology of Palestine,* AP, 1960, 271
pp., Pb $1.25; PEL, Pb 4s 6d. Al-
bright gives us a helpful introduction
to the techniques of archaeology and
the labors and results of expeditions
which have been excavated in Palestine. A series of chapters presents the
history of Palestine chronologically,
with insights gained from archaeological research. See also, W. F. Albright,
*Archaeology and the Religion of
Israel,* JH, ED 4, 1956, 246 pp.,

$6.00; OUP, RE, 1954, 28s; and N.
Glueck, *Rivers in the Desert,* WN,
1959, 320 pp., 30s.

3. Archaeological Institute of America, *Archaeological Discoveries in the
Holy Land,* TYC, 1967, 220 pp.,
$12.95. Twenty-three chapters by
Palestinian archaeologists and biblical
scholars have been collected—many
from the pages of the magazine
"Archaeology"—by the Archaeological Institute of America. Included
are chapters by Frank M. Cross, Jr.
on the Dead Sea Scrolls, by Yigael
Yadin on Masada, by James B. Pritchard on Gibeon, and by Kathleen Kenyon on Jericho.

4. BRIGHT, John, *A History of Israel,* WP, 1959, 512 pp., $7.50;
SCMP, 1960, 50s. John Bright takes
Old Testament history seriously. He
draws upon archaeological sources in
presenting a history of Israel based
upon contemporary Near Eastern
scholarship. Extensive footnotes provide documentation for further research.

5. DeVAUX, Roland, *Ancient Israel:
Its Life and Institutions,* 2 V., MH,
ET, 1961, 592 pp., Hb $10.95, Pb
$2.95 each; DLT, 55s. (OoP) A study
of family, civil, military, and religious
institutions in ancient Israel is here
presented by a Roman Catholic
scholar who is widely known for his
work in the excavation of the Qum-
ran community center. Literary criticism, archaeology and philology are
tools which DeVaux uses judiciously
in his research.

6. FINEGAN, Jack, *Light from the
Ancient East,* PUP, ED 2, 1959, 638
pp., $10.00; PUP, 676 pp., 70s. Fine-
gan's purpose was to give a connected
account of the archaeological background of Judaism and Christianity.
He begins with Mesopotamian village
culture of 5000 B. C. and continues
his narrative through early Christian

times. The student will do well to read the book through, then keep it with the reference books he uses most frequently. The text is highly readable, and footnotes will prove useful for more detailed study.

7. GORDON, Cyrus H., *The Ancient Near East*, WWN, 1965, 312 pp., Pb $1.75. Earlier editions of this work bore the titles, *The World of the Old Testament* and *Introduction to Old Testament Times*. The book discusses the ancient Near East with particular reference to biblical history. The author, a world authority on Canaanite literature, brings interesting sidelights from archaeology.

8. *Everyday Life in Bible Times*, NGS, 1967, 448 pp., $9.95. This is a lavishly illustrated book with text prepared in part by members of the staff of the National Geographic Society staff. A series of special chapters by recognized authorities adds to the value of the book. James Pritchard writes on the work of the archaeologist; S. N. Kramer, the Sumerologist, writes on the World of Abraham. The Egyptologist John Wilson provides a chapter on the World of Moses. George Ernest Wright of Harvard, excavator of Shechem and President of the American Schools of Oriental Research, has written the chapter on the World of David and Solomon.

9. *PFEIFFER, C. F., *Baker's Bible Atlas*, BR, 1962, 333 pp., $7.95; OB, 25s. The Baker Atlas contains, in addition to its collection of maps, a description of the Bible lands and an attempt to follow the events of biblical history from Patriarchal times through the Book of the Revelation. There are chapters on Bible Lands Today and Biblical Archaeology in the Twentieth Century. See also, C. F. Pfeiffer, ed., *The Biblical World*, BBH, 1966, 612 pp., $8.95.

10. PRITCHARD, J. B., ed., *Ancient Near Eastern Texts Relating to the Old Testament*, PUP, ED 2, 1955, 516 pp., $20.00; OUP, 1958, 400 pp., 45s. Scholars in various fields of Near Eastern studies have translated texts which parallel or provide data for understanding the Old Testament. This is a large and expensive volume, but it is indispensable for serious Old Testament study.

11. PRITCHARD, J. B., ed., *The Ancient Near East in Pictures Relating to the Old Testament*, PUP, RE, 1955, 351 pp., $20.00; OUP, 1954, 370 pp., 160s. A companion volume to the above. It contains 769 illustrations classified according to the following categories: peoples and their dress; daily life; writing; scenes from history and monuments; royalty and dignitaries; gods and their emblems; the practice of religion; myth, legend and ritual on cylinder seals; views and plans of excavations. Maps and a catalogue are appended. See also, an abridged edition of Dr. Pritchard's two reference volumes (above), entitled *The Ancient Near East*, PUP, 1965, 380 pp., Hb $7.50, Pb $2.95. It contains the most significant texts and photographs and is available in handy paperback format.

12. THOMAS, D. W., ed., *Documents from Old Testament Times*, TN, 1958, 302 pp., $5.00; HRP, 1961, $1.75; TN, 1958, 328 pp., 25s. This volume contains a collection of translations of cuneiform, Egyptian, Moabite, Hebrew, and Aramaic documents which are of particular interest to Old Testament students. Useful introductions and notes are included.

13. WRIGHT, G. E., *Biblical Archaeology*, WP, RE, 1963, 291 pp., Hb $10.95, Pb $1.65; DUC, RE, 1962, 289 pp., Hb 50s, Pb 12s 6d. Dr. Wright tells us that his purpose is "to summarize Biblical discoveries which directly illumine Biblical history, in

order that the Bible's setting in the ancient world and its relation to its environment may be more readily comprehended." This is an authoritative volume by a man who has devoted his life to archaeological work.

1EB. ARCHAEOLOGY AND GEOGRAPHY: NEW TESTAMENT
W. J. Martin

If archaeology was concerned only with architectural remains and objects of arts, then there would be no archaeology of the New Testament. Early Christians met in private houses, which were not considered as sacred. For them the consecration of a material building would have seemed a pagan custom. Their sanctuary was in heaven (Hebrews 9:24). Abraham, too, their great example in faith, had erected no temple, and Jacob had called a barren spot on a desolate hillside, Bethel, "House of God."

It was probably not until after the Milan decree of Constantine the Great in 312 that Christians began to associate the act of worship with consecrated buildings. Objects of ecclesiastical art, too, do not begin to appear until after this time. On the other hand, archaeology can provide information on such matters as the topography of Jerusalem in New Testament times. That city now lies 12-20 feet below the present surface. The walls in their present form were built between 1536 and 1539 by Suleiman the Magnificent.

Archaeology of the New Testament is chiefly concerned with documentary remains relating to New Testament writings. Among such remains, Greek papyri from sites in Egypt are of considerable importance. For the New Testament background should also be mentioned the remains of Herodian and Graeco-Roman buildings.

Geography provides information on the physical features of the country. It has done important work

in the identification of sites. That of some traditional sites still awaits corroboration.

1. ALBRIGHT, W. F., *The Archaeology of Palestine,* AP, 1960, 271 pp., Pb $1.25; PEL, 4s 6d. This work, by a scholar whose knowledge of the ancient East is unrivaled, has a value out of all proportion to its size. It covers the whole biblical background and contains within a comparatively small compass all the essential information.

2. *BALY, Denis, *The Geography of the Bible,* HRP, 1957, 303 pp., $6.95; LU, 35s. Here is a work by a trained geographer long a resident in Palestine. It is well-written and contains a vast amount of essential information. There is no better book on the subject.

3. *BRUCE, F. F., *Second Thoughts on the Dead Sea Scrolls,* WBE, RE, 1961, 144 pp., Pb $1.65; PP, RE 2, 1956, 160 pp., 6s. A lucid re-evaluation of the significance of the scrolls. For an equally judicious and succinct account by a scholar associated with the publication of the scrolls, see J. T. Milik, *Ten Years of Discovery in the Wilderness of Judea,* AL, 1959, 160 pp., Hb $5.35, Pb $2.85; SCMP, 12s 6d.

4. DEISSMAN, G. A., *Light from the Ancient East,* BBH, ET, RE, 1966, 535 pp., $7.95. This standard work by the pioneer in papyriological studies is a mine of information. For anyone wishing to do serious reading in this field it is indispensable.

5. FINBERT, E. J., *Israel,* Paris, Hachette, 1956, 456 pp., 45s. For traveling a pocket guide is virtually indispensable. This is one of the most recent. While it seems reliable geographically, some will find the political comments distasteful. A comprehensive, accurate pocket guide is an

urgent desideratum. For a geographical background of the Bible by a non-specialist, see J. H. Kitchen, *Holy Fields,* PP, 1956, 160 pp., 10s 6d.

6. FINEGAN, Jack, *Light from the Ancient Past,* PUP, ED 2, 1959, 500 pp., $10.00; OUP, ED 2, 1960, 638 pp., 63s. Approximately half of the work is concerned with the New Testament background. For the more advanced reader it will be found invaluable. It is an excellent and comprehensive survey of the whole archaeological background of the Bible.

7. *GROLLENBERG, L. H., *Atlas of the Bible,* NE, ET, 1959, 166 pp., $5.00; NE, 1956, 90s. This atlas is superbly illustrated and the maps have excellent annotations. A thorough study of it could well prove as rewarding as a trip to the Holy Land. It is suitable for readers of all grades. See also, *Shorter Atlas of the Bible,* NE, 1960, 195 pp., $3.95; NE, 12s 6d.

8. KENYON, F., *Our Bible and the Ancient Manuscripts,* HRP, 1958, 352 pp., $5.00; ES, RE 5, 42s. Kenyon was recognized as one of the greatest scholars in the field of biblical manuscripts. This is a masterly account of the extant material. The later edition abandons in places Kenyon's high standard of objective scholarship. See also, C. K. Barrett, *The New Testament Background: Selected Documents,* SPCK, 1957, 316 pp., 21s.

9. LANKESTER, H. G., *The Antiquities of Jordan,* PRA, RE, 1959, 223 pp., $7.50; Ri, LU, 1967, 35s. A description by a field archaeologist in nontechnical language of some important sites. He writes with firsthand archaeological knowledge, and this makes his comments on the finding of the Dead Sea Scrolls of unusual importance. See also, D. J.

Wiseman, *Illustrations from Biblical Archaeology,* WBE, 1959, 112 pp., $3.50; TP, ED 3, 1958, 12s 6d.

10. *MAY, H. G. and R. W. Hamilton, *Oxford Bible Atlas,* OUP, 1962, 142 pp., Hb $4.95, Pb $2.50; OUP, 25s. A well-illustrated compact work with excellent maps, this is one of the most useful atlases of its kind. There is a handy index of place names.

11. *MILLIGAN, George, *Here and There Among the Papyri,* HS, 1923, 180 pp., $2.00; DOR, 1922, 7s 6d. (OoP) This is one of the most delightful and readable books on the survey of the earlier discoveries and their importance for the New Testament. It is full of valuable information communicated in a readily assimilated form.

12. RAMSAY, W. M., *Historical Geography of Asia Minor,* Amsterdam, Adolf M. Hakkert, 1962, 495 pp., fl 60. This is solid reading but it is indispensable for anyone studying the spread of Christianity. Ramsay was the greatest authority in this field and this is the finest work on Asia Minor. See also, H. Metzger, *St. Paul's Journeys in the Greek Orient,* SCMP, ET, 1956, 76 pp., 8s 6d.

13. SMITH, G. A., *The Historical Geography of the Holy Land,* HRP, RE, 1966, 713 pp., Pb $3.75; FO, RE, 512 pp., 21s. For long the standard work in the field and still well worth study, or as a valuable work of reference. Its bulk might deter the beginner.

14. UNGER, M. F., *Archaeology and the New Testament,* ZPH, 1962, 353 pp., $5.95 (OoP); Ri, PI, 1965, 352 pp., 30s. This is a good comprehensive survey of the relevant material. It is suitable for either beginners or advanced readers. The sections on the historical background enhance

the value of this work. See also, C. F. Pfeiffer, *Jerusalem Through the Ages,* BBH, 1967, 94 pp., Hb $7.80, Pb $1.95.

15. *VAN DER MEER, F. and C. Mohramann, *Atlas of the Early Christian World,* NE, ET, 1958, 216 pp., 70s. This is an excellent and magnificently illustrated introduction to the life of the early Church.

16. WRIGHT, G. E., *Biblical Archaeology,* WP, RE, 1963, 288 pp., Hb $10.95, Pb $1.65; DUC, 1960, Hb 50s, Pb 12s 6d. The greater part of this book deals with Old Testament archaeology, and only some fifty to sixty pages with the New Testament. It is well-written, and the illustrations are carefully chosen. It is an excellent and comprehensive presentation of the material.

17. WRIGHT, G. E. and F. V. Filson, *The Westminster Historical Atlas to the Bible,* WP, RE, 1956, 130 pp., $7.50; SCMP, 1958, 148 pp., 50s. This is again an invaluable tool for any student of the Bible. The quality of the maps is not quite so good as the Oxford Atlas, but the information is more detailed.

1F. INSPIRATION AND AUTHORITY
Bernard Ramm
Certain topics in theology very closely implicate each other and it is hard to discuss one without the other. Thus revelation, inspiration, illumination, interpretation, canon, and authority are of one piece. Strictly speaking, inspiration is the process or activity of the Holy Spirit to retain and preserve the revelations of God first, perhaps, in the form of authentic oral traditions (e.g., the time of the patriarchs until Moses), and then in a written form. Thus in our modern methods of technology the product of inspiration comes out as a printed Book, the Holy Scriptures.

The Holy Scripture being inspired of the Holy Spirit is thus the only authoritative and canonical writing permitted within the Christian Church.

If a revelation is God's Word, and if its written form is created by divine inspiration, then that written version of the Word of God is the solemn authority of God in the Church. Speaking in perspective of sheer numbers and continuity through the centuries, the overwhelming majority of Christians have accepted the divine authority of Holy Scripture within the Church. Even when the concept of tradition allows other kinds of materials (as is believed by some churches) this does not diminish within these churches the concept of the divine inspiration and divine authority of Holy Scripture.

1. BARTH, Karl, *Church Dogmatics,* 2 V., Ri, AL, 1961, $12.50 each; 4 V., TTC, 1956, 40-60s each. This work contains Barth's definitive views on revelation, inspiration, authority, and biblical interpretation. As a critic of the views of religious liberalism or modernism he is devastating. He is also critical of many aspects of the older orthodox views of the Bible. Although there is much we would not agree with in this volume, it nevertheless is a storehouse of theological information that no student who wishes to be very thoroughly informed can afford to miss even though the sheer reading of Barth at times is an enormous intellectual adventure.

2. BEEGLE, D. M., *The Inspiration of Scripture,* WP, 1963, 223 pp., $4.50. This is an attempt to restate the doctrine of the inspiration of Scripture in the light particularly of Old Testament studies. While granting that there are some errors in Scripture which cannot be resolved by any kind of apologetic, Beegle still maintains continuity with the his-

toric and evangelical view of the authority of Holy Scripture.

3. BRUNNER, H. E., *Revelation and Reason*, WP, 1946, 440 pp., $6.00; SCMP, 1947, 25s. (OoP) Although this is formally a book on apologetics or eristics, it contains Brunner's own rather sharp views on character of revelation. See also, P. K. Jewett, *Emil Brunner's Concept of Revelation*, TTC, 1954, 204 pp., 18s. It is a scholarly conservative critique.

4. BULTMANN, Rudolph, *Existence and Faith*, LA, 1960, 320 pp., Hb $4.00, Pb $1.45; HS, 1961, Hb 21s; Ri, CO, 1964, 384 pp., Pb 8s 6d. Bartsch, H. W., ed., *Kerygma and Myth*, 2 V., AL, ED 2, 1964, V. 1, $5.25, V. 2, 1962, $6.50; SPCK, 1953, pp. 240-368, 22s 6d. (VT) C. W. Kegley, *The Theology of Rudolph Bultmann*, HRP, 1966, 320 pp., $5.75; SCMP, 45s. We lump all three of these books together as there is not in English as yet a systematic presentation of Bultmann's views on inspiration, authority, and revelation. What he believes on these subjects must be gleaned from his writings and materials about him. But in that the Bultmannian school has been exerting such an enormous influence on theology and biblical scholarship, he must be mentioned.

5. DAVIES, R. E., *The Problem of Authority in the Continental Reformers*, EP, 1946, 158 pp., 12s 6d. This book clearly reflected the new mood in theology created by neo-orthodoxy in a greater appreciation of biblical thought of the Reformers. Thus it attempts to show the connection of present-day thought with that of the Reformers and thus indicates that religious liberalism was a by-path.

6. *FORSYTH, P. T., *The Principles of Authority*, AL, 1952, 430 pp., Hb $5.50; IP, 432 pp., 21s. Forsyth has

been called the Barth-before-Barth. Forsyth liked neither the orthodox versions of authority nor the newer religious liberal views of authority. So he wrote a book which in many ways is the best book we have on the subject of authority. He attempts to show the unique supremacy in authority of Jesus Christ and how this is objectively mediated to us through the apostles and then through the New Testament.

7. GAUSSEN, L., *Theopneustia: The Plenary Inspiration of Holy Scriptures*, BICA, ET (OoP); *Inspiration of the Holy Scriptures*, Ri, MP, 1949. (OoP) In many ways this has been the classic exposition of the doctrine of inspiration as held by theologians who are conservative or evangelical or fundamental or orthodox. It reflects a great deal of the biblical learning of the time. It also rebuts many of the common objections to inspiration. Although still valuable, it must be brought up to date by more recent studies.

8. GELDENHUYS, J. N., *Supreme Authority*, WBE, 1954, 128 pp., $2.00 (OoP); MMS, 1953, 10s 6d. An important study of the authority of Christ, the apostles and the New Testament.

9. *HENRY, C. F., ed., *Revelation and the Bible*, BBH, 1958, 413 pp., Hb $6.00, Pb $3.95; TP, 1959, 416 pp., 17s 9d. This book is a series of essays by the best of contemporary evangelical scholarship written around several themes about the issues of inspiration and authority. In general the essays are an attempt to justify the historic view of the inspiration and authority of the Bible in the light of recent biblical and theological scholarship.

10. JOHNSON, R. C., *Authority in Protestant Theology*, WP, 1959, 224 pp., $4.50. This is a very capable sur-

vey (but not exhaustive) of opinions on authority in Protestantism from Luther to Barth. It is therefore a very valuable source book for the study of biblical authority both contemporary and historical.

11. KIERKEGAARD, Soren, *On Authority and Revelation*, PUP, 1955, 205 pp., Hb $4.50; HRP, Pb $2.25; OUP, 36s. (OoP) The book was written by Kierkegaard in response to the Danish Church's censoring of a certain Mr. Adler who claimed private revelations. It is important in that it anticipates certain views of revelation and authority as later held by the neo-orthodox, but also in taking a stance against the views of religious liberalism which at that time were in the process of formation. It is not to be understood that Kierkegaard knew of these views and attempted to refute them but rather what he said as a matter of fact did refute them even though he might not have been familiar with him. Especially important in this book is the defense of the precise authority of an apostle.

12. KUYPER, Abraham, *Principles of Sacred Theology*, WBE, 1954, 684 pp., $6.95. This volume is selected from the heart of a three-volume theological encyclopedia in the Dutch language and translated into English. Many consider Kuyper the greatest theologian in the Reformed tradition since Calvin. From a theological standpoint this is perhaps the most profound treatment of the historic views of inspiration, revelation and authority that we have in the evangelical and Reformed tradition. Although perhaps difficult to understand at first reading, it is well worth the patience to master its content.

13. *MACHEN, J. G., *Christianity and Liberalism*, Ri, WBE, 1960, 188 pp., Pb $1.75; VP, 1964, 200 pp., 12s 6d. A brilliant exposition of the place of authority in Christianity.

14. *MANLEY, G. T., ed., *The New Bible Handbook*, IVP, 1950, 480 pp., $4.95; TP, ED 3, 15s. This is a solid, compact handbook on the various topics of Holy Scripture adhering to a real evangelical position yet in good scholarship.

15. McDONALD, H. D., *Theories of Revelation*, HP, 1960, 384 pp., $7.50; AU, 1963, 42s. Although the title seems to restrict the volume to revelation, this is not true. There are important and contemporary chapters on both inspiration and authority. The book treats both evangelical and non-evangelical positions.

16. ORR, James, *Revelation and Inspiration*, WBE, 1953, 224 pp., $3.00. (OoP) Kuyper, Warfield, and Orr were the three greatest reformed theologians of their era. This is a learned book and a sensible one and in some ways prophetic of the later views about Holy Scripture. Although not holding to the precise view of Scripture as Warfield, he nonetheless defended a very high view of the inspiration and authority of Holy Scripture.

17. *PACKER, J. I., *Fundamentalism and the Word of God*, WBE, 1958, 192 pp., Pb $1.25; TP, 4s 6d. This is a reply to theologians in general and to Gabriel Hebert in particular (*Fundamentalism and the Church*) that in rejecting the so-called fundamentalist view of the Bible they are as a matter of fact rejecting the Church's historic view that the Bible is the inspired Word of God.

18. *RAMM, Bernard, *The Pattern of Religious Authority*, WBE, 1957, 117 pp., Pb $1.50. This is an effort to show that there is no single doctrine of authority for Christians but a pattern of authority, namely, the interlocking authority of Holy Scripture, the Holy Spirit and Jesus Christ. A bibliography at the end of the vol-

ume lists most of the important works on authority of Scripture up to the time that the book was written.

19. RODGERS, J. B., *Scripture in the Westminster Confession,* WBE, 1967, $6.75. The new confession of faith by the Presbyterian Church in America created a fresh controversy over the doctrine of the inspiration of the Scriptures and the status of the Westminster Confession in the light of recent biblical and theological scholarship. Rodgers gives us a very comprehensive survey of the opinions of the men who wrote the Westminster Confession and thereby enables us to understand what the Confession means. In the final part of the book he examines the statement of the new confession and urges us to bring our understanding of the inspiration of Holy Scriptures up to date.

20. RUNIA, Klaas, *Karl Barth's Doctrine of Holy Scripture,* WBE, 1962, 225 pp., $4.00. This book is very valuable because it gives a very objective account of Barth's view of inspiration; it gives relevant criticism of this view; and it indicates the sort of thing that an evangelical can salvage from Barth for the enrichment of his own theology of Holy Scripture.

21. STONEHOUSE, N. B. and P. Woolley, *The Infallible Word: A Symposium,* PGPC, 1946. (OoP) This book is a series of closely reasoned essays in the general character of Holy Scripture as inspired, canonical, and authoritative. It works very carefully within the general framework of the so-called Hodge-Warfield school of biblical inspiration.

22. WALVOORD, J. F., ed., *Inspiration and Interpretation,* WBE, 1957, 280 pp., $4.50. The book consists of a series of essays around many topics by many evangelical scholars. The essays are informative and reflect the high view of Holy Scripture, its inspiration, and authority as is characteristic of the evangelicals.

23. WARFIELD, B. B., *The Inspiration and Authority of the Bible,* PRPC, ED 2, 1948, 422 pp., $3.75; MMS, 1951, 25s. (OoP) This volume is a compilation of a series of essays. No man in the history of Christian theology has so painstakingly researched the Scripture to see what the Scripture has to say of itself. Warfield is generally considered as having made the best case for a high doctrine of inspiration from the standpoint of historic or evangelical theology. This work has been a standard and will continue to be so for some years to come.

Special Note
The outstanding Dutch Reformed theologian, G. C. Berkouwer has written a book on the inspiration of the Bible in his series of Studies in Dogmatics. This is not yet in English translation but it is expected that it shortly will be. We will not only have a great theologian's interpretation of the doctrine of inspiration in the light of modern criticism and theology, but also a somewhat alternate view than that of the Warfield view which has predominated in American evangelical circles.

CHRISTIAN DOCTRINE

2. CHRISTIAN DOCTRINE: INTRODUCTION

Clark H. Pinnock

The mentality of the twentieth century towards religious matters shows a distinct preference for ambiguity over precision, dialogue over debate, and peace over truth. This is the age of the ecumenical love-in, in which all questions of truth are sacrificed to the plea for unconditional love. The weather vane is its symbol indicating the need for sensitivity to the winds of human change. In fact, it represents the spinelessness of contemporary Christianity to heed the Word of God and declare it.

The sermon has become the Sunday morning editorial, and preachers are experts at putting their finger to the wind. The Christian witness who is not grounded in the doctrines of the Bible is like a doctor who allows his patients to diagnose their own illness and prescribe their own remedies. There is a famine of hearing the words of the Lord. In order to be meaningful, man drowns out God's voice with his own answers.

Paul saw it as his duty to master and proclaim the whole counsel of God. With this truth he fed the Church of God (Acts 20:27ff). Christian doctrine is milk to the baby and strong meat to the mature believer (I Peter 2:2, I Corinthians 3:2). The Apostle found it in the God-breathed Scriptures (II Timothy 3:15-17), and through the revelation of Jesus Christ which he received (Galatians 1:12).

He was a militant when it came to Christian doctrine. He condemned false teaching vigorously at Galatia (Galatians 1:6-9). He even went to the extent of publicly refuting Cephas when he behaved inconsistently (2:11). The reason why Paul became so upset when doctrine was perverted was because he feared the effect upon the Church and her mission.

False teaching has a poisonous effect on the soul. It leaves sinners still under the curse. It destroys evangelism altogether. There is no evangelism where the truth of the gospel is not imparted. The good news is a message about Jesus Christ whose content is divinely revealed and deposited in Scriptures. If we do not master our message, we will be unable to introduce others to our Lord. What men need is not faith as such, but faith in a competent Savior. Christian doctrine is the study which equips us to explain the dimensions of divine salvation.

For this reason, every Christian is called to be a theologian. Christian doctrine is too important to be left to the professionals. Understanding the things of God is part of our royal priesthood. Like the noble Bereans, we ought to search the Scriptures to test the teaching we receive. For there is a danger of being deceived. The apostles warn us on numerous occasions about denials of the gospel which will afflict the Church during these days (I Timothy 4:1; II Timothy 4:3ff; II Peter 2:1).

We cannot be saved without understanding divine truth to some degree (II Thessalonians 2:13), and we certainly cannot be effective witnesses to others if we do not grasp God's Word ourselves. Titus was told that he ought to be able to teach sound doctrine and in addition to confute those who contradict it (1:9). We only partly comprehend the truth if we cannot defend it.

It is a sad fact that many martyrs have given their very lives for truths which we in our complacency have not bothered to master. Error goes unchecked in pulpit and seminary, and the cults thrive in the midst of the professing Church simply because we have not made ourselves skillful in biblical truth. It is high time to sharpen the sword we wield. Its dull edge accounts for much of our ineffectiveness.

We are ambassadors for Christ, not politicians. It is our obligation to make the Gospel known. To do that we must understand what it is. We will not rescue the perishing if the lifeboat is sinking. Evangelism, truth, and the Christian life are all bound up in this issue. God will not honor a half-hearted and empty-headed witness to Christ. Genuine revival will come to the Church when the Holy Spirit moves us to recover scriptural truths.

2A. GENERAL
Philip E. Hughes
This section deals, in the main, with Christian doctrine as a whole, as distinct from the treatment of particular Christian doctrines which are the concern of the remaining sections of this division. Christian doctrine in general is commonly referred to as Theology. More specifically, it is Systematic Theology, that is, theology which is systematized by the study of the available sources and organized under particular doctrinal heads. The main heads of systematic theology are (1) the doctrine of God (theology proper), (2) the doctrine of man (anthropology), (3) the doctrine of the person of Christ (Christology), (4) the doctrine of the work of Christ for man's salvation (soteriology), (5) the doctrine of the Church (ecclesiology) and (6) the doctrine of the last things (eschatology). It need hardly be said that all these themes are intimately associated with each other.

The systematization of Christian doctrine or theology is an important and logical task because the Bible is not systematically arranged and consequently what it has to say on different themes has to be gathered by the comparison and bringing together of many separate passages. Systematic theology is the complement of biblical exegesis, that is, the expounding and interpretation of the various books of the Bible verse by verse. Finally, theology conceived in this systematic or "dogmatic" manner may be treated under the categories either of Biblical Theology, that is, in relation to the biblical teaching alone, or of Historical Theology, that is, in relation to the fortunes and formulations of the different doctrines during the course of the history of the Church.

Fourth Century
1. *ATHANASIUS, Saint, The Incarnation of the Word of God, MC, 1946, 120 pp., Pb $1.75 (OoP); MO, 1963, 96 pp., 8s 6d. A little classic by one of the great leaders of the Church in the early centuries. "It is his glory that he did not move with the times," says C. S. Lewis of Athanasius in his Introduction. "It is his reward that he now remains when those times, as all times do, have moved away. When I first opened his De Incarnatione I soon discovered by a very simple test that I was reading a masterpiece . . . only a master mind could, in the fourth century, have written so deeply on such a subject and with such classical simplicity."

Fifth Century
2. AUGUSTINE, Saint, City of God, OUP, 1963, 428 pp., $4.80; DC, 1958, 545 pp., Pb $1.65; OUP, 30s. A defense of Christianity against the charge that Christianity was to blame for the misfortunes which led to the collapse of the Roman Empire and the first major development of a Christian theology of history. A work of perennial significance. "The book has its faults," as Marcus Dods observed nearly a hundred years ago; "but it effectually introduces us to the most influential of theologians, and the most popular teacher; to a genius that cannot nod for many lines together; to a reasoner whose dialectic is more formidable, more keen and sifting, than that of Socrates or Aquinas; to a saint whose ardent and genuine devotional feeling bursts up through the severest argumentation; to a man whose kindliness and wit, universal sympathies and

breadth of intelligence, lend piqu-ancy and vitality to the most abstract dissertation."

Sixteenth Century

3. LUTHER, Martin, *Reformation Writings of Martin Luther,* 2 V., PL, V. I, 1953, 402 pp., $6.00; V. II, 1956, 340 pp., $7.50; LU, V. I, 1953, 402 pp., 27s 6d; V. II, 1956, 340 pp., 31s 6d.

4. LUTHER, Martin, *A Compendium of Luther's Theology,* WP, 1943, 253 pp., Pb $2.00. (OoP) It is above all in his expository sermons and lectures that the genius of Martin Luther is seen and perhaps particularly in his lectures on the book of Genesis and on the Epistles to the Romans and to the Galatians. These in themselves provide a wonderful, though not systematic, declaration of his theology. The two volumes edited by Woolf contain the most important treatises from the Reformer's pen, including of course the Ninety-Five Theses, a documented account of the proceedings at the Diet of Worms, a number of sermons and expositions, and a selection of his prefaces to different books of the Bible. Kerr's volume is valuable because it arranges appropriate extracts from Luther's writings under eleven theological heads.

5. LUTHER, Martin, *Day by Day We Magnify Thee,* FP, 1950, 437 pp., Pb $3.95; EP, 440 pp., 12s 6d. A rich treasury of anthology of memorable passages, one for each day of the year.

6. CALVIN, John *Institutes of the Christian Religion,* 2 V., WP, 1960, 1734 pp., $12.50 set; WBE, Pb $6.95; SCMP, 1961, 900 pp., 6s 6d. For force, clarity, and logic of intellect Calvin was without peer among the many notable scholars of the Reformation. His *Institutes* continues up to the present day to be the finest

work of systematic theology ever written. The genius of his character, pure and brilliant as a diamond, is enshrined in this master-work which is indispensable for the serious student of Christian doctrine. See also, B. B. Warfield, *Calvin and Augustine,* Ri, TP, 508 pp., 25s.

7. HUGHES, P. E., *Theology of the English Reformers,* WBE, 1965, 283 pp., $5.95; HS, 30s. The teaching of the leaders of the Reformation in England expounded with the aid of numerous quotations from their writings and systematically arranged under the heads of Holy Scripture, justification, sanctification, preaching and worship, ministry, the sacraments, and Church and state.

8. TYNDALE, William, *The Work of William Tyndale,* FP, 1965, 406 pp., $6.25; SCP, 1964, 446 pp., 42s. Through his translation of Holy Scripture Tyndale has left an indelible stamp on the English language. His genius for his native tongue is amply demonstrated by the writings assembled in this book, also the strength and depth of his theological perception.

9. CRANMER, Thomas, *The Work of Thomas Cranmer,* FP, 1965, 370 pp., $6.25; SCP, 1964, 325 pp., 42s. Cranmer, like Tyndale a great scholar, was the liturgical genius of the Reformation. The Book of Common Prayer, for which he was chiefly responsible, has enriched the English language forever. The writings reproduced in this book bear testimony to the stature of Cranmer as a theologian.

10. LATIMER, Hugh, *Sermons of Hugh Latimer,* CAUP, 1844, 551 pp. (OoP) Bishop Latimer, the outstanding preacher of the English Reformation, was not a systematic theologian; but he was a learned man and his sermons are a mine of theological wis-

dom and practical Christianity. The study of them cannot fail to bring great benefit.

11. HOOKER, Richard, *The Works of Richard Hooker,* 3 V., OUP, 1845, 488, 610, 755 pp., 31s 6d. (OoP) The "judicious" Hooker is famous for his main work on the *Laws of Ecclesiastical Polity,* which occupies the major portion of these three volumes. Systematically conceived, carefully reasoned, and written in classic prose, it is a defense of the "middle way" of reformed Anglicanism between the extremes of Romanism on the one hand and "puritan" sectarianism on the other.

Seventeenth Century
12. *BAXTER, Richard, *The Saint's Everlasting Rest,* V. XXII and XXIII of the Practical Works, Ri, AL, 1962, 540, 480 pp., $3.50; Ri, EP, 1961, 187 pp., 18s 6d. A classic work from the Caroline period on the doctrine of the last things, or eschatology, characteristically discursive, devotional, and hortatory as well as theological in content.

13. OWEN, John, *The Doctrine of Justification by Faith,* BTT, 1851, 400 pp. (OoP) Owen, Vice-Chancellor of the University of Oxford in Cromwell's time, wrote extensively on many different theological subjects. His work on justification is a good example of the thoroughness of his scholarship and the scripturalness of his position.

Eighteenth Century
14. EDWARDS, Jonathan, *Puritan Sage: Collected Writings of Jonathan Edwards,* LP, 1953, 640 pp., $7.50. (OoP) A collection of the main works, the longer ones in part only, of the notable New England thinker and preacher. Edwards possessed one of the outstanding minds of his day. His parish of Northampton was the center of a remarkable revival of

evangelical religion and his first-hand studies of the theology of revival are of perennial importance.

15. OUTLER, A. C., ed., *John Wesley,* OUP, 1964, 516 pp., $7.50. A collection of writings by John Wesley designed to exhibit the theological thought of the great evangelist and systematically arranged under specific headings.

16. WHITEFIELD, George, *Select Sermons of George Whitefield,* Ri, BTT, 1964, 192 pp., 4s 6d. George Whitefield was undoubtedly the greatest preacher of his own age and very possibly of the whole Christian era. As Dr. D. M. Lloyd-Jones says in the Foreword: "Of few men can it be said that their preaching was "apostolic" in character; but it certainly can be said of Whitefield." Bishop Ryle's essay on "George Whitefield and his Ministry" is a little classic, and the summary of Whitefield's doctrine which is also included is taken from a sermon preached at the great evangelist's funeral. The half-dozen sermons which follow admirably illustrate the theology of grace which he preached indefatigably to the blessing of countless multitudes of his hearers.

Nineteenth Century
17. CUNNINGHAM, William, *Historical Theology,* 2 V., TTC, 1870, 639, 614 pp. (OoP); and James Orr, *The Progress of Dogma,* WBE, 1952, 365 pp., $3.50. (OoP) Valuable works for serious students by two noted Scottish professors of last century. As the titles indicate, theology is viewed under its most important heads within the perspective of its development and elaboration during the centuries of the Church's history.

18. *HODGE, Charles, *Systematic Theology,* 3 V., Ri, WBE, 1952, 648, 732, 880 pp., $17.50 set; JC, 1960, 25s each. The nineteenth century saw

the production of a large number of major works on systematic theology, many of them of a voluminous nature. Of these, Charles Hodge's three-volume work is a comprehensive exposition from the pen of a Reformed scholar. It represents the peak of evangelical "scholasticism" of the Princeton school.

19. RYLE, J. C., *Light from Old Times,* WH, 1898, 488 pp. (OoP) Bishop Ryle was a man of strong Reformed convictions with a great gift for expressing sound theology in simple language. The studies in this volume are mainly biographical in form, but they concern men who cannot be understood apart from their theology. Accordingly it is a work of theological edification as well as historical worth. Apart from the first chapter, which is devoted to John Wycliffe, "the morning star of the Reformation" (fourteenth century), the men portrayed are some of the great Christian figures of the sixteenth and seventeenth centuries.

20. LITTON, E. A., *Introduction to Dogmatic Theology,* JC, 1960, 608 pp., 27s 6d. As with most books, this one has some weaknesses; but it is a valuable work, systematically presented, by a fine Anglican scholar. See also A. H. Strong, *Systematic Theology,* Ri, PI, 1962, 1166 pp., 50s.

21. KUYPER, Abraham, *Principles of Sacred Theology,* WBE, 1953, 684 pp., $6.95. An important work in the Reformed tradition by the great Dutch theologian and statesman. Kuyper, who at one time was prime minister of the Netherlands, was the founder of the Free University of Amsterdam.

Twentieth Century
22. BAVINCK, Herman, *Our Reasonable Faith,* WBE, 1956, 568 pp., $6.95. A compendium of theology,

being in effect a condensation of Bavinck's three-volume work on Reformed Dogmatics (not available in translation). Bavinck was professor of theology in the Free University of Amsterdam.

23. *WARFIELD, B. B., *Biblical and Theological Studies,* PRPC, 1952, 580 pp., $4.95; Ri, TP, 25s. One of the most notable Reformed scholars of his day, Warfield, though he wrote much, never produced a systematic theology. This volume brings together seventeen theological essays from his pen and four of his sermons. There is also a biographical introduction by the editor on Warfield as man and theologian.

24. *FORSYTH, P. T., *Positive Preaching and the Modern Mind,* AL, 1964, 228 pp., $3.50; WBE, Pb $2.25; IP, 1949, 260 pp., 15s; and James Denney, *The Atonement and the Modern Mind,* HS, 1910, 117 pp. (OoP) Forsyth and Denney were two of the finest theological minds of their day. Forsyth indeed may well be regarded as the most creative Christian thinker of this century. Both recalled the Church to see the cross in its true perspective, at the very heart of the Christian faith. These two books are fine examples of their effectiveness in speaking to the spirit of their age.

25. VOS, Geerhardus, *Biblical Theology,* WBE, 1948, 453 pp., Hb $5.00, Pb $2.95. A thorough study, historically presented, of the successive periods of biblical revelation, namely, the Mosaic, the prophetic, and the New Testament epochs. The consideration of the New Testament period is not carried beyond the four Gospels. As the author says in his preface, his work might be more suitably named a history of special revelation.

26. *MACHEN, J. G., *The Christian Faith in the Modern World,* WBE,

RE, 1965, 243 pp., Pb $1.95; and *The Christian View of Man,* WBE, 1947 (OoP); Ri, BTT, 1965, 254 pp., Pb 5s. Two books, addressed to a wide readership, by the founder of Westminster Theological Seminary, Philadelphia. Clearly and incisively written, together they cover the wide field of Christian theology.

27. THOMAS, W. H. G., *The Principles of Theology,* LO, 1930, 540 pp., $4.25 (OoP); CBRP, ED 5, 1956, 547 pp., 30s. A valuable study of the great themes of theology presented in sequence under the heads of the Thirty-Nine Articles of Religion of the Church of England. For a concise and compact compendium of Reformed Theology, see Louis Berkhof, *Systematic Theology,* Ri, BTT, 1958, 784 pp., 30s.

28. LECERF, Auguste, *An Introduction to Reformed Dogmatics,* LU, 1949, 408 pp., 25s. (OoP) An important work from the pen of a French Reformed theologian. An excellent book for the serious reader who likes his thinking to be stimulated. See also J. O. Buswell, Jr., *A Systematic Theology of the Christian Religion,* ZPH, 1962, 600 pp., $16.95.

29. BRUNNER, Emil, *Dogmatics,* 3 V., WP, 1950, 361 pp., $6.00; 1952, 386 pp., $6.50; 1962, 457 pp., $6.50; LU, 1949, 376 pp., 35s; 1952, 444 pp., 42s; 1952, 472 pp., 42s. One of the major works on systematic theology of our time. Its worth is enhanced by the clarity of its style and the penetration of its thought. The strength of Brunner's position is compromised by the ambivalence of his attitude to Scripture.

30. *HUGHES, P. E., ed., *Creative Minds in Contemporary Theology,* WBE, ED 2, 1968, 488 pp., $6.95. A symposium by evangelical scholars. A careful exposition and evaluation of the thought of fourteen modern thinkers: Barth, Berkouwer, Bonhoeffer, Brunner, Bultmann, Cullmann, Denney, Dodd, Dooyeweerd, Forsyth, Gore, Reinhold Niebuhr, Teilhard de Chardin, and Tillich, preceded by a chapter by the editor on the Creative Task of Theology. The first edition lacks the chapter on Bonhoeffer and carries a different chapter on Teilhard de Chardin from that which appears in the second edition.

31. *HENRY, C. F., ed., *Basic Christian Doctrines,* HRW, 1962, 302 pp., $6.00; HRW, 48s. Forty-four short chapters by as many evangelical scholars covering the wide range of Christian theology. An admirable book for the non-specialist reader.

32. *LOANE, M. L., *Do You Now Believe?,* CHP, 1966, 11 pp., Pb 5s; and J. R. W. Stott, *Basic Christianity,* IVP, 1958, 144 pp., Pb $1.25; TP, Pb 3s 6d. Two excellent little books suitable for new Christians and for study groups of different kinds. The one by the Archbishop of Sydney is a development of the doctrine of the creed. The other, by John Stott, is also suitable for handing to non-Christians. See also, T. C. Hammond, *In Understanding Be Men,* IVP, ED 5, 1954, $3.00; TP, 7s 6d.

2B. GOD AND CREATION
Harold B. Kuhn

Many have been temporarily distrubed by the strident pronouncement that "God is dead" which was fashionable sometime ago. Although this death-of-God theology is now on its way out, it is clear that we are at a critical stage in Christian thinking. It matters greatly how men think of God and his creation, of his relation to his world and of his attitude toward men.

Here are set forth several volumes dealing with the related subjects of God's existence and God's nature, in-

cluding two anthologies containing relevant entries. In the latter part are found titles and brief entries dealing with the Christian view of creation, including a critical discussion of alternate views, particularly those rooted in organic evolution.

1. BAVINCK, H., *The Doctrine of God*, WBE, ET, 1951, 408 pp., $5.00. (OoP) A great and scholarly work from the Reformed viewpoint.

2. *BERKOUWER, G. C., *The Providence of God*, WBE, ET, 1952, 294 pp., $3.50. Like the rest of the volumes in the series, this is soundly evangelical and dispersed with many exciting ideas.

3. DEMARAY, D. E., *Basic Beliefs: An Introductory Guide to Christian Theology*, BBH, 1958, 140 pp., Pb $1.50. Here is a handbook designed to afford an overview of the Christian faith. It is designedly concise and simple; its first three chapters are a worthy contribution to the subject of God, particularly the second, "Who is God?" which is carefully divided into topics.

4. COTTON, J. H., *Christian Knowledge of God*, MC, 1951, 180 pp. (OoP) Two major questions concern the author of this work: How may God be known? and With what degree of certainty may a Christian expect to hold this knowledge? The committed Christian will find much in this volume to challenge him amid much with which he must be in disagreement.

5. FABER, F. W., *The Creator and the Creature*, PRC, 1961, 370 pp., Hb $4.50, Pb $2.95; BO, 372 pp., 10s 6d. This author, a Roman Catholic, reaches over the confessional chasm and unites heart with heart as he attempts to show man his role as creature and to persuade him that he is homeless until he finds his home in God.

6. GOLLWITZER, Helmut, *The Existence of God as Confessed by Faith*, WP, ET, 1965, 245 pp., $5.75; SCMP, 35s. Here is a carefully structured volume, dealing primarily with similarities and differences between the two Continental writers, Karl Barth and Rudolf Bultmann. The author stands much nearer to the former. One must expect to invest much intensive study if he is to master this work.

7. HAMILTON, F. E., *The Basis of Christian Faith*, HRP, RE, 1964, 364 pp., $5.00. Chapters II, III, and IV of this volume deal with the origin of the universe and embody an able defense of the creationist position. It is a work of abiding worth, affording a highly rewarding adventure in reading.

8. HENDRY, G. S., *God the Creator*, HS, 1937, 194 pp. (OoP) To the question, "How can God be known?" this Scottish divine replies that God is known only through historically-based revelation. Two key themes pervade the work, the personality of God and the creatorhood of God. To faith, God as personal is relational to man; God as creator moves 'beyond' this and becomes the God of mystery.

9. HENRY, C. F., ed., *Basic Christian Doctrines*, HRW, 1962, 302 pp., $6.00; HRW, 48s. This is a valuable symposium containing forty-three separate articles, plus introduction and postscript, each dealing with some major phase of Christian truth. It contains three chapters on "The Knowledge of God," one on "The Trinity," and one on "Creation" in addition to thirty-eight others. The authors have been carefully chosen, with a view to presenting a coherent

46

view of God, the universe, and redemption.

10. HENRY, C. F., *The God Who Shows Himself*, WB, 1966, 138 pp., $3.50. The major thrust of this volume is that in our age of uncertainty in theology, there remains available a vital stream of revelation, within which one can discern God's presence as an epistemological reality. The volume traces ably God's effective action in the several areas of man's life and endeavor.

11. HODGSON, Leonard, ed., *God and the World Through Christian Eyes*, SCMP, 1933, 172 pp. (OoP) This symposium is shaped by the editor's concern to bring within one volume a series of discussions helpful to the reader who wishes to construct a *Weltanschauung* which is typically Christian. A work for the mature Christian.

12. HULSBOSCH, A., *God in Creation and Evolution*, SHE, ET, 1966, 240 pp., $4.95. This work has value for the evangelical for two reasons: first, it acquaints him with an attempt to reconcile a type of evolution with Christianity; and second, it familiarizes him with the Catholic approach to the question of a possible severance of the development of man's body from the conferral of his soul.

13. JENKINS, Daniel, *The Christian Belief in God*, WP, 1963, 226 pp., $4.75. This book is in some ways an irritant. One soon learns, however, that the author seeks to face the typical anti-theistic arguments current in university circles. The reader who is willing to live with some concessiveness, in order to see at last the shallowness of agnosticism, will find it helpful.

14. LEVER, Jan, *Creation and Evolution*, KR, ET, 1958, 244 pp. (OoP)

Produced by an eminent zoologist of the Free ·University of Amsterdam, the work combines a deep familiarity with the natural sciences and a sincere and vigorous biblical faith.

15. *MIXTER, R. L., *Evolution and Christian Thought Today*, WBE, 1959, 224 pp., $4.50. This symposium has for its central task the investigation of the doctrine of organic evolution in the light of Christian faith. It is recommended that the reader begin with Chapter Eleven, "Theology and Evolution," then proceed to Chapter Ten, "A Creationist Interpretation of Prehistoric Man," before reading the remaining nine chapters.

16. SOPER, D. W., *God Is Inescapable*, WP, 1959, 128 pp. (OoP) This volume challenges by means of irritation. It seeks to speak the Word of the gospel in today's language, but may defeat its own purpose by turning the mind from that which really makes God inescapable, namely a genuinely divine Christ.

2C. MAN AND SIN
Fred H. Klooster
True wisdom involves the knowledge of God and of ourselves. The two are so interrelated that man cannot have one without the other. The true grandeur of man is seen in the light of God's revelation as man created in the image of God. But man's present plight and sinful misery can only be rightly known from the revelation of man's fall and the nature of sin which has disrupted his relation with God. The gospel reveals God's gracious work in Jesus Christ for meeting man's sinful need and redeeming him, restoring him to fellowship and communion with God through the working of the Holy Spirit. Thus a biblical doctrine of man requires the distinction between man as he was created and man redeemed through Jesus

Christ in the fellowship of the Holy Spirit.

1. KLOOSTER, F. H., "The Nature of Man" in *Christian Faith and Modern Theology,* CHAP, 1964, 426 pp. (pp. 145-173), $5.95. An overview is presented of the biblical doctrine of man as created, fallen, and redeemed together with a survey of major differences between the biblical, the liberal, and the neo-orthodox views of man and sin.

2. BUSWELL, J. O., Jr., "The Nature of Sin" in *Christian Faith and Modern Theology,* CHAP, 1964, 426 pp. (pp. 177-189), $5.95. A survey of the revolt in modern theology with respect to the doctrine of sin and an examination in the light of Scripture.

3. LLOYD-JONES, D. M., *The Plight of Man and the Power of God,* PI, 1945, 94 pp. (OoP); Ri, WBE, 1966, $2.50. A diagnosis of the present state of man and its remedy.

4. *BERKOUWER, G. C., *Man: The Image of God,* WBE, 1962, 376 pp., $6.00. A comprehensive study of the biblical doctrine of man in the light of history and especially contemporary theology from a Reformed perspective emphasizing the uniqueness of man as the image of God.

5. *MACHEN, J. G., *The Christian View of Man,* WBE, 1947 (OoP); BTT, 1965, 254 pp., Pb 5s. A popular and lucid presentation of the view of man in relation to God originally presented as radio addresses by the champion of evangelicalism in the heyday of liberalism. See also, James Orr, *God's Image in Man,* Ri, WBE, 1948, 326 pp., $3.00 (OoP); S. B. Babbage, *Man in Nature and in Grace,* WBE, 1957, 115 pp., $1.50.

6. PREUS, H. A., and E. Smits, eds., *The Doctrine of Man in Classical Lutheran Theology,* AUP, 1962, 245 pp., $5.00. A translation of sections of the theology of Johann Gerhard and Martin Chemnitz together with an introduction providing historical and theological perspective on these seventeenth century Lutheran views of man.

7. MURRAY, John, *The Imputation of Adam's Sin,* WBE, 1959, 95 pp., $2.00. (OoP) A concise biblical-theological study of the relation of Adam's sin to that of his posterity based on Romans 5, evaluating conflicting views as well.

8. *DOOYEWEERD, Herman, *In the Twilight of Western Thought,* PRPC, 1960, 195 pp., Pb $2.50. The co-founder of an important new school of Christian philosophy contends that the nature of man can only be known from Scripture and shows how modern nihilism and man's loss of self-understanding stems from an apostate root. (Cf. "What is Man?" pp. 173-195)

9. *SAUER, Erich, *The King of the Earth,* WBE, 1962, 256 pp., $3.95; PP, 16s. The nobility of man according to the Bible is expounded by the great German Bible teacher. Man is shown to be the kingly instrument of God with strength of character and optimism and consciousness of divine dignity.

10. SCHARLEMANN, M. H., ed., *What, Then, Is Man?* CON, 1958, 356 pp., $3.50. A stimulating symposium by a group of Lutherans representing the historic Lutheran viewpoint in an interdisciplinary study.

11. DONIGER, S., ed., *The Nature of Man in Theological and Psychological Perspective,* HRP, 1962, 264 pp., $5.00 (OoP); HRP, 45s. A symposium by a wide variety of writers representing various views of man from the theological and psychological perspectives.

12. ·BARTH, Karl, *Christ and Adam: Man and Humanity in Romans 5*, HRP, 1956, 96 pp., $2.00; COL, 1956, Pb 95¢; OB, 46 pp., 6s. A succinct statement by the major voice in neo-orthodoxy whose position is better understood from the massive *Church Dogmatics*.

13. NIEBUHR, R., *The Nature and Destiny of Man*, 2 V., CSS, 1941, 300, 332 pp., Hb $5.95 each, Pb $1.65 each; NI, 1941-1943, 324, 340 pp., 20s each. The famous Gifford Lectures (1939) by America's foremost representative of realistic theology in the neo-orthodox tradition.

14. *LUTHER, Martin, *The Bondage of the Will*, REV, 1957, 323 pp., $3.50; JC, 324 pp., 15s. This is Martin Luther's magnum opus and one of the basic documents of the Reformation period. The vigor, pungency, and dialectical skill of the author would involve a mental and spiritual revolution for many Christians. It presents an outstanding biblical view of man, written as a rebuttal to the humanism of Erasmus.

2D. PERSON AND WORK OF CHRIST G. W. Grogan

It has been well said that "Christianity is Christ," and the person and work of Christ constitute the very heart of the Christian faith. For this reason they have always occupied a large and important place in theological writing and in theological debate. The most dangerous heresies are those which go astray here, for such error affects the nature of the gospel itself. All evangelistic literature worthy of the name dwells much on these central themes, for conversion is repentant and trustful response to Christ.

Literature intended for the encouragement of Christians in spiritual progress also finds its center here, for growing faith is nourished as it feeds on Christ, the Bread of Life. Some of the books on the subject cover both the person and the work of Christ (although there are comparatively few of these), many of them deal with the person or work alone, while there are some which deal with a more restricted although important field such as the virgin birth or the resurrection.

1. COUSINS, Peter, *A Christian's Guide to the Death of Christ*, HS, 1967, 192 pp., Pb 3s 6d. The Christian's Guide Series is "a series of short, simply-written books, dealing with basic Christianity . . . designed for the ordinary Christian." This one accomplishes this purpose well and would be suitable for young people, Christian or non-Christian.

2. *STALKER, James, *The Life of Jesus Christ*, REV, RE, 1909, 162 pp., $1.95; TTC, 1891, 155 pp., 9s. (OoP) This book has been reprinted over and over again, and this is not surprising for it is a model of compression and lucidity. It is perhaps the best simple account of our Lord's life written in modern times.

3. *MORRIS, Leon, *The Lord from Heaven*, WBE, 1958, 112 pp., Pb $1.45; TP, Pb 4s 6d. Here is a helpful introduction to the serious study of our Lord's person. It proceeds through the New Testament section by section and concludes by drawing the threads together in the concluding chapter. See also, Leon Morris, *The Story of the Christ Child*, WBE, 1960, 108 pp. (OoP); MMS, 128 pp., 10s 6d; and P. C. Simpson, *The Fact of Christ*, Ri, JC, 1952, 115 pp., 4s 6d.

4. GREEN, Michael, *Man Alive!*, IVP, 1967, 96 pp., Pb $1.25; TP, 3s 6d. It examines the evidence for the resurrection of Christ in terms of the event itself and of its effect upon those who know the risen Christ. The author's style is attractive and the book is to

be recommended as an evangelistic tool for work among students.

5. MORRISON, Frank, *Who Moved the Stone?*, ZPH, 1956, 192 pp., $3.95; FF, Hb 9s 6d, Pb 5s. This is an exciting piece of apologetics. The author investigated the evidence for the resurrection expecting to come to negative conclusions but was brought to faith in the resurrection by the facts themselves.

6. FINLAYSON, R. A., *The Cross in the Experience of Our Lord,* PJ, 1955, 95 pp. (OoP) Based on a series of conventional Bible readings, these chapters examine sensitively and devotionally the cost of our redemption to the Savior himself. The author is a Scottish evangelical theologian.

7. GUILLEBAUD, H. E., *Why the Cross?* IVP, 1946, 208 pp., Pb $1.50; TP, 6s. This book has two parts: "Is a Substitutionary Atonement Christian?" and "Is Substitution Immoral or Incredible?" It is written untechnically and would be helpful to a thoughtful inquirer. The answers it gives to objections are sane and helpful.

8. MORRIS, Leon, *Glory in the Cross,* HS, 1966, 96 pp., Pb 3s 6d. This is a title in the "Christian Foundations" series and is a product of the Evangelical Fellowship in the Anglican Communion. In it an acknowledged expert on the subject writes popularly but thoughtfully for the general reader.

9. MORGAN, G. C., *Crises of the Christ,* REV, 1945, 334 pp., $5.95; PI, 25s. This is perhaps the author's greatest book. It deals successively with the birth, baptism, temptation, transfiguration, crucifixion, resurrection, and ascension of Christ and shows how he meets man's many-sided need.

10. LIDDON, H. P., *The Divinity of Our Lord and Saviour Jesus Christ,* RIV, 1855, 535 pp. (OoP) This is a great classic on the subject by an Anglo-Catholic writer who was conservative in his attitude to the Bible. Much of the space is given to a consideration of the New Testament material but the Nicene formula is also considered and defended. The wedding of scholarship and devotion in it makes it heartwarming as well as instructive.

11. MURRAY, John, *Redemption Accomplished and Applied,* WBE, 1955, 192 pp., Pb $1.95; BTT, 1961, Pb 3s. This book, by a well-known evangelical theologian, is concerned not only with the atonement but with the doctrine of grace, and it shows clearly the links between the two. It is Calvinistic in standpoint and there is a chapter on particular redemption.

12. STIBBS, A. M., *The Finished Work of Christ,* TP, ED 2, 1964, 40 pp., 2s. This sets out in a scholarly way to answer those who maintain that "Christ's earthly passion was but an expression in time or history of something which happens only fully in eternity and that the eternal Son of God is therefore to be thought of as continually offering himself to God in order to secure our acceptance in God's presence."

13. *FORSYTH, P. T., *The Work of Christ,* AL, 1958, 191 pp., $4.00; IP, 1946, 244 pp., Hb 15s, Pb 7s 6d. Forsyth was trained under liberalism and reacted against it in the direction of a much more positive and biblical theology without becoming completely conservative. This book originated in lectures given to young ministers and is more simply written than some of the author's work. It lays special stress upon the holiness of God.

14. GREEN, E. M. B., *The Meaning of Salvation,* WP, 1965, 256 pp., $4.50; HS, 30s. The aim of this scholarly work is not to explore the doctrine of salvation in all its many-sidedness but to consider the use of the actual term "salvation" in Scripture. This means that it does on a larger scale for this word what Leon Morris' *Apostolic Preaching of the Cross* (see below) does with other great biblical terms applied to the Cross.

15. *MORRIS, Leon, *The Cross in the New Testament,* WBE, 1964, 454 pp., $6.95; PP, 1965, 30s. A very valuable piece of work. It could be said with justice that this does for the nineteen-sixties what Denney's *Death of Christ* did for an earlier generation. It proceeds through the New Testament writings systematically. The closing chapter gives a very clear and balanced statement of the doctrine of the atonement. A useful appendix gives a classified arrangement of all New Testament references to the death of Christ. See also, *The Story of the Cross,* WBE, 1957, 128 pp., $2.00; MMS, 10s 6d.

16. THOMPSON, J. G., *The Praying Christ,* TP, 1959, 159 pp., 12s 6d. Excellent doctrinal study on Jesus' pattern and teaching of prayer as revealed in the Gospel records.

17. *TENNEY, Merrill C., *The Reality of Resurrection,* HRP, 1963, 221 pp., $4.00; HRP, 30s. A modern treatment which is both intellectually stimulating and spiritually enriching. This clear and well-organized presentation covers pre-Christian concepts, historical developments, and present theological and experiential patterns. Recommended.

18. SMITH, W. S., *Great Sermons on the Death of Christ,* WAWC, 1965, 244 pp., $4.00. Sermons by celebrated preachers, past and present, on this profound subject. Includes biographical sketches and useful bibliographies.

19. TAYLOR, Vincent, *The Cross of Christ,* SM, 1956, 108 pp., $3.00; MC, 15s. The author has written several larger books on this theme. Here he surveys the New Testament evidence briefly, considers modern theories of the significance of the cross and gives his own estimate of its meaning. As in his earlier works, he treats the category of sacrifice as central and moves closer to penal substitution than he had done earlier, without really embracing it.

20. *DENNEY, James, *The Death of Christ,* IVP, RE, 1951, 208 pp., $3.50; TP, RE, 10s 6d. One of the greatest books on the subject in English and long regarded as a classic exposition of the evangelical doctrine of the atonement. It consists largely of detailed exegesis of the leading New Testament passages. The final chapter, "The Atonement and the Modern Mind," is an abridgement of what was originally a separate book. See also, *The Christian Doctrine of Reconciliation,* Ri, AL, 1959, 339 pp., $3.50; Ri, JC, 17s 6d.

21. MORRIS, Leon, *Apostolic Preaching of the Cross,* WBE, 1956, $5.95; TP, 1955, 296 pp. This is a very thorough study of the great biblical words in which the doctrine of the atonement is set forth in the Bible. It considers redemption, covenant, blood, propitiation, reconciliation, and justification. The two chapters on "propitiation" are especially helpful for they provide a scholarly attack on modern tendencies to eliminate the wrath of God and to reduce "propitiation" to "expiation."

22. TAYLOR, Vincent, *The Person of Christ in New Testament Teaching,* SM, 1958, 322 pp., $5.50; MC, 30s. From a moderately liberal stand-

point, this book surveys the New Testament evidence in two ways. First of all it deals with it exegetically and then historically and theologically. The author is particularly interested in the divine sonship of Jesus as presented in the New Testament and in the consciousness of our Lord himself.

23. MACINTOSH, H. R., *The Doctrine of the Person of Christ*, TTC, ED 2, 1913, 540 pp. (OoP) This is perhaps the most comprehensive book in English on this subject. It deals with the New Testament evidence, with the history of the doctrine and gives a reconstructive statement of it. This last section reflects the debates of Macintosh's day and his own construction of the doctrine is not wholly acceptable. See also, for the greatest of nineteenth-century works, T. J. Crawford, *The Doctrine of Holy Scripture Respecting the Atonement*, Ri, BBH, 1954, 545 pp., $4.95. (OoP)

24. BAILLIE, D. M., *God Was in Christ*, CSS, 1956, 231 pp., Hb $3.95, Pb $1.45; FF, ED 2, Hb 21s, Pb 9s 6d. From a standpoint that is generally positive but not completely conservative, Baillie deals with both the person and the work of Christ, although much more fully with the former. He also relates the person of Christ to the doctrine of the Trinity. He provides some useful criticism of certain modern views but is less helpful in his own positive construction.

25. FORSYTH, P. T., *The Person and Place of Jesus Christ*, Ri, WBE, 1964, 357 pp., Pb $2.25; IP, 1946, 360 pp., 15s. Considered by many to be Forsyth's greatest work. For his general outlook, see the comment on his *The Work of Christ* above. His style does not appeal to all readers, but it is worth persevering with this bracing exposition of his belief that Christ is the center of the gospel.

26. CULLMANN, Oscar, *A Christology of the New Testament*, WP, RE, 1964, 346 pp., $6.50; SCMP, ED 2, 1959, 45s. A major work by an important continental scholar. From a moderately liberal standpoint, he explores the Christological titles of the New Testament and expounds their background, use, and significance. Cullmann believes that the person and work of Christ cannot be divorced from each other and his book reflects this conviction.

27. BRUNNER, Emil, *The Mediator*, WP, 1934, 624 pp., Pb $3.25; LU, 47s. This is one of the few works which deals both with the person and the work of Christ and it is a massive treatment of each. It assumes a fairly considerable knowledge of Scripture and some knowledge of the modern history of theology. Brunner accepts the deity of Jesus, the doctrine of the incarnation and penal substitution, but rejects the virgin birth.

28. *HENRY, C. F., ed., *Jesus of Nazareth: Saviour and Lord*, WBE, 1966, 277 pp., $5.95. This conservative symposium opens with two chapters showing the Christological trends of the present time and the remainder of the essays deal with pressing issues, especially those which concern the relationship between faith and history so far as this affects Christology. Here is evangelical scholarship at its best.

29. GRILLMEIER, A., *Christ in Christian Tradition*, SHE, 1965, 528 pp., $8.50; MO, 75s. This is an extremely detailed treatment, by a Roman Catholic, of the history of Christology up to the Council of Chalcedon (451 A.D.). It is quite heavy going but is invaluable for close study of the subject.

30. PARKER, T. H., ed., *Essays in Christology for Karl Barth*, LU, 1956, 297 pp. A number of Chris-

tological themes are treated here by a group of British theologians, all influenced in varying degrees by Barth's approach to Christology. Some of its contributors are more conservative than Barth while others are more liberal.

31. *MACHEN, J. G., *The Virgin Birth of Christ*, Ri, BBH, 1958, 415 pp., Hb $5.95, Pb $3.95; Ri, JC, 1958, 432 pp., 25s. A masterpiece of conservative apologetics. It explores all important aspects of the subject with great thoroughness and combats all views which do not take the biblical evidence sufficiently seriously or which do not interpret it in the way the Bible itself does. See also, James Orr, *The Virgin Birth of Christ*, HS, 1907, 302 pp. (OoP)

32. FULLER, D. P., *Easter Faith and History*, WBE, 1964, 288 pp., $4.95; TP, 1967. This is an outstanding work on the subject by an evangelical scholar. He surveys the history of scepticism concerning the resurrection of Christ in modern theology and meets it ably and persuasively. A distinctive feature is his emphasis upon the writings of Luke and his testimony to the resurrection.

33. FRANKS, R. S., *History of the Doctrine of the Work of Christ*, 2 V., HS, 444, 437 pp. (OoP); *Work of Christ*, Ri, NE, 1962, 728 pp., 30s. This is the standard history of the doctrine and traces it in some detail from New Testament times to 1901. It is an invaluable reference book, indispensable for serious study of the subject.

34. *WARFIELD, B. B., *The Person and Work of Christ*, Ri, PRPC, 1950, 575 pp., $4.50. This work, by the greatest evangelical theologian of his day, shows his immense skill as an exegetical and polemic theologian. He was incapable of writing an unclear sentence. His work demolishes

liberal qualifications and denials of evangelical truth about our Lord's person and work. It concludes with three doctrinal sermons. See also, *The Lord of Glory*, HS, 1907, 304 pp. (OoP)

35. *BERKOUWER, G. C., *The Person of Christ*, WBE, 1953, 286 pp., $5.00; *The Sacraments*, WBE, 1967, $7.00. Penetrating studies in the reformed tradition by one of the foremost leaders of contemporary theology. The author considers the historical deliverances of the ecumenical councils, Christian confessions, the scriptural data, the reformers and recent theological literature. Recommended for study in depth.

36. *OWEN, John, *The Death of Death in the Death of Christ*, Ri, BTT, 1963, 318 pp., 15s; *The Glory of Christ*, Ri, MP, 1949, 285 pp., $3.50 (OoP); OL, 286 pp. (OoP) John Owen, most learned of the Puritans and perhaps the greatest British theologian of all time, wrote voluminously. These two are his masterpieces. The author treads circuitous paths, but his interpretation of the texts is sure, and his power of theological construction is superb, and his treatment is thorough. In spite of difficult text, the reading can be most rewarding. The first volume written in the author's early career deals with the question of universal redemption. The second volume, his last work, derives as much from his love for Christ and seems to soar into heavenly places.

2E. SALVATION AND SANCTIFICATION
M. Eugene Osterhaven
The salvation which Jesus Christ has wrought out for men was planned by God and is applied to them by the Holy Spirit. The New Testament teaches the sovereignty of God's grace. It is he who saves, he unites men to Christ, he gives them a new

nature, he calls, he justifies, he gives faith, and he sanctifies. As God draws men to himself, they are not passive; rather, the Holy Spirit moves them to respond so that they believe, seek to work out their own salvation, struggle against sin, pray for the Holy Spirit, and try to do God's will.

God's will is made known in his law which, first having shown man his sin, now comes to exercise a positive influence in his life. Even while the Christian knows that he cannot keep the law perfectly he sees it as the standard towards which he must strive out of gratitude for the redemption which he has in Jesus Christ.

1. *BERKOUWER, G. C., *Divine Election*, WBE, 1960, 336 pp., $5.00; *Faith and Justification*, WBE, 207 pp., $4.00; *Faith and Sanctification*, WBE, 193 pp., $4.50; *Faith and Perseverance*, WBE, 256 pp., $4.50. Each of these studies by the famous contemporary Dutch Reformed theologian is excellent. The point of view is that of the historic protestant faith, and the author shows his acquaintance with varying positions and seeks to set forth the conservative biblical point of view. Berkouwer's works are especially helpful because of his competence in the history of doctrine. He sees man as a sinner wholly unable to save himself and in need of the grace of God which is given him freely in Jesus Christ. Man is justified by grace, not works, but he seeks to do good because of the new nature which has been given him in Christ. His salvation is grounded in eternity and he has assurance of being a child of God forever because of God's faithfulness to his promise.

2. *BUCHANAN, J., *The Doctrine of Justification*, BBH, 1955, $4.95; BTT, 1961, 524 pp., 21s. An excellent treatment of the subject, arranged historically and dogmatically.

The point of view is Reformed. There is biblical emphasis on imputation of Christ's righteousness to the believer and brilliant defense of forensic categories.

3. CHAMBERLAIN, W. D., *The Meaning of Repentance*, WP, 1943, 238 pp., $2.00. An American Presbyterian New Testament theologian studies a much neglected doctrine and produces a book which is biblical and conservative theologically. After showing the need for the study, he gives a survey of the New Testament material followed by a chapter on the implications of repentance. There is also included a discussion of the mind of the flesh and the mind of Christ in the Christian, and the way in which repentance is produced. The answer to the latter is that it is by the Holy Spirit, who motivates the human will.

4. CRABTREE, A. B., *The Restored Relationship*, JP, 1963, $4.50; CK, 1963, 208 pp., 21s. A treatment of the doctrine of salvation by a contemporary British Baptist who has specialized in the theology of Jonathan Edwards and man's relationship to God. He asks how the relationship between God and man, which has been vitiated by sin, can be rectified. He states that the cardinal question of soteriology is how the sinner can be put right with God. Although the treatment contains numerous references to positions taken by theologians in the history of the church, it is readily understandable and faithful to the biblical positions. There is a comparison of Protestant and Roman Catholic positions in the matter of justification.

5. FLEW, R. N., *The Idea of Perfection in Christian Theology*, OUP, 1934, 422 pp., $3.75; 15s. A brilliant historical study, from the Methodist viewpoint, of the Christian's ideal for the present life.

6. *HALLESBY, O., *Prayer*, AUP, 1931, 137 pp., Hb $2.00, Pb $1.50; TP, 1956, 6s. An excellent treatment setting forth a definition of prayer, its difficulties, the misuse of prayer, and various forms of prayer. The position is consistently biblical and the style is simple and practical. A strong strain of piety pervades the treatment.

7. HULME, W. E., *The Dynamics of Sanctification*, AUP, 1966, 194 pp., $4.75. A Lutheran professor of pastoral theology discusses sanctification from a pastoral point of view. He shows an avid interest in the problems of mental and emotional health and the difference between true biblical sanctification, motivated by the Holy Spirit, and cheap substitutes thereof. The book is well outlined, the style is clear, and there are helpful references to other theological literature.

8. *HUGHES, P. E., *But for the Grace of God: Divine Initiative and Human Need*, WP, 1964, Pb $1.25; HS, 94 pp., 3s 6d. An excellent brief statement of the meaning of grace as set forth in the New Testament. The discussion covers the relation of grace to faith, works, law, the covenant, the sacraments, bishops, Mary, and election. Controversial issues concerning grace are not avoided.

9. JONES, O. R., *The Concept of Holiness*, MC, $3.75; AU, 1961, 200 pp., 21s. A British scholar offers a rather sophisticated treatment of his subject to try to arouse the interest of those philosophically and theologically motivated. The treatment is not primarily biblical, although the author moves within the sphere of biblical and evangelical Christian thinking, but is directed more toward a philosophical discussion of the subject. He asks what holiness is, its relation to the will, to moral goodness, and concludes with a discussion on divine personality and the perfect vision. The author is well-read theologically and makes many references to the positions of others.

10. KEVAN, E. F., *The Grace of Law: A Study of Puritan Theology*, BBH, 1965, $4.95; CK, 1964, 294 pp., 30s. A leading British evangelical sets forth the Reformed conception of the law of God as having a positive function in the Christian's life. The law shuts up the sinner to Christ and, once he has been saved, it becomes a help to him in showing him the will of God for Christian living. This study is an historical-dogmatic one, written as a dissertation, but giving an emphasis which is much needed in evangelical circles where law is disparaged except for its role in driving the sinner to the Savior.

11. KEVAN, E. F., *The Evangelical Doctrine of Law*, TP, 1956, 28 pp., Pb 1s 6d. A short treatment of the same subject as found in Kevan's larger work. It is scholarly, biblical, and clear.

12. KOBERLE, Adolph, *The Quest for Holiness*, AUP, 1936, 268 pp., Pb $2.50. An excellent statement on man's justification before God through the word of forgiveness and his sanctification by the Holy Spirit. The author, a professor at the University of Basel, writes a volume which is mildly heavy theologically, but also admirably biblical and clear.

13. *KUYPER, Abraham, *The Work of the Holy Spirit*, FW, 1900; Ri, WBE, 664 pp., $6.95. A comprehensive study of the work of the Holy Spirit in plain language by the great Dutch theologian which is still unsurpassed. Treatment covers the work of the Holy Spirit in creation, the giving of Scripture, in the history of salvation, and particularly in the application of the salvation wrought out by Christ to sinful men.

14. *LLOYD-JONES, D. M., *Conversions: Psychological and Spiritual,* IVP, 40 pp., Pb 60¢; TP, Pb 2s 6d. The British physician-preacher evaluates the phenomenon of conversion and argues that mass evangelism does not necessarily mean brainwashing, as used in certain totalitarian countries of our time. Mass conversion, as well as the conversion of the individual, may be genuine and motivated by the Holy Spirit. The style is clear and crisp and the point of view is evangelical.

15. *MACHEN, J. G., *What is Faith?* WBE, RE, 1962, 263 pp., Pb $1.95. An excellent study of the subject by the great New Testament scholar of Princeton and Westminster. Faith is seen as consisting of knowledge and trust in Christ. Its relation to hope and good works is discussed and it is proclaimed the only antidote for the modern drift of skepticism.

16. MARSHALL, I. H., *Christian Beliefs,* IVP, Pb $1.25; TP, 1963, 96 pp., Pb 3s. A brief guide which surveys Christian doctrine and has many helpful suggestions for further study.

17. MILLER, Alexander, *The Renewal of Man: A Twentieth-Century Essay on Justification by Faith,* DC, 1955, $2.95; GAL, 1956, 184 pp., 12s 6d. A contemporary discussion of an old Christian topic which takes an essentially evangelical position. The style is crisp and the treatment impresses one as being highly relevant. The author knows how to hold attention and shows himself to be an adept student of human psychology as well as theology.

18. MURRAY, John, *Redemption—Accomplished and Applied,* WBE, 1955, 192 pp., $1.95; BTT, 1961, 236 pp., Pb 3s. The first part of the book is on the atonement with more than one-half of the volume on the

application of salvation, covering the various steps in the order commonly associated with Reformed or evangelical theology. The style is clear and the treatment is what one might expect of a conservative Presbyterian theologian.

19. MURRAY, John, *The Covenant of Grace,* TP, 1953, 32 pp., Pb 1s 6d. A good brief treatment of the subject emphasizing the sovereignty of grace as God takes a people into covenant with himself. The relation of the various biblical covenants to each other is discussed and the unity of the Covenant of Grace is emphasized so that the Church is seen as the continuation of Old Testament Israel.

20. NEILL, Stephen, *Christian Holiness,* HRP, $3.00; LU, 1960, 134 pp., 15s. A contemporary Anglican Bishop sets forth the biblical idea of holiness and refutes the perfectionist and conformist errors. Bishop Neill is one of the more excellent conservative theological writers of our time, with a facility to write simply even while expounding difficult themes. Deeply involved in the ecumenical movement, he is at the same time consistently evangelical.

21. PINK, A. W., *The Doctrine of Sanctification,* BBH, 1955, 206 pp., $3.00. A well-known evangelical author discusses the doctrine of salvation as to its meaning for Christian life. There is a fine emphasis on the divine source of the Christian's sanctification and his union with Christ. The style is relatively simple and the author stays with his subject without allusions to or illustrations from contemporary life.

22. *RYLE, J. C., *Holiness: Its Nature, Hindrances, Difficulties, and Roots,* KR, 1962, 333 pp., $4.50; JC, 1952, 15s. The author, an Anglican Bishop, is in the line of Puritan divines in a general theological posi-

tion. He writes in a very readable style for the layman as well as more sophisticated readers. The point of view is strictly scriptural and evangelical and there is constant appeal to Scripture throughout. The author's own warmth and piety are much in evidence in the book. See also, J. S. Stewart, *A Man in Christ*, HRP, 331 pp., $2.50; HS, 1935, 12s 6d.

23. WARFIELD, B. B., *Perfectionism*, PRPC, 1932, 611 pp., $4.95; OUP. (OoP) Stimulating and brilliant essays by a great Presbyterian theologian on modern holiness movements. The text is sophisticated and difficult.

2F. PERSON AND WORK OF THE HOLY SPIRIT
John F. Walvoord

The doctrine of the Holy Spirit has attracted attention in the twentieth century not only as the key to the doctrine of the Trinity, but is of central importance in the debate between neo-orthodoxy and orthodoxy. The Holy Spirit is related to any discussion of sanctification and the place and importance of spiritual gifts. The ministry of the Spirit is vital in teaching the Scriptures and is relevant to biblical epistemology.

The deity of the Spirit and his personality are essential to the doctrine of God, and his work in inspiration accounts for the unique character of the Bible as the Word of God. The Holy Spirit is indispensable to the salvation of the lost, to growth in knowledge and holiness of the believer, and to power in spiritual life and service.

1. CHAFER, L. S., *He That Is Spiritual*, ZPH, 1918, 193 pp., $3.50; OL, 11s. (OoP) This popular presentation of the doctrine of the Holy Spirit as it relates to the salvation and spiritual life of Christians has introduced thousands to the simple basic principles of being a spiritually-minded

Christian. For young Christians, this volume, written by a great man of God, is an essential introduction to the Holy Spirit.

2. CHAFER, L. S., *Systematic Theology*, V. 6, DASP, 1948, 298 pp., $3.95; MMS, 25s. (OoP) Designed for mature students, this theological treatment presents a comprehensive study of the person and work of the Holy Spirit.

3. *KUYPER, Abraham, *The Work of the Holy Spirit*, FW, 1900; Ri, WBE, 664 pp., $6.95. This major contribution is a classic written by a famous Dutch theologian. It will introduce the student to traditional Reformed theology as related to the Holy Spirit.

4. MARSH, F. E., *Emblems of the Holy Spirit*, KR, RE, 1957, 257 pp., $2.95; AS, 1965, 27s 6d. This standard work on the typology of the Holy Spirit in Scripture is an important collateral study of the many figures in the Bible speaking of the Holy Spirit.

5. *MORRIS, Leon, *Spirit of the Living God*, IVP, 1960, 102 pp., Pb $1.50; TP, 104 pp., 4s. The important teachings of the Bible and the Holy Spirit, presented in a non-technical way, are an excellent introduction to the whole field. The author is a recognized and competent evangelical scholar.

6. MOULE, H. C. G., *Veni Creator*, HS, 1895; Ri, PI, 252 pp. Scholarly and deep insights into the person and work of the Holy Spirit.

7. MURRAY, Andrew, *The Spirit of Christ*, Ri, OL, 1963, 272 pp., 18s 6d. A series of profound and penetrating meditations. The two-fold working of the Holy Spirit in the Old and New Testaments. There are also

useful notes on the usage of the word *Spirit* in the Bible.

8. OWEN, John, *A Discourse Concerning the Holy Spirit,* from the *Works of John Owen,* 4 V., PEBS, 1862; Ri, *The Holy Spirit, His Gifts and Power,* KR, 1967, 356 pp., $4.50. As an early puritan treatise and a theological classic, this work is one of the most thorough treatments of the subject in early American theology.

9. PACHE, Rene, *The Person and Work of the Holy Spirit,* MP, 1954, 219 pp., $3.50. Representing the best in evangelical scholarship from Europe, this thorough presentation of the doctrine of the Spirit is suited for lay study on the college level.

10. PENTECOST, J. D., *The Divine Comforter,* REV, 1963, 256 pp., $3.95. This series of sermons treats all the important doctrines relating to the Holy Spirit including his essential character, ministry and gifts, the nature of regeneration and sanctification and the Holy Spirit as the spiritual power in the life of a Christian.

11. RIDOUT, Samuel, *Person and Work of the Holy Spirit,* LB, 224 pp., Pb $1.50. Representative of thoroughly biblical studies in the Holy Spirit, presented from the viewpoint of the Plymouth Brethren, this study is a good introduction to the doctrine of the Holy Spirit.

12. SMEATON, G., *The Doctrine of the Holy Spirit,* Ri, BTT, 1959, 372 pp., 13s 6d. A rich theological exposition which is as useful now as it was 85 years ago.

13. *THOMAS, W. H. G., *The Holy Spirit of God,* Ri, WBE, 1963, 303 pp., Pb $2.25. The writings of Griffith Thomas continue to bless evangelical Christians. This work is one of the best Anglican treatments.

14. *WALVOORD, J. F., *The Holy Spirit,* ZPH, 1958, 288 pp., $5.95. The entire doctrine of the Holy Spirit is presented in this standard textbook used in college and seminary. The Holy Spirit is studied from a biblical and theological point of view. Completely indexed, it also includes an analysis of the history of the doctrine of the Holy Spirit and the Holy Spirit in contemporary theology.

2G. CHRIST AND FELLOWSHIP
William C. Robinson
Robert P. Roth

The plan of God for the salvation of his fallen creatures calls for the election of some for the task of saving all. Before the coming of Jesus this was established in the Covenant God made with Israel which produced a fellowship that lived by hope in the promised Redeemer. After Jesus this fellowship became renewed in the new Covenant which lives by faith in his resurrection and hope in his coming again. This fellowship is called and gathered by the Spirit to glorify God and to shed his love abroad by being servants in the world. The literature on the Church is abundant. We list here a cross-section of books dealing with the biblical teaching about the Church, the history of this unique fellowship and the significance of the Church for society today.

1. BANNERMAN, James, *The Church of Christ,* 2 V., BT, 480, 468 pp., $7.50; BTT, RE, 1960, 30s. The Reformed doctrine of the Church as wrought out in Scotland is here presented.

2. BEST, E., *One Body in Christ,* MC, 1955, 249 pp., $4.00 (OoP); SPCK, 264 pp., 25s. (OoP) A thoughtful study of the Pauline doctrine of the Church, corrective of some recent theories.

3. BOSC, Jean, *The Kingly Office of the Lord Jesus Christ,* OB, ET, 1959, 166 pp., 16s. (OoP) Here Christ is presented in his offices of prophet, priest, and king and the need for a balanced emphasis upon each is maintained. Christ uses his ministers, but only he can reform his Church. See also, T. F. Torrance, *Royal Priesthood,* IR, 1955, 108 pp., Pb $2.00; OB, Pb 9s.

4. *BRUCE, F. F., *The Spreading Flame,* WBE, 1953, 191, 192, 160 pp., $5.00; PP, 1958, 432 pp., 21s. This is a fresh approach to the advance of the Christian fellowship in the early centuries. See also, Oscar Cullmann, *The Early Church,* WP, 1956, 271 pp., $4.50; Ri, WP, 1966, 162 pp., Pb $1.95; SCMP, 1956, 271 pp., 25s; Ri, SCMP, 1966, 162 pp., Pb 12s 6d.

5. BURTNESS, James, and John Kildahl, *The New Community in Christ,* AUP, 1963, 207 pp. (OoP) This is a collection of essays on the corporate Christian life or what it means to belong to the body of Christ.

6. COLE, R. A., *The New Temple,* TP, 1951, 56 pp. (OoP) A rewarding study of the earliest catechetical teaching of the Church as reflected in the New Testament.

7. FLEW, R. V. N., *Jesus and His Church,* AL, 1956, 272 pp., $3.00; EP, 1938, 192 pp., 15s; and *The Nature of the Church,* HRP, 1952, 347 pp., $4.00; MUS, 21s. This able English Methodist scholar shows that Jesus and his Church belong together. A good survey of the New Testament teaching.

8. HORT, F. J., *The Christian Ecclesia,* MC, 258 pp., Pb $1.75. (OoP) This English scholar shows that Jesus did establish the Church, or that he re-founded the Old Church as the New Israel by faith in his own Messi-

ahship. An indispensable study of the connotation of the word *Church* in the New Testament.

9. JENKINS, Daniel, *The Strangeness of the Church,* DC, 1955, 188 pp. (OoP) Here is a realistic assessment of the nature and function of the Church today as it is expressed in the present cultural climate; see also, *The Reality of the Church,* CSS, 1958, 245 pp., $2.45. (OoP)

10. *KÜNG, Hans, *The Council in Action,* SHE, 1963, 276 pp., $4.50. Here is a guide to the exciting deliberations of the Second Vatican Council written by a Roman Catholic professor who was daily involved in its debates. The intellectual basis for the issues of ecumenicity is discussed.

11. KUYPER, R. B., *The Glorious Body of Christ,* WBE, 1955. (OoP) The glory of the Church is set forth against all efforts to belittle its dignity. "It is Christ Himself who governs the Church through its officers." Their task is to declare and apply the laws of Christ, not to legislate for the Church.

12. *MORRIS, Leon, *Ministers of God,* IVP, 1964, 128 pp., Pb $1.50; TP, Pb 4s. As Christ came to minister so he calls his Church and her officers to minister by proclaiming the work he accomplished for men. His is the one essential ministry, ours are continuations of his only as we faithfully point to him and what he has done for us. See also, Michael Green, *Called to Serve,* WP, 1965, 95 pp., Pb $1.25; HS, 3s 6d.

13. MURRAY, John, *Christian Baptism,* PRPC, 1952, 94 pp., $2.00. A valuable discussion of the significance of baptism.

14. NEWBIGIN, Leslie, *The Household of God,* FR, 1954, 177 pp., Pb $2.75; SCMP, RE, 1964, 160 pp., 9s

6d. This book discusses the nature of the Church in the light of the current ecumenical debate. It examines the three traditions of Church life and structure: Catholic, Protestant, and Pentecostal.

15. NYGREN, Anders, *Christ and His Church,* WP, 1956, 125 pp. (OoP); SPCK, 1957, 10s 6d. This book is a penetrating study of the central and critical issues involved in the Church's search for unity. See also, G. T. Manley, *Christian Unity,* MEB, 1956, 96 pp., Pb $1.25.

16. NYGREN, Anders, *This Is the Church,* MUP, 1952, 353 pp. (OoP) This is a collection of essays by Swedish scholars on the nature of the Church. There are three sections dealing with biblical, historical, and doctrinal aspects of the Church.

17. SCHLATTER, Adolf, *The Church in the New Testament Period,* AL, 1955, 347 pp., $4.50; SPCK, 21s. The treatment of the several New Testament leaders, e.g., James, Peter, Paul and of the early congregation is illuminating. See also, A. T. Hanson, *The Pioneer Ministry,* WP, 1961, 176 pp., $3.75; SCMP, 21s.

18. SCHWEIZER, Edward, *Church Order in the New Testament,* AL, 1961, 239 pp., Hb $6.45, Pb $3.50; SCMP, 229 pp., Pb 16s. "In the Church there is really only one single authority—that of Christ Himself (or alternatively of God or of the Holy Spirit), only a Christocracy."

19. STÄHLIN, Wilhelm, *The Mystery of God,* CON, 1964, 224 pp., $3.50. It is God who became flesh and lives on in the Church through preaching and sacraments and, therefore, the divine presence can never be substituted by a sentimentalizing or spiritualizing of the human or of the things of this world.

20. STANLEY, D. M., *The Apostolic Church in the New Testament,* NP, 1965, 472 pp., $6.95. This is a scholarly study of the origin of the Church. The book is composed of four parts: 1) the formation of the Church and Scripture through early preaching, 2) the work of liturgy in shaping both Church and Scripture, 3) the meaning of the written Gospel and 4) the work of Paul among the Gentiles. See also, P. T. Forsyth, *The Church and the Sacraments,* AL, 1955, 308 pp., $4.00; Ri, IP, 1953, 12s 6d; and *A. M. Stibbs, *God's Church,* IVP, 1959, 128 pp., Pb $1.50; TP, Pb 4s.

21. VAN DEN HEUVEL, A. H., *The Humiliation of the Church,* WP, 1966, 192 pp., Pb $2.25; SCMP, 15s. A collection of essays on the crisis of the Church including such topics as experimental preaching, worship in a secularized world, ecumenicity, the Honest to God debate, and problems of the new morality.

22. WARNS, J., *Baptism: Its History and Significance,* PP, 1958, 352 pp., 15s. (OoP) A thorough work arguing for believer's baptism.

2H. LAST THINGS
William M. Arnett

"Last Things" (eschatology, the technical term, from eschatos, *meaning "the last") is that phase of the Christian message which deals with events in the future. For the Christian, it embraces the blessed hope of Christ's second coming and the living hope of resurrection and life everlasting. There is a two-fold aspect to last things: (1) with relation to the individual, it includes death, resurrection, judgment, the conditions of rewards and punishments, and existence after death; (2) with relation to the world, it involves the second coming of Jesus Christ and the end of the world as we now know it. Views of the millennium, based on the thousand years*

of Revelation 20:1-7, are also included; the intermediate state, or the condition and state of the soul between death and the resurrection; and the "great gulf" between heaven and hell. It is a fascinating area of the Christian faith.

1. *MANLEY, G. T., *The Return of Jesus Christ,* IVP, 1960, 104 pp., Pb $1.50; TP, 1960, Pb 4s. The author has designed this book to help young Christians by confirming belief in Christ's promise to return, by showing that it was a living hope in the early Church, and by instilling a love for his "appearing" in Christians today. It is biblical, evangelical, and affirmative. Various interpretations and some difficulties are presented to inform, but not always to resolve them. It is an excellent introductory study.

2. *DERHAM, A. M., *Shall These Things Be?* IVP, 1956, 39 pp., Pb 50¢; TP, Pb 2s. In six brief chapters, this booklet deals with the important aspects of the basic fact of Christ's second coming rather than with particular matters of interpretation. Our Savior's return is seen as a definite, personal, and glorious act, and the doctrine itself is presented as a very practical, vital truth.

3. BLACKSTONE, W. E., *Jesus Is Coming,* REV, 1908, 252 pp., Hb $2.95, Pb $1.95. This volume is a classic presentation concerning the personal, premillennial coming of Jesus Christ. It was first published nearly a century ago and is probably the most widely circulated book on the subject with a correspondingly great influence. It has been in print almost continuously since the first edition.

4. LUDWIGSON, C. R., *Bible Prophecy Notes,* ZPH, ED 3, 1951, 172 pp. (OoP) This work affords an excellent summary of the differing positions in

modern evangelicalism on major prophetic themes, with helpful charts and documentation. It reflects a careful study of a wide range of literature and of the biblical data. It will aid greatly those who seek to arrive at some conviction of their own regarding these great truths.

5. SAUER, Erich, *The Dawn of World Redemption,* WBE, 1951, 206 pp., Pb $1.95; PP, Hb 10s 6d, Pb 6s. The late author was one of the outstanding spokesmen of biblical Christianity in our time. This volume is the first of his famous trilogy of books on the divine purposes, plan, and history of salvation, and presents a survey of the history of salvation in the Old Testament. This study combines a profound knowledge of the biblical text and an unusual theological insight, coupled with gifts of original thought and vigorous expression.

6. SAUER, Erich, *The Triumph of the Crucified,* WBE, 1951, 207 pp., Pb $1.95; PP, 1951, Pb 5s. This volume, companion to *The Dawn of World Redemption,* is a survey of salvation in the New Testament. It includes an illuminating study of the antichrist. The core of the survey is the redemptive work of Christ, which moves to his culminating triumph when God shall be all in all. There are 3,700 Scripture references in this work.

7. SAUER, Erich, *From Eternity to Eternity,* WBE, 1954, 207 pp., Pb $2.25; PP, 10s 6d. This is the third volume in the author's trilogy of biblical exposition, in which he sets forth an outline of the ways of God with men through seven periods of salvation, culminating in the eternal plan for the Kingdom and the Church. A colored chart illustrates the main themes of this part of the book. The inspiration of Scripture is also discussed, as well as problems

raised concerning the prophecies of the coming Kingdom of God.

8. BAXTER, Richard, *The Saint's Everlasting Rest,* AL, 1962, 187 pp., $3.50; EP, 18s 6d. Although written in the seventeenth century by the great Puritan, it is a classic and a glorious book about heaven.

9. WOOD, A. S., *Prophecy in the Space Age,* MMS, 1964, 159 pp., 12s 6d. The aim of this book, written from a premillennial perspective, is to relate the eternal truth of prophecy to the flow of current events in the space era. First presented as addresses, each chapter is helpfully outlined and is based on an informed exegesis of the Word. The author, an evangelical, presents a ringing challenge to vigorous Christian activity since he firmly believes the end of the age is near.

10. LADD, G. E., *The Gospel of the Kingdom,* WBE, 1959, 143 pp., $2.75; PP, 10s 6d. This volume comprises a proclamation of various aspects of the Kingdom of God which is interpreted as belonging to the present as well as to the future. First delivered as addresses in the pulpit and in Bible conferences, these studies are simple and direct in style. The ultimate perfection of the Kingdom is seen in God's final victory at the end of the millennium.

11. WALVOORD, J. F., *The Return of the Lord,* ZPH, 1955, 160 pp., $2.50. The series of messages in this carefully written volume discusses various topics related to Christ's second coming from a premillennial point of view. Each chapter is designed to be sufficient in itself while contributing to Christian doctrine as a whole, and is presented in popular sermonic form. The author is a capable exponent of dispensational pretribulationism.

12. LADD, G. E., *The Blessed Hope,* WBE, 1956, 167 pp., Pb $1.95. The central thesis of this book is that the Blessed Hope is the second coming of Jesus Christ, not a pre-tribulation rapture. The author, an evangelical scholar and a diligent student of the Word, favors post-tribulationism (that is, the Church is taken out of the world *after* the tribulation, not *before*).

13. HUGHES, Archibald, *A New Heaven and a New Earth,* PRPC, 1958, 233 pp., $3.75; MMS, 1958, 17s 6d. This study surveys the prophetic element in Scripture relating to Jesus Christ, and sets forth His second coming as the consummation of God's eternal plans. The book abounds with quotations from the Scriptures, not mere citations. Part II considers significant, relevant questions for which biblical illumination is sought. The author is evangelical, but rejects dispensationalism and millennialism. See also, W. M. Smith, *The Biblical Doctrine of Heaven,* MP, 1968, $4.95.

14. BOETTNER, Loraine, *The Millennium,* PRPC, ED 4, 1958, 380 pp., $4.50. This volume makes available a systematic treatment of the three general systems which profess to set forth the teaching of Scripture regarding the second coming of Christ and the future course of the Kingdom, namely postmillennialism, a-millennialism and premillennialism. The author, a conservative scholar and a postmillennialist, points out that each of these systems is consistently evangelical, but the diverse methods used in interpreting Scriptures give rise to variations in belief.

15. *TENNEY, M. C., *Interpreting Revelation,* WBE, 1957, 220 pp., $3.50. The author presents methods and interpretative principles, as well as "schools" of interpretation, rather than giving a detailed commentary.

The approach is from a premillenial and moderate futurist standpoint, and is a scholarly, evangelical work.

16. *BOETTNER, Loraine, *Immortality*, PRPC, ED 7, 1956, 161 pp., $2.50. Three main topics are discussed from an evangelical point of view in this work: physical death, immortality, and the intermediate state (that is, the realm or condition in which souls exist between death and the resurrection). Other related topics are also considered, including soul sleep, annihilation, purgatory, spiritualism, prayers for the dead, burial, and cremation.

17. *RAMM, Bernard, *Them He Glorified*, WBE, 1963, 148 pp., $3.25. The author presents a systematic study of the doctrine of glorification, showing the eschatological character of our present salvation and its fruition in final glorification. In this evangelical work, one of the richest veins of biblical truth is tapped and explored, centering in the biblical concepts of glory and future glorification.

18. SCHEP, J. A., *The Nature of the Resurrection Body*, WBE, 1964, 252 pp., $4.95. This is an exhaustive study of the biblical data relating to one of the most controversial areas in the field of biblical theology today, namely, the nature of the resurrection body. It is painstaking, evangelical scholarship in biblical and contemporary literature. The author rejects the spiritualizing interpretations of the resurrection which abound in our time.

19. BUIS, Harry, *The Doctrine of Eternal Punishment*, PRPC, 1957, 148 pp., $2.75. The author traces belief in the doctrine of eternal punishment historically from the age of the Old Testament to the present. The biblical teaching is carefully expounded, and numerous variations therefrom in past and contemporary thought are cited. The teaching of the Bible on the reality and eternity of punishment is clearly supported by this book.

20. KAC, A. W., *The Rebirth of the State of Israel*, MP, 1958, 383 pp., $4.95; MMS, 1958, 22s 6d. In this outstanding volume, the author, a Jewish Christian, presents an in-depth study of the teaching of the Bible concerning Israel. On the background of an intimate acquaintance with Jewish history and thought, he traces events which have led to the establishment of present-day Israel. The significance of contemporary headlines is observed in conjunction with the prophetic Scriptures.

21. *MORRIS, Leon, *The Biblical Doctrine of Judgment*, TP, 1960, 72 pp., 5s. An evangelical scholar presents an Old and New Testament study of judgment in this concise book by getting at the heart of the meaning of words that are used to express the judgment. The author views the judgment in the New Testament in a two-fold manner: as a present reality and as a future certainty.

22. SMITH, W. M., *World Crises and the Prophetic Scriptures*, MP, 1952, 384 pp. (OoP) The author is an outstanding Bible scholar and student of prophecy. The twelve chapters of this book relate to various phases of world affairs, including such topics as "Prophecies of and Preparation for a World Government," "The Coming World Religion," "The Significance of Russia in the Closing Days of This Age," and "At the Center of the Earth—Jerusalem."

23. PAYNE, J. B., *The Imminent Appearing of Christ*, WBE, 1962, 191 pp. (OoP) The focus of this study concerns the temporal connection sustained between the glorious appearing of Christ and the rapture of

the Church, its being "caught up in the clouds" to meet him, and the possibility of an immediate, imminent occurence of these events. It is a very carefully documented, evangelical work, within a premillennial, post-tribulation framework.

24. CULLMANN, Oscar, *Immortality of the Soul or Resurrection of the Dead?* AL, 1958, 60 pp., Pb $1.50; EP, 1958, Pb 6s. Examination of the scriptural evidence in exciting manner.

25. BRUNNER, Emil, *Eternal Hope,* WP, 1954, 232 pp., $3.50. This volume is characteristic of current discussions in the field of eschatology in contemporary European theology. Its theological perspective is neo-orthodox. The element of uncertainty is indicative of the struggle between an older type of liberalism and the new attempt to take the Bible more seriously. It veers sympathetically to universalism.

26. BERKHOF, Louis, *The Kingdom of God,* WBE, 1951, 178 pp., $2.50. (OoP) Development of the kingdom idea including liberal, social, and neo-orthodox conceptions.

27. LADD, G. E., *Crucial Questions about the Kingdom of God,* WBE, ED 3, 1952, 193 pp., $3.00. This scholarly work presents a brief survey of the history of interpretation relating to the kingdom of God, and discusses various aspects and problems relating to the kingdom such as its relation to time, the linguistic interpretation, and objections to the millennial interpretation. There is great fidelity to the Word of God.

28. MINEAR, P. S., *Christian Hope and the Second Coming,* WP, 1954, 220 pp. (OoP) This work has been described as "an example of modern ecumenical perplexity, in the attempt to deal with eschatology apart from a

full commitment to Scripture." It represents a neo-liberal attempt to chart a middle course between fundamentalism and modernism, seeking to avoid both literalism and total spiritualization. The result is often a lack of clarity.

section 3
CHRISTIAN WITNESS

3. CHRISTIAN WITNESS: INTRODUCTION
C. Stacey Woods

The chief priority and unquestioned imperative for the Christian in the man-ward or horizontal direction of his life on earth is witness and evangelism. Witnessing is as much what we are as it is what we do or say. "Ye are my witnesses." Only the person who has experienced Christ can bear witness to him.

Evangelism is the task of heralding the good news of Jesus, the Son of God, to every man with a view to his conversion. In its broadest and truest sense, the evangel or the message is the total New Testament revelation. The ultimate objective of evangelism is not only conversion, but beyond that, to present every believer perfect in Christ Jesus. The message of the gospel today must not only be proclaimed. It must be demonstrated and authenticated to an unbelieving world by the life of the herald lived among men. The one who tells out the gospel must live the gospel, so that in a sense the man becomes his message.

To fulfill the double ministry of witness and evangelism, we must know how others who have preceded us have succeeded or failed. They have many lessons to teach us, and we can only really understand the challenge and need of today in the context of yesterday and in the promise of tomorrow. Hence, the importance of a working knowledge of the history of the churches, which for the most part is a tragic one. It is also important to understand how these churches have defined their belief in terms of their creeds and confessions. The history of the succeeding waves of missionary endeavor also should be studied, from the first thrust of the early Church down to today, when missions are no longer the white man's burden alone, and in reality never should have been so considered.

As we go to mankind with the message of Christ, we must also understand the faiths of other peoples. Hence, a working knowledge of the great non-Christian ethnic religions is an essential, if we are to communicate meaningfully and if our message is to be related to people where they are.

3A. HISTORY OF CHURCH
Joel L. Samuels
The apostle Paul prays that believers may comprehend "with all the saints what is the breadth and length and height and depth, and to know the love of Christ . . ." (Ephesians 3:18, 19). The heritage of the Christian today includes men and movements, institutions and ideas from many periods of the history of Christianity. The reading of Church history is a valuable part of appreciating this great heritage. Unfortunately, wisdom and nonsense accumulate together, and the reading of history may assist one to discriminate between the positive and negative factors in the contemporary Church.

The books under "General Works" are arranged according to the degree of difficulty with which they may be read—from the least to the most difficult. Those under "Historical Periods" are normally arranged according to the chronological development of the history of Christianity.

General Works
1. *LATOURETTE, K. C., *Christianity through the Ages*, HRP, 1965, 321 pp., $2.45; HRP, 19s. A broad survey of the history of Christianity in the setting of world history. The author frankly confesses that its writing sets forth Christian convictions, both in the understanding of Christian origins and in the appraisal of events. The value of the work is that the reader may obtain an overall view of the subject.

2. BETTENSON, Henry, ed., *Documents of the Christian Church,* OUP, ED 2, 1963, 489 pp., Hb $3.75, Pb $2.50; OUP, 510 pp., 18s. This is a selection of documents, in English translation, which is of greatest significance for understanding the history of Christianity.

3. WALKER, Williston, *A History of the Christian Church,* CSS, 1959, 585 pp., $7.50; CLA, 1960, 42s. This is a revised edition of a textbook in Church history which has been used for many years. It is factually accurate and, in most instances, presents the most important information on the leading events in the history of Christianity. Its viewpoint is that of Protestant liberalism.

4. *LATOURETTE, K. S., *A History of Christianity,* HRP, 1953, 1516 pp., $10.00; ES, 1544 pp., 63s. This encyclopedic survey of the history of Christianity in its global setting is most valuable as a reference type work. The viewpoint is theologically conservative although the author may be considered as a little more optimistic than what history or Scripture seems to justify. Good bibliographies are appended to each chapter.

5. HUGHES, Philip, *A History of the Church,* 3 V., SHE, 1935, 397, 517, 556 pp., $15.00; SHE, 95s. Designed as a comprehensive survey of the history of Christianity, these three volumes cover the period from Christian origins to the time of Martin Luther. The point of view is Roman Catholic.

6. SCHAFF, Philip, *History of the Christian Church,* 8 V., Ri, WBE, 1960, $49.50. Covering the history of Christianity only to and including the continental Reformation, these eight volumes are the most comprehensive treatment of Church history available from the Protestant viewpoint. The edition cited herein is an unaltered reprint of the 1910 edition;

its bibliographies, therefore, are not up-to-date.

7. CROSS, F. L., ed., *The Oxford Dictionary of the Christian Church,* OUP, 1958, 1492 pp., $20.00; OUP, 1957, 1512 pp., 90s. An alphabetical arrangement of entries on subjects of interest in both theology and Church history. The articles are concise and good bibliographies are appended to many of the important entries. The use of asterisks within the article serves as an excellent system of cross references. The orientation is to English Church history, especially the Church of England. Nonetheless, this is an excellent and comprehensive reference work.

8. MONTGOMERY, J. W., *The Shape of the Past,* EB, 1962, 382 pp. Although much of the history as written deals with the *what* of history, this work deals with the *why* of history. Sub-titled "An Introduction to Philosophical Historiography," this volume seeks to demonstrate that only orthodox Christianity can adequately explain history.

Major Periods
9. RAMSAY, W. M., *The Church in the Roman Empire,* HS, 1892; Ri, BBH, 1954, 510 pp., $4.95. Detailed discussion of Church history from the time of Christian origins to A.D. 170 sets Christianity in the context of Roman imperialism. Sir William Ramsay was an archaeologist who wrote many important works on the archaeology and geography of the New Testament. For historical sketches of great insight, see E. Stauffer, *Christ and the Caesers,* SCMF 1955, 294 pp., 25s (OoP); for stimulating and original study of the early Church preaching, see J. Foster, *After the Apostles,* SCMP, 1951, 128 pp., 6s. (OoP)

10. *BRUCE, F. F., *The Spreading Flame,* WBE, 1958, 432 pp., $5.00;

PP, 21s. The best description of the content of this volume is found in the sub-title, "The Rise and Progress of Christianity from its First Beginnings to the Conversion of the English." See also, for the documents illustrative of the history of the Church to A.D. 337, James Stevenson, ed., *A New Eusebius,* SPCK, 1957, 448 pp., 35s.

11. SCHMEMANN, Alexander, *The Historical Road of Eastern Orthodoxy,* HRW, 1963, 368 pp., $6.50; HARV, 1965, 72s. A general survey of the Eastern Orthodox churches culminating with a discussion of Russian Orthodoxy. The emphasis is placed upon the formative period of Eastern Orthodoxy in the ancient period. It was this period which produced the great creeds accepted by the Reformers and subsequent spokesmen for evangelical Christianity.

12. ATIYA, A. S., *A History of Eastern Christianity,* ME, 1968. A fuller account of the Eastern churches than Schmemann. This book gives the most detailed attention to Christianity in Egypt (Coptic Church), the Jacobites, Nestorians, Armenians, and the Church of South India. Concentrating on the origins of these churches, Atiya (who is a Copt), surveys the status of these groups in modern times.

13. *WALKER, G. S. M., *The Growing Storm,* WBE, 1961, 251 pp., $4.00; PP, 16s. Although the period of A.D. 600 to A.D. 1350 is often described as "the dark ages," one ought not forget the positive contribution of this period to our heritage. Walker attempts to offer a judicious appraisal of this period of Church history. While there are more detailed works on this period available, none give quite as good a broad introduction as does this work. See also, M. Deansley, *A History of the Medieval*

Church 590-1500, ME, ED 9, 1957, 284 pp., 18s.

14. BROWNE, L. E., *The Eclipse of Christianity in Asia,* FER, 1967, 198 pp., $6.50. The rise of Islam certainly was one of the decisive factors in the emergence of "the dark ages" in the history of Christianity. The work is significant for both gaining an understanding of the origins of Islam and the medieval period of the history of Christianity. See also, J. M. Hussey, *The Byzantine World,* Ri, HU, 1967, 176 pp., 11s 6d.

15. *PARKER, G. H., *The Morning Star,* WBE, 1965, 248 pp.; PP, 21s. Most persons acquainted with Church history move from the medieval period to the Reformation without carefully studying the influential figures and events which directly contributed to the Reformation. Parker gives particular attention to the two centuries prior to the Reformation, especially to John Wycliffe.

16. *BAINTON, R. H., *The Reformation of the Sixteenth Century,* BP, 1952, 276 pp., $3.75; HS, 1953, 20s. Perhaps this is the best introduction to the Reformation from the standpoint of providing a connected account of the major events during this time.

17. HARBISON, E. H., *The Christian Scholar in the Age of Reformation,* CSS, 1956, 177 pp., Pb $1.25. Harbison offers a general survey of scholarship as a Christian calling in the ancient and medieval Church but concentrates on Erasmus, Luther and Calvin.

18. GRIMM, H. J., *The Reformation Era,* MC, 1954, RE, 1965, 675 pp., $7.95; CM, 1966, 30s. The particular contribution of this study of the Reformation is that the author attempts to delineate the historical and cultural context of the Reformation.

See also, A. Hyma, *The Renaissance to Reformation,* WBE, RE, 1955, 592 pp., $6.00.

19. *CHADWICK, Owen, *The Reformation,* WBE, 1965, 463 pp., $5.95; PE, 7s 6d. Included in this general survey of the Reformation is a discussion of the Counter-Reformation (Roman Catholic Church) and the Eastern Orthodox Church. The author also orients some of his treatment to a discussion of the results of the Reformation for the ministry, worship, and liturgy.

20. *ATKINSON, James, *The Great Light: Luther and Reformation,* WBE, 1968, 287 pp., $5.00. Emphasizing the theological significance of the Reformation, the author organizes his material according to the chief Reformers. Special attention is given to Luther with sketchy discussion of Zwingli and Calvin. There is a good section on "the Reformation in Britain." See also, E. G. Schwiebert, *Luther and His Times,* CON, 1950, 892 pp., $12.95; CON, 70s.

21. DOUGLAS, J. D., *Light in the North,* WBE, 1964, 220 pp.; PP, 16s. Continuing at the point where Atkinson ended, Douglas provides a detailed account of Scottish Convenanters.

22. WILLIAMS, G. H., *The Radical Reformation,* WP, 1962, 924 pp., $15.00; WN, 928 pp., 70s. Until the twentieth century, this subject has not been given the attention it deserves. There were a number of movements contemporary with the Reformation which believed that the Reformers "did not go far enough." This included the biblically-oriented Anabaptists, rationalistically-inclined humanists, and the mystically-inclined Spiritualists. Williams writes with personal affinity for Unitarians.

23. NICHOLS, J. H., *History of Christianity 1650-1950,* RP, 1956, 493 pp., $6.00. This is a broad survey of the history of Christianity since the post-Reformation period. Nichols sets forth the thesis that western Christendom has gradually been secularized.

24. STOEFFLER, F. E., *The Rise of Evangelical Pietism,* Leiden, Netherlands, E. J. Brill, 1965, 257 pp. "Pietism" is often a misunderstood and frequently maligned expression. The fact is that this movement has had a subtle influence upon many segments of contemporary Christendom. Stoeffler gives attention to the English Puritans and Continental Pietism. Since the account ends with P. J. Spener, one may expect at least an additional volume. See also, G. R. Ballerne, *A History of the Evangelical Party in the Church of England,* Ri, CBRP, 1951, 290 pp., 12s 6d.

25. *WOOD, A. S., *The Inextinguishable Blaze,* WBE, 1960, 256 pp.; PP, 15s. The Wesleyan revival in the eighteenth century and its abiding influence is the topic of this work. See also, S. C. Carpenter, *Eighteenth-Century Church and People,* MU, 1959, 296 pp., 35s.

26. OLMSTEAD, C. E., *History of Religion in the United States,* PH, 1960, 628 pp., $9.95. A detailed account of the history of Christianity in the United States. The author does justice to the difficult subjects of the wide variety of denominations and sectarian groups.

27. SMITH, H. S., R. T. Handy, and L. A. Loetscher, *American Christianity,* 2 V., CSS, 1960-63, 615, 634 pp., $10.00 each. The editors have selected documents which they believe to be most important for understanding the course of American Christianity. The documents are placed in their appropriate historical context.

28. MAYER, F. E., *The Religious Bodies of America*, CON, 1954, 578 pp., $9.95; CON, 1960, 591 pp., 60s. This handbook of denominations, sectarian groups, interdenominational trends, and cults in America provides information of the origin and teaching of these movements. The author's viewpoint is conservative Lutheran and this affects his discussion.

29. SHELLY, Bruce, *The Cross and Flame*, WBE, 1967, 191 pp., $3.95. A history of martyrdom and exploration of why some Christians are willing to face torture and death.

3B. CREEDS AND DENOMINATIONS
John H. Gerstner
The Church of Jesus Christ is a tree with many branches (Matthew 13:31,32), a body with many members (Romans 12:5), many folds but one flock (John 10:16, RV). "Denominations" is our contemporary word for "branches," "members," or "folds" which unfortunately does not suggest the scriptural unity that these biblical metaphors show. However, we should see that these many and separate denominations are at the same time the undivided, visible Church of our one Lord Jesus Christ. The proof of this is in their separate creeds wherein they officially, spontaneously, clearly, and emphatically affirm, amidst many variations, that there is "one body, and one Spirit, even as ye are called in one hope of your calling; one Lord, one faith, one baptism, one God and Father of all, who is above all and through all, and in you all" (Ephesians 4:4-6).

1. BINDLEY, T. H., ed., *The Oecumenical Documents of the Faith*, BN, 1950, 246 pp., $4.50; ME, ED 4, 25s. Helpful discussions with extensive notes on the early creeds.

2. *COXHILL, H. W., and K. G. Grubb, *World Christian Handbook*, FR, 1962, 400 pp., $7.50; WDP, 27s 6d. By no means as adequate as Grundler (see below) it is nonetheless the most extensive world-survey of denominations appearing in English (about every five years).

3. DENZINGER, Henry, *The Sources of Catholic Dogma*, BHC, 1957, 653 pp., $8.50. (OoP) For Roman Catholic dogma this book is the closest approximation we have to an official collection of officially recognized deliverances of popes and councils.

4. EMPIE, P. C., and J. I. McCord, eds., *Marburg Revisited: A Reexamination of Lutheran and Reformed Traditions*, APH, 1967, 193 pp., Pb $1.75. Papers and addresses given as part of official Lutheran and Reformed discussions taking place from 1962 to 1966. They deal with the historical issues between the two traditions such as the eucharist and Christ's glorified humanity.

5. GERRISH, B. A., ed., *The Faith of Christendom: A Source Book of Creeds and Confessions*, WPC, 1963, 371 pp., Hb $4.00, Pb $1.95. This is a very wide selection of creeds of all traditions in all ages with useful introductions.

6. GREEN, Benjamin, *A Harmony of the Westminster Presbyterian Standards*, JKP, 1951, 231 pp., $5.00. (OoP) The Westminster standards constitute the most extensive and scientific doctrinal creeds ever produced by a Reformed Church and Green's work is especially useful because of the harmony format, not to mention the informative notes.

7. GRUNDLER, Johannes, *Lexikon der Christlichen Kirchen und Sekten unter Berücksichtigung der Missionagesell schaften und Zwischenkirchlichen Organisationen*, 2 V., Herder, Freiburg, 1961, 1599 pp. We men-

tion this invaluable German work because it has no parallel in English. It is the most comprehensive and up-to-date handbook available of the history, doctrine, and statistics of the denominations of the world.

8. HALL, Peter, *The Harmony of Protestant Confessions*, SH, 1854, 640 pp. (OoP) An old work available in many libraries, convenient for comparing the treatment of various doctrines, such as justification, in the different creeds of Protestantism.

9. KELLY, J. N. D., *Early Christian Creeds*, HRP, ED 2, 1960, 446 pp., $12.00; LO, 1950, 42s. One of the greatest contemporary students of the early Church, Kelly gives a very learned but readable history and analysis of the definitive early creeds.

10. LACKMANN, Max, *The Augsburg Confession and Catholic Unity*, HH, 1963, 159 pp., $4.50. The Augsburg Confession of 1530 was the definitive statement of Lutheranism vis-a-vis Roman Catholicism and is here studied in that light today. This creed was endorsed by many sixteenth-century Reformed theologians and qualifies as the most Protestant ecumenical creed.

11. LEITH, J. H., ed., *Creeds of the Churches: A Reader in Christian Doctrine from the Bible to the Present*, ALP, 1963, 589 pp., $7.50; DC, Pb $1.95. Probably the most valuable single volume in inexpensive paperback that one can easily obtain for a general coverage of creeds.

12. MAYER, F. E., *The Religious Bodies of America*, CON, RE 4, 1961, 591 pp., $9.95; CON, 60s. By a conservative Lutheran, this standard book contains a great deal of information, historical and especially theological, of many denominations in this country.

13. *MEAD, F. S., *Handbook of Denominations in the United States*, ABP, ED 4, 1965, 271 pp., $2.95. This work is more compendious than Mayer's volume and more up-to-date but not so informative theologically.

14. *NEUFELD, V. H., *The Earliest Christian Confessions*, WBE, 1963, 166 pp., $4.00. A solid conservative scholar examines the early creeds in a scholarly fashion but much less extensively than Kelly. Too technical for some, this book is nonetheless within the range of serious-minded college students.

15. *ROUTLEY, Erik, ed., *Creeds and Confessions: From the Reformation to the Modern Church*, WP, 1963, 158 pp., $3.50; DUC, 1962, 159 pp., 15s. This is particularly valuable not only because of its bibliographical notes but also its concentration on the modern creeds which interest most college students. See also, *Runia Klaas, *I Believe in God*, IVP, 1964, 80 pp., Pb $1.25; TP, Pb 6s.

16. SCHAFF, P., *The Creeds of Christendom with a History and Critical Notes*, 3 V., RE 4; *The Evangelical Protestant Creeds, with Translations*, 3 V., HRP, RE 6, 1919, 949, 634, 966 pp., V. 1,3 $12.95 each, V. 2 $7.95. This remains the greatest collection of creeds in the English language. Schaff was an erudite Church historian and his introductions show it. Volume 3 contains modern evangelical creeds.

3D. MISSIONS
H. Wilbert Norton
Mission is the individual and collective proclamation and expression by the Church of the life of Christ. The proclamation is personally received and so appropriated by the Church that its over-flowing witness and service in love reaches throughout the world. It takes root in all cultures as

salvation through the death and resurrection of Jesus Christ and draws disciples together in Christ into growing cells of Christian witness among all peoples. Jesus Christ as Lord of life and death calls his disciples to obedient submission in sharing himself with all sinners world-wide and inviting all men to find forgiveness of sin, abundant living, and meaning in union with him.

1. ADOLF, Paul E., *Missionary Health Manual*, MP, 1964, 188 pp., $2.50. A concise manual of the basic elements of missionary health written by a missionary doctor whose experiences in China and whose later services to missionaries on furlough qualify him eminently to counsel missionaries and missionary candidates in physical, mental, and emotional health.

2. BARLOW, Sanna, *Mountains Singing*, MP, 1952, 352 pp., $3.50. The incredible story of two American women, Joy Ridderhof and her colleague, Anne Sherwood, making gospel recordings in the tribal languages of remote Filipino tribesmen. This is the story of unsophisticated faith expressed in the lives of two of Christ's disciples in the face of critical cultural problems, linguistic barriers, and transportation obstacles graphically and realistically told in the contemporary "pilgrim's progress." Good reading for students who feel that the church is composed of a middle-class mentality and morality and who need the challenge of two Christians who ". . . were always living on the ragged edge of nothing; and on the threshold of everything."

3. BROW, Robert, *Religion: Origins and Ideas*, IVP, 128 pp., $3.50. For twenty years the author lived in India as an army officer, studying Hinduism and Eastern religions firsthand. He bases his study on the presupposition that the world's religions have

strayed from man's original religion which was based on God as Creator and on sinful man with his sacrifices approaching God in his alienation. Ancient atheism, Buddhism, ethicism, and monism were four distinct elements in the revolt of man against the evaluation of a degenerated priestcraft. Brow sketches the historical development of the Hindu Scriptures, the concepts of reincarnation, incarnations and saviours, and the ancient origin of unitarianism in reformers such as Zoroaster and Mohammed in modern Judaism.

4. COOPER, Clay, *Nothing to Win—But the World*, ZPH, 152 pp., $2.95. Twenty-seven chapters successively presenting one theme from each of the twenty-seven New Testament books in sermonic style giving an elementary and informative presentation of contemporary missionary opportunities for the church.

5. DAVIS, Raymond J., *Fire on the Mountain*, ZPH, 1966, 253 pp., $3.95. The stirring story of the acts of the Holy Spirit among the Wallamo tribe of southern Ethiopia, the saga of contemporary church growth among a people deprived of their missionary friends who were expelled after nine years of pioneer evangelism at the time of the Italian invasion in the mid-1930's. A handful of Wallamo Christians withstood persecution with only a fragment of Scripture in their Wallamo language. The returning missionaries in the post-World War II period discovered a living church composed of thousands of committed Wallamo believers, self-instructed, self-governing, and self-propagating. The Wallamo church is a contemporary African church with a New Testament charisma!

6. FIFE, Eric S., and Arthur F. Glasser, *Missions in Crisis*, IVP, 1961, 269 pp., Pb $1.95. Writing in a stimulating style, the authors present three

considerations: (1) the church on the defensive in a revolutionary world seeking justice, expressing itself in the upsurge of nationalism while Christian missions learn the hard lessons of communism's takeover in China, (2) the church, caught in the throes of the desire for unity, now faced with the theological and organizational problems of the ecumenical movement, (3) the church on the offensive in the struggle against racism, the opportunities of non-professional missionaries, the challenges of missionaries, urban needs and inner-city ghettos, and the turmoil of student unrest. Meanwhile the channels of the mass media provide the means of sharing the gospel with the world. See also, E. S. Fife, *Man's Peace God's Glory*, IVP, 144 pp., $3.50.

7. FORSBERG, Malcolm, *Last Days on the Nile*, LC, 215 pp., $3.95. This is a story of the seed of the gospel which fell on "the good soil" of the southern Sudan transforming Sudanese lives as individually men came to a saving knowledge of Jesus Christ and collectively the church of Christ blossomed in the desert heat. But caught in the mid-twentieth century political and ideological tensions of East Africa, the church was crushed, Christians were murdered, and the heralds of the gospel expelled. The author's thirty years of personal involvement in this dramatic account make his report all the more meaningful as he skillfully underscores the problems of the contemporary witness to Jesus Christ which, in the Sudan as in many parts of the world, is confronted by the tidal wave of nationalism and the undertow of post-colonial independence. The book gives rare historical insights into some of the colonial activities and policies which contributed to difficulties for the church.

8. ISAIS, Juan, *The Other Side of the Coin*, WBE, 1966, 104 pp. Pb

$1.45. An honest, straightforward presentation of the tensions which exist in varying degrees between missionaries and Christian nationals in Latin America, shocking at times, but sincere and spiritually helpful. Isais helps the missionary to see himself through Latin eyes and understanding. Himself a Latin with many years' experience in working with missionaries, the author leads the reader to realize it is possible for Christians to work together.

9. KRAEMER, Hendrik, *Why Christianity of All Religions?* WP, 1962, 125 pp., $2.75. The person of Jesus Christ alone is absolute and Christianity along with other systems is judged by him and needs renewal from him constantly. A warm-hearted presentation of the uniqueness of Christ by one of the great scholars in the history and phenomenology of religion.

10. LATOURETTE, Kenneth, *A History of the Expansion of Christianity*, 7 V., HRP, 1946. This superb classic, scholarly in every point, presents Christian missions and their historic growth throughout the ages with due regard for Roman Catholic and Orthodox missionary expansion as well as the Post-Reformation Protestant worldwide witness to Jesus Christ. Each volume contains its own exhaustive index and annotated bibliography.

11. LINDSELL, Harold, ed., *The Church's World-Wide Mission*, WB, 1966, 289 pp., $3.95. This is the editor's report of the proceedings of the Congress of the Church's Worldwide Mission, held at Wheaton College, Wheaton, Illinois, April 9, 1966, and sponsored by the Interdenominational Foreign Mission's Association. The Report is divided into four parts including an appendix presenting the background of the IFMA and EFMA, the committee and program personnel as well as the Congress con-

sultants and a listing of the denominations and missionary organizations represented at the Congress.

12. LYALL, L. T., *Come Wind, Come Weather*, MP, 1960, 95 pp., $2.00; HS, Pb 4s 6d. A missionary resident of China for more than twenty years, the author frankly tells the story of the Protestant church from the time of the Communist take-over in 1950 until the report of the last missionary to leave China in 1959. The policies and procedures of the Red Chinese government in dealing with liberal as well as conservative Christians is documented.

13. McGAVRAN, D. A., *The Bridges of God*, FP, 1957, 158 pp., Pb $2.50; WDP, Pb 5s. A study in mission strategy, provocative in its emphasis on "people movements" and mass conversion with spontaneous church growth based on the organized cells within the movement of a people. McGavran's theory stands in opposition to the "mission station strategy" which he feels has failed to produce dynamic, growing churches for meaningful penetration of people within their particular culture. See also, *How Churches Grow*, FP, 1966, 188 pp., Pb $2.50.

14. McGAVRAN, D. A., ed., *Church Growth and Christian Mission*, HR, 1965, 252 pp., $5.00. Assisted by a team of three missions experts (Professor Robert Calvin Guy of Southwestern Baptist Theological Seminary, Melvin L. Hodges, Executive Secretary for Latin America of the Assemblies of God, and Eugene A. Nida, Secretary for Translation of the American Bible Society), Dr. McGavran leads his colleagues in presenting his church growth principle on the basic issues of theology, sociology, methodology, and administration. The growth of the church is the basic problem in missionary strategy in the contemporary world. See also, R. P.

Beaver, *Envoys of Peace*, WBE, $3.00.

15. NEILL, Stephen, *A History of Christian Missions*, PE, 622 pp., Pb $2.25; PEL, Pb 10s 6d. Neill's brilliantly written book is volume six of the Pelican series on the history of the church. The author, a prodigious writer on mission themes, divides his one-volume history into two parts, treating the missionary events of the church during the first seventeen centuries in Part I (240 pp.) and the development of modern missions in Part II (334 pp.). The author is ecumenically oriented giving generous treatment to the Roman Catholic and Orthodox missions but only a brief mention of the independent "faith missionary" movement. An extensive bibliography and index help to make this one-volume work extremely valuable.

16. ROBERTS, W. D., *Revolution in Evangelism*, MP, 1967, 127 pp., $2.00. The story of Evangelism-in-Depth, the total mobilization of the church in its evangelistic outreach as initiated by Dr. Kenneth Strachan, the late General Director of the Latin America Mission.

17. SMALLEY, W. A., ed., *Readings in Missionary Anthropology*, Practical Anthropology, Inc., Terrytown, N. Y., 1967, 368 pp. This is a collection of the articles previously published in *Practical Anthropology* between 1953 and 1959 plus two from 1960. The works of twenty-one authors, including Dr. Smalley, are organized under four headings: Cultures of Man and the Communication of the Gospel, Christianity in Human Cultures, The Missionary in an Alien Culture, Anthropology: Role and Method. The articles are written by scholars whose practical experiences as missionaries and field workers make this volume an extremely valuable contribution to those interested

in resolving the cultural problems confronted in the world-wide witness of the church. See also, Bengt Sundkler, *The World of Missions,* WBE, $6.95.

18. STRACHAN, R. K., *The Inescapable Calling,* WBE, 1968, 127 pp., $1.65. The late General Director of the Latin America Mission presented the content of these lectures during the last year of his earthly response to the calling from which he himself never escaped. Essentially Dr. Strachan's posthumous work presents the theology of Evangelism-in-Depth, a revolutionary concept in evangelism which calls for the total mobilization of the church in witness.

19. WALLIS, E. E., and M. A. Bennett, *Two Thousand Tongues to Go,* MP, 1959, 308 pp., Hb $3.95, Pb $1.95; HS, Pb 7s 6d. The story of Wycliffe Bible Translators from 1917 when its founder, William Cameron Townsend, began his missionary career in Guatemala. At the time of the book's publication a host of linguistic pioneers had penetrated 175 language groups in 11 countries. Meanwhile Wycliffe continues to train over 500 translators annually who seek to share the Bible and its Lord with the unreached minorities of the world.

3E. NON-CHRISTIAN RELIGIONS
James W. Reapsome
While some Christian theologians are positing the thesis that God is dead, the ancient religions of the past are far from it. Hinduism, Islam, and Buddhism especially are experiencing a resurgence of interest and vitality, not only in their countries of origin but around the world, even in the West. At the same time there is a prevailing spirit of syncretism abroad that would seek to find common ground between all religions, and Christians have entered into dialogue with representatives of these ancient faiths.

The historic Christian position of antithesis between religions is being questioned as never before. Therefore, whatever road one takes, he must be acquainted with not only the old traditional stances of these faiths but their modern expressions and appeals.

1. *BRADEN, C. S., *The World's Religions, a Short History,* ABP, 1954, 256 pp., Hb $3.00, Pb $1.00. This is probably the best popularly-priced, non-technical introduction to the subject available. It is brief, readable, comprehensive, and includes the most important features of the major faiths: central aim, founding, personalities, institutions, sacred books, divisions, spread and influence, and present status. Good bibliography and portions of Scriptures of various religions.

2. *ANDERSON, J. N., ed., *The World's Religions,* WBE, 1950, 208 pp., $3.50; TP, ED 3, 1955, 10s 6d. The standard introduction from an evangelical viewpoint. Short factual accounts of the history, philosophy, and practices of animism, Judaism, Islam, Hinduism, Buddhism, Shinto, and Confucianism. Eight authors contribute. The epilogue discusses attitudes to these religions in the light of Christianity.

3. *JAMES, E. O., *Christianity and Other Religions,* HS, 1968, 191 pp., Pb 15s. Without denigrating "God-given truths in other religions," James attempts to determine the uniqueness of Christianity. He discusses the common ground and aims it shares with other religions, going first into the prehistoric background of religion, then to monotheism, pantheism, salvation, sacrifice, immortality, and revelation. His investigation is from a liberal theological stance. See also, Edmund Perry, *The*

Gospel in Dispute, DC, 1958, 230 pp., $3.95.

4. VOS, H. F., ed., *Religions in a Changing World,* MP, 1959, 441 pp., $5.95. The editor chose thirteen writers, most of them missionaries (they had personal dealings with adherents of the religion they wrote about), to contribute about Animism, Judaism, Islam, Hinduism, Zoroastrianism, Jainism, Sikhism, Southeast Asian Buddhism, religions of China and Japan, Communism, Eastern Orthodoxy, Roman Catholicism, and Protestantism. They give facts about the religion's founding, where it falls short of Christianity, advice about how to convert adherents, and political cross-currents in these religions. Evangelical viewpoint.

5. FERM, Vergilius, ed., *Forgotten Religions,* TPL, 1950, 392 pp. (OoP) Highlights of old religions, some of them still alive, for the layman's understanding. Essays were written on the basis of the religion's complexity, importance, interest, and representative viewpoint. Here are areas not covered in books on major religions, such as Babylonian, Canaanite, Norse, and Eskimo religion, plus the religions of North and South American Indians and Australian Aborigines.

6. *BROW, Robert, *Religion: Origins and Ideas,* IVP, 1966, 128 pp., $3.50; TP, 6s. A clear, sound analysis of religion and the theories about its early development. Majors on Buddhism and Hinduism and the modern philosophical expressions of both. Excellent introduction by evangelical writer.

7. NOSS, J. B., *Man's Religions,* MC, ED 3, 1963, 812 pp., $7.95; CM, ED 3, 63s. An outstanding liberal scholar provides one of the most comprehensive volumes available, with adequate amounts of descriptive and inter-

pretive details from original sources. He does justice to the religion's development as well as its origin, thus making a bridge between founding and present state. He writes about Hinduism, Jainism, Buddhism, Sikhism, Taoism, Confucianism, Shinto, Zoroastrianism, Judaism, Christianity, and Islam.

8. SLATER, R. L., *World Religions and World Community,* COLP, 1963, 299 pp., $6.00; COLP, 45s. The role of religion in attaining world political solidarity is ambiguous; it can be either unifying or divisive. This is a fascinating discussion of a little-noticed problem: political attitudes as shaped by religion. The book gives a wider view of religious movements as they affect prospects for world peace and an in-depth view of what influences religious behavior.

9. VICEDOM, G. F., *The Challenge of the World Religions,* FP, 1963, 161 pp. This is world religion, not in historical form, but in current pronouncements, or, as the author believes, world religions on the offensive. Therefore, he wants to acquaint Christians with what is happening as the propaganda of world religions moves into the vacuum of the West's lack of supporting, formative ideas. He allows the propaganda to speak for itself, but tells what Christians must do to combat it.

10. VISSER'T HOOFT, W. A., *No Other Name,* WP, 1963, 128 pp., $2.50; SCMP, 8s 6d. The first general secretary of the World Council of Churches writes with creative vigor about the exclusive, universal validity of the historic Christian faith. He assaults religious syncretism and describes the tensions between the Church and syncretistic movements, especially in Hinduism and Bahaism.

11. NIDA, Eugene, and W. A. Smalley, *Introducing Animism,* FR, 1959,

64 pp., Pb 90¢. The basic concepts of animism and the cultures in which it predominates are discussed by two evangelical scholars. Animism, they say, is not a unified faith but a mass of primitive religious beliefs and practices, some of which persist in major faiths. Also includes a discussion of how and why Christianity has made a profound impact on the animistic world.

12. BERSTEIN, Philip, *What the Jews Believe,* FSG, 1951, 100 pp., $2.50. An elementary study of the beliefs and practices of Jews in America and their differences with Christianity. There is no binding creed all Jews accept, nor a supreme ecclesiastical body. Hence, there is diversity of practice and latitude of beliefs.

13. COHON, B. D., *Judaism in Theory and Practice,* BPC, 1954, 246 pp. (OoP) This is a search for the heart of religious Israel and the mind of the synagogue; what the Jews believe and why and what they mean to be in the world. Orthodox, reformed, and conservative Judaism are seen against their historic background and the pattern of the Jew's adjustment to the modern world. Also answers why the Jews rejected Jesus. Jewish theology, ethics, institutions, rituals, and holy days are discussed.

14. COOLEY, J. K., *Baal, Christ and Mohammed: Religion and Revolution in North Africa,* HRW, 1964, 384 pp., HB $8.95; JM, 1967, 50s. The three major religious figures of North African history serve as the basis for the interaction between Islam and Christianity. Islam, through the consolidation of Arab-Muslim power, is seen to be on the offensive as a rejuvenated religion, while Christianity is pictured as being on a "new retreat." See also, for a penetrating study of Islam in relation to Christianity, K. Cragg, *The Call of the Minaret,* OUP, 1956, 376 pp., Hb $6.50, Pb $1.95;

OUP, 37s 6d; OUP, RE, 1965, Pb 12s 6d.

15. MORGAN, K. W., ed., *Islam— The Straight Path,* RP, 1958, 453 pp., $6.00. This is Islam as interpreted by eleven Muslim contributors from Egypt, Iran, Turkey, Pakistan, China, and Indonesia, but not done defensively or in comparison with other religions. Covers Islam's origins, history, beliefs and laws, mystical elements, unity and diversity, and culture. Includes a glossary of terms.

16. VERHOEVEN, F. R., *Islam, Its Origin and Spread in Words, Maps and Pictures,* SM, 1962, 87 pp. (OoP); *Islam,* RO, 120 pp., 15s. A brief history of the spread of Islam together with Muslim beliefs and practices. Helpful introduction and valuable for dates, references and symbols. Pictures and maps highlight the book.

17. RADHAKRISHAN, S., *The Hindu View of Life,* MC, 1927, 92 pp., $3.00, RE, 1962, Pb $1.45; AU, Hb 10s 6d, Pb 4s 6d. While Hinduism is complex, here are the underlying beliefs that unify and guide the ordinary Indian family in the nature and content of its religious experience. There are no limits to fixed intellectual beliefs; intellect is subordinated to intuition, dogma to experience. The author writes about the Hindu attitude to other religions and defends the much-maligned law of Karma. For a more in-depth study, see *A. L. Basham, *The Wonder That Was India,* GP, 1959, 568 pp., Pb $3.95.

18. SUZUKI, D. T., *Zen Buddhism, Selected Writings,* DC, 1956, 294 pp., Pb $1.45. Zen, from the Japanese *zazen* ("to sit and meditate") is making a strong appeal as a meditative sect of Buddhism. Here are selections of one of its most popular adherents and exponents, showing that

this 2,500-year-old religion is still alive and growing; it can't be dismissed as either bizarre or frivolous. Barrett's introduction both defends and explains Suzuki's appeal.

19. THOMSEN, Harry, *The New Religions of Japan,* CET, 1963, 280 pp., $5.00; PH, 40s. There are 171 new religions in Japan drawing a following of one-fifth of the people there. This is an accurate assessment of their origins, beliefs, and practices. It is factual, scholarly, and well-arranged. What accounts for the appeal of these religions is carefully analyzed.

20. EKVALL, R. B., *Religious Observances in Tibet,* UCP, 1964, 313 pp., $8.50; UCP, 63s. For those especially concerned with Buddhism, this is both a study of religious terms and a description of practices, as contrasted to the ideology of Mahayana Buddhism. Subjective responses, behavior of society, and personal needs are discussed.

21. ELIADE, Mircea, *Shamanism, Archaic Techniques of Ecstasy,* PUP, 1964, 610 pp., $8.50; *Shamanism,* RO, 45s. Set in the general history of religion, this is an advanced treatment of the entire phenomenon of Shamanism, its techniques, symbolism and mythologies. The author puts together the approaches of psychology, sociology, and ethnology. He talks most about the shaman as magician, medicine man, healer, miracle-doer, priest, and poet in Siberia and Central Asia, but includes other parts of Asia, Oceania, and the Americas in his discussion.

22. BROWNE, Lewis, ed., *The World's Great Scriptures,* MC, 1946, 559 pp., Hb $7.95, RE, 1962, Pb $2.95; CM, Hb 63s, RE, 1962, Pb 25s. This is an anthology of what seems to the editor the most vital in the world's holy books, selected from the Scriptures of Babylonia, Egypt,

Hinduism, Buddhism, Confucianism, Taoism, Zoroastrianism, Judaism, Christianity, and Islam. He concentrates on ethics, not theology or ritual, and leaves out what he calls creation stories, miracles, and liturgy.

23. CHAMPION, S. G., *The Eleven Religions and Their Proverbial Lore,* EPD, 1945, 340 pp. (OoP) The eleven are Buddhism, Christianity, Confucianism, Hebraism, Hinduism, Islam, Jainism, Shinto, Sikhism, Taoism, and Zoroastrianism. This is a fully-referenced source book for comparative study. It has 4,890 quotations mainly on tolerance, brotherhood, charity, and love. There is a brief introduction to each religion by different authorities.

section 4
CHRISTIAN LIFE

4. CHRISTIAN LIFE: INTRODUCTION
Calvin Malefyt

Jesus, who called himself the Light of the world, came to expose the darkness in individuals and society and to release men from chains of self-delusion. The truth he proclaimed centered in himself, yet it cannot be fully understood unless seen in historical, social, and liturgical perspective.

Christians today have a bond with Christian believers through the centuries. Their struggles and temptations are those common to historic humanity. Others who have walked in the Way can be a source of encouragement, as their understanding and experience confirm the illumination that comes from a triune God. May not those ignorant of religious history be condemned to repeat some of the mistakes of the past?

Their insights given us by our Lord are of intensely practical help in the fundamentals of daily life. God's help can prevent the difficulties of communication between parents and children, or between husband and wife. Surely it is in the home that we first learn the meaning of judgment, grace, and forgiveness. In this microcosm of society we learn by precept and example to overcome evil and to express his life of light.

Even worship can be enriched by an appreciation that corporate liturgy expresses the praise of One who has called us out of darkness into his marvelous light. The music and hymns of the Church through the centuries are an enriching heritage. Transformation of a community can come from the broader perspective induced by gratitude for God's tangible and transforming love. This is Christian living.

4A. BIOGRAPHY, JOURNALS AND AUTOBIOGRAPHY
Joseph Bayly

What does it mean to be a great man? One who has achieved self-fulfillment, one who has made a permanent contribution to society, one who has come closest to realizing his potential, one who is a servant. Most of the men and women represented by the books noted here are great in these ways. Their exemplary lives and insights are open to us through their own writing (journals, letters, diaries, autobiographies) or through what others have written about them. Reading the experience of others is one of the happiest ways to learn. The lives of these men and women teach.

Biography
1. *BAINTON, R. H., *Here I Stand —A Life of Luther*, ABP, 1951, 422 pp., $6.00; MENT, 336 pp., Pb 50¢; AC, 1950, 386 pp., 20s. This life of the great reformer gives historical perspective and interpretation of Luther's work and writings and experiences. A brilliant biography. See also an equally good and more recent biography written with the historical perspective, V. H. Green, *Luther and the Reformation*, PUT, 1964, 208 pp., $5.95, Pb $1.65; BAT, 30s.

2. CHESTERTON, G. K., *Saint Thomas Aquinas*, DC, 1957, Pb 75¢; HS, 1962, 159 pp., Pb 5s. A superb and scintillating introduction to the work and personality of the medieval church philosopher, theologian and "Angelic Doctor." See also, G. K. Chesterton, *St. Francis of Assisi*, DC, 1957, Pb 65¢; HS, Pb 3s 6d.

3. *ELLIOT, Elisabeth, *Shadow of the Almighty*, HRP, 1958, 256 pp., $3.95; HS, 1959, Hb 18s, Pb 6s. The biography of Jim Elliot, one of the five missionaries killed by Auca Indians in South America in 1955. Extensive excerpts from Elliot's

diary—especially the college years—afford many well written spiritual insights.

4. ELLIOT, Elisabeth, *Who Shall Ascend? The Life of R. Kenneth Strachan of Costa Rica*, HRP, 1968, 171 pp., $5.95. The evangelical world looked up to Ken Strachan, director of Latin America Mission and Evangelism-in-Depth, as a strong Christian leader. But throughout life Strachan was beseiged by feelings of failure and inadequacy. Drawing heavily from his correspondence, Mrs. Elliot shows us the man from the inside—the faltering servant God chose to be a leader.

5. GELZER, D. G., *Calvin*, JC, 1959, 174 pp., 13s 6d. This short and authoritative study of the life and times of John Calvin is lively and picturesque. The pale, frail "man of Geneva" is portraitured as a man with iron will, utter dedication to his task, and super-human capacity to work. For other short studies, see also, J. Cadlier, *The Man God Mastered*, TP, 1960, 180 pp., 8s 6d; and T. H. L. Parker, *A Portrait of Calvin*, SCMP, 1954, 124 pp., 7s 6d.

6. GILL, F. C., *Charles Wesley: The First Methodist*, ABP, 1964, 234 pp., $5.00. This thorough but readable account of the less well-known cofounder of Methodism provides an historical probe into Methodism with well-integrated excerpts from his journal and letters.

7. *HERCUS, John, *David*, IVP, 1968, $1.25; TP, 144 pp., Pb 4s 6d. The David of the Bible—shepherd boy, outlaw, king—comes alive in this imaginative but basically true-to-Scripture account of his life. The reader finds he knows himself better after knowing David.

8. HITT, R. T., *Jungle Pilot*, HRP, 1959, 303 pp., $4.95; HS, RE, 1964, Pb 6s. The biography of one of the men killed by Auca Indians is subtitled, "The Life and Witness of Nate Saint—The Inventive Genius of Operation Auca." Especially interesting to activists.

9. HITT, R. T., *Sensei*, HRP, 1965, 240 pp., $3.95; HS, 1966, 256 pp., 18s. Irene Webster-Smith made a home for eighty-seven little Japanese girls whom she saved from the immoral life of a geisha. Heart-warming as stories involving children often are, this book shows God's faithfulness to those who come as little children.

10. HOUGHTON, Frank, *Amy Carmichael of Donavur*, CL, 1953, 390 pp., $3.95; SPCK, 12s 6d. Irish-born Amy Carmichael was "mother" to hundreds of "unwanted children" in India. Her beautiful life which taught them to love God and one another is an example to us through this biography. Her devotional writings have been a gift to the Church.

11. LOANE, M. L., *Masters of the English Reformation*, CBRP, 1956, 246 pp., 12s 6d; *Pioneers of the Reformation in England*, CBRP, 1964, 185 pp., 15s 6d. Engaging and well-documented short biographies of Bilney, Tyndale, Latimer, Ridley, Cranmer, Frith, Barnes, Rogers, and Bradford. For excellent short biographies of Henderson, Rutherford, Bunyan, Baxter, Martyn, Whitefield, Newton, and others, see books by M. L. Loane, *Makers of Religious Freedom in the Seventeenth Century*, TP, 1960, 240 pp., 4s 6d; *Oxford and the Evangelical Succession*, LU, 1950, 312 pp., 15s; *Cambridge and the Evangelical Succession*, LU, 1952, 276 pp., 12s 6d.

12. *MARSHALL, Catherine, *A Man Called Peter: The Story of Peter Marshall*, MH, 1951, 332 pp., $5.95; FAW, 1964, Pb 75¢; FO, 254 pp., Pb 3s 6d. The readable story of an ear-

nest young man from Scotland who
became pastor of an influential Presbyterian Church in Washington D. C.
and chaplain of the United States
Senate without losing his vision, his
commitment, or his sense of humor.

13. MOULE, H. C., *Charles Simeon,*
IVP, 192 pp., $2.00; Ri, TP, 1965,
Pb 5s. This is a biography of a sane
saint without affectation of piety or
self-conscious sanctimony. In fulfill-
ing the ministry for fifty-four years
at Holy Trinity Church in Cambridge,
he exerted immense influence
throughout England, especially in the
academic circles. There was manliness
about his ministry which is most attractive.

14. PETERSON, W. J., *Another
Hand on Mine,* MH, 228 pp., $5.50.
Dr. Carl K. Becker left a successful
practice in Pennsylvania to become a
medical missionary in the Congo
where he is still serving after 35
years. This hard-to-put-down biography includes an account of the
Congo rebellion.

15. PIERSON, A. T., *George Müller
of Bristol,* REV, 375 pp., $4.50; Ri,
PI, 1954, 383 pp., 15s. George Müller's life proved the faithfulness of
God again and again as he trusted
God to provide for his own needs and
those of the two thousand children
he cared for during more than 60
years of orphan work.

16. POLLOCK, J. C., *Hudson Taylor
and Maria,* MH, 1962, 207 pp.,
$3.50; HS, 1965, 189 pp., Pb 5s. An
outstanding China-missionary biography. Taylor is human in this book
—the mistakes and shortcomings are
as real as the triumphs of this spiritual giant. It is a good balance to
Hudson Taylor's Spiritual Secret discussed below.

17. POLLOCK, J. C., *Moody: A Biographical Portrait of the Pacesetter in*

Modern Mass Evangelism, MC, 1963,
318 pp., $5.95; ZPH, 1967, 336 pp.,
Pb $1.95. *Moody Without Sankey,*
HS, RE, 1966, 288 pp., Pb 6s.
Dwight L. Moody did everything
with gusto—whether it was selling
shoes, recruiting street-boys for Sunday school or preaching to great
crowds in Great Britain and the
United States. This biography evokes
the feeling of Moody's colorful life.
For a biography of the modern evangelist see, *Billy Graham,* MH, 1966,
$4.95; ZPH, 1967, Pb 95¢; HS, 1967,
359 pp., 25s; Pb 7s 6d.

18. STONEHOUSE, N. B., *J. Gre-
sham Machen,* WBE, 1955, 520 pp.,
$4.95. (OoP) Excellent biography of
the brilliant leader of the modern
evangelical movement and the author
of many classical works of apologetics. Machen was responsible for
raising the intellectual acuteness of
Protestant orthodoxy to a high level.

19. *TAYLOR, Dr. and Mrs.
Howard, *Hudson Taylor's Spiritual
Secret,* MP, 1950, Pb 89¢. In this
biography, with many quotes from
letters and journals, the focus is on
the missionary's spiritual life. His
secret: "The drawing for every need
. . . upon Christ."

20. TAYLOR, M. G., *Behind the
Ranges,* MP, 1964, 343 pp., Pb
$1.29; CI, 256 pp., 10s 6d. The life
of J. O. Frazer, pioneer missionary to
the mountain people of China, taken
mostly from his diary and letters.
The classic chapter on prayer is
worth the whole book.

21. WILSON, D. C., *Dr. Ida,* MH,
1959, 358 pp., $6.50; HS, 1964, 125
pp., Pb 6s. Ida Scudder battled
taboos and ignorance to bring medical care and the gospel to the people
of India. Her singular dedication won
the respect of many who had questioned the place of a woman as a missionary doctor.

22. WILSON, D. C., *Ten Fingers for God*, MH, 1965, 247 pp., $5.90; HS, 1966, 256 pp., 25s. Paul Brand, son of missionaries in India, returned to that country as a doctor and pioneer in research and surgery techniques for rehabilitation of lepers. He has become a world-renowned leprologist without losing his Christian vision.

23. WYNBECK, David, *David Brainerd, Beloved Yankee*, WBE, 1961, 242 pp., $3.75. Exerpts from and commentary on the journal of colonial America's missionary to the Indians who died as a young man. The book contains insights into the great awakening and leaders such as Jonathan Edwards, Brainerd's father-in-law, and George Whitefield.

Autobiography

24. AUGUSTINE, *The Confessions of St. Augustine*, DC, RE, 1960, 429 pp., Pb $1.25; FO, 1957, 256 pp., Pb 2s 6d. The classic spiritual autobiography of this great Church Father shows a life of self-denial and devotion to Christ. Augustine wrote his *Confessions* so that others could benefit from his experience and give glory to God.

25. *CAILLIET, Emile, *Journey into Light*, ZPH, 1968, $3.95. One of America's leading evangelical scholars tells his own story of a pilgrimage from intellectual atheism to child-like faith in Christ. See also, the autobiographical account of K. S. Latourette, *Beyond the Ranges*, WBE, 1967, 161 pp., $3.95.

26. GROSSE, Edmund, *Father and Son*, WWN, 1963, 250 pp., Pb $1.65. Conflict between the generations is not new. Victorian Edmund Grosse recollects the influence of his rigorously pietistic father over the first seventeen years of his life and his struggle for identity and personal faith.

27. KUHN, Isobel, *By Searching*, MP, 1963, 128 pp., $2.95, Pb 59¢; LU, 5s. This is the China-missionary's helpful story of her early agnosticism, conversion, call to the mission field, of obstacles overcome and lessons learned.

28. LeTOURNEAU, R. G., *Mover of Men and Mountains*, PH, 1967, 257 pp., $3.95; MP, 290 pp., Pb $1.25. The contemporary autobiography of a man of action—inventor, engineer, millionaire-philanthropist—who never forgot God in times of depression or affluent success.

29. *LEWIS, C. S., *Surprised by Joy*, HA, 1956, 238 pp., $4.50, Pb $1.65; FO, 190 pp., Pb 2s 6d. In an autobiography that is also an excellent apologetic, Lewis writes candidly of his search for joy in childhood and as an adult atheist, until he reluctantly accepted theism (for him the beginning of becoming a Christian). Finding Christ, he discovered the joy he had been seeking all his life. The book is especially valuable for those with philosophical-intellectual questions about Christianity.

Letters and Journals

30. BONHOEFFER, Dietrich, *Letters and Papers from Prison*, MC, 1962, $4.50, Pb $1.45; FO, 1959, 192 pp., Pb 2s 6d. The Nazis imprisoned Dietrich Bonhoeffer for his outspoken opposition to Hitler and then hanged him. His correspondence reveals his sensitivity, his faith in God, his creative thinking. It has a relevant message for the Church today.

31. *FRANK, Anne, *Anne Frank: Diary of a Young Girl*, DC, 1952, 285 pp., $4.50; POB, RE, 1953, Pb 75¢; DC, 1952, 281 pp., 12s 6d. An unusually sensitive Jewish teenager keeps a diary while in hiding with her family and others for three years from the Nazis. The special problems of a strictly curtailed existence are

joined with the joys and miseries of being an adolescent.

32. *HAMMARSKJOLD, Dag, *Markings,* AAK, 1964, 221 pp., $4.95; FF, 186 pp., Pb 6s. The journal entries of Dag Hammarskjold, United Nations General Secretary, reveal the private feelings and insights of a man in the public domain. In language that is often poetic, Hammarskjold admits fear, loneliness, searching, and a pervading spiritual commitment. This book is for meditation.

33. *LEWIS, C. S., *A Grief Observed,* SP, 1963, 60 pp., $2.50; FF, 1966, Pb 5s. Lewis' unselfconscious journal records his painful progress through grief after his wife's death. He struggles with reason-paralyzing sorrow and Job-like questions before he returns to faith and acceptance. Completely honest.

34. LEWIS, C. S., *Letters,* HA, 1966, 308 pp., $5.95; BLES, 30s. C. S. Lewis' correspondence was extensive and he relished to write to his friends and former pupils. He received a flood of letters from strangers, and each received a full and personal reply. Those who know him only as a brilliant and illuminating writer will be surprised at his wit, wisdom and humanity. See also, *Letters to Malcolm, Chiefly on Prayer,* HA, 1964, 124 pp., $3.50; BLES, 159 pp., 12s 6d; and *Letters to an American Lady,* WBE, 1968, $3.95; C. S. Kilby, *The Christian World of C. S. Lewis,* WBE, 1964, 211 pp., $4.50.

35. PEPYS, Samuel, *Diary,* MC, 1963, 246 pp., $4.00, Pb $1.95. Acquaintance with this intimate journal of the seventeenth-century Londoner is one mark of a liberal education. Pepys wrote with gossipy candor about the affairs of daily life. His account of the great London fire is especially noteworthy.

36. TROBISCH, W., *I Loved a Girl,* HRP, Pb $1.25. This exchange of letters between a young African and his missionary friend gives a clear statement of the Christian view of sex, courtship and marriage, and at the same time explains the problems of fitting this ethic into African tribal life.

37. WESLEY, John, *The Journal of the Rev. John Wesley,* 8 V., EP (OoP); PUT, 1963, Pb $1.85. In 8 volumes, the private diary of the founder of Methodism. Random browsing through these books provides insight into a towering leader who changed a nation's social patterns and affected its history in a crisis-period of history not unlike our own. For a scholarly biography, see A. G. Outler, *John Wesley,* OUP, 1964, 516 pp., $7.50; for abridged journals see, *Journal of John Wesley,* MP, Pb 89¢.

4B. FAMILY AND MARRIAGE
Dwight H. Small

The human life cycle incorporates all the stages of individual personal growth within the framework of the family. The subject is generally approached from the first established family unit, husband and wife as a couple. The study of marriage concerns itself with factors leading to mate selection, family, and social forces influencing the possible success of the relation, the forms of love and pseudo-love, and the psychology and mores of sexuality.

In our changing times the adjustments and conflicts of married life, family goals, child rearing, and the crises of the changing years call for analysis and guidelines. The books listed below range from popular treatments to college texts, from evangelically oriented to secular writers. Special subjects have not been singled out for separate listing, but will be found adequately covered in the books selected. From a wealth of literature only samples can be included, but the following represent the best books available. Titles divide equally, leading from marriage to family.

1. *BOVET, Theodor, *A Handbook to Marriage,* DC, 1958, 157 pp., Hb $2.50, Pb 95¢. David Mace, Executive Director, American Association of Marriage Counselors, says, "I believe that no serious student of marriage, no teacher or counselor in the family field can afford to ignore the contribution Dr. Bovet has to make to our quest for a wholesome, balanced understanding of the true nature of the relationship between man and woman." A sensitive, easy to read, evangelical approach.

2. WHITE, Ernest, *Marriage and the Bible,* BR, 1965, 149 pp., $3.50. A comprehensive survey of biblical teachings on marriage, combining biblical interpretation, theology, and psychology. Begins with a survey of biblical anthropology, then considers the nature, purposes, and functions of sexuality as a basic expression of the personal self. Examines secondary purposes such as fellowship, procreation, and edification. Discusses the roles of husband and wife, and deals with conflicts in marriage such as religion, in-laws, and sexual incompatibility. Interprets biblical teaching on divorce and remarriage.

3. HULME, W. E., *Building a Christian Marriage,* PH, 1965, 120 pp., $3.95. Fine discussion of marital roles, identity in distinction, and the biblical pattern of mutual subservience with the husband as the head and the wife as the heart. Easy style, evangelical, basic.

4. *SMALL, D. H., *Design for Christian Marriage,* REV, 1959, 221 pp., $3.95. A basic text on the biblical view of marriage, reviewing such questions as the Christian goal of marriage, the nature of love, Christian view of sex, and the morality of contraception. Section on dating, extended discussion of the psychology of petting, all in readable style, aimed at the college level.

5. *FROMME, Allan, *The Ability to Love,* FSG, 1963, 366 pp., Hb $5.95, Pb 75¢; AU, 30s. One of the most practical and helpful books on love available, of greater helpfulness than Erich Fromm's *The Art of Loving,* HRP, 1963, 133 pp., $2.75; BAB, Pb 60¢; AU, 1957, 143 pp., Hb 12s 6d, Pb 4s 6d. Describes our neurotic and pseudo-loves, love's changing expressions, our growth in patterns of non-love, what makes for freedom to love, and the contribution to personality strengths and weaknesses on our ability to love. A provocative book, not spiritually oriented, skillfully combining theoretical understanding and practical counsel.

6. HAVEMANN, Ernest, *Men, Women and Marriage,* DC, 1962, 226 pp., $3.95. A wise, balanced view that demolishes common myths about marriage. Practical perspective is refreshing, counsel is sound. Common guilts are removed in the realistic acceptance of marriage as a very human relationship. Not religious but a good counter to false religious idealism.

7. *TOURNIER, Paul, *To Understand Each Other,* JKP, 1967, 63 pp., $2.00; SCMP, Pb 5s. One of Tournier's best, on the need for empathic understanding in marriage. Sensitive discussion of husband-wife differences, how each may express himself to the other in a wide variety of conditions, how to understand the specific needs of love in one's partner, and how understanding can pave the way to major mutual helpfulness.

8. *HUNT, Morton, *Her Infinite Variety: The American Woman as Lover, Mate and Rival,* HRP, 1962, 333 pp., $6.95; HRP, 45s. A contemporary look at modern woman's life from childhood through old age, thoughtfully examining the various roles she is required to play, her problems and conflicts, triumphs and satisfactions. Provocative for both men and women to consider the many faces of women, the myths of the feminine character, the seven disconnected ages of women, the reluctant nymph, the married mistress, the not-quite-ideal mother, man's best friend and beloved enemy. Also discusses the more-or-less career wife.

9. BLOOD, R. O., Jr., *Marriage,* FRP, 1962, 515 pp., $6.95; CM, 55s. Up-to-date survey of marriage as a personal relationship. Marriage is considered within the social environment of the family. Occupational roles thoroughly examined, also mixed marriages, financial managements, extended family networks, sources of conflict, family planning, parental roles. College text.

10. BOWMAN, H. A., *Marriage for Moderns,* MH, ED 5, 1965, 709 pp., Hb $8.50, Pb $1.50; MH, 68s. Up-to-date revision of one of the great classic college texts. Comprehensive, not too technical, basic to any thorough study of premarital steps, marriage in all its dimensions, and family.

11. *SMALL, D. H., *After You've Said I Do,* REV, 1968, 256 pp., $4.95. Comprehensive study of communication in marriage. Why communication fails, verbal and non-verbal communication development, blocks in the relationship, personal transparency, creative listening, what is dialogue, empathic rapport, semantic difficulties and adequate feedback, sexual communion, use of conflict and crisis, etc. Many engaging chapters such as "Buttoned Lips and

Boxed-in Lives." Fully referenced to contemporary psychological literature and biblically oriented.

12. PIPER, O. A., *The Biblical View of Sex and Marriage,* CSS, 1960, 239 pp., $3.95; NI, 17s 6d. Complete revision of earlier work treating the nature of sex and the unity of the flesh in marriage, sexual standards in marriage, the purpose and virtues of marriage within the biblical context, the way of reconciliation through forgiveness. Mature, evangelical, theological. Compare with advanced theological treatments such as Helmut Thielicke's *The Ethics of Sex,* HRP, 1964, 338 pp., $4.95; JC, V. 3, 352 pp., 30s. Part 4 of Karl Barth's *Church Dogmatics,* AL, 1936-1962, $9.50-$13.50 each; TTC, 12 V., 40s-60s.

13. *MURRAY, John, *Divorce,* OPC, 1953, 117 pp., $2.50. Excellent, scholarly volume. It brings the whole question of marital separations and divorce within the biblical perspective. The subjects considered are the Old Testament provision, the teaching of our Lord, the teaching of Paul, specific issues such as rights of the woman, problems of remarriage and adultery, and several case studies. The book is essentially an exposition to promote a better understanding of the scriptural view of divorce.

14. BAILEY, D. S., *Sexual Relation in Christian Thought,* HRP, 1959, 312 pp. (OoP) Like his earlier book, *The Mystery of Love and Marriage,* a study in depth. Both are basic to a theological understanding of the "one flesh" relation of marriage in the divine order. Somewhat difficult but worth the effort.

15. FAIRCHILD, R. W., *Christians in Families,* CLCP, 1964, 264 pp., Pb $2.25. An excellent basic text on Christian family values against the background of social forces that have

changed the American family. Particularly fine as a biblically sound study of the family as the school for learning Christian relationships and ministry.

16. SCUDDER, C. W., *The Family in Christian Perspective,* BR, 1962, 167 pp., $3.50. An overall picture of the Christian family, God's ideal, responsible parenthood, responsible family relationships, provision for the elderly, ruptured family relations, delinquent behavior, in-law problems, the church, and the home. Evangelical and helpful.

17. WYNN, J. C., *How Christian Parents Face Family Problems,* WP, 1955, 144 pp., $2.50. Excellent self-help for many common problems of child-rearing. Here are precepts every parent can practice. Non-technical in style. Underlying the study is the conviction that Christian families, though plagued by the concerns common to most homes, do have uncommon ways of meeting them.

18. DREIKURS, Rudolf, *The Challenge of Parenthood,* DSP, 1948, 334 pp., $5.95. Old but classic text still helpful in a vast array of family concerns. The parental situation is seen from many aspects (including the generation gap), and the child situation is seen in the struggle for identity. Methods of training are taken up in detail. Various expressions of the difficult child are examined with case studies suggesting ways of guidance.

19. *MOW, A. B., *Your Child from Birth to Rebirth,* ZPH, 1963, 152 pp., Hb $2.95, Pb 95¢. This searching book delves deeply into the solemn questions which face parents and teachers today. What is the basic responsibility Christian parents have toward their children? Do Christians know exactly what they want their children to learn? With simplicity and tact, Dr. Mow exposes the failures

and inadequacies in the Christian education of our children. Practical, down-to-earth advice combines with real life examples. Especially helpful in showing the place of imaginary play in developing faith in God and his Word.

20. GINOTT, H. G., *Between Parent and Child,* MC, 1965, 223 pp., $4.95. The book has an ambitious purpose to make life between parent and child less irritating and more rewarding. It offers concrete suggestions for dealing with daily situations and problems faced by all parents. It presents a new approach to conversation with children, praise and criticism, expression of anger, achievement of independence and assumption of responsibility in all matters of importance in a child's life. There is clear and detailed advice on discipline and limits, sex education, children's fears and anxieties, and on situations which call for professional help. The book helps parents to understand their children's feelings, deal with their conduct, and live with them in mutual respect and dignity.

21. DUVALL, Evelyn, *Family Development,* LC, 1962, 532 pp., $8.75. Emphasis on the family life cycle. Dynamic, functional approach to family relationships, strengthened by the author's employment of the developmental task concept. Examines both expanding and contracting families.

22. WINTER, Gibson, *Love and Conflict,* DC, 1958, 191 pp., Pb 95¢. Discusses new patterns in family life forged in the changing milieu of our day. The abdication of the father's role, the diminishing of intimacy, and the alienation of youth are treated in easy-to-read style. Excellent sociological background for understanding today's family.

23. ANDERSON, W. J., *Design for Family Living,* DEC, 1964, 384 pp., $5.95. An important book bridging the technical and the popular approaches. Written in readable style, with apt illustrations, amusing anecdotes, and convincing case material. Excellent section on middle-aged living. Also good on understanding teenagers.

24. ELLZEY, W. C., *Preparing Your Children for Marriage,* AP, 1964, 159 pp., $3.95. Rightly called "A Manual for Parents." Offers practical guidelines for achieving a maturity in married life which will reflect itself in a child's future marital relationship. Considers such subjects as helping children live their own lives, easing their struggle with rules and regulations, stimulating self-discovery, dealing with reality, fostering feelings of affection, balancing work and play. An important guide to all parents.

25. MEHL, Roger, *Society and Love: Ethical Problems of Family Life,* WP, 1964, 223 pp., $4.50; HS, 1965, 224 pp., 25s. One of few books fully acquainted with the modern social situation of the family, yet rooted in an informed biblical perspective. It is not an ethical guide, but a consideration of the meaning of the family, of married life, and the presence of children. Takes up the problem of authority and present-day family functions.

26. WYNN, J. C., ed., *Sex, Family, and Society in Theological Focus,* AP, 1966, 256 pp., $2.25. Eleven contributors clear away the confusion about sex ethics and family stability. Scintillating essay by Harvey Cox on today's sex mores. Basic essay by Peter de Jong on Christian anthropology as it bears upon a biblical view of the sexual relation. Parental authority keenly discussed by Dr. and Mrs. Dale Harris. Divorce and remarriage viewed under the concept of realized forgiveness by James Emerson, Jr. Gibson Winter voices fresh, perceptive ideas on the nature of marriage.

27. DENTON, Wallace, *What's Happening to our Families,* WP, 1963, 222 pp., $4.00. Discusses the changing family structure, shifting and uncertain roles, the influence of Protestantism on the family. Problems examined include that of emasculated man and unfulfilled woman, anxious parents, accelerated living, longer retirement, decline of religious basis of family behavior, and family isolation. Family strengths rest upon new roles, matured marriage concepts, a proper use of leisure, and modern flexibility. A final section considers new horizons for church and family.

28. WILLIAMSON, R. C., *Marriage and Family Relations,* JW, 1966, 618 pp., $8.50. Here is a major technical work covering all phases of family development. An excellent book of the most thorough nature for advanced students of marriage and family.

29. KEPHART, W. M., *The Family, Society and the Individual,* HM, ED 2, 1966, 666 pp., Hb $8.25, Pb $1.10. Another thorough text for advanced students who would study the place of the family in the larger societal patterns of our day.

30. *KIRKPATRICK, Clifford, *The Family as Process and Institution,* RP, ED 2, 1963, 1132 pp., $8.00. It would be difficult to surpass this updated classic text by one of the foremost scholars in the field of marriage and family. Every subject is fully treated with impressive documentation. It is family sociology at its best.

31. FAIRCHILD, R. W., and J. C. Wynn, *Families in the Church: A Protestant Survey,* AP, 1961, 302

pp., $5.75. (OoP) A study of middle-class Protestant families. Churches assess family influence and shifting family patterns. Parents speak to the Church and the Church responds. Could be studied along with *Helping Families in the Church* by Oscar Feucht, CON, 1957, 334 pp., $3.50; CON, 25s.

4C. CHRISTIAN CLASSICS
Paul M. Bechtel,
Joseph C. Holbrook, Jr.
Harish D. Merchant
Few books escape the fate of being discarded on the scrapheap of history. Christian books are no exception. For a Christian book to gain the designation of "classic" it must have struck a responsive chord in the hearts and minds not only of its own generation, but of succeeding generations until now. It has been said that a Christian, a Jew and a Muslim of the thirteenth century could more easily understand each other than a Christian of the second, thirteenth and twentieth century. There are thought patterns that are the common property of an age that are discarded by thinking men of all religious belief in succeeding ages.

The volumes listed below have broken through these thought patterns. They have spoken a universal language that links Christian men together in the "communion of saints" across the centuries of the Christian era. They continue to reflect the response of man as man to the revelation of God's mighty act in Jesus Christ. Like the Bible, they need to be translated anew into today's idiom.

Many of them need a J. B. Phillips to render them into modern English. But even if couched in an English that was spoken by our great grandfathers, they continue to pay rich dividends to those who will take the time to settle back in an easy chair, forget for a moment the particular form that our twentieth century *problems come packaged in and will link their mind and heart with those of the author in grappling with the issues of life and death, God and Satan, love and hate, sin and salvation, heaven and hell.*

1. ANDREWES, Lancelot, *The Private Devotions of Lancelot Andrewes,* ABP, 1950, 146 pp., $1.50; SCMP, 1957, 126 pp., 9s 6d. The chaplain to Queen Elizabeth and James I, also a King James Bible translator, prepared private devotions for his own use in Hebrew, Greek, and Latin. Discovered after his death, they are a beautiful mosaic of Bible and devotional passages arranged by the days of the week.

2. *ST. AUGUSTINE, *Confessions,* ZPH, 1967, 429 pp., Pb $2.95; WSP, Pb 45¢; Ri, FO, 1957, 256 pp., Pb 2s 6d. Written in A.D. 400, this book is one of the world's great spiritual autobiographies. It surveys Augustine's early worldliness, his doubts, his conversion at thirty-three, and subsequently the working of God's grace in his life. Spiritually profound, it is also a work of great spiritual beauty. It begins with that famous line, "Thou hast made us for Thyself, and our hearts are restless till they rest in Thee."

3. ST. AUGUSTINE, *The City of God,* OUP, 1964, 452 pp., Hb $4.80; DC, 1958, 551 pp., Pb $1.65; OUP, 1963, 30s. St. Augustine is probably the most influential Christian thinker after Paul. This book is his masterpiece, a vast synthesis of religious and secular knowledge. There is wealth of evidence produced here that paganism bore within itself the seeds of its own destruction, and hence was the real cause of the decline of the Roman empire. This is the first cosmic interpretation of history in terms of the struggle between good and evil. An abridgement of the original twenty-two volume treatise.

4. BANGSTER, Jonathan, *Daily Light on the Daily Path*, ZPH, Hb $2.50, Pb $1.00. One of the best known of all evangelical devotional manuals. There are daily readings for the year which bring scriptural passages together under selected topics.

5. BAXTER, Richard, *The Saints' Everlasting Rest*, REV, 1962, 187 pp., $3.50; EP, 18s 6d. This English chaplain during the English Civil War notes for those facing death on the battlefield and others that man's hope is not in this world. Those who would achieve the higher goal must seriously examine their present position.

6. BONHOEFFER, Dietrich, *Letters and Papers from Prison*, MC, 1962, 253 pp., Pb $1.45; FO, 1959, 192 pp., Pb 2s 6d. These letters to his parents and friends during his imprisonment, 1943-44, show Bonhoeffer's deep spiritual insights and his concern for others. His early hope for release from prison waned when he knew execution was near, but he never lost courage and faith.

7. *BONHOEFFER, Dietrich, *Life Together*, HRP, 1954, 122 pp., $2.50; SCMP, 96 pp., Pb 6s 6d. This simple and yet powerfully convincing book was written when Bonhoeffer was the head of a seminary of the German "Confessing Church." The insights into fellowship with God and with men are startling and unforgettable. The first chapter delineating the distinction between the human and spiritual love is very much worth the whole book. Highly recommended.

8. *BONHOEFFER, Dietrich, *The Cost of Discipleship*, MC, 1949, 198 pp., Pb $2.50; SCMP, 1964, 285 pp., Pb 13s 6d. Bonhoeffer condemns "cheap grace;" that is, grace which requires only an intellectual assent. Discipleship means following Christ

into the world in his suffering love. We are called into the world through the preaching of the Word, and we are incorporated into his Body through baptism.

9. BUNYAN, John, *Grace Abounding to the Chief of Sinners*, OUP, 1966, 412 pp., $7.00; OUP, 1955, 412 pp., 30s; SCMP, 1955, 148 pp., Pb 9s 6d. A spiritual exercise somewhat like Augustine's *Confessions*. Bunyan notes that the memory of past mercies helps the Christian in times of trial, that temptation and sorrow alternate with joy and peace, compelling the Christian to rely absolutely on Christ. See also, *Spiritual Riches of John Bunyan*, WPC, 1952, 352 pp., $1.75.

10. *BUNYAN, John, *The Pilgrim's Progress*, BBH, 1967, $4.95; ZPH, Pb 95¢; JMD, 1954, 328 pp., Pb 6s 6d. A book that both children and adults have loved for some three hundred years. A tinsmith, whose real gift was writing, tells the story of the Christian's walk, with all its temptations and joys, until he reaches the celestial city. Every Christian ought to read this book often.

11. CALVIN, John, *Institutes of the Christian Religion*, 2 V., WP, 1960, 1732 pp., $12.50; WBE, 1962, 1286 pp., Pb $5.50; JC, 1957, 1314 pp., 42s. The carefully thought-through, systematic presentation of the full scope of Reformation theology. Calvin was primarily a masterful biblical scholar, but he brought to his Bible study a mind that was able to set forth its teachings in an orderly manner.

12. CHAMBERS, Oswald, *My Utmost for His Highest*, Ri, DODD, 1965, 384 pp., $3.50. A much admired and much used daily devotional manual. Each selection begins with a Scripture passage and is followed by illuminating interpretation.

The meditations are talks given in London and in Egypt.

13. *DEFENELON, François, *Christian Perfection,* HRP, 1947, 208 pp., $3.50. This book is a gem. The instructions from the spiritual writings of Fenelon are wise, simple and devout. Fenelon has a calm insight into the laws of spiritual life and the conflicts in the human heart. Mere skimming or ferreting will not do; quiet the intellect and approach the book with expectancy. Humility will accomplish what cleverness or pride cannot. See also, *Letters and Reflections of François de Fenelon,* WPC, Pb $1.50.

14. DONNE, John, *Devotions Upon Emergent Occasions,* UMIP, 1959, Pb $1.65. Donne imagines that he has become gravely ill, which reminds him of his soul's illness from sin. The king sends his private physician and the patient begins to recover. Since all men have their origin in God, no one can escape involvement in the life of others. Source of the "no man is an island" passage.

15. EDWARDS, Jonathan, *The Diary of David Brainerd,* MP, 1955, Pb 89¢. This spiritual autobiography traces out some of Brainerd's career as student and missionary to the Indians. It is the record of a devout soul struggling to know and do the will of God. A Christian's prayer and hope for the reign of Christ throughout the earth.

16. FOX, George, *The Journal of George Fox,* CAUP, $4.50; PUT, 1963, 578 pp., Pb $1.95; JMD, 1962, 359 pp., Pb 9s 6d. The founder of the Society of Friends wrote a remarkable account of his itinerant preaching, his hardships, his spiritual visions. As a mystic in some ways, he depended upon the "inner light."

17. HENRY, Matthew, *The Secret of Communion with God,* Ri, REV, 1963, 118 pp., $2.50. The famous Bible commentator writes about the secret of beginning, continuing, and ending each day with God. In spite of the fact that the book was written almost two hundred and fifty years ago, it is simple, lucid, and very practical. In fact, it is a guide to help discipline the mind and direct the heart, and should bring spiritual refreshment to many needy hearts.

18. HERBERT, George, *Poems,* OUP, 1961, 308 pp., Pb $2.25; OUP, Pb 7s 6d. Many regard this seventeenth century English Anglican, who spent most of his career in a country parsonage, as the finest devotional poet in English.

19. *HERMAN, Nicolas, *The Practice of the Presence of God,* Ri, REV, 1958, Hb $1.00, Pb 35¢; SCMP, 1956, 176 pp., 9s 6d. This is a memoir of the life and thought of a lay monk who was a kitchen worker in a french monastery of the seventeenth century. God can be served as well in the kitchen or on the battlefield as in a worship service. Worship is a matter of the consecrated will rather than the understanding. By his own testimony he found that the reading of books and listening to sermons had not brought him the sense of presence of God. The "unspeakable riches of God and of Jesus Christ" were his through a life of prayer while performing his daily tasks.

20. JOHNSON, Samuel, *Prayers,* HRP, 1958. (OoP) This collection of prayers, assembled and arranged by topics by Elton Trueblood, is elevated by the earnestness and beauty of style of the celebrated eighteenth-century English author. See also for the excellent collection by the English novelist, Elizabeth Goudge, *A Diary of Prayer,* COM, 1966, 377 pp., $6.95; HS, 287 pp., 16s.

21. JONES, E. S., *Abundant Living,* ABP, 1942, 372 pp., $2.00. A simple, devotional manual with daily readings elaborating passages of Scripture. Jones is always clear, readable, and sensitively aware of the Christian's responsibility to act out the principles of his convictions.

22. JULIAN of Norwich, *A Shewing of God's Love,* LO, RE, 1958, 100 pp., 9s 6d. A fourteenth-century spiritual document of sound and consoling doctrine and radiant faith should bring help and joy to all who desire to live in closer union with God. These are reflections on the author's "visions" when she was thirty and a recluse at St. Julian's Church, Norwich. For an unabridged version see, Julian of Norwich, *Revelations of Divine Love,* PE, 224 pp., Pb $1.45; ME, 288 pp., Hb 12s 6d; PE, Pb 6s.

23. KELLY, Thomas, *A Testament of Devotion,* HRP, 1941, 124 pp., $2.00. Kelly was a twentieth-century American Quaker and teacher at Haverford College, whose *Testament of Devotion* has been much admired for its exploration of the inner life. There have been a number of printings of this work.

24. *KEMPIS, T. á, *The Imitation of Christ,* BRUP, 1962, 257 pp., Hb $2.00; DC, 1955, 227 pp., Pb 65¢ (VE); JMD, 1960, Hb 11s 6d; PE, Pb 3s 6d. Issued in thousands of editions and translated into hundreds of languages, no book of devotion has been so widely read as this one since its appearance in 1441. Although à Kempis tends to be a bit ascetic, he is a profound explorer of the inner life and writes with beautiful simplicity.

25. KROMMINGA, John, ed., *Thine is My Heart,* ZPH, 1958, 384 pp., $3.95. (OoP) A collection of daily devotional readings selected from the writings of John Calvin. The title is part of the inscription on the Calvin family crest. Selections come from the commentaries, sermons, letters, and *Institutes.*

26. *LAW, William, *A Serious Call to a Devout and Holy Life,* WBE, 1966, 313 pp., Pb $1.95; EP, 255 pp., Pb 3s 6d. Although Law lived in "The Age of Reason," he calls upon everyone to devote his life to God. The first half of the book suggests a pattern for serving God in external affairs. The second half is a guide to prayer and the interior life which would honor God. Through use of imaginary characters, he describes how professing Christians fall short of their high calling. He lays great stress on the use of the will in living the Christian life. See also, A. W. Hopkinson, *The Pocket William Law,* WP, 1952, Pb $1.50; EP, 1957, 160 pp., 6s.

27. LUTHER, Martin, *On Christian Liberty or the Freedom of a Christian,* FP, 1943, Pb 50¢. Not so much a doctrinal treatise of the great reformer, but a recital of his own personal faith and of how he attained it. Written as an answer to Pope Leo X who sought to obtain a recantation from Luther. See also, Martin Luther, *Table Talk,* FP, 1967, 464 pp., $6.50; WPC, Pb $1.50.

28. *M'INTYRE, D. M., *The Hidden Life of Prayer,* BEF, 1962, 94 pp., Pb $1.50. This short and splendid book is both scholarly and devotional. It was written by a man who had traveled the steep and lonely path of prayer. Not a reading book, it is meant to be studied and contemplated upon.

29. MURRAY, Andrew, *The Lord's Table,* CL, 1962, 96 pp., $2.00; *The Lord's Supper,* OL, 8s 6d. There is proper balance in this devotional book between the doctrine and the

devotion. Divided into three parts, "The Week before the Supper," "The Communion Sabbath," and "The Week after the Supper," the book delves deep into the meaning of communion for a Christian. See also, *Waiting on God,* Ri, OL, 1961, 110 pp., 8s 6d.

30. NEWMAN, J. H., *Apologia Pro Vita Sua,* OUP, 1964, Hb $3.00; DC, 1956, Pb 95¢. If a Protestant can get over his initial obstacle to reading with pleasure the writing of one who left the Protestant fold and went over to Rome, he will find the story of this gracious Englishman more than rewarding. It will also serve, in this ecumenical age, to demonstrate that God touches the lives of people in different ways, and our ways are not necessarily the only ways he works.

31. PASCAL, Blaise, *Pensées,* EPD, 1951, 543 pp., Pb $1.25; HARV, 1962, 448 pp., 35s; JMD, 1960, 308 pp., Pb 12s 6d. These fragmentary notes and thoughts were intended to be an "apology for the Christian Religion." They begin by examining the human condition to show the need for God. Pascal sees the heart rather than the mind as the more important agency in disclosing the reality of God. Both apologetic and devotional in nature.

32. PEERS, E. A., ed., *The Life of Theresa of Jesus,* DC, Pb 65¢; PE, 316 pp., Pb 3s 6d. The autobiography of one of the great women of Christian history. Theresa was a Spanish noblelady of the very purest and gentlest character. Her words of devotion and love for Christ make her books a classic in the strain of Christian mysticism.

33. *QUOIST, Michel, *Prayers,* SHE, 1963, 177 pp., $3.95. There is no outmoded rhetoric in these compelling and relevant prayers by a French Catholic priest. The book has enjoyed phenomenal sales in Europe, but is virtually unknown in the evangelical community. The stinging simplicity of these conversations should change many prosaic and self-centered prayer habits.

34. RUTHERFORD, Samuel, *Letters,* MP, 1951. (OoP) This devout Scottish preacher, cast into a dungeon for his faith, wrote many beautiful letters of encouragement and spiritual insight to others.

35. SIMEON, Charles, *Let Wisdom Judge,* IVP, 1959, 190 pp., $2.95; TP, 9s 6d. A selection of University addresses and sermon outlines by the eighteenth-century vicar of Holy Trinity, Cambridge, are clear, penetrating and fresh. Arthur Pollard in the introduction says, "He turned Cambridge upside-down in his own time, and Cambridge was all the better for it."

36. TAYLOR, Jeremy, *Holy Dying,* WPC, 1952, 384 pp., Pb $1.75; and *Holy Living,* WPC, 1956, 384 pp., Pb $1.75. A high churchman and a royalist in the seventeenth century, Taylor prepared a manual of instruction for both holy living and holy dying. Holy living consists in remembering our heavenly calling while practicing a just and godly life on earth. Holy dying must be prepared for while one is still in his strength and can see the limited attraction of earthly things.

37. *THIELICKE, Helmut, *The Silence of God,* WBE, 1962, 92 pp., $2.50. These sermons by a modern German preacher and theologian were written during the crisis years of the Second World War. The Scriptural "existentialism" of the author shows the eternal Word encompassing and sustaining through the times of anxiety, guilt, suffering, and death. See also by the same author, *Out of the Depths,* WBE, 1962, 89 pp., $2.50.

38. *TOZER, A. W., *Pursuit of God,* CHPU, 1948, 128 pp., Pb $1.50. A modern classic by a Christian and Missionary Alliance pastor decries the activism of Christians and exhorts them to spend time with God: "As the heart panteth after the water brooks, so panteth my soul after Thee, O God" (Psalms 42:1). A stirring and eloquent book which will cut deep into the "holy masquerade" of those who will take time to read it. For reflections on the attributes of God written in the same vein, but somewhat more profound, see *The Knowledge of the Holy,* HRP, 1963, $3.00.

39. WATKINS, J. M., ed., *The Cloud of Unknowing,* JUP, 1957, $4.00; PE, ED 6, 1956, 270 pp., 10s; PE, Pb 4s 6d. A German mystical work of unknown authorship which appeared in the fourteenth-century. Luther translated the work and expressed great admiration for it. The theme is that one must empty his mind of its baggage and wait in a cloud of unknowing in order to achieve perfect union with God.

40. WATSON, Thomas, *A Body of Divinity,* BTT, RE, 1965, 316 pp., 15s. (OoP) Little is known about Watson who like other Puritans in seventeenth-century England suffered persecution; however, unlike the others he is both logical and readable. This treatise deals with the foremost doctrinal and practical truths of Christian faith, written in original, rich and pungent style.

41. WESLEY, John, *A Plain Account of Christian Perfection,* AL, 116 pp., $2.00; Ri, EP, 1960, 7s 6d; *Christian Perfection,* WPC, $1.50. (OoP) Answers pertinent questions such as "Can man be perfect?" and "What is perfection?" There is impassioned confidence in these pages that God commands only what he wills his servants to do. See also, William

Guthrie, *The Christian's Serving Interest,* KR, RE, 1958, 192 pp., $2.95 (OoP); and John Newton, *Cardiphonia: The Voice of the Heart,* Ri, OL, 1950, 432 pp. (OoP).

42. WESLEY, John, *Journal,* PUT, 1963, 433 pp., $1.85; EP, 1952, 436 pp., 10s 6d. As if to put us to shame for our few accomplishments, Wesley's *Journal* is the account of a man who rose early and worked late in the untiring labor of winning England for Christ. A good antidote for those who think they are doing more than others in the service of Christ.

4D. HYMNS AND PSALMS

J. Buchanan MacMillan

Only in rare circumstances have Christians met regularly for corporate worship without engaging in some sort of singing. The Psalms of the Old Testament passed from Jewish worship directly into that of the early Church and provided a major source of sung texts. In the beautiful Latin version of the Reformation churches and the metrical paraphrases of those traditions which sprang from Calvin's leadership, Psalm texts have resounded forth from choir and congregation through the centuries.

Paul specifically enjoins Christians to sing "psalms, hymns and spiritual songs" to the Lord (Ephesians 5:19-20, Colossians 3:16). Freely composed metrical hymns began to appear in the fourth century, but only after the Reformation did they become the primary musical expression of the congregation. Only in recent times has an adequate and scholarly literature dealing with psalmody and hymnody grown up. In the following list, an attempt has been made to bring together titles that will prove both readable and reliable in information.

1. MESSENGER, R. E., and H. E. Pfatteicher, "A Short Bibliography for the Study of Hymns," in *The*

Papers of the Hymn Society of America, THS, 1964, 31 pp., Pb 60¢. This excellent bibliography is the twenty-fifth in a series of pamphlets that may be obtained complete for about $7.00 from The Hymn Society, 475 Riverside Drive, New York, New York. While no critical estimate of individual titles is included, the list is selective and provides a helpful starting point for wide ranging study.

2. *PFATTEICHER, H. E., *In Every Corner Sing,* FP, 1954, 214 pp., $2.50. For the reader who is looking for a brief, authoritative account of the development and scope of Christian hymnody this work is heartily recommended.

3. MACMILLAN, Alexander, *Hymns of the Church,* UCPH, 1945, 323 pp., $4.00. (OoP) Designed as a companion to *The Hymnary* (1930), the book is cast in the form of a concise and most readable history of Christian hymnody that loses little if used as an independent work. It is to be highly recommended. See also, C. E. Whittemore, *Hymn Writers of the Church,* HS, Pb 3s 6d.

4. *ROUTLEY, Erik, *Hymns and Human Life,* PL, 1953, 346 pp., $6.00; WBE, ED 2, 1966, Pb $3.95. This is a book about hymns for relaxed reading. It covers the historical field, but avoids an historical approach and is chatty and anecdotal with a good leavening of humor. One chapter, for instance, deals with bishops who wrote hymns. The author is a widely acknowledged authority on hymnody.

5. BAILEY, Albert, *The Gospel in Hymns,* CSS, 1950, 600 pp., $7.50. The author develops his book around 313 hymns that constitute the common possessions of five or more of a selected group of the most important American, British, and Canadian denominational hymnals. A wealth of information about the authorship of the hymns and their historical and theological background is assembled into chapters dealing with the eras of Church history in a lively and interesting manner.

6. RYDEN, E. E., *The Story of Christian Hymnody,* FP, 1959, 670 pp., $7.50. This book presents the text of the hymn discussed before each section of commentary; thus it provides the reader with an extensive anthology of hymnic verse, as well as with much information about the hymns.

7. HAEUSSLER, Armin, *The Story of Our Hymns,* EDEN, 1952, 1088 pp., $7.75. Most major denominational hymnals have companion volumes of pertinent information, which are all too often too little publicized and frequently allowed to go out of print. This work is the companion to the Hymnal of the Evangelical and Reformed Church. It contains an article on each text and tune in that hymnal and a biographical sketch of each author and composer.

8. *REYNOLDS, W. J., *A Survey of Christian Hymnody,* HRW, 1963, 320 pp., $7.95; HRW, 48s. The survey is brief but commendable and is followed by 160 hymns, text and music presented as in a normal American hymnal. Brief informative footnotes appear below each hymn. The format is exceedingly attractive.

9. *NOSS, Luther, ed., *Christian Hymns,* MEB, 1962, 255 pp., Pb $1.95. One hundred eighteen hymns of historical importance and excellence are presented with music. Each hymn is followed by brief notes by the editor. Highly recommended. See also, *D. Kidner, ed., *Christian Praise,* IVP, 466 pp., $3.50; TP, 468 pp., 18s 6d.

10. *ROUTLEY, Erik, *I'll Praise My Maker,* IP, 1952, 280 pp., 15s. The subtitle to this fine study reads: "A study of the hymns of certain authors who stand in or near the tradition of English Calvinism, 1700-1850." Such important writers as Philip Doddridge, John Cennick, Augustus M. Toplady and over a dozen others who have contributed significant hymns to the standard heritage are discussed in this interesting book, with liberal quotations that illustrate their styles.

11. MANNING, B. L., *The Hymns of Wesley and Watts,* EP, ED 7, 1960, 143 pp., 7s 6d. Here are five informal papers of great excellence which precipitate soul stirring passion of the evangelical faith and experience. See also, J. E. Rattenbury, *The Evangelical Doctrines of Charles Wesley's Hymns,* EP, 1941, 365 pp., Hb 15s, Pb 7s 6d.

12. LOVELACE, Austin, *The Anatomy of Hymnody,* ABP, 1965, 112 pp., $2.75. This slim volume presents in handy form the details of poetic meter and rhythm as found in English hymns. Examples are given of each type. A final chapter deals with rhetorical devices; it is based on a fuller account which may be consulted in Frank Baker, *Representative Verse of Charles Wesley,* ABP, V. 1, 1963, introduction lxi pp., 415 pp., $11.00; EP, 480 pp., 63s.

13. McCUTCHAN, R. G., *Hymn Tune Names, Their Sources and Significance,* ABP, 1957, 206 pp., $3.75. An interesting reference book. While far from exhaustive, it is the only one of its kind.

14. ROUTLEY, Erik, *The Music of Christian Hymnody,* IP, 1957, 308 pp., 30s. Apart from various handbooks to specific denominational hymnals, which deal only with the tunes in those collections, this is one

of the only books in English bearing on the subject of hymn tunes in historical and critical perspective. It completely overlooks much of the American repertory and is sometimes biased and over-dogmatic. Nevertheless, it is an important study in the field.

15. JACKSON, G. P., *The Spiritual Folksongs of Early America,* Ri, PS, 1964, 254 pp., Hb $4.00. Pb $2.00; DO, 16s. A long introduction contains much information about this interesting music. The tunes and texts of 250 religious ballads, folk hymns, and revival songs are included.

16. JACKSON, G. P., *White Spirituals in the Southern Uplands,* Ri, FA, 1964, 444 pp., $9.50; DO, 1965, Pb $2.50; DO, 1964, 20s. An authoritative book about the history, transmission and use of religious folksongs.

17. FOOTE, H. W., *Three Centuries of American Hymnody,* HUP, 1940, 418 pp. (OoP); BAIB, 70s. Although not currently listed in *Books in Print,* no list of hymnological works would be complete without this important study, which traces American congregational song from the days of the Pilgrims.

18. BRITT, Matthew, *Hymns of the Breviary and Missal,* BENB, 1948, 416 pp. (OoP) Protestant hymnody is much indebted to the many translations of the Latin hymns of the early middle ages. This fine study by a Catholic scholar presents a rich selection of great Latin hymns together with one or more of the best English paraphrases. Each text is followed by a historical-critical article and a stanza-by-stanza commentary.

19. PATRICK, Millar, *Four Centuries of Scottish Psalmody,* OUP, 1949, 234 pp. (OoP) This is an engaging account that should appeal even

to those who do not boast of Scottish ancestry. Beside providing a scholarly account of the development and use of the Scottish Psalter, it gives many insights into the religious life of that country in earlier times, particularly in relation to the practice of Church music.

20. ROUTLEY, Erik, *The English Carol*, OUP, 1958, 272 pp., $5.00. Here the reader will find a discussion of carols from those of the fifteenth century to the present. Reference is often made to that excellent modern collection, ˉ*The Oxford Carol Book* by Percy Dearmer, OUP, 1928, 491 pp., Hb $5.00, Pb $1.75; OUP, RE, 1964, 454 pp., Hb 18s 6d, Pb 6s, which every lover of sacred song should know.

21. BENSON, L. F., *The Hymnody of the Christian Church*, Ri, JKP, 1956, 310 pp., $4.50. Six lectures delivered at Princeton constitute the substance of this excellent work. Anyone with an interest in the purpose of hymnody in Christian worship ought to read this book. The author thoughtfully examines the scriptural warrant for singing hymns, their literary and scriptural implications and their use in services.

22. *BENSON, L. F., *The English Hymn*, Ri, JKP, 1962, 624 pp., $4.50. An unexcelled classic in the field by the foremost American hymnologist. Hymnody, including metrical Psalmody, is investigated from its beginnings. Its development and use is traced, with careful documentation, to the beginning of the present century and set forth in an excellent literary style.

23. JULIAN, John, ed., *A Dictionary of Hymnology*, 2 V., Ri, DO, 1958, 1768 pp., $17.50; DO, 12s 6d. Although out of date and inadequate for American hymnody, "Julian" remains the only encyclopedia reference work in the field of English hymn texts and their authors. The original part of the work is followed by two supplement sections, so that some items must be sought in two or three places. The whole is adequately indexed. Although new works are in process in both the United States and Great Britain to bring it up to date, the original will remain of vital importance.

section 5
CHRISTIAN ETHICS

5. CHRISTIAN ETHICS: INTRODUCTION
J. Oliver Buswell, Jr.

Ethics is the subject which deals with right and wrong, good and evil. The words right and wrong imply a standard of comparison, and the words good and evil imply a goal or purpose to be realized. The biblical standard of ethics is the revealed will of God, especially as expressed in the ten commandments (Exodus 20:1-17). The biblical goal is the glory of God (I Corinthians 10:31) or the kingdom, or household, of God (Matthew 6:33; Ephesians 2:19; Galatians 6:10).

"Morality and Conduct" as a subtopic may be thought of as summarized by Christ (Matthew 22:40) and by Paul (Romans 13:8-10) in terms of love toward God and love toward our neighbors. Sex morality is strongly emphasized in the seventh and tenth commandments and in the Sermon on the Mount, especially Matthew 5:28. Social responsibility is an important theme throughout the Bible from Genesis 4:9 with Cain's evasion, "Am I my brother's keeper?" to Christ's Great Commission of Matthew 28:18-20 and Paul's concern for our testimony toward "those who are without" (I Corinthians 5:12; Colossians 4:5; I Thessalonians 4:12; Ephesians 5:11).

Urban society is assumed as a part of Christian ethical responsibility toward society in general. It is assumed that Christians buy and sell and work productively in their neighborhoods. We are in the world (I Corinthians 5:10) though not of the world (John 17:18). Poverty and hunger as aspects of Christian ethics are an important feature of the Book of Proverbs. The heart of New Testament economics is expressed in such texts as Ephesians 4:28 and I Timothy 5:1.

On the subject of racial conflict, the Bible clearly and uniformly teaches that all men are created in the image of God, and are derived from one common stock. As for war, Paul clearly teaches that it is the God-given function of government to "bear the sword, not in vain" against lawlessness and disorder (Romans 13:1-4). Fellowship and group dynamics as an ethical method is supported by such texts as James 5:16.

5A. SEX, MORALITY AND CONDUCT
Robert K. Bower

Christians believe that sex and sexuality are gifts of God which find their true meaning and fulfillment when guided by the One who created man both male and female. It is the Christian faith which provides the kind of environment which adequately nourishes sexual love and causes it to be fruitful, joyous, and satisfying as God intended it to be.

There are voices today which would seek to lead people away from a biblical anthropology of sex with its established principles of sexual morality. However, it is only as faith in the God of the Bible is exercised and the guidelines of his revelation are followed that the tension will be resolved between individual and social responsibility in matters of sexual relations and the divine plan for each person will be realized fully.

Easy
1. *BABBAGE, S. B., *Christianity and Sex*, IVP, 1963, 59 pp., Pb 95¢. The nature and problems of sex viewed from a theological and historical perspective. Treatment of the subject matter is set within a consistent and conservative framework based on crucial biblical passages. Interestingly written.

2. BABBAGE, S. B., *Sex and Sanity*, WP, 1967, 98 pp., Pb $1.45; HS, 1965, 94 pp., Pb 3s 6d. Aware of the present problems of Christian young adults today, Dr. Babbage examines

in an understanding fashion the prevalent attitudes toward sex, marriage, promiscuity, homosexuality, and the new morality. Thoroughly biblical and evangelical in perspective. Comprehensive and straightforward in style.

3. BAINTON, R. H., *What Christianity Says about Sex, Love and Marriage,* AP, 1957, 124 pp., Pb 75¢; *Sex, Love and Marriage,* CO, 1958, 128 pp., 2s 6d. An interesting, accurate, and very informing historical survey of the church's attitude toward sex, love, and marriage from New Testament times to the present day. The conflicts, the misunderstandings, and the misinterpretations of Scripture regarding the nature and fulfillment of sex are described in terms of the sacramental, romantic, and companionable views of the marriage state.

4. BARCLAY, O. R., *A Time to Embrace,* IVP, 1964, 61 pp., Pb 60¢; TP, Pb 2s. Aimed at avoiding legalism at specific levels but providing guidelines for Christian behavior, this book takes note of cultural factors while seeking to retain biblical objectives and norms.

5. CAPPER, W. M., and H. M. Williams, *Toward Christian Marriage,* IVP, 1958, 144 pp., Pb 95¢; *Heirs Together,* TP, 1956, 128 pp., Pb 3s 6d. Written for college age persons in the period of courtship prior to engagement, this book by two doctors in the field of medicine covers basic information on sex physiology and function, guiding principles of conduct and the ideals of Christian marriage. Sex problems of the single young person handled in conservatively Christian ways.

6. *DUVALL, E. M., *Why Wait Till Marriage?* ASP, 1965, 128 pp., Pb 75¢; HS, 1966, 15s. Quoting case studies as well as her counseling experiences with youth on over 100 campuses, the author gives her carefully formulated views on the problems and dangers inherent in premarital sex relations. Interesting style, conservative in orientation.

7. *GRIMM, Robert, *Love and Sexuality,* ASP, 1964, 127 pp., $3.50; HS, 1965, 128 pp., 15s. An inspirational and biblically-sound exposition of sexuality by a Swiss university chaplain which presents a high view of sex and marriage. Love is seen as adequately protected and nurtured only within the institution of marriage as seen in Christian perspective. More general than specific in application.

8. SCORER, C. G., *The Bible and Sex Ethics Today,* IVP, 1966, 128 pp., Pb $1.50; TP, Pb 6s. A quite conservative, biblio-historical treatment of contemporary views of sexual conduct with popular questions answered on the basis of rather broad, as opposed to specific, principles derived from Scripture.

9. WEATHERHEAD, L. D., *Mastery of Sex,* ABP, 1962, 190 pp., Pb $1.00; SCMP, 1965, 192 pp., Pb 7s 6d. Though written in the 1930's, this volume on the psychology and theology of sex is still relevant and is one of the best for guidance in the control of the sex impulse. The author's views toward sex and marriage are conservative with few exceptions.

Moderately difficult
10. *BARNETTE, H. H., *The New Theology and Morality,* WP, 1967, 120 pp., Pb $1.85. One of the finest and most conservative books available for the Christian providing explanations of, as well as the pros and cons on, such controversial themes as the new morality, death of God, secular society, and the Christian's attitude toward war. Highly recommended.

11. *BERTOCCI, P. A., *The Human Venture in Sex, Love and Marriage,* ASP, 1949, 143 pp., $2.50; LO, 10s 6d. An excellent philosophical-psychological defense of traditional morality by a professor of philosophy at Boston University. Petting, pre-marital intercourse, love, and marriage treated without "appeal to religious conviction or doctrine." Not a substitute for, but a helpful supplement to, a Christian theology of sex and marriage.

12. DEMANT, V. A., *Christian Sex Ethics,* HRP, 1965, 127 pp., $2.75; *Exposition of Christian Sex Ethics,* HS, 1963, Pb 4s 6d. A series of lectures to undergraduate university students on sex ethics by a professor at Oxford in which he outlines a generally conservative philosophy of sex relationships necessary for happiness both before and throughout the lifetime of a marriage. Practical and interesting.

13. Group for the Advancement of Psychiatry, *Sex and the College Student,* ATH, 1966, 178 pp., Hb $4.50, Pb $2.45. Information gathered from medical and college administrative files by psychoanalytic psychiatrists, a psychologist and several college officials providing guidance for institutions of higher education in setting policies governing student sexual conduct. Orientation is non-religious, and data appear to be inadequate and lack comprehensiveness.

14. HILTNER, Seward, *Sex and the Christian Life,* ASP, 1957, 129 pp., Pb 75¢. In this brief volume, the author has drawn the guidelines of Christian conduct from his larger work, *Sex Ethics and the Kinsey Reports,* ASP, 1953, 238 pp. (OoP), and provides the reader with a philosophy of sex based upon biblical insights. Psychological and physiological data are also considered in the light of the guidelines and principles which he presents.

15. Lutheran Church, Missouri Synod, *Engagement and Marriage,* CON, 1959, 194 pp., $3.00; CON, 256 pp., 21s. Traces the development of engagement and marriage from Old Testament concepts and practices to the present period. Excellent analysis using the insights from two Lutheran theological faculties for the formulation of principles governing Christian engagement and marriage. Graphs included.

16. *MURRAY, John, *Principles of Conduct,* WBE, 1957, 272 pp., Hb $3.50, Pb $2.25; TP, 25s. The bibliotheological method is employed to explore the organic unity and the continuity of divine revelation in various aspects of biblical ethic. The specific subjects discussed are creation ordinance, marriage, procreation, and the sanctity of life.

17. Lutheran Church, Missouri Synod, *Sex and the Church,* CON, 1961, 271 pp., $3.50; CON, 25 s. One of the most scholarly studies of sex produced by a church group in the United States. Responses from over 3,000 couples and 1,000 pastors who participated in a sex attitude inventory are integrated into a Christian interpretation of sex, reflecting biblical principles. Lutheran, Reformed, and Roman Catholic views included.

18. *LEWIS, C. S., *The Four Loves,* HA, 1960, 192 pp., $3.75; CO, 1963, 128 pp., Pb 2s 6d. In his inimitable style, the author provides us with a literary, theological, and somewhat psychological treatment of the types of love and affection experienced in life for objects, animals, friends of the opposite sex and God. Distinguishing between these, he brings each into a proper relationship with that love which is for God himself.

19. PIPER, O. A., *The Biblical View of Sex and Marriage*, CSS, 1960, 239 pp., $3.95; NI, 17s 6d. Written by a former professor at Princeton Theological Seminary, this book treats, biblically, the origin, nature, purpose, and problems of sex and sexuality with special attention given to the significance of sexual union by unmarried or married individuals. A high view of sex and marriage is set forth.

20. JONES, H. K., *Toward a Christian Understanding of the Homosexual*, ASP, 1966, 160 pp., $3.00. The book brings together the best scientific information about male homosexuality available to date. After surveying the Judeo-Christian attitudes, the author suggests guidelines which the local pastor and congregation can follow in building their ministries to these people.

Advanced

21. BAILEY, Sherwin, *Sexual Ethics*, MC, 1963, 159 pp., Pb $1.45; *Common Sense about Sexual Ethics: A Christian View*, GOL, 1962, 175 pp., 12s 6d. After considering the generally confused attitude of the Church in past history and the conflicting pronouncements of Church bodies today on the nature of sex and marriage, he outlines a philosophy which is moderately liberal at some points and conservative at others. Should be read carefully or one may draw unjustified conclusions.

22. BOVET, Theodor, *A Handbook to Marriage*, DC, 1958, 157 pp., Pb 95¢; *Handbook to Marriage and Marriage Guidance*, LO, 152 pp., 12s 6d. A Swiss Protestant physician with extensive clinical experience in dealing with marital problems discusses the nature of love, the selection of a mate, the psychology of the male and female, and the crises in marriage.

Designed for those who are married or about to be married.

23. British Council of Churches, *Sex and Morality*, FP, 1966, 77 pp., Pb $1.00; SCMP, 80 pp., Pb 3s 6d. A controversial report which states very ambiguously the conclusions of a group appointed by the British Council of Churches. Divorce, pre-marital, and extra-marital relations are viewed from a rather liberal perspective, with the possibility of exceptions to the rules traditionally governing such practices. The British Council itself states in the preface that it disagrees with the principle of exceptions and reaffirms the rule that sexual relations should be confined to marriage.

24. COLE, W. G., *Sex and Love in the Bible*, AP, 1959, 448 pp., $6.50; HS, 1960, 25s. Cultural and historical factors influencing the people of God are presented within a weak and subjective framework of biblical inspiration. An inadequate understanding of the nature of biblical betrothal equates this with modern engagement practices resulting in a vacillating view of premarital chastity.

25. *FLETCHER, Joseph, *Moral Responsibility*, WP, 1967, 256 pp., Pb $1.95. A volume designed to apply more fully the principles laid down by the author in his earlier work, *Situation Ethics*. A liberal philosophy of sex and morality is outlined, going beyond the position, it would appear, of that held by John A. T. Robinson.

26. FLETCHER, Joseph, *Situation Ethics*, WP, 1966, 176 pp., Pb 95¢; SCMP, 25s. Through a lengthy presentation of *exceptions* to the rules of conduct, the author raises such exceptions to the level of a rule (that there are no general rules). Paul Ramsey capably and completely refutes this view in his volume, *Deeds and Rules* (given elsewhere in this section).

27. GENNE, Elizabeth and William, *Christians and the Crisis in Sex Morality*, AP, 1962, 123 pp., 75¢. A well-documented report by both the head of the Department of Family Life for the National Council of Churches (USA) and his wife which grew out of the Conference on Family Life, sponsored by the Canadian and National (USA) Councils of Churches. Crucial questions discussed frankly within a rather broad-minded but Christian context.

28. MUELDER, W. G., *Moral Law in Christian Social Ethics*, JKP, 1966, 189 pp., $5.00. The author holds that morality must be based jointly on theology, philosophy, and science. Following the idealism of Edgar S. Brightman, he emphasizes a sense of responsibility which includes both society and the individual, thus arguing in part against situational ethics. Traditional in attitude toward moral standards but more liberal than conservative in theology. For advanced students.

29. PEMBERTON, P. L., *Dialogue in Romantic Love*, JP, 1961, 64 pp., Pb $1.00. A sociological and developmental analysis of dating patterns within a general Protestant framework emphasizing methods of dealing with highly sophisticated young adults so that romantic love is adequately guided and maintained in terms of a scientific and yet biblically-oriented value system. Useful and generally conservative in perspective.

30. *RAMSEY, Paul, *Deeds and Rules in Christian Ethics*, CSS, 1967, 245 pp., Pb $3.50; OB, 1965, 120 pp., 10s. Perhaps the best theoretical analysis of, and reply to, the "New Morality" in print. Incisive critique by this Princeton University professor of the writings of John A. T. Robinson, *Honest to God*, Joseph Fletcher, *Situation Ethics*, and

others. Difficult to read because of philosophical emphasis but not too advanced for anyone willing to think deeply and seriously. Eminently worthwhile.

31. *ROBINSON, J. A. T., *Christian Morals Today*, WP, 1964, 47 pp., Pb 65¢; SCMP, Pb 2s 6d. The author seeks to clarify (or make corrections in) his position in *Honest to God*. Rather than considering individual needs only as a basis for ethical action, he suggests corporate and social action as well. The result, however, is that exceptions to corporate needs (as expressed in rules or laws) are stressed so strongly that they are easily ignored and the fulfillment of individual needs (and desires) encouraged under the inadequately described criterion of love.

32. ROBINSON, J. A. T., *Honest to God*, WP, 1963, 143 pp., Pb $1.65; SCMP, 144 pp., Pb 5s. Borrowing from the radical new theologians, the author presents their non-traditional views in a popular and rather sensational form. Questions are raised regarding the system of morality held by the Church as well as the meaning and validity of the commonly accepted important events in the life of our Lord. Liberal in orientation.

33. *THIELICKE, Helmut, *The Ethics of Sex*, HRP, 1964, 338 pp., $4.95; JC, 352 pp., 30s. Ethical principles are derived from a biblical anthropology and applied within an empirically determined context of specific circumstances involving such problems as divorce, birth control, abortion, homosexuality, etc. An outstanding work, well-written and thorough. Should be read by all students seriously considering ethical questions of sex and sexual behavior.

5B. SOCIAL RESPONSIBILITY
David O. Moberg

Christian love and justice demand a

concern for the welfare of our fellow-men. Christ's "Great Commission" to teach His people "to observe all things whatsoever I have commanded you," the example of God who loved men collectively ("the world" of John 3:16) as well as individually, and numerous direct instructions and implicit teachings of the Bible indicate our social responsibility. Social problems which affect multitudes are also the problems of each member. Loving persons individually necessitates loving them collectively, so social action and reform are fully as important as social welfare. Neutrality on social issues is impossible.

Despite their significant role in social welfare and reform in the past, evangelicals in this century have been aloof from most direct forms of social concern until recently. Their literature on the subject is therefore limited, but they can benefit from judicious use of the work of others. Only a few of the most important works are listed here; others may be found in other sections of this book.

1. *KEITH-LUCAS, Alan, The Church and Social Welfare, WP, 1962, 84 pp., Pb $1.25. Confusion and heresies in many Protestant approaches to current welfare problems are exposed constructively. This is "required reading"; its six brief but insightful chapters can help to make one a better citizen, a more understanding Christian and a more truly loving person.

2. *MOBERG, D. O., Inasmuch: Christian Social Responsibility in the Twentieth-Century, WBE, 1965, 216 pp., Pb $2.45. This evangelical survey covers all major aspects of Christian social concern, including its scriptural basis, the needs of society, channels, programs and activities by which Christians can implement social concern and methods for evaluating success. Suggestions for discussion and further study in each of its ten chap-

ters make it a useful resource for religious education and discussion groups as well as for individual readers.

3. *WIRT, Sherwood, The Social Conscience of the Evangelical, HRP, 1968, 117 pp., $4.95. The editor of Decision magazine deals here with the revival of evangelical social concern. He offers biblical perspectives on contemporary social issues and contends that true evangelical faith leads to sensitive social concern.

4. *RAUSCHENBUSCH, Walter, Christianity and the Social Crisis, HRP, 1964, 429 pp., Pb $2.75; HRP, 18s. This classic of the "social gospel" movement is a passionate plea for social repentance and social reconstruction to cope with "the social crisis." It recognizes the importance of personal regeneration as well as social reform and remains relevant, interesting, and easy to read despite occasional "dated" passages and an underlying respect for Christian Socialism.

5. SMITH, T. L., Revivalism and Social Reform, ABP, 1957, 253 pp., $4.00; HRP, RE, 1966, Pb $1.95; HRP, RE, 1966, 254 pp., 16s. As an historical study of the influence of revivalistic religion and of the quest for Christian perfection in mid-nineteenth-century America, this is a stimulating account of the political and social "liberalism" of evangelical Christians a century ago.

6. CAIRNS, E. E., Saints and Society, MP, 1960, 192 pp., $3.25. (OoP) Evangelical contributions to social reforms through the eighteenth-century English revivals are the primary focus of this book. Its strong conclusion, "Revival should, as it has in the past, result in service to society as well as the salvation of souls," is somewhat vitiated by the socio-economic and

political conservatism of its recommendations for action.

7. GRANT, F. B., *Ministries of Mercy,* FR, 1962, 167 pp., Hb $2.95, Pb $1.75. This is a brief survey of church-sponsored services for children and youth, the aged, the physically and mentally ill, the handicapped, economic dependents, migrants, and law violators. It includes brief summaries of the religious origins of social work and why Christians minister to persons in need.

8. HARRINGTON, J. T., and M. S. Webb, *Who Cares?* FR, 1962, 160 pp., Pb $1.75. As a project guidebook on the church's mission to persons with special needs, this may be used either independently to stimulate discussion or as a resource accompanying Grant's *Ministries of Mercy.*

9. RAHTJEN, B. D., *Scripture and Social Action,* ABP, 1966, 144 pp., Pb $1.50. This "guide to understanding the social witness of the church" teaches that evangelism and social action are not alternatives from which to choose; both are necessary in the Christian witness today.

10. BARNES, R. P., *Under Orders,* DC, 1961, 138 pp., Pb $2.95. The role of Christian churches in public affairs ("all the interests of the community as a whole and the social forces that impinge upon persons") is the focus of this book. Barnes concludes that the churches' special responsibility is to interpret the truth of the gospel in such a way as to make it obviously relevant to man's needs. He gives practical suggestions for doing so.

11. **Report of the National Advisory Commission on Civil Disorders,* EPD, 1968, $7.95; BAB, 609 pp., Pb $1.25. This report of the so-called U.S. Riot Commission is the most im-

portant document dealing with the problems of race, violence, and disorganization in contemporary American life. It describes what happened in recent riots, summarizes their causes, and suggests what can be done by communities, cities, police departments, the news media, schools, welfare departments, employers, government, and other agencies to correct the problems of racial disorder, violence, and disorganization in contemporary American life.

12. WILLIAMSON, Margaret, ed., *Concern and Response,* FR, 1962, 223 pp., Pb $3.50. This report of the Second National Conference on the churches and social welfare summarizes statements on goals and policies, methods of implementing goals, and recommendations for action. Fifteen denominational reports and other materials also are included. Despite outline-like brevity, it is a good basis for thought and discussion.

13. KRAEMER, Hendrik, *The Bible and Social Ethics,* FP, 1965, 38 pp., Pb 75¢. The need for a new social ethic and for the Kingship of Christ in the present world is presented in the belief that the ecumenical movement and the quickening of Christian social conscience are related. General principles are set forth more clearly than specific directions and actions demanded by the Christian social conscience.

14. MILLER, H. M., *Compassion and Community,* ASP, 1961, 288 pp., $3.50. (OoP) Miller's survey of the church's changing role in social welfare surveys the historic background, problems and policies of church welfare activities, relationships between churches, social workers and community agencies, and special areas demanding Christian concern.

15. NIEBUHR, Reinhold, *Moral Man and Immoral Society,* CSS, 1932, 284 pp., Hb $4.95, Pb $1.45; SCMP, 1963, 13s 6d. A sharp distinction is drawn between the moral behavior of individual persons and the ethical-moral activities of national, racial, economic, and other groups to which they belong. All Christians should consider these seminal ideas of this prominent neo-orthodox theologian.

16. BENNETT, J. C., *Social Salvation: A Religious Approach to the Problems of Social Change,* CSS, 1935, 220 pp. (OoP) Despite its non-evangelical theological orientation, this renowned book can stimulate any Christian's thinking on the "theological preface to social action." It deals with the relationships between sin and social evil, individual salvation and social conditions, Christology and social change, moral behavior and human welfare, and the work of God and responsibility of man in society.

17. *RASMUSSEN, A. T., *Christian Social Ethics: Exerting Christian Influence,* PH, 1956, 318 pp., $10.00. One of the best general textbooks on Christian influence in the oppressive moral climate of American society, this covers both the philosophical basis for Christian social ethics and some principles or guidelines for implementing them.

18. HORTON, P. B., and G. R. Leslie, *The Sociology of Social Problems,* ACC, ED 3, 1965, 742 pp., $7.95. This college-level work is the most widely used social problems textbook. It summarizes data on current American problems and interprets them from three theoretical perspectives (social-disorganization, value-conflict, and personal deviation). Its presentations on the misinterpretation of data, techniques of successful lying (both with and without statistics), and powerful propaganda techniques of pressure groups are especially helpful.

19. *NIEBUHR, H. R., *Christ and Culture,* MUS, 1951, $3.25; HRP, 1956, 259 pp., Pb $1.75; FF, 1952, 156 pp., 21s. Five basic types of answers to problematic relationships between Christ and culture (the "total process of human activity and . . . total result of such activity") are presented and analyzed. A sixth position is presented as more consistent with the fact that "Christ is risen from the dead and is not only the head of the Church but the redeemer of the world."

20. NAYLOR, H. H., *Volunteers Today—Finding, Training and Working with Them,* ASP, 1967, 192 pp., $5.50. Volunteer services by laymen to supplement professional welfare are an increasingly important outlet for Christian social concern. This practical how-to-do-it book is written for leaders in organizations which require the unpaid work of citizens in administration and program services. It covers motivations, recruitment, orientation and training, supervision, communications, volunteer-staff relations, and many other pertinent topics.

21. TROELTSCH, Ernst, *The Social Teaching of the Christian Churches,* 2 V., MC, 1931, 1019 pp. (OoP); Ri, HRP, 1960, V. 1, $2.25, V. 2, $2.45 (OoP); AU, 1931, 1022 pp., 63s. This classical work first published in German in 1911 surveys the great variety of social and ethical responses of Christians to social and ethical questions in the primitive church, early and medieval Catholicism, and the various branches of Protestantism. Important also for sociological concepts of the Church, sect, and mysticism, these volumes provide a solid historical work on Christian social responsibility.

22. *BRUNNER, Emil, *Justice and Social Order,* HRP, 1945, 304 pp., $4.00. Meaning and significance of justice are examined in the Western culture and in the revelation of the Scriptures. These principles are applied to justice in the economic, political, and international orders. A theoretical work, pregnant with many practical implications.

5C. URBAN SOCIETY
David S. Schuller

The city has become the residential or gravitational center for virtually every North American. The rapid shift from rural dominance to an overwhelmingly urban economy and mind-set has taken place within a brief half-century. Metropolis is the new form of our society.

For a long time the Church ignored the change. Only when her failure to reach increasing numbers of urban people and whole spheres became institutionally threatening, did the Church rediscover her mission to the city. In some situations the change came too late.

The task of the Christians is not to divert the flow of American life from the main street to the side street where the church building stands. Their task is to move the Church, composed of those who consciously call themselves by the name of Jesus Christ, out into the marketplaces of the emerging metropolis. There they meet the world in honest dialogue, seeking to convey God's Word as he speaks judgment and grace.

1. *COX, Harvey, *The Secular City,* MC, 1965, 276 pp., Hb $4.95, Pb $1.45; SCMP, 1966, 13s 6d. This is the manifesto that called American Christendom to enter the secular city with joy. As one of the most highly praised and sharply condemned books of this decade, it is one which a Christian must know. While loaded with overstatement, weak argument,

and "wild theology," it is a germinal work that has forced all Christians to re-examine their concept of the secular and the meaning of the contemporary city.

2. GOODMAN, Paul and Percival, *Communitas: Means of Livelihood and Ways of Life,* RH, 1960, 248 pp., Pb $1.45. This book represents advanced reading with no particular Christian interpretation. It is a classic guide to the planning of cities that re-examines first principles. This is a book for the reader who wants an analysis of the past and alternatives for the future that moves beyond the popular level. A fresh, theoretical contribution to the art of building cities.

3. KENRICK, Bruce, *Come out the Wilderness,* HRP, 1962, 220 pp., Pb $1.60; CO, 25s. This is the dramatic story of the East Harlem Protestant Mission as told by one of its participants. Since the work of this enlarged parish has had a profound influence upon churches throughout this country and the world, any Christian concerned with social action and a strong witness to Christ in the inner city should know of the successes and failures of this project.

4. LEE, Robert, *Cities and Churches,* WP, 1962, 356 pp., Pb $3.50. This book provides an excellent sampling of the writings of some of the leading thinkers in the area of the urban church in the early sixties. While one wishes the book had a more virile theological base, the material it does present is highly useful.

5. LEE, Robert, *The Church and the Exploding Metropolis,* JKP, 1965, 125 pp., Pb $1.50. A slightly more advanced selection of seven essays dealing with theological, biblical, and sociological perspectives on the essence of the new urban America. In this small volume, these distinguished

authors raise a number of significant issues about the contemporary city and suggest possible paths of action.

6. LEIFFER, M. H., *The Effective City Church,* ABP, RE 2, 1961, 214 pp., $4.00. Originally published in 1949, this book has become a classic introduction to the church in the city. The book focuses upon the necessity for inter-relations between the church and its community. Part III provides some guidelines for a church's examination of its ministry to the needs of people in its particular area.

7. MOORE, R. E., and D. L. Day, *Urban Church Breakthrough,* HRP, 1966, 183 pp., $4.50. In contrast to those who foresee only the death of the parish, especially in the inner city, this book celebrates a new day for the urban church. While working with a minimal theological statement, the book fulfills the promise of its subtitle: *A Practical Guide for Sparking New Vitality in Today's Churches.*

8. *NORTON, P. L., *Church and Metropolis,* SP, 1964, 128 pp., $2.95. Norton is a Christian layman who is Professor of Planning in the Graduate School of New York University. With deep concern for the role of the Church in the city, he describes "the creation of community" as the contemporary challenge to the Christian world.

9. SCHALLER, L. E., *Community Organizations: Conflict and Reconciliation,* ABP, 1966, 176 pp., Pb $1.95. Written by a city planner who later was ordained into the Methodist ministry, this book contains an appraisal of one of the most controversial issues facing the church today: the church's participation in community organization. He provides a clear and readable background for understanding the present situation,

concluding with a set of twenty-five key questions that the churchman concerned about community organization should ask himself.

10. *SCHULLER, D. S., *The New Urban Society,* CON, 1966, 101 pp., Pb $1.00. An excellent short introduction, this book portrays the twentieth century urban sprawl and helps Christians see it and all its paralyzing problems under God's creating hand. The call is to proclaim Christ to the institutions and issues where the major decisions of life are made.

11. *SHIPPEY, F. A., *Protestantism in Suburban Life,* ABP, 1964, 221 pp., $4.50. Rejecting common stereotypes of suburbia, the author probes the role of the church in modern suburbs. This is *must* reading for any Christian interested in re-examining the role of the church in a suburban community. It provides useful outlines of the specific characteristics a church must have if it is to serve suburban society.

12. *STRINGFELLOW, William, *A Private and Public Faith,* WBE, 1962, 93 pp., Hb $3.00, Pb $1.45. The work of a brilliant Christian lawyer, this volume charges that religion in America is characteristically atheistic or agnostic. He calls Christians and their churches to a thoughtful reappraisal of their role in the world. In his own life, the author has demonstrated that the Church must be free to be poor in order to minister the gospel to the poor.

13. WEBBER, G. W., *God's Colony in Man's World,* ABP, 1960, 152 pp., Hb $2.75, Pb $1.25. Another "graduate" of the East Harlem Protestant parish describes the Church as essentially a colony in which men are strengthened for their task in the world. While not compromising the centrality of worship and the power of the gospel, he emphasizes the

Christian's vocation in the world as a witness to the work of the Holy Spirit.

14. *WINTER, Gibson, *The Suburban Captivity of the Churches,* MC, 1962, 209 pp., Hb $3.50, Pb $1.45; SCMP, 21s. This book more than any other, caused American churches to re-examine their role over against modern society. The author speaks a sharp judgment upon the institutional Church that has lost its mission. Renewal of the dying Church can be effected only as it repents of a false principle of exclusiveness which it has adopted. Winter advocates a ministry to sectors of the city as an attempt to renew its mission to all men. Indispensable for understanding the struggles of the contemporary urban church.

15. YOUNGER, G. D., *The Church in Urban Renewal,* LC, 1965, 216 pp., $4.50. A knowledgeable urban pastor addresses one of the most pressing problems facing the church today: how churches should relate themselves to urban renewal programs. The book is based on studies in depth, made in urban renewal areas in several of the largest cities in the U. S. The book contains a realistic appraisal of the situation and provides a guide to potential action.

5D. POVERTY AND HUNGER
James W. Reapsome

Books written from a specifically evangelical Christian viewpoint about poverty and hunger are hard to come by. Most of those in the following list are standard secular works on the subject. There are, of course, a growing number of books about Christian social concern, and these should be consulted for their references to poverty and hunger. Christians through the ages have been vitally involved in alleviating poverty and hunger ever since the first Christians at Antioch sent relief to the believers at Jerusa-

lem (Acts 11:29, 30). Therefore, the information contained in the following works should help to arouse a similar concern today, not only for those of the household of faith, but for all men.

1. *SIMON, Paul, *The Christian Encounters a Hungry World,* CON, 1966, 101 pp., Pb $1.00. A brief, elementary survey of hunger and poverty in the United States and the world. Shows what efforts have been made to feed the hungry. There are practical suggestions and group discussion questions about what Christians can do.

2. *BELGUM, H. J., *Poverty and the Christian Conscience,* APH, 1964, 32 pp. This is a leader's guide for a church study-action course based on six lessons. It covers attitudes toward poverty, scriptural relevance, what the Church has done in the past, conditions today and what the Church can do politically and socially. Brief but pertinent introduction to the subject.

3. SIMON, Arthur, *Faces of Poverty,* CON, 1966, 113 pp., $3.75. Profiles of the poor in a parish on Manhattan's lower east side. Personal, emotional, sympathetic, without more clamor for welfare. Pleads for help in the form of concrete economic proposals that would enable the poor to help themselves. A beginning to acquaint the smug with the terrors of poverty.

4. GARST, Jonathan, *No Need for Hunger,* RH, 1963, 182 pp., $3.95. Here is a professor-farmer-government official who believes farmers can feed the world, but they will need the help of the scientist, industrialist, and salesman. His own farming has made him a sought-after consultant in food problems in Latin America, India, and other parts of Asia. The race is between population

growth and food production. A nice, non-technical style.

5. MAY, Edgar, *The Wasted Americans*, HRP, 1964, 227 pp., $4.50; HRP, 1966, 250 pp., 36s. This newspaperman turned social worker has now become a government advisor on the subject. His account of actual cases and experiences in Buffalo created a nationwide stir at the time of publication. Highly interesting, non-professional approach, but terribly depressing.

6. *FULLER, R. H., and B. K. Rice, *Christianity and the Affluent Society*, WBE, 1967, 191 pp., Pb $2.45; HS, 1966, 192 pp., 30s. These men take a look at affluence in the context of eternity, two worlds, the Bible's and ours. It is essentially a critique of the premises, goals, and achievements of affluence. Though not directly related to poverty and hunger, the book obviously shows what a segment of the world—the United States and Great Britain—has at its disposal to meet human needs.

7. DUNNE, G. H., ed., *Poverty in Plenty*, PJK, 1964, 142 pp., $4.95. These are the seven addresses given at a conference on Poverty in Plenty: the Poor in our Affluent Society, at Georgetown University. Here you can find the causes of poverty, proposed economic, social, and political weapons to combat poverty, a description of federal anti-poverty programs and what is wrong with them, the role of education in the problem and a proposed solution: accelerate economic growth to combat unemployment. Conferences rarely present a balanced picture of a problem, but there are useful insights here.

8. McCORMACK, Arthur, ed., *Christian Responsibility and World Poverty*, NP, 1963, 314 pp. From a Roman Catholic viewpoint, both clerical and lay, a group of European experts write about the extent of poverty, underdeveloped areas, demographic studies, marriage and parenthood, the communist solution and the Christian solution. It is a call for both personal and corporate Christian responsibility and international justice. Specific needs are presented in Asia, Africa, and South America. Actual projects are described. The earth can feed its people, these contributors believe. Whether one agrees with the undergirding dogmatic Roman Catholic natural theology or not, the facts demanding a Christian response are devastating.

9. GORDON, M. S., ed., *Conference on Poverty in America*, CPC, 1965, 465 pp., Pb $2.95. This is a comprehensive volume of thirty learned, technical papers. For factual resources this is unsurpassed. It covers the nature of poverty in the United States, economic and social views; antipoverty programs, income distribution policies, education policies, full employment and the labor market, income maintenance, welfare and rehabilitation, urban renewal, rural poverty, the role of the poor and a program to combat poverty.

10. HARRINGTON, Michael, *The Other America: Poverty in the United States*, MC, 1962, $4.95; AP, 1964, 191 pp., Pb 95¢. This authoritative portrait of poverty in America has earned wide acclaim. Harrington describes what he calls the faces behind the statistics: unskilled workers, migrants, the aged, and the minority groups who make up this nation's forty to fifty million poor. He talks about the newness of contemporary poverty and why the "economic underground" is both socially and politically "invisible." His conclusion is an ethical proposition: in a nation that has the technology and wealth to eradicate poverty, it is an outrage and a scandal that there should be such social misery.

11. BORGSTROM, Georg, *The Hungry Planet*, MC, 1965, 487 pp., Hb $7.95, Pb $2.95; CM, 496 pp., 75s. For the more advanced reader this Michigan State University professor describes what it will take to feed the world adequately: double food production overnight. Perhaps this will happen in forty to fifty years, but by then world population will have doubled. His conclusions are the result of a twenty-year study. He holds scant hope for the future. Proposed solutions have been short-sighted, he feels. Not pleasant reading for an evening, but loaded with facts and figures.

12. THEOBALD, Robert, *The Challenge of Abundance*, CNP, 1961, 235 pp., Hb $4.50; NAL, 1962, Pb 60¢. Continuation of our old patterns of selfishness will ensure mankind's not surviving, says this author. The implications of economic and social revolutions show that some kind of world citizenship is not a dream but a necessity. From this kind of a political stance Theobald passionately tells about the problems of abundance and the relations between rich and poor nations.

5E. RACIAL CONFLICT AND WAR
Jaymes P. Morgan, Jr.
As the Church of Jesus Christ enters the last third of the century, it is apparent that the problems of racial conflict and war hold center stage for all of mankind. At the same time, these two issues together provide painful documentation of the degree to which the Church has been domesticated by the prevailing attitudes of the culture. The result of this acculturation is a wide-spread ignorance among Christians concerning the dimensions of both problems as well as massive confusion as to the proper response to the issues. Therefore, it becomes necessary to embark on an information-gathering process as well as undertaking the task of Christian interpretation and evaluation. The materials suggested are designed both to provide information and to assist in evaluation.

1. BAINTON, R. H., *Christian Attitudes Toward War and Peace*, ABP, 1960, 299 pp., Pb $2.25; HS, 1961, 25s. A substantial discussion of the origins and adaptations of the various Christian responses to the problem of war—pacifism, the ethic of the just war and the crusade—together with a critical evaluation calling for a recovery of the ethic of pacifism.

2. CADOUX, C. J., *The Early Church and the World*, TTC, 1925, 675 pp., $8.00; TTC, 32s. A magisterial discussion by periods of the attitudes of the Church of the first three centuries toward the major social questions, including slavery and war, providing helpful background material for those concerned to address the social issues from a biblical perspective.

3. FRANKLIN, J. H., *From Slavery to Freedom*, AAK, ED 3, 1967, 639 pp., $7.50. The classic history of the Negro peoples, describing the African roots, the role of the black man in the New World, the character of slavery, the struggle for freedom both from slavery and the subsequent second-class citizenship and an inventory of progress to date.

4. *HAMILTON, Michael, ed., *The Vietnam War: Christian Perspectives*, WBE, 1967, Hb $3.50, Pb $1.65. Most of the essays included were presented at a symposium at the Washington Cathedral by leading scholars and theologians. In discussing the ethical and moral implications of U.S. involvement in Vietnam, a broad range of political, ethical, and doctrinal positions are represented.

5. *HASELDEN, Kyle, *Mandate for White Christians,* JKP, 1966, 127 pp., $3.00. Editor of the *Christian Century* asks and answers some pointed questions. Why does not the Church do something about the racial crisis? Why is there such a great gulf between what Christians say and what they do? Why, despite the ferment of racial activity among the Church's leaders, are so few individual white Christians involved?

6. HERSHBERGER, G. F., *War, Peace and Nonresistance,* HE, RE, 1953, 375 pp., $3.50. A comprehensive discussion of the problem of military conflict from a Mennonite peace perspective, tracing the history of warfare and non-resistance, distinguishing Christian non-resistance from modern pacifism and defending the contribution of Christian non-resistance to society. See also, Jean Lasserre, *War and the Gospel,* HE, 1962, 245 pp., $3.75; JC, 15s.

7. *KELSEY, G. D., *Racism and the Christian Understanding of Man,* CSS, 1965, 178 pp., Hb $4.50, Pb $2.95. In the finest theological discussion of the problem of racism available, a Negro professor of Christian ethics engages in serious analysis of the theological assumptions implicit in racism, demonstrating the genocidal logic of racism and the fundamentally idolatrous character of racial pride and prejudice.

8. *KING, M. L., Jr., *Where Do We Go from Here: Chaos or Community?* HRP, 1967, 209 pp., Hb $4.95; BP, Pb $1.95. Dr. King's last book, eloquently posing the question anew as to whether the black man shall be America's liability or her opportunity, calling for a worldwide fellowship acknowledging our common humanity.

9. LAURENTI, Luigi, *Property Values and Race,* UOCP, 1960, 256 pp.,

$6.00. The result of massive studies of neighborhood change in seven major cities, this the authoritative discussion of the relationship of property value to race demonstrates that the idea that racial change is responsible for the loss in property values is simply a red herring hiding the tracks of the real villain, white prejudice, and panic selling.

10. LONG, E. L., Jr., *War and Conscience in America,* WP, 1968, 130 pp., Pb $1.65. A brief and readable discussion of the alternatives which conscience faces in its response to military conflict, outlining the various forms of conscientious participation and religious opposition, together with a call for calm discussion and mutual respect among those concerned.

11. *MONTAGU, Ashley, *Man's Most Dangerous Myth: The Fallacy of Race,* TWPC, RE 4, 1964, 499 pp., Hb $7.50; TWPC, 1965, Pb $2.65. This classic analysis of the concept of race by the author of the UNESCO statement on race rescues the term from the mythology with which it is so often cluttered and thoroughly discredits the thesis of racial superiority. It includes an exhaustive bibliography for further reference.

12. PARSONS, Talcott, and K. B. Clerk, eds., *The Negro American,* HM, 1966, 781 pp., Hb $9.50; BP, Pb $3.95. Gunnar Myrdal's *An American Dilemma,* 2 V., MH, 1964, 324 pp., Pb $3.45 each, revisited twenty years later, this is the comprehensive analysis of the condition of the American Negro, documenting both the social and the personal effects of racism and outlining prospects and suggestions for the resolution of the American dilemma, by a large company of eminently qualified contributors.

13. RAMSEY, Paul, *War and the Christian Conscience,* DUP, 1961,

331 pp., $6.00. An eminently rational defender of the ethic of the just war engages in exhaustive—and sometimes exhausting—discussion of the theory of the just war, both in its classic and contemporary expressions, and in an analysis of the question whether modern war—including thermo-nuclear conflict—can be conducted justly.

14. REIMERS, D. M., *White Protestantism and the Negro,* OUP, 1965, 236 pp., $5.00; OUP, 1966, 248 pp., 35s. A relatively brief history of the attitudes of the Protestant Churches toward the black man as a person and as a "problem" from before the Civil War to the present, documenting the degree to which churches tend to become social institutions dominated by cultural commitments.

15. **Report of the National Advisory Commission on Civil Disorders,* BAB, 1968, 609 pp., Pb $1.25. The exhaustive analysis by the President's Commission of the events of the 1967 urban riots in the United States and their underlying causes, with recommendations for the alleviation of the tension which is rapidly creating a nation of two separate societies. In calm, dignified prose, the Report uncovers the sickness that could destroy a nation.

16. *SILBERMAN, C. E., *Crisis in Black and White,* RH, 1964, 370 pp., Hb $5.95, Pb $1.95; CAPE, 1965, 384 pp., 30s. The most readable introduction to the problem of racial conflict in the United States, by an editor of Fortune magazine who is diligently fair in his analysis.

17. SIMPSON, G. E., and J. M. Yinger, *Racial and Cultural Minorities,* HRP, ED 3, 1965, 582 pp., $9.50. A massive and scholarly attempt to synthesize the contributions of the scores of studies dealing with prejudice, discrimination, and the role of racial and cultural minorities in American society, relating these materials to the developing sciences of human behavior.

18. TILSON, C. E., *Segregation and the Bible,* ABP, 1958, 176 pp., Hb $2.50, Pb $1.75. A brief, readable attempt to discuss whether the Bible demands segregation or gives precedents for the practice and to outline the implications of the biblical understanding of creation and redemption for the issue of segregation, concluding that the practice has no support in Holy Scriptures. See also, T. B. Maston, *The Bible and Race,* BR, 1959, 117 pp., $2.50; J. O. Buswell, III, *Slavery, Segregation and Scripture,* WBE, 1963, 101 pp., $2.50.

19. *WASHINGTON, J. R., Jr., *Black Religion: The Negro and Christianity in the United States,* BP, 1964, 308 pp., Hb $5.00, Pb $2.45. A searing and controversial indictment of the expression of the Christian faith as it is found in the black churches of America, designating it as atheological, simplex, and irrelevant to the world in which the Church is called to serve. This should be required reading for all who think that the Negro should be ministered to by "his own" churches.

5F. FELLOWSHIP AND GROUP DYNAMICS
Ivan J. Fahs
Group dynamics is one of those areas of interest that is more often applied to various groups than theoretically written about. But when the subject is treated, it is often in the "how-to-do-it" pamphlets, "what-we-did" case studies, or "guides" to group discussion. While these are useful, only samples are included in this array of publications because of their brevity and narrow scope.

As a social-psychological phenomenon, group dynamics is analyzed by psychologists, and uniformly their academic treatment of the subject is excellent. However, these academics are not likely to use the term group dynamics *since the label has a "Madison Avenue" flavor professors studiously avoid; their nomenclature is more likely to include "syntality," "social self," "sociometry," "centrality," and "cognitive dissonance". Individuals motivated to learn more will find perceptive analyses of these concepts in professional journals.*

The sources cited here may be the beginning point for a better understanding of how persons act in groups.

1. *LITTLE, Sara, Learning Together in the Christian Fellowship,* JKP, 1956, 104 pp., Pb $1.25. A description that would serve as a good introduction to the field of group dynamics, especially as it applies to Christian groups. Consideration given to the place of the Bible and Christian fellowship in a group. Various reliable sources pulled together in a readable, orderly manner.

2. TRECKER, A. R. and H. S., *How to Work With Groups,* ASP, 1952, 167 pp., $3.50. Written primarily for the adult leader who is just beginning some leadership experiences. A how-to-do-it book, helping one get started as a president, committee member, fund raiser, publicity director. Appendix has information on parliamentary law.

3. UTTERBACK, W. E., *Group Thinking and Conference Leadership,* HRW, RE, 1964, 244 pp., Hb $6.50, Pb 50¢. A straightforward, easily comprehended treatment of techniques of discussion including radio and television discussion, discussion in the classroom, the business conference, and large group discussion. Case problems included in the appendix.

4. *WHYTE, W. H., Jr., *The Organization Man,* SS, 1956, 429 pp., $5.95; DC, 1957, 417 pp., Pb $1.75; PE, 1956, 429 pp., Hb 25s, Pb 5s. Not strictly a book about group dynamics but thunderous with implications to the structure of a group. What happens to an individual who has no personal identity apart from that which the organization gives him? A classical warning against overstructuring groups.

5. THELEN, H. A., *Dynamics of Groups at Work,* UCP, 1963, 379 pp., Hb $6.75, Pb $2.45; PB, 1954, 379 pp., 50s; UCP, 1954, 379 pp., Pb 17s. Useful suggestions for organizer, leader, and member of group are given in the following areas: citizen action, education, faculty self-training, administration and management, human relations, and public meetings. Concepts such as needs of group members and leadership development are presented as background.

6. *GOLDING, William, *Lord of the Flies,* COM, 1962, $5.75; CA, 1959, Pb $1.25; FF, 1954, 248 pp., 18s; MC, 1966, Pb 4s 6d. A thought-provoking literary portrayal of what happens to a group left without an adult world to "guide." Raises the questions of individual freedom and group structure. Excellent for discussion of group dynamics.

7. *GORDON, Thomas, *Group-Centered Leadership: A Way of Releasing the Creative Power of Groups,* HM, 1956, 366 pp., $6.95; MC, 1966, 298 pp., Pb 4s 6d; FF, 1966, Pb 2s 6d. Well-written with many perceptive insights into the phenomena of leadership and groups. Makes use of case studies from a variety of settings. Probably one of the best single sources to look at for an understanding of group dynamics. Has inspirational value.

8. LIFTON, W. M., *Working With Groups; Group Process and Individual Growth,* JW, ED 2, 1966, 238 pp., $6.95; JW, 302 pp., 56s. Consideration given to typical problems in group process and group techniques applied. The group process is documented in diary form with interpretive comments added. Each section has a carefully developed bibliography worth referring to.

9. CARTWRIGHT, Dorwin, and Alvin Zander, eds., *Group Dynamics; Research and Theory,* HRP, ED 2, 1960, 826 pp., $10.50; TA, ED 2, 1961, 654 pp., 45s. A symposium of articles by most of the leaders in the field. Consideration given to group cohesiveness, group pressures and group standards, individual motives and group goals, leadership and group performance, and the structural properties of groups.

10. HARE, A. P., E. F. Borgatta, and R. F. Bales, *Small Groups; Studies in Social Interaction,* AAK, RE, 1965, 666 pp., $7.95. A symposium of articles including historical and theoretical background, the individual in social situations, and the group as a system of social interaction. Annotated bibliography included.

11. HOPKINS, T. K., *The Exercise of Influence in Small Groups,* BEP, 1964, 205 pp., $6.50. A scholarly treatment small groups theory with examples taken from discussion and dormitory groups. Concepts discussed and tested. Special section on the rank-influence process.

12. THIBAUT, J. W., and H. W. Kelley, *The Social Psychology of Groups,* JW, 1959, 313 pp., $7.95. No doubt the most complex of the books in this section, but done in the best tradition of scholarship. Nearly half the book is concerned with dyadic relationships—relations between two persons. Of great importance to theory and practice of small groups.

section 6

DEFENSE OF THE FAITH

6. DEFENSE OF THE FAITH: INTRODUCTION
Harold Lindsell

Christianity is not, never was, and never will be free from attack. It is both biblical and logical for Christians to offer a defense of their faith. Peter says: "Always be prepared to make a defense to any one who calls you to account for the hope that is in you . . ." (I Peter 3:15, RSV). To defend the Christian faith is to engage in the task of apologetics, which may be defined as a systematic statement of the basic beliefs of Christianity with the implications and rational grounds for those beliefs. Apologetics deals especially with these issues and problems that arise when the Christian faith clashes with the prevailing intellectual climate.

Today Christianity is under assault on every hand. In part this is a result of new knowledge in astronomy, biology, history, sociology, and philosophy. In addition, values have shifted profoundly and a communications gap of gigantic proportions has arisen. Amid the clamor of a new age, men are increasingly aware of the fact that science and technology are producing more problems than they solve, and learned men are looking for some unifying force, some ethical and moral principles that can bind things together. This does not mean that Christianity is an enemy of true knowledge. Rather, it welcomes such knowledge and should do all that it can to incorporate this knowledge into the apologetic framework of the faith.

The defense of the Christian faith has a twofold purpose. First, it is essential for the Christian himself to develop a consciously thought-through world and life view. Such a coherent philosophy will do as much for him as for others. He needs to understand things. In turn, understanding becomes the basis for concrete action. Men act on what they believe. Secondly, the Christian faith must be vindicated against those who oppose it, in order to demonstrate the inadequacy of erroneous notions and to direct men toward Christianity.

Christianity belongs in the marketplace and must always compete for the allegiances of men. In order to challenge other viewpoints and to defend his own, the Christian must fearlessly face all branches of human learning; first to understand them, then to relate them to Christian standpoints, and finally, to establish the superiority of Christianity over its opponents.

6A. GENERAL
Gordon R. Lewis

Christians claim: (1) that a loving Lord of history lives today, (2) that God was in Christ reconciling fallen man to himself, and (3) that the Bible is God's Word to a needy world. Theology and related disciplines develop the implications of these presuppositions. Apologetics defends them over against non-Christian truth-claims. Some Christians doubt that they should prepare an answer (apologian, I Peter 3:15) for those who question their basic beliefs.

The general biblical support for an apologetic is well stated by F. F. Bruce's work, The Defence of the Gospel in the New Testament, WBE, 1965, 105 pp., Pb $1.25; Apostolic Defence of the Gospel, TP, 1959, 96 pp., 3s 6d. For a more extended consideration of Paul's most significant defense before the educated Athenians (Acts 17) see the four-part series "Gospel on Campus," HIS, October, 1966—January, 1967. In accord with biblical precedent the following books do more than expound the faith, in one way or another they defend it. Care has been taken to include representatives of different apologetic approaches.

1. *LITTLE, Paul E., *Know Why You Believe,* IVP, RE, 1968, 120 pp., $1.25. A readable restatement of classical answers to basic questions about God, Christ, his resurrection, the reliability of the Bible, miracles, science, the problem of evil, and other religious and Christian experiences. See also, his *How to Give Away Your Faith,* IVP, 1966, Chapter 5, "Why We Believe," pp. 63-81, $3.50, for the most useful single chapter in defense of Christianity.

2. PHILLIPS, J. B., *The Ring of Truth,* MC, 1967, 125 pp., $2.95; HS, 96 pp., 3s 6d. Having spent the best years of his life in close and constant contact with the New Testament, the translator decided to speak out for the truth revealed in and through Jesus Christ. "I found," he says, "that once one gets to grips with the actual stuff of the New Testament its vitality is astonishing . . . here was I confronted by eternal truths which my soul, however reluctantly, felt bound to accept."

3. GROUNDS, V. C., *The Reason for Our Hope,* MP, 1945, 128 pp., Pb 39¢. Effective radio addresses given in the aftermath of the second World War on such subjects as Creation or Chance? Liar, Lunatic, or Lord of All? Prophetic Proof, the Why of War and Redemption Versus Religion, by the president of Conservative Baptist Theological Seminary.

4. SHORT, A. R., *Why Believe?* IVP, 1958, 112 pp., $1.25; TP, 96 pp., 3s 6d. Chapters on belief in God, Christ, the Bible, man's relation to God, Christ's death, and the way to faith. The medical doctor seeks to harmonize science and Scripture in *Modern Discovery and the Bible,* IVP, 1949, 244 pp., 5s. (OoP)

5. *PIKE, K. L., *With Heart and Mind,* WBE, 1962, 140 pp., Pb $1.95. Although stressing limitations and relativities of logical processes, the professor of linguistics nevertheless maintains that "fruitful discourse in science or theology requires us to believe that *within* the contexts of normal discourse *there are some true statements.* Man *must* sometimes act as if he believed it—or die." See also, *Stir-Change-Create,* WBE, 1967, 164 pp., $2.65.

6. BOWMAN, Allen, *Is the Bible True?* FRP, 1965, 189 pp., $3.95; PI, 1966, 192 pp., 17s 6d. Succinct, well-written chapters by a professor of history and political science arguing that the Bible's claims for itself are valid, its promises reliable, its ethics sound, its spiritual remedy effective, its prophecies reliable, its philosophy of origins reasonable, and its history credible.

7. *PINNOCK, C. H., *Set Forth Your Case,* CP, 1967, 94 pp., Pb $1.50. A forthright challenge of the popular notion that truth about God and Christianity is totally non-rational and unverifiable. Non-Christian presuppositions can be changed by setting forth Christian claims, showing their correlation with evidence which the Holy Spirit attests.

8. CLOSE, H. T., *Reasons for Our Faith,* JKP, 1962, 103 pp., $1.45. A brief introduction to varied apologetic approaches starting with miracles, nature, religious experience, man's needs, and God himself. Includes questions and suggested readings.

9. CLARK, G. H., et al., *Can I Trust My Bible?* MP, 1963, 190 pp., $3.50. Eight evangelical scholars answer questions about miracles, science, the canon, fulfilled prophecy, the reliability of the biblical text, the accuracy of biblical history, and the basis of belief in inspiration.

10. *MACHEN, J. G., Christianity and Liberalism,* WBE, 1964, 189 pp., Pb $1.75; VP, 200 pp., 12s 6d. A perceptive analysis with continued relevance for distinguishing authentic Christianity from liberal religions. Against the Bible writers' alleged dependence upon mystery religions see Machen's *The Origin of Paul's Religion,* Ri, WBE, 1967, 189 pp., $1.95. On the relation of faith to knowledge see Machen's *What is Faith?* WBE, RE, 1962, 250 pp., Pb $1.95.

11. *LEWIS, C. S., Mere Christianity,* MC, 1952, 175 pp., Hb $3.50, Pb $1.25; BLES, 1952, 178 pp., 12s 6d; CO, 1955, 192 pp., Pb 3s 6d. Broadcast talks by late Oxford professor taking right and wrong as a clue to the meaning of the universe. A defense of Christian beliefs and Christian behavior as well as the doctrine of the trinity. See also, *The Problem of Pain,* MC, 1948, 148 pp., Hb $3.95, Pb 95¢; BLES, 1940, 148 pp., 7s 6d; and *Miracles,* MC, 1948, 220 pp., $3.00; MC, 1947, Pb 95¢; BLES, 1947, Hb 13s 6d; CO, 1960, 192 pp., Pb 2s 6d.

12. GUILLEBAUD, H. E., *Some Moral Difficulties of the Bible,* TP, 1941, 208 pp., 5s. (OoP) Discussions of the origin of sin, suffering, the choice of Israel, predestination, God's wrath and jealousy, imprecatory psalms, the cursing of the fig tree, and other New Testament problems. See also, *Why the Cross?* IVP, 1946, 208 pp., Pb $1.50; TP, ED 2, Hb 7s 6d, Pb 6s. Discusses whether a substitutionary atonement is immoral, incredible, or Christian.

13. *GERSTNER, J. H., Reasons for Faith,* HRP, 1960, 245 pp., Hb $2.95; BBH, 1966, Pb $1.95; HRP, 1960, 28s. A popular statement of traditional arguments for the existence of God. The case for Christianity moves from support for the Bible as sound history to the deity of Jesus Christ and from Christ's authority to the Bible as the inspired Word of God. See also, S. C. Neill, *Christian Faith Today,* PE, 1955, 272 pp., Pb 3s 6d. (OoP)

14. HAMILTON, F. E., *The Basis of Christian Faith: A Modern Defense of the Christian Religion,* HRP, RE, 1964, 364 pp., $5.00. The prominent contribution of this book is its extensive treatment of the Bible's remarkable ethic, unity, historical accuracy, preservation, and fulfilled prophecy. The only adequate cause of these biblical phenomena, Hamilton argues, is supernatural inspiration.

15. CARNELL, E. J., *An Introduction to Christian Apologetics,* WBE, RE, 1955, 379 pp., $5.00. An assertion about the triune God or biblical truth is a hypothesis to be confirmed or disconfirmed, according to the late professor of apologetics. The test of true hypotheses is their consistency and coherence with facts. The Christian hypothesis is not self-contradictory and answers to affairs of the heart (internal experience) and of history (external experience). So Christianity is true and worthy of our trust. See also, T. C. Hammond, *Reasoning Faith: An Introduction to Christian Apologetics,* TP, 1943, 276 pp. (OoP)

16. CARNELL, E. J., *A Philosophy of the Christian Religion,* WBE, 1952, 523 pp., $5.00. (OoP) The Christian hypothesis is to be accepted, according to the thesis of this work, because it supplies the most satisfying values for which to live. Seek first the kingdom of God and his righteousness and all other values will be added—pleasures, economic needs, science, logic, service of fellow men, forgiveness, and reconciliation. Christianity alone brings fulfillment to the complete person.

17. CARNELL, E. J., *Christian Commitment: An Apologetic,* WBE, 1957, 314 pp., $5.00. The Christian hypothesis fits our moral experience as persons. God is the indispensable condition of our dignity, rights, and freedom. But we offend God when we fail to respect the dignity and rights of others. How can a man who violates the laws of justice, consideration, and love be just before God? Only Christianity answers that question. The Christian doctrine of Christ's atonement alone meets man's moral need.

18. *CARNELL, E. J., *The Kingdom of Love and the Pride of Life,* WBE, 1960, 164 pp., $3.50. (OoP) The Christian hypothesis best meets human psychological needs. The Bible calls for utter honesty and humility before God. Then believers in Christ may accept themselves as accepted of God. The Holy Spirit strengthens the inner man to bear misunderstanding in patience and hope. Destructive anxiety can be replaced by constructive service to others. Christians need not prove themselves all the time, but leave the work of salvation to God. Acceptance of Christianity brings amazing resources for psychological health.

19. RAMM, Bernard, *Protestant Christian Evidences,* MP, 1954, 252 pp., $3.95. The truth of Christianity is verified, Ramm argues, by fulfilled prophecy, miracles, the supernatural character of its founder, Christ's resurrection, Christian experience, and the supernatural character of the Bible.

20. RAMM, Bernard, *Varieties of Christian Apologetics,* WBE, 1961, 199 pp., $4.95. Valuable for comparing and contrasting the apologetic approaches of classical Christian thinkers on some of the perennial problems in the field: the nature of revelation, faith and philosophical

reasoning, the effects of sin, common ground, and the kind of certainty possible.

21. *CLARK, G. H., *A Christian View of Men and Things,* WBE, 1952, 325 pp., $2.45. (OoP) Arguing that Christianity is more consistent than any alternative world-view, Clark sketches a Christian philosophy of history, politics, ethics, science, and religion. He also develops a rational epistemology.

22. ORR, James, *The Christian View of God and the World,* WBE, 1947, 480 pp., $3.50. (OoP) This is an old classic which presents an evangelical Christian world-view. In spite of its age, it is relevant and useful.

23. DeBOER, Cecil, *Responsible Protestantism,* WBE, 1957, 247 pp. (OoP) A sensitive apologetic by a professional philosopher discusses the relevancy of Christian faith in the secular society. Covering a variety of subjects including science, ethics, politics, ecumenicity, labor union education, and race problems, the author brings to bear immediacy and directness upon these timely topics.

24. VAN TIL, Cornelius, *The Defence of the Faith,* PRPC, 1955, 436 pp., $3.00. The primary source of Van Til's thought to date, this book contains a summation of the theology he seeks to defend as professor of apologetics. He considers the point of contact with non-Christians, the problem of method, authority and reason, and the significance of common grace. Over two hundred pages reply to the critics of this authoritarian apologetic.

25. BARRETT, E. E., *A Christian Perspective of Knowing,* BP, 1965, 224 pp., $3.95. Christianity is held to be true, not so much on grounds of logical consistency or factual adequacy, but personal, mystical experi-

ence by the professor of philosophy and religion at Olivet Nazarene College. He seeks to develop a "Christian mysticism."

26. BUSWELL, J. O., *A Christian View of Being and Knowing*, WBE, 1960, 214 pp., $3.50. (OoP) Subtitled "An Introduction to Philosophy," this book employs an inductive method of knowing and defends a substantial soul as distinct from the body and brain.

27. FREEMAN, D. H., *A Philosophical Study of Religion*, PRPC, 1964, 270 pp., $5.00. A professor of philosophy (University of Rhode Island) examines the nature of religion, religions claiming revelation and particularly Christian revelation-claims for the Bible in view of science, the problem of evil, and personal testimony.

28. HACKETT, S. C., *The Resurrection of Theism: Prolegommena to Christian Apology*, MP, 1957, 381 pp., $5.00. (OoP) A closely reasoned defense of traditional arguments for the existence of God by a Wheaton College philosophy professor. Develops a theory of knowledge considered foundational to apologetic endeavors called rational empiricism.

29. *SCHAEFFER, F. A., *Escape from Reason*, IVP, 1968, 96 pp., Pb $1.25; TP, Pb 3s 6d. A perceptive challenge to a non-rational fantasy of absurd experience, drugs, and pornography tracing the trends in literature, art, music, movies, television, and the theater. The popular lecturer in Europe and the United States effectively presents Christianity as the most live option to make sense of life. See also, *The God Who Is There*, HS, 1968, Pb 15s; IVP, 1968, 194 pp., Hb $4.50, Pb $2.50.

6B. PHILOSOPHY
Arthur F. Holmes
The extent and quality of Christian

involvement in philosophy is often underestimated. Not only in medieval but also in modern times, some of the major philosophers of the West were either Christian or else strongly motivated by Christian ideas and values. This is the case with Bacon, Locke, Berkeley, Leibnitz and to some extent also Descartes and Kant. Today, involvement in philosophy is just as urgent if not always as distinguished.

The literature cited below ranges from studies of past relationships of Christianity and philosophy to current attempts to develop theistic perspectives in such branches of the discipline as philosophy of religion, metaphysics, epistemology, philosophy of science, and ethics. A considerable Roman Catholic literature on the subject has, for reasons of space, been omitted.

Christianity and Philosophy
1. *HOLMES, A. F., *Christianity and Philosophy*, IVP, 1960, 39 pp., Pb 95¢; TP, 1964, 28 pp., Pb 2s 6d. A brief and introductory attempt to explore the relationship between philosophy and the Christian faith on the basis of their respective definitions.

2. CASSERLEY, J. V., *The Christian in Philosophy*, CSS, 1951, 266 pp.; FF, 1949. (OoP) This book has two parts: the first an analysis of the historical role of Christianity in Western philosophy, the second an exposition of the present situation facing Christian thinkers. The problems of subjectivity and individuality are stressed. The book is readable, provocative, and rewarding; one of the best works in this area.

3. GILSON, Etienne, *Reason and Revelation in the Middle Ages*, CSS, 1938, 114 pp., $1.25. (OoP) A classic survey of major patristic and medieval views of the relation of revelation and reason, that brings the prob-

lem into focus and maps the major alternatives.

4. *NEDONCELLE, Maurice, *Is There a Christian Philosophy?* HAW, 1960, 154 pp., $3.95; BO, 160 pp., 9s 6d. This book summarizes an important discussion begun in France in the early 1930's that is of perennial concern to both Catholic and Protestant thinkers. It is partly historical and partly constructive; the best introduction to the subject available in English translation.

5. *DOOYEWEERD, Herman, *In the Twilight of Western Thought,* PRPC, 1960, 195 pp., Hb $2.50, Pb $1.75. A Dutch thinker, influential in Reformed circles for his Christian philosophy of divinely ordained law spheres, presents a series of lectures tracing the plight of Western philosophy to its apostate roots. Christian philosophy is rooted in the regenerate heart and grounded in the sovereignty of a creator—and redeemer—God. Probably the most readable and introductory of Dooyeweerd's works.

Christian Perspectives

6. CARNELL, E. J., *A Philosophy of the Christian Religion,* WBE, 1954, 523 pp., $5.00. A leading American evangelical thinker takes stock of varied religious and pseudo-religious options, from Marxism and hedonism to Catholicism and Kierkegaard. The book is written for the beginning student and in a persuasive manner. It is outdated in its omission of recent existentialist and post-positivist analysis.

7. *CLARK, G. H., *A Christian View of Man and Things,* WBE, 1952, 325 pp., $2.95. (OoP) A Christian world and life view is spelled out in a range of areas: science, ethics, politics, religion, epistemology. The author establishes his conclusions by setting their logical coherence in contrast to the inconsistencies of conflicting views.

It is introductory; fruitful reading regardless of one's attitude to particular positions adopted.

8. CLARK, G. H., *Religion, Reason, and Revelation,* PRPC, 1961, 241 pp., $3.75. A carefully argued attempt to refute current and traditional philosophies of knowledge, religion, and morality, and to present strongly Calvinistic theology as the only remaining alternative.

9. FREEMAN, D. H., *A Philosophical Study of Religion,* CP, 1964, 270 pp., $3.75. An introduction to the philosophy of religion which argues that while religion in general may be the projection of man's hopes and illusions, Christianity is different. God's self-revelation gives it the quality of objective truth.

10. JOAD, C. E., *The Recovery of Belief,* HHP, 1952, 250 pp., $3.50; FF, 1952, 18s. A British philosopher, formerly an agnostic, gives a philosophical *apologia* for his newly-found Christian faith. The decisive issue, originally, for his unbelief and subsequently for his belief, was the problem of evil. Competent but non-technical.

11. YOUNG, W. C., *A Christian Approach to Philosophy,* BBH, 1954, 252 pp., $4.00. A basic introduction defining the classic philosophical problems and positions, with an attempt to indicate directions for conservative Christian thought.

12. *FARRER, Austin, *Faith and Speculation,* NYUP, 1967, 175 pp., $5.00; ACB, 1967, 12s 6d. A distinguished British philosopher brings together his developing thought of twenty-five years in metaphysical theology. He attempts to show the conceivability of divine action in the world, in terms of the paradox of double agency, divine and creaturely, in the three fields of grace, nature,

and history. The relation of the created act to the transcendent Creator, he holds, remains indefinable, but this is neither an obstacle to faith nor a scandal to reason.

13. TRESMONTANT, Claude, *The Origins of Christian Philosophy,* HAW, 1963, 123 pp., $3.95; BO, 128 pp., 9s 6d. A Catholic writer explores the metaphysical implications of the biblical ideas of creation and man, as these were developed in the patristic period.

14. FOSTER, M. B., "The Christian Doctrine of Creation and the Rise of Modern Natural Science," *Mind,* 43 (1934), 446; 44 (1935), 439; 45 (1936), 1. This is a series of articles arguing that modern science, and consequently, early modern philosophy, are rooted in the contingency and rationality of nature, a basis that must be traced to Christian confidence in the Creator.

15. GILSON, Etienne, *The Spirit of Medieval Philosophy,* CSS, 1936, 490 pp., $3.95. Gilson attempts to show the possibility of Christian philosophy by the transformation of Greek ideas in medieval thought. A classic study, topically arranged, that is essential to the student who wants to explore the philosophical implications of Christian belief. Somewhat technical but superbly written.

16. KRONER, Richard, *Speculation in Pre-Christian Philosophy,* WP, 1956, 251 pp. (OoP); *Speculation and Revelation in the Age of Christian Philosophy,* WP, 1959, 269 pp., (OoP); *Speculation and Revelation in Modern Philosophy,* WP, 1961, 361 pp. (OoP) This trilogy explores the historical interrelation of reason and revelation. The concept of revelation is more existential than propositional, but the series merits the attention of the serious student of philosophic history. It makes good reading, sometimes entertaining, although it is at times obviously interpretive.

17. TEMPLE, William, *Mens Creatrix,* SM, 1917, 367 pp., Hb $6.00, Pb $2.25; MC, 1917, 21s; and *Nature, Man and God,* SM, 1934, 530 pp., $6.75; MC, 35s. A classic attempt to develop Christian theism as a kind of evolutionary idealism, by a former Archbishop of Canterbury. The author rejects Descartes' subjectivism as history's *grand faux pas,* and opts for a more dialectical method. The chapters on epistemology and on freedom are especially rewarding, but the theology is more immanentistic than many readers will like.

18. TENNANT, F. R., *Philosophical Theology,* V. 2, 1928, CAUP. (OoP) The author develops an extended teleological argument for the existence of God, based on the possibility of scientific knowledge, of aesthetic and moral experience, etc. This is the classic reformulation from the days of realistic epistemology and still has value.

19. BENDALL, Kent, and Frederick Ferré, *Exploring the Logic of Faith,* ASP, 1962, 219 pp., $2.25. Conversations exploring the logical meaning and truth-criteria of Christian belief. Cast in the spirit of linguistic analysis, they provide an informal and highly readable basis for further discussion.

20. PLANTINGA, Alvin, *God and Other Minds,* CUP, 1967, 277 pp., $8.50. An evangelical thinker, highly respected for his competence as a philosophical analyst, presents essays on the existence of God, on evil and freedom, and on the problem of other minds. Somewhat technical, and written in contemporary philosophic style, it is an outstanding piece of work from anyone's viewpoint.

21. McDONALD, H. D., *I and He,* EP, 1966, 123 pp., 16s. An extension of the old moral argument towards a philosophical theology. We can understand the God of grace on the basis of our moral self-knowledge. The author is well read and alert to contemporary philosophy.

22. RAMSEY, I. T., ed., *Christian Ethics and Contemporary Philosophy,* MC, 1966, $7.95; SCMP, 396 pp., 50s. An impressive collection of essays on the relation between religion and ethics, this volume involves the reader in a vigorous and informative dialogue between Christian and non-Christian philosophers, both of whom are about as diverse in their own beliefs as could be. For students of contemporary ethical theory, it is likely to be a fruitful study.

The Logic of Religious Belief

23. HICK, John, ed., *The Existence of God,* MC, 1964, 298 pp., Pb $1.95; CM, Pb 15s. This is a book of readings, classical and contemporary, on the theistic arguments. It contains the important source materials on this topic.

24. FERRÉ, Frederick, *Language, Logic and God,* HRP, 1961, 184 pp., $3.50; ES, 1962, 192 pp., 15s. A comprehensive discussion of the religious language problem, its development since the decline of logical positivism and the paths taken by the discussion of the 1950's. Ferré's own proposals draw together strains of thought that contribute to evangelical thought on the subject. Somewhat technical but very rewarding.

25. HERDERN, William, *Speaking of God,* MC, 1964, 209 pp., $4.95; EP, 224 pp., 21s. A theologian surveys the philosophic issue and articulates his point of view on the religious language problem. He insists on including both personal language (I-Thou) and the language of mystery in religious language, but criticizes Buber and others for excluding cognitive propositions from personal discourse. The book is introductory, yet is one of the more helpful items on this subject.

26. FOSTER, M. B., *Mystery and Philosophy,* AL, 1957, 96 pp., $2.75; SCMP, 12s 6d. The author underscores the concept of mystery, neglected in both analytic and rationalistic philosophy, as an essential ingredient of both religion and life.

27. MITCHELL, Basil, ed., *Faith and Logic,* HP, 1958, $4.00; AU, 1957, 230 pp., 21s. A group of Anglican philosophers and theologians present a collection of essays arising from regular discussions of changes in philosophy and their relation to theology. The essays touch religious language, theological method, and the logic of such concepts as revelation, the soul, grace, and "we."

28. RAMSEY, I. T., ed., *Prospect for Metaphysics,* PL, 1961, 240 pp., $6.00; AU, 25s. A collection of essays by Christian philosophers of varied persuasion regarding the role of metaphysics and its relation to religion in the context of ordinary language analysis.

29. TOULMIN, Stephen, et al., *Metaphysical Beliefs,* SCMP, 1957, 216 pp. (OoP) Three essays on three aspects of the logic of contemporary metaphysics, one in relation to scientific theory, one on poetic imagery and religious belief, one on the verification of religious belief. Together they afford fresh ways of looking at the relation between science, metaphysics, and religion; ways that are influential and provocative if not wholly acceptable.

30. DILLERY, Frank, *Metaphysica and Religious Language,* COLP, 1964, 173 pp., $4.00; COLP, 176

pp., 30s. A creative attempt to incorporate into the religious language discussion the concept of metaphysics as world-hypotheses, and to show on this basis both the cognitive and the existential nature of religious symbolism. A book for the serious student of recent philosophy.

31. RAMSEY, I. T., *Models and Mystery*, OUP, 1964, Pb $1.55; OUP, 74 pp., 9s 6d. An intriguing analysis of the role of conceptual models in scientific and religious knowledge, and consequently a helpful piece of epistemological map-work. The style is lively and the argument pointed.

Existentialism

32. *COLLINS, James, *The Existentialists*, REG, 1959, 224 pp., Pb $1.45. A Catholic philosopher gives a thorough examination to some key existentialists, and focuses some important themes. It is both more thorough and more technical than Roberts' book, and more penetrating.

33. ROBERTS, D. E., *Existentialism and Religious Belief*, OUP, 1957, 341 pp., Pb $1.95; OUP, 352 pp., 12s 6d. What is existentialism, and why should Christians pay any attention to it? The author explores this question as an aspect of the struggle between contemporary Christianity and secularism. Starting with Pascal, he discusses Kierkegaard, Heidegger, Sartre, Jaspers, and Marcel. He is both critical and appreciative.

6C. LIBERALISM
Kenneth Hamilton

Liberal theology has been variously defined. In general, liberals insist that religious faith must be prepared to adapt itself to current views of the world, even at the expense of dropping previous beliefs if these seem to have become outmoded. There is thus no one liberal theology; but liberal thought tends to mirror the secular attitudes that happen to be influ-

ential at the time, holding it vitally important to keep abreast of "the modern mind."

At the beginning of the century liberals felt confident that liberal Christianity would triumph spectacularly. Today the movement has been split by the confused ideologies of our times and few religious thinkers continue to call themselves liberals without qualification. However, in the many efforts to find a new theology or a contemporary form of Christianity, the liberal program continues even though it may lack the name.

The following selection from the great variety of books expounding liberal views or estimating liberalism is divided into two. Books reflecting the older liberalism are given first and followed by examples of recent liberal thinking.

Old Liberalism

1. HARNACK, Adolf, *What is Christianity?* PS, 1958, 224 pp., $3.50; HRP, 1957, Pb $1.75; EB, 1958, 224 pp. (OoP) These lectures, given in Berlin at the turn of the century, exhibit liberalism at its most confident. Still very readable, Harnack's account of the "essence" of the Christian faith being in the message of Jesus about the infinite worth of the human soul strikes the modern reader as being somewhat implausible.

2. FOSDICK, H. E., *The Living of These Days: An Autobiography*, HRP, 1956, 324 pp., Hb $4.50; Pb $1.95; SCMP, 1957, 336 pp., 25s. The foremost liberal preacher between World Wars I and II, Dr. Fosdick through his many writings provides us with a kind of barometer of the fluctuations in the liberal climate during his lifetime. His autobiography, written when he was seventy-eight, is a fascinating account of the change in the temper of liberalism from the optimistic moralism of Harnack to a more sober outlook under

the pressure of disillusioning events. But, while changing his emphasis, Fosdick preserves intact his faith in liberalism.

3. *MACHEN, J. G., *Christianity and Liberalism,* WBE, RE, 1960, 189 pp., Pb $1.75; VP, 1964, 200 pp., 12s 6d. The most uncompromising opponent of liberalism of his time, and one of the most perceptive, Dr. Machen in this study attempts to probe beneath the surface to uncover the basic theological assumptions of liberalism. Published in 1923, *Christianity and Liberalism* contains insights still well worth pondering.

4. VAN DUSEN, H. P., *The Vindication of Liberal Theology: A Tract for the Times,* CSS, 1963, 192 pp., $3.50. Written after his retirement as President of Union Theological Seminary, New York, Dr. Van Dusen's book is an impassioned defense of liberalism acknowledging that liberal theology has been under serious attack for more than thirty years. It ends with a valuable historical essay, "Theology in the Nineteenth-Century."

5. SCHLEIERMACHER, Friedrich, *On Religion: Speeches to its Cultured Despisers,* PS, 287 pp., $3.75; HRP, ET, 1958, Pb $1.60. Schleiermacher's lectures, first appearing in 1799, are an historic landmark in the history of liberalism. Indeed, this book may be regarded as the manifesto of the movement and an indispensable source of modern liberal ideas.

6. RAUSCHENBUSCH, Walter, *A Theology for the Social Gospel,* Ri, ABP, 1961, 279 pp., Pb $2.00. Rauschenbusch was not only one of the pioneers of the social gospel but also more aware of the theological basis of his position than were others who tried to apply Christian principles to the problems of modern industrial society. While many social gospelers were naively optimistic about the perfectibility of man, he tried to grapple with the reality of human sin —especially in this book, first published in 1917.

7. NIEBUHR, Reinhold, *Moral Man and Immoral Society: A Study in Ethics and Politics,* CSS, 1932, 284 pp., Hb $4.95, Pb $1.45; SCMP, 1963, Hb 13s 6d. This book caused a great impression when it first appeared, dismaying many liberals by its pessimistic conclusions about the impossibility of reforming society by preaching a humanitarian gospel of love. It is the best introduction to Niebuhr's "Christian realism," in which he departed from the social gospel by moving, as he said, "politically to the left, theologically to the right."

8. DeWOLF, L. H., *The Case for Theology in Liberal Perspective,* WP, 1959, 206 pp., $3.50. A staunch supporter of a rational approach to faith, Dr. DeWolf advocates a moderate liberalism which he believes holds fast to historic Christianity but also takes into account modern man's understanding of himself and his world.

9. NIEBUHR, H. R., *The Meaning of Revelation,* MC, 1960, 196 pp., Hb $3.50, Pb $1.95; CM. (OoP) First published in 1941, this book remains the most complete statement of the liberal concept of revelation as deriving from the experience of the Christian community rather than from the objective truth of God's Word to man.

10. *MACKINTOSH, H. R., *Types of Modern Theology: Schleiermacher to Barth,* CSS, 1937, 334 pp., $4.00; CO, 1964, 320 pp., 9s 6d. Recognized from its publication in 1937 as a scholarly and yet plainly-written survey of the historical background of liberalism, this book remains the best introduction to its subject. It is

without equal both for its panoramic view of theological history and also for the fairness of its treatment of individual thinkers.

11. CAUTHEN, Kenneth, *The Impact of American Religious Liberalism,* HRP, 1962, 290 pp. (OoP) A detailed and accurate history of liberalism in the American scene, this book is both illuminating and readable. Its handling of its complex subject matter is quite admirable.

12. BARTH, Karl, *Protestant Thought: From Rousseau and Ritschl,* HRP, 1959, 435 pp., $7.00; *From Rousseau to Ritschl,* SCMP, 432 pp., 42s. This translation of eleven chapters of *Die Protestantische Theologie im 19. Jahrhundert (Protestant Theology in the 19th Century)* is far from easy reading, being entirely concerned with theologians and philosophers on the European Continent. It is rewarding, however, to the reader who wishes to study in depth the history of modern liberalism.

13. TILLICH, Paul, *Perspectives on 19th and 20th Century Protestant Theology,* HRP, 1967, 252 pp., $5.95. This historical study is shorter and less detailed than Barth's. Yet, because it takes for granted some previous acquaintance with the men and ideas it describes, it is just possibly harder to read. Prepared after Tillich's death from tapes of spoken lectures, it is a good guide to Tillich's outlook and interests. It actually goes back to the seventeenth century to explain nineteenth-century thought, and it touches only very briefly on twentieth-century developments.

14. MACQUARRIE, John, *Twentieth-Century Religious Thought: The Frontiers of Philosophy and Theology, 1900-1960,* HRP, 1963, 415 pp., $5.00; SCMP, RE, 1966, 392 pp., 21s. This is a most useful reference book, though hardly the kind of work that can be read through from cover to cover. Dr. MacQuarrie divides the thinkers in his survey—which omits very few philosophers or theologians of note—under headings indicating the "school of thought" they belong to, and gives us potted yet fair summaries of the thinking of each. At the end of each section he makes some judicious comments on the "school." Although the survey comes down to the present decade, the bulk of the thinkers included belong to the earlier years of this century.

New Liberalism
15. BARNETTE, H. H., *The New Theology and Morality,* WP, 1967, 120 pp., Pb $1.85. This is a brief introduction to the various types of theological thinking and ethical teaching that seek to find radical "contemporary" forms for Christianity. It is written in plain language and includes both exposition and assessment. There is a useful section on the issue of the Christian approach to war and peace.

16. OGLETREE, T. W., *The Death of God Controversy,* ABP, 1966, 127 pp., Pb $1.45; SCMP, Pb 5s. Dr. Ogletree presents a well-thought-out exposition of the movement and a careful assessment of the three leading "Christian atheists." He seeks to be constructive and to avoid a condemning attitude, although he does not hold back from criticism.

17. *ROBINSON, J. A. T., *Honest to God,* WP, 1963, 143 pp., Pb $1.45; SCMP, 144 pp., Pb 5s. The Anglican Bishop of Woolwich's book created an unprecedented stir throughout the world when it appeared, and the commotion it caused is not yet stilled. Dr. Robinson did not try to be original, but to draw some conclusions from the thinking of three European thinkers: Bultmann, Bonhoeffer, and Tillich.

Whether his presentation of traditional Christian thinking and of his chosen trio was accurate is still being disputed. The importance of the issues he raised cannot be denied. This is a fairly easy book to read, but a much harder one to digest.

18. ROBINSON, J. A. T., and David Edwards, *The Honest to God Debate,* WP, 1963, 287 pp., Pb $1.65; SCMP, Pb 6s. This follow-up to *Honest to God* was rather hastily put together from letters written to Bishop Robinson, reviews of his book, and some additional essays on it. Dr. Robinson's contribution, "The Debate Continues," does little to clarify issues, but some of the reviews make illuminating reading.

19. BRUCE, Michael, *No Empty Creed,* SP, 1965, 144 pp., Pb $1.45; PS, 1964, 143 pp., 7s 6d. While this is a book intended primarily to set forth a traditional view of Christian faith from an Anglican standpoint and not to "answer" *Honest to God,* it is one that contains incidentally a decisive criticism of Bishop Robinson's standpoint. It also raises other issues connected with commending Christianity to "the modern mind."

20. *MORRISON, J. M., *Honesty and God,* SAP, 1966, 172 pp., 7s 6d. This book is the most thorough response to *Honest to God* that has so far appeared. While clearly written, it is rather tightly packed in its argument and requires close attention. It has much to say about the moral implications of Dr. Robinson's teaching.

21. BAKER, T. G. A., et al., *The New Theologians: Bultmann, Bonhoeffer, Tillich, Teilhard de Chardin,* MO, 1964, 47 pp. (OoP) The essays in this book are short and to the point, though better in exposition than in criticism. They furnish a useful starting point for readers who

wish to go further in the study of these four theologians.

22. MEHTA, Ved, *The New Theologian,* HRP, 1965, 219 pp., $5.95; WN, 192 pp., 36s. Originally a series appearing in *The New Yorker* magazine, this book begins with a review of the issues raised by *Honest to God.* The author then gives a record of interviews with representative "new" theologians in America, Britain, and Continental Europe. Long on anecdote and short on critical insight, the book's best section is 81 pages of Bonhoeffer's life with extracts from his writings.

23. JENKINS, D. E., *Guide to the Debate About God,* WP, 1966, 111 pp., Pb $1.45; LU, 128 pp., 8s 6d. In order to deal with the central concerns raised by *Honest to God,* Jenkins tells the story of liberalism from the time of Schleiermacher. The telling is lucid, uncluttered with details, and drives home the point that Robinson's rejection of theism stems from the early liberal rejection of traditional Christianity.

24. HORDERN, William, *A Layman's Guide to Protestant Theology,* MC, RE, 1958, 266 pp. (OoP); CM, RE, 1962, Hb 30s, Pb 5s. Hordern has a gift for simple exposition. First published in 1955, this survey has been brought up to date. The additions, however, are rather too brief to match the rest in clarity.

25. BONHOEFFER, Dietrich, *Letters and Papers from Prison,* MC, 1962, 192 pp., Hb $4.95, Pb $1.45; SCMP, RE, 1967, 240 pp., Hb 22s 6d, Pb 3s 6d. These last writings of Bonhoeffer, who was executed by the Nazis in 1945, have inspired the recent enthusiasm for a "religionless" or "secular" Christianity. The reader of this moving testament can judge for himself how far Bonhoeffer has

been used or misused by his professed followers.

26. HAMILTON, William, *The New Essence of Christianity*, AP, 1961, 159 pp., $3.50. Written before he began to advocate death-of-God theology, this book explains Dr. Hamilton's move to "Christian atheism" better than do his subsequent writings. Here the influence of Bonhoeffer is most marked.

27. VAN BUREN, Paul, *The Secular Meaning of the Gospel*, MC, 1963, 205 pp., Hb $4.95, Pb $1.95; SCMP, 224 pp., Hb 15s, C1 25s. Usually linked with the death-of-God theology, Dr. van Buren here makes use of an oddly-yoked combination: Bonhoeffer and British linguistic philosophy. The result is a theology without God—a humanism highly reminiscent of old-style liberalism.

28. *COX, Harvey, *The Secular City: Secularization and Urbanization in Theological Perspective*, MC, 1965, 276 pp., Hb $4.95, Pb $1.45; SCMP, RE, 1966, 13s 6d. This book has been extremely influential as the most extreme and ambitious statement of "secular Christianity." Dr. Cox appeals to Bonhoeffer, but also to many other thinkers (principally European). Here the optimism and faith in progress that marked liberalism at the beginning of the century makes a spectacular come-back.

29. CALLAHAN, Daniel, ed., *The Secular City Debate*, MC, 1966, 218 pp., Hb $5.95, Pb $1.45; Ri, CM, 1967, Hb 50s, Pb 11s 6d. Like so many of the "debate" books appearing these days, this one contains more superficial than perceptive criticism. Dr. Cox's own "Afterword" and his appended essay, "Beyond Bonhoeffer," are instructive, though.

30. PEERMAN, D. F., *Frontline Theology*, JKP, 1967, 172 pp.,

$4.50; SCMP, 1965, 15s. The essays in this book are collected from the pages of *The Christian Century:* the series "How I am Making up My Mind." While some of the eighteen contributors represent a more traditional outlook, the majority are from the religious *avant-garde* and their opinions provide a cross section of contemporary liberalism.

31. RICHARDSON, Alan, *Religion in Contemporary Debate*, WP, 1966, 216 pp., $2.75; SCMP, 1966, 128 pp., 6s 6d. A penetrating criticism of the whole spectrum of "religionless" and "atheistic" Christianity. It is written in simple and direct language, but is a little too compressed to make easy reading.

32. MASCALL, E. L., *The Secularization of Christianity: An Analysis and a Critique*, HRW, 1966, 286 pp., $6.00; DLT, 1965, 312 pp., 32s. The author concentrates chiefly upon Robinson and van Buren, but extends his criticism to other exponents of the "new" Christianity. A forceful and well-documented attack from the position of traditional Anglo-Catholicism, the argument is somewhat overloaded with details—the trees tend to obscure the wood.

33. JENKINS, D. E., *The Glory of Man*, WP, 1967, 118 pp., $3.50; SCMP, 18s. On the basis of the Christology of the early Church, Dr. Jenkins looks at the contemporary "exclusion of God" and concludes that a non-Christian vision of the world has perverted the traditional Christian message. He points out that the consequence of seeing God apart from the scriptural revelation is a deification of man that finally loses man also.

34. BROWN, D. M., ed., *Ultimate Concern: Tillich in Dialogue*, HRP, 1965, 234 pp., $3.95; SCMP, 25s. This book is the record of a seminar

in which Dr. Tillich answered questions posed by faculty members and students at the University of California, Santa Barbara. It is perhaps the best introduction to the complex thought of Tillich, who sought to reconcile Christianity and philosophy within a broad liberal tradition.

35. TILLICH, Paul, *My Search for Absolutes*, SS, 1967, 144 pp., $4.95. The lectures contained in this book (one in the "Credo Perspectives" series) were given by Dr. Tillich shortly before his death in 1965. They are interesting both because of the autobiographical material they present and because they deal with the central issue in Tillich's thinking. Tillich's writings are never easy to follow, but here he speaks with unusual directness.

36. ALTIZER, T. J., ed., *Toward a New Christianity: Readings in the Death of God Theology*, HA, 1967, 374 pp., $3.95. One of the leading "Death of God" theologians presents an anthology of sources of radical theology over the past two centuries. The bibliography supplied is a valuable guide to readers interested in the subject.

37. *BOWDEN, John, and James Richmond, eds., *A Reader in Contemporary Theology*, WP, 1967, 190 pp., Pb $1.95; SCMP, 192 pp., 7s 6d. This is a valuable guide to contemporary movements in religious thought, not only because of the extracts given from famous thinkers' writings but because of the editors' "Historical Introduction" and explanations. Final "Comments and Reactions" are given by H. D. Lewis, David Jenkins, and John Macquarrie.

6D. NATURE OF PHYSICAL UNIVERSE
David L. Dye
A modern person needs to understand something of the nature of the physical universe in order to be able to see his physical environment as a part of the total reality. The Christian faith provides such a comprehensive view, capable of including, and setting a proper context for, the descriptions science gives of the physical universe. The laws of the physical universe, some of which have been elicited by scientific methods, are God's laws, established and continued according to his purposes. (These purposes transcend the laws, just as eternal, spiritual realities, some of which are revealed, are qualitatively different from physical realities and thus subject to different ways of knowing them.) The literature of this field undergoes turnover as science develops and tends to be either purely scientific or philosophical. The books listed here include also several that discuss Christian views of the universe in connection with the relations between science and Christianity.

1. *MACKAY, D. M., ed., *Christianity in a Mechanistic Universe, A Symposium*, IVP, 1965, 125 pp., Pb $1.25; TP, 128 pp., Pb 4s. Here are four essays by British scientists, two of which address questions concerning the nature of the universe. Science describes patterns in the physical universe and is neutral about purpose. The Christian sees purpose as well, which provides meaning to life that cannot be obtained from mere description of physical phenomena. The concepts are profound but not difficult for a student who has begun to ponder his total environment. Recommended highly for both the advanced thinker and the beginner.

2. MASCALL, E. L., *Christian Theology and Natural Science*, LOG, 1957, 300 pp., $7.50. This remarkable book examines the conflicts and rapprochements between science and theology, the nature of science and of the universe it describes, and

the purpose in the universe as seen in the Christian view. Among the conclusions are (1) that a complete description of the universe should include references to purpose and only theology or metaphysics can provide this reference; and (2) that the new discoveries and more complete descriptions of the advancing science should complement revealed truth in building a Christian view of the universe. The author is well-educated in modern physics as well as in theology. The book is recommended as worthy critical study.

3. *CARNELL, E. J., *An Introduction to Christian Apologetics*, WBE, 1948, 378 pp., $5.00. Within the larger context of a Christian world view, the late Professor Carnell has beautifully analyzed the basic nature of the universe, the scientific methods used to prove it, and the knowledge one may have of it. He deals with natural theology, natural laws, Christian rationalism, the criteria of verification, and the necessary assumptions to think at all about the nature of the universe. It is not a difficult book for a thoughtful student and is worth careful reading. Although there are more recent books, none have outdated it. Highly recommended.

4. *RAMM, Bernard, *The Christian View of Science and Scripture*, WBE, 1954, 367 pp., $4.00; PAP, RE, 1964, 256 pp., Pb 6s. This contemporary classic summarizes the state of the problems between science and Christianity and tensions within Christendom on the place of science. It then formulates solution approaches acceptable to modern minds. The nature of the universe is discussed in the contexts both of the philosophical arguments and of the ways of interpreting data from various scientific fields. Highly recommended.

5. *LEWIS, C. S., *Miracles, a Preliminary Study*, MC, 1947, 220 pp., Pb 95¢; BLES, Hb 13s 6d; FO, 1960, 192 pp., Pb 2s 6d. The nature of the universe is here presented from the point of view of the propriety of miracles. Lewis' characteristic lucidity of style belies the penetrating depth of the analysis, as he shows the inconsistency of a purely naturalistic view, the meaning of natural laws, and the need for a theistic assumption to undergird the notion of uniformity in the physical universe. Recommended basic reading for every student who wonders about the meaning of the world in which he lives. For a more advanced and equally lucid treatment of the uniformity in geology, biology, and theology, see Reijer Hooykaas, *Natural Law and Divine Miracle*, BRL, 1959, 238 pp. (OoP)

6. HOLMES, A. F., *Christianity and Philosophy*, IVP, 1960, 39 pp., Pb 95¢; TP, 1964, 32 pp., Pb 2s. Although not a discourse on the nature of the universe, this short book introduces the basic concepts of a world view, which is certainly a prerequisite for such a study. The book is recommended for one beginning his quest for understanding of the universe and also for the continuing student who may need his perspective refreshed.

7. CLARK, G. F., *The Philosophy of Science and Belief in God*, CP, 1964, 95 pp., Pb $1.50. This little book summarizes reasons for the widespread antipathy toward religion by scientists, presenting views of ancient, Newtonian, and modern scientists and philosophers. The author's own evangelical Christian position does not obtrude obviously into the presentation. He concludes that science does not and cannot imply nonexistence of God or of spiritual realities. It is relatively easy reading for a person who is interested in the subject and recommended to students as an introduction to a way of thinking

about science. A fuller presentation of Dr. Clark's position is to be found in his *A Christian View of Man and Things*, WBE, 1952, 325 pp. (OoP)

8. BARBOUR, I. G., *Issues in Science and Religion*, PH, 1965, 400 pp., $5.95; SCMP, 1953, 264 pp., 25s. This book presents a wide-ranging analysis with historical perspectives and a physicist's insight into problems. He discusses issues rather than pat answers, though laying a foundation for a Christian viewpoint. He takes effective issue with the "god-of-the-gaps" notion, and the nature of the universe described by science is an ever-present backdrop for the discussions. This book is detailed enough not to be quick easy reading, but to be rewarding to a serious student who, because he is himself wrestling with these issues, will devote himself to studying them.

9. *DYE, D. L., *Faith and the Physical World*, WBE, 1966, 214 pp., Pb $2.95. The nature of the physical universe and of the scientific methods used to elicit descriptions of it are presented, with the view that "all truth is God's truth." The book has a few places where a background in science would help the reader, but the main argument is not difficult to follow. Students with the problems of reconciling biblical Christian faith with scientific thinking could profit from this book.

10. SHORT, A. R., *Modern Discovery and the Bible*, TP, ED 3, 1952, 246 pp. (OoP) Among the matters discussed in this well-written book are the nature of the universe and the evidences justifying the Christian view that there is plan and purpose in it. A student by reading this can certainly gain an appreciation of the consistency and comprehensiveness of his faith.

11. EDDINGTON, A. S., *The Nature of the Physical World*, AAB, 1958, 360 pp., Pb $1.95; JMD, 352 pp., 15s. In the field of physics, any book still referred to that was written in 1929 must almost by definition be a classic. This book qualifies for that distinction by being understandably written, containing the essential views of quantum mechanics and relativity after their first settling-out and before some of the later controversy over their philosophical meanings. There is also some good common sense from this distinguished theoretical physicist on the nature and limitations of science as a means of knowing. Recommended to all as an introduction to the scientific approach to the nature of the universe.

12. SMETHURST, A. F., *Modern Science and Christian Belief*, ABP, 1955, 300 pp. (OoP); NI, 21s. (OoP) This book treats systematically the relationships of science and Christian faith, with the overall view that these two disciplines are interdependent: the assumptions of science are most sensibly based on a theological view; the objectivity and honesty of a scientist are manifestations of Christian morality. The author was a geologist and theologian and combines these disciplines quite effectively with a theologically oriented book. See also Karl Heim, *Christian Faith and Natural Science*, HRP, 1957, 256 pp., Hb $3.25, Pb $1.60; SCMP, ET, 1953, 25s.

13. COULSON, C. A., *Science and Christian Belief*, UNCP, 1955, 127 pp. (OoP); CO, 1958, 160 pp., Pb 2s 6d. This little book of lectures presents a general way of approaching the common challenges by science to Christianity. The author, a mathematician, points out that scientists appeal to metaphysical assumptions in their studies. Thus science and religion jointly may seek to know different aspects of a central unified di-

vine truth, so that science may be considered a religious activity. The view of the book is syncretic, and there is much left to the reader to think through. While quite general, i.e., non-specific, it is neither elementary nor difficult and will give a student a starting point for further inquiry.

14. MARGENAU, Henry, *The Nature of Physical Reality—a Philosophy of Modern Physics,* MH, 1950, 471 pp., Pb $3.95; MH, 1959, 32s. Professor Margenau has given a tightly reasoned and full presentation of an epistemology of science that allows for the observable results of modern quantum physics without abandoning the idea of an objective reality "really down there" under the formalism. While not a simple book, it is complete enough in itself not to require an extensive technical background in physics. Causality, measurements, the meaning of the exclusion and uncertainty principles, and the shortcomings of empiricism, operationalism, and positivism are discussed. Recommended for mature students of philosophy and science who have digested the simpler books on this list.

15. VON WEISSACKER, C. F., *The World View of Physics,* UCP, 1952, 219 pp. (OoP); RO, 14s. Here is a rather difficult book on scientific philosophy by a top-ranking German theoretical physicist, a book well worth reading for its insights and approaches. The book communicates the fallacies of a self-sufficient, all-embracing scientism and the "dangers of a merely scientific approach to the fundamental questions of life." Theology is not discussed, *per se,* and Christianity is seen more as a mystical, ethical system than as the revealed way of experiencing God. Yet the author expresses the basic human need to experience God and the inherent inability of science as a means

to achieve this experience. This book raises many "fundamental questions," without answering them. (The revelation of God in Christ points us in the direction of many of the answers.) In this sense, the book is a little disappointing, but it should serve as a stimulus for a mature Christian student to dig deeper. Often in research one can get direction to the right answers only when the right questions have been asked.

16. BOHM, David, *Causality and Chance in Modern Physics,* PUP, 1957, 200 pp., $5.95; RO, 184 pp., 21s. In this book (and in articles in *Reviews of Modern Physics*) Bohm states a view of the nature of the universe, challenging the so-called "orthodox interpretation" of the indeterminacy principle in quantum mechanics. It is not easy reading for a person unfamiliar with modern quantum theory, nor is it written with any specifically Christian perspective. However, this view (shared by De Broglie, Margenau and Einstein) is holistic, sees the universe as having some objective absolute reality and flatly contradicts the concepts of irrational non-causal reality which has been used as ammunition by some atheists. A Christian physicist would find this book useful and could reformulate the arguments in his terms as another example of the consistency and comprehensiveness of the Christian world view. See also, Louis de Broglie, *Non-Linear Wave Mechanics,* AMEL, 1960, 304 pp., $14.50; AMEL, 75s, for mathematical formulations of these ideas.

6E. SCIENCE AND TECHNOLOGY
Richard H. Bube

A Christian views science as a discipline for interpreting the revelation of God in nature and as a means for developing a technology that fulfills man's office as the one who is to have dominion over the earth. Since the Christian receives both the natural revelation and the biblical revelation of God as trustworthy and reliable in the areas for which they were given and in which they are relevant, he attributes the many historical and current apparent conflicts between science and Christian theology to differences between two interpretations of these revelations, either one of which—or both—could be in error. He is also sensitive to the Christian responsibility of guiding the application of scientific technology to the lives of men.

1. VAN DER ZIEL, Albert, *The Natural Sciences and the Christian Message*, DEC, 1960, 259 pp., $4.50. A sweeping and readable survey of science and Christianity based on the conviction that the natural sciences and the Christian message are properly used when they complement one another.

2. *BUBE, R. H., ed., *The Encounter between Christianity and Science*, WBE, 1968, 303 pp. A treatment of the basic concepts of science and Christianity, of natural revelation and biblical revelation, and of some of the most vital issues in astronomy, geology, physical science, biology, psychology, and social science.

3. BARBOUR, I. G., *Christianity and the Scientist*, ASP, 1960, 128 pp. (OoP) A treatment of the scientific profession from a Christian point of view. Includes discussion of applied science and human welfare, science teaching, and the relationship between science and the social order.

4. VAN DER ZIEL, Albert, *Genesis and Scientific Inquiry*, DEC, 1965, 209 pp. An attempt to show how a theological interpretation and a scientific interpretation of the early chapters of Genesis can be made to complement each other. The author

adopts the documentary hypothesis of these chapters.

5. *POLLARD, W. G., *Physicist and Christian*, SP, 1961, 178 pp., Pb $1.65. Science and Christianity are each viewed in terms of the "community of the faithful" by the American physicist-priest in order to emphasize the importance of realizing the involvement of the individual in both disciplines.

6. DYE, D. L., *Faith and the Physical World: A Comprehensive View*, WBE, 1966, 214 pp., Pb $2.95. An attempt to treat the whole spectrum of Christianity and science by a Christian physicist who believes that science and Christianity present a total life view which can and should be integrated.

7. *RAMM, Bernard, *The Christian View of Science and Scripture*, WBE, 1955, 368 pp., $4.00; PAP, RE, 1964, 256 pp., Pb 6s. A classic in the field in the modern day idiom and one of the first clear statements on science by an evangelical Christian. Treats basic presuppositions and particular problems in astronomy, biology, geology, and anthropology. Includes a five-and-a-half page classified bibliography.

8. YARNOLD, G. D., *The Spiritual Crisis of the Scientific Age*, MC, 1959, 207 pp., $3.75; AU, 18s. A treatment of some of the basic problems underlying interaction between Christian faith and science in the modern day and a treatment of Christian ethics in an industrialized and nuclear age.

9. LACK, David, *Evolutionary Theory and Christian Belief*, BN, 1957, 128 pp., $2.50; ME, Pb 3s 6d. A brief and readable little book that treats the issues relating Christianity and evolution in a helpful way.

10. CLARK, R. E. D., *The Christian Stake in Science,* MP, 1967, 160 pp.; PP; *Christian Belief and Science,* FP, 1961, 160 pp., Pb $2.25; EUP, 1960, 168 pp., 12s 6d. An attempt to show that the Christian world view is more consistent with the findings of science than opposing world views.

11. SCHILLING, H. K., *Science and Religion,* CSS, 1962, 272 pp., $4.50. Another approach to the presentation of Christianity and science in terms of the characteristics of two similar communities.

12. *POLLARD, W. G., *Chance and Providence,* CSS, 1958, 190 pp., $3.50. An attempt to correlate the Christian doctrine of the providence of God with basic conclusions of modern quantum theory in physics.

13. *MIXTER, R. L., ed., *Evolution and Christian Thought Today,* WBE, 1959, 224 pp., $4.50; PP, 21s. An inquiry by thirteen members of the American Scientific Affiliation into the relationship between Christianity and evolutionary thought; all authors hold to an evangelical Christian position and also speak with authority in the scientific topic of their choice.

14. *TEILHARD DE CHARDIN, Pierre, *The Phenomenon of Man,* HRP, 1961, 318 pp. Pb $1.75; HRP, 1959, $5.00; CO, 1961, 320 pp., 25s; Ri, FO, 1965, Pb 5s. Because of his impact on modern thought, this book by Teilhard de Chardin should be included although it is quite different from the other selections. The author seeks to set out a complete evolutionary interpretation of life with Christian overtones.

6F. EDUCATION
J. Marion Snapper
Next to the home no set of institutions has more influence on the forming of persons and culture than the
schools. They do not by themselves form the future but they are the public arena in which the various forces in a society come to focus on the next generation. Therefore responsible Christians have always been vitally concerned with education wherever it is found. The entries given here represent a sampling of literature on education; some are concerned generally with philosophy of education, some urge specific programs of action in either religious or day school education; others written within the perspective of the Christian faith, both Catholic and Protestant, have become seminal works for various groups in the Christian community as they wrestle with problems of education. Although the spectrum of viewpoints is broad, all of the books represent efforts by Christian-oriented minds.*

1. BEAVER, R. P., ed., *Christianity and African Education,* WBE, 1966, 233 pp., Pb $2.65. Essays on subjects like evangelism and education, Protestant and Roman Catholic educational programs, African intellectuals, theological education, and future of Christian education in Africa.

2. BENNETT, J. C., *Christians and the State,* CSS, 1958, 302 pp., $4.50. A well-balanced analysis of the church-state problem in America. The author's study leads him to reject the theory of an absolute separation of church and state. He supports health and welfare benefits for non-public schools while rejecting direct state aid for such institutions.

3. BRYSON, Lyman, et al., ed., *Goals for American Education,* HRP, 1950. (OoP) A symposium (Conference of Science, Philosophy, and Religion—1948) containing major papers by some twenty outstanding American scientists, philosophers, and theologians. Focuses on higher education, but seeks to relate all edu-

cation to changing and perpetual needs in a society that education must serve.

4. COGLEY, John, ed., *Religion in America*, MEB, 1958, 288 pp., Pb $2.25. Includes essays by such diverse authors as Reinhold Niebuhr, Leo Pfeiffer, Will Herberg, Stringfellow Barr, Gustav Weigel, Paul Tillich. The principal concern is with the place and significance of religion in a free society. Outstanding material on the question of public policy toward the parochial school is included.

5. CULLY, K. B., *Basic Writings in Christian Education*, WP, 1961, 350 pp., $4.95. Thirty-one selections from the early church fathers through the middle ages, Reformation, and eighteenth century to the middle of the twentieth century, ending with Mann, Bushell, Dewey, and Coe.

6. CULLY, K. B., *The Search for a Christian Education since 1940*, WP, 1965, 205 pp., $4.50. A companion volume to the immediately preceding title. Presents a broad continuum of philosophies of Christian Education by means of brief introductions and discussions of the contributions of the leaders of each school of thought.

7. DAVIES, R. E., ed., *An Approach to Christian Education*, AL, 1957, 159 pp., $2.75; EP, 1956, 168 pp., Pb 5s. A symposium by nine British educators and commentators concerned to relate a vigorous evangelical faith to solid education in and through the disciplines that make up the school's curriculum. Well written and both educationally and religiously provocative.

8. DAWSON, Christopher, *The Crisis of Western Education*, SHE, 1961, 246 pp., $3.95; DC, 1965, 197 pp., Pb 95¢; SHE, 1961, 256 pp., 18s. A Harvard social historian and a Catholic, the author analyzes the sickness of western civilization as a consequence of cutting itself off from its Christian and classical roots. He proposes a renaissance to be effected through the schools, including several concrete recommendations.

9. DUNN, W. K., *What Happened to Religious Education?* JH, 1958, 346 pp., $6.00; OUP, 40s. To get at the problem of the place of religious education in public schools, the author tries to get behind Supreme Court decisions and state legislation to what he calls the "grass roots": practices of school systems, controversies, the writings of religious leaders, and the like, to find out historically how religious education was treated on the elementary levels of education, and why.

10. ELIOT, T. S., *Christianity and Culture*, HA, 1949, 202 pp., Pb $1.95. A penetrating and stimulating discussion of culture. Eliot's definition of the culture of a people as an incarnation of its religion is most provocative for thinking about Christian and secular education.

11. FERRÉ, N. F., *Christian Faith and Higher Education*, HRP, 1954, 251 pp., $3.00. (OoP) Focusing on higher education, but seeking to speak also to the lower forms, this contemporary theologian, although not an evangelical, seeks to relate some of the valuable new insights into the nature of Christian calling to problems of education and culture. Readable and stimulating.

12. FULLER, Edmund, ed., *The Christian Idea of Education*, YUP, 1957, 265 pp., $6.50; YUP, 2 V., 1957-62, 265, 345 pp, Hb 48s, 30s, Pb 14s, 9s 6d. Contains papers presented at the Kent School Seminar held in 1955. Among the eight major papers are those presented by W. G. Pollard, E. H. Harbison, Alan Paton,

W. H. Shepherd, Jr., John Courtney Murray, J. Maritain, R. Neibuhr, and G. Florovsky. Not always easy reading, but it contains excellent samples of concern for Christianity and education by scholars of various backgrounds. Pollard's essay is probably the most interesting to the average reader.

13. GAEBELEIN, F. E., *Christian Education in a Democracy*, OUP, 1951, 318 pp., Hb 31s 6d. This is a basic book for those interested in the relevance and need for Christian education, the biblical and evangelical basis for Christian education, and the norms for judging a Christian educational institution. It deals with education at all levels, both in the day school and in the church.

14. GAEBELEIN, Frank E., *The Pattern of God's Truth: Problems of Integration in Christian Education*, OUP, 1954, 118 pp., $2.50 (OoP); MP, 1968, Pb $1.25; OUP, 1954, 16s 6d. Those who are wrestling with the problems of integrating education with a Christian philosophy will find here a clear delineation of the problems with practical solutions for making education both scholarly and Christian. This is an important book for all who believe that education ought to have a living relation with God's truth at all points.

15. HUNTER, David, *Christian Education as Engagement*, SP, 1963, 128 pp., $3.50. Using insights from both theology and psychology, the author shows the necessity of intense personal involvement if any educational program is going to interest people enough to change them significantly. The emphasis on interpersonal relations and dialog is supported as being the most defensible in terms of biblical theology and modern psychology. A provocative, informed, interdisciplinary discussion with direct applica-

tion to curriculum and teaching in Christian Education.

16. JAARSMA, Cornelius, *Human Development, Learning, and Teaching*, WBE, 1961, 301 pp., $6.00. A textbook for an introductory course in educational psychology. In it the author attempts to explain the nature of the learner and the learning process from a Christian and biblical point of view. The emphasis is on education as personality development. The presentation is somewhat theological and heavy at times.

17. KENNEDY, W. B., *The Shaping of Protestant Education*, ASP, 1968, 78 pp., Pb $2.50. This monograph concentrates upon the development of Protestant educational strategy over the last eighty years. Special attention is given to the Sunday School and its changing role in its relationship to both public schools and to the organized church, focusing on the shift from being primarily an instrument of missionary evangelism to an instrument of nurture for each denomination.

18. LEWIS, C. S., *The Abolition of Man*, MC, 1947, 61 pp., Pb $1.25; BLES, 64 pp., Pb 4s 6d. In this terse treatise the author exposes some of the basic flaws in existing pedagogy. He specifically denounces the importance placed upon developing the intellect at the expense of fortifying the moral and spiritual character. Lewis suggests that unless man builds the intellect upon the base of moral values his victory over nature will end in defeat for man.

19. LYNN, Robert, *Protestant Strategies in Education*, ASP, 1965, 96 pp., Pb $2.50. A perceptive analysis of the glaring inadequacies of Protestant oriented public school education augmented by traditional Sunday School training in Protestant churches. An historical sketch is giv-

en, leading to the contemporary crisis and the need for new answers. The outlines of an educational response are offered.

20. MARITAIN, Jacques, *Education at the Crossroads*, YUP, 1943, 120 pp., $4.75; YUP, 1960, Pb 95¢; YUP, 1943, Hb 30s, Pb 8s 6d. The most eminent twentieth-century Catholic philosopher of education gives us an analysis of American education through the eyes of one committed to a Christian classical philosophy of education. This book should be read by all concerned for democracy, Christianity, and education. See also, Nicholas Wolterstorff, *Religion and the Schools*, WBE, 1965, 46 pp., Pb 75¢.

21. McCLUSKEY, N. G., S. J., *Catholic Viewpoint on Education*, Hanover House, 1959, 192 pp. (OoP) An excellent book for Protestants who want to know how a leading Catholic educator views the many problems of education. The reader who wishes to work in primary sources is referred to his book of source materials, *Catholic Education in America*, COLP, 1964.

22. MICKELSEN, A. B., *Interpreting the Bible*, WBE, 1963, 425 pp., $5.95. A good book for teachers, offering basic principles for understanding the Scriptures. Following a brief introduction to the problem of hermeneutics, the author presents some general guidelines for interpretation. He then discusses various literary forms and gives principles and procedures for interpreting each major form.

23. MURCH, J. D., *Teach or Perish!* WBE, 1966, 117 pp., Pb $1.65. Evaluation of the Christian education at the local church level and a call for revitalization, expansion and advance.

24. PANOCH, J. V., and D. L. Barr, *Religion Goes to School*, HRP, 1968, 183 pp., $5.95. This book is written for the classroom teacher, and is intended to clarify the relations between religion and public education, as well as to suggest methods and materials adaptable for classroom use. Its recommendations are all made within the spirit and intent of the U.S. Supreme Court decisions on religion and public schools. It contains an extensive bibliography of materials for the public school teacher.

25. PHENIX, P. H., *Education and the Common Good*, HRP, 1961, 271 pp., $5.00. Written by a professor at Teachers College, Columbia University, this book argues that religion can inform and shape contemporary public education and present a "moral philosophy of the curriculum." Religion is presented not as a creed, ceremony, or institution, but as man's ultimate concern and commitment. Given this broader perspective, the book is persuasive and is well-written in a popular style.

26. PIKE, K. L., *With Heart and Mind*, WBE, 1962, 140 pp., Pb $1.95. Can evangelical Christianity be synthesized with sound scholarship? The author, a learned professor of linguistics, shares the personal struggles involved in reaching that synthesis in his own life.

27. SHERRILL, L. J., *The Rise of Christian Education*, MC, 1944, 349 pp., $4.50; CM, 1950, 35s. A classic historical study of religious education in the Hebraic-Christian tradition from Hebrew origins to the fifteenth century. The method used examines "convictions regarding the nature of the Supreme Being, his most significant manifestations of himself, his will for men, and the supreme values of existence." A final chapter is devoted to an evaluation of the education surveyed.

28. SIZER, T. R., ed., *Religion and Public Education,* HM, 1967, 361 pp., Pb $4.50. The volume consists of seventeen papers presented at the Conference on the Role of Religion in Public Education on the subject of the significant contemporary relationships between religion and schooling.

29. SMART, J. D., *The Teaching Ministry of the Church: An Examination of the Basic Principles of Christian Education,* WP, 1954, 207 pp., $3.00. A discussion of the theological foundations of the church's educational program. A brief historical section is followed by a re-definition of the goal of Christian teaching in terms of the doctrine of the Trinity and its implications for curriculum, program, and the growth of persons. For theory and practice of administering church educational programs, see also R. K. Bower, *Administering Christian Education,* WBE, 1964, 227 pp., $4.50.

30. TAYLOR, M. J., *An Introduction to Christian Education,* ABP, 1966, 412 pp., $6.50. The four parts of the book cover the major aspects of Christian Education: theoretical foundations, administration, programs, methods, materials, agencies and organizations. Individual chapters are written by thirty-one specialists in Christian Education. See also, Arnold DeGraaf, *The Educational Ministry of the Church,* WBE, Pb $3.50.

31. WATERINK, Jan, *Basic Concepts in Christian Pedagogy,* WBE, 1954, 139 pp., $2.00. (OoP) The concepts developed show how unity in the individual can be brought to life in all of its parts; how both child and educator, in serving God and knowing his ordinances, can serve both God and man. The author, a European psychologist, develops his pedagogy in a Christian philosophical-psychological framework.

32. WITHERINGTON, H. C., *Psychology of Religion,* WBE, 1955, 344 pp., $3.50. A well-written and biblical treatment of man as a religious being. The book is lucid and can be readily understood by those who have not had much training in the field of psychology. Many of the concepts developed are novel and refreshing to those who believe in biblical Christianity.

33. ZYLSTRA, Henry, *Testament of Vision,* WBE, 1961, 144 pp., Pb $1.45. A collection of writings and addresses by a professor of English. Written in a richly varied style, this anthology is the product of a Christian mind. The author reveals a deep commitment to Christ and to the liberal arts and sound tradition.

6G. PSYCHIATRY AND MEDICINE

E. Mansell Pattison

Psychiatry is the specialty within medicine dealing with the diagnosis and treatment of the emotionally ill. The practice of psychiatry covers an immense array of activities—from the hospital treatment of acutely ill persons, where drug therapy and electroshock therapy may be used, to psychotherapy and psychoanalysis which are essentially explorations in the understanding of human conflict, to social and community psychiatry which is concerned with social and cultural attitudes and community action programs.

During the first half of the twentieth century most attention was paid to the neurotic uses of religion. However, in the past twenty years greater attention is being paid to the healthy functions and uses of religion. In fact, the clergy and churches are now considered to be a major community mental health resource. Therefore the bibliography focuses on discussions of the healthy use of religion and the neurotic use of religion. The more theologically oriented books explore Christian understanding of human emotional problems seen in the terms of contemporary psychological research.

Listing is arranged in sequence: bibliographic resources, psychological studies of religious personality, Church organization and mental health, Christian approaches to emotional health, including the topics of sin, morality, guilt, and anxiety, general discussions of psychiatry and religion, Freud and religion, studies on psychopathology and religion, and medicine and religion.

1. MEISSNER, W. W., *Annotated Bibliography in Religion and Psychology,* 1961, 235 pp. The most complete reference resource available, containing 2905 annotated entries up to 1960, mostly journal articles. For subsequent and further resources one may consult compilations by the Academy of Religion and Mental Health, the National Institute of Mental Health, the Religious Education Association, and the volumes in the Successful Pastoral Counseling series published by Prentice-Hall.

2. STRUNK, Orle, Jr., *Readings in the Psychology of Religion,* ABP, 1959, 288 pp., $4.50. Contains brief selections from almost all the early pioneer investigators in the psychology of religion, whose work is often unavailable. Also brief selections from current investigators and a survey history of the development of research in this field.

3. PRUYSER, P. W., *A Dynamic Psychology of Religion,* HRP, 1968, 384 pp., $10.00. An eminent psychologist, devout churchman, and a leading theoretician in the psychology of religion examines religious experience in terms of the "part-processes" of personality function. Religion is viewed from a functional point of view, but not as a singular aspect of life. Pruyser insists that reli-

gion can now no longer be seen as an isolated item or parcel of experience but as a quality of an individual's experiencing the world and himself.

4. STEWART, C. W., *Adolescent Religion: A Developmental Study of the Religion of Youth,* ABP, 1967, 318 pp., $6.00. A careful case study of a group of normal adolescents, tracing their total development from birth, with an examination of the dynamic psychological factors that bring them to their individual religious attitudes. Views religion in large part as serving certain normal psychological needs.

5. *ROBERTS, D. E., *Psychotherapy and a Christian View of Man,* CSS, 1960, 161 pp., Pb $1.25. An early, and still superior, analysis of how the task of restoring a human to emotional "wholeness" and "holiness" is shared by the healing function of psychotherapy and the healing function of church. No sloppy thinker, Roberts skillfully blends psychoanalytic, existential and classic theological concepts into an integrated view of man.

6. MAVES, P. B., *The Church and Mental Health,* CSS, 1953, 303 pp., $4.50. (OoP) A symposium which covers the many areas and activities where the Church can foster mental health. The theological basis for this area of church concern is well presented, along with very practical and specific examples of how a local church can both nurture healthy growth of its members and help those in crisis and distress.

7. *DITTES, J. E., *The Church in the Way,* CSS, 1967, 358 pp., $7.50. An unusual provocative, timely book by a theological professor with a doctorate in psychology. It is a psychological analysis of the purpose of the Church as ideally conceived and as a realistic interpretation of man's participation in it. In response to the criti-

cism that the Church is irrelevant, unreal, preoccupied with organization, the author suggests that the confrontation of these human obstacles may provide the occasion for the Church to realize its mission.

8. KLAUSNER, S. Z., *Psychiatry and Religion,* FRP, 1964, 299 pp., $7.50; CM, 55s. A fairly complex, but insightful study, by a professor with doctorates in both sociology and psychology. The first half of the book is a description of the pioneering Religio-Psychiatric Clinic at the Marble Collegiate Church founded twenty-five years ago. The second half of the book examines the roles and goals of psychiatrically-oriented ministers and religiously-oriented psychiatrists. They have a joint endeavor, yet frame their work in competitive ideologies. For advanced readers. See also Victor White, *Soul and Psyche,* CHP, 1960, 132 pp., 21s. (OoP)

9. *WHITE, Ernest, *Christian Life and the Unconscious,* HRP, 1955, 190 pp., $3.00 (OoP); HS. (OoP) A serious attempt by an English psychiatrist to demonstrate that religion and psychology, so far from being mutually antagonistic, are both of immense value in the attainment of the integration of the mind and the health of the soul. He explores traditional Christian ideas about sin, evil, guilt, conversion, baptism, and sanctification in relation to Freudian and Jungian psychoanalytic concepts like unconscious motivation, emotional conflict, archetypes, and complexes. Not difficult in spite of the content.

10. *TOURNIER, Paul, *The Meaning of Persons,* HRP, 1957, 238 pp., $3.75; SCMP, RE, 1962, Pb 13s 6d. A Swiss physician who has spent much of his practice helping people to find themselves as persons, Tournier has won wide acclaim for his devout Christian commitment, penetra-

ting psychological insight, and simple convincing style. Among his many books, this one stands out for its description of how to develop genuine human relations in a Christian perspective. He takes Martin Buber's seminal concepts of I-It and I-Thou relationships and makes them applicable to everyday life. See also, *Guilt and Grace,* HRP, 1962, 224 pp., $3.75; SCMP, 21s; and *Escape from Loneliness,* WP, 1961, 192 pp., $4.00; Ri, SCMP, 1966, Pb 10s 6d; and H. B. Walker, *To Conquer Loneliness,* HRP, 1966, 172 pp., $3.95.

11. ORAISON, Marc, et al., *Sin: A Symposium,* MC, 1962, 177 pp., $4.50; CM, 35s. A group of French Roman Catholic theologians with clinical training address themselves to a fresh understanding of the concept of sin that does justice to both theological and psychological concepts. Their European continental theology closely approximates the best of American classic theology in a refreshing manner. They discuss the relationship of responsibility and blameability to sin in a manner which opens new vistas to any reader.

12. HARTMANN, Heinz, *Psychoanalysis and Moral Values,* IUP, 1960, 121 pp., $3.00. A simply written, brief monograph by America's leading psychoanalytic theoretician. He addresses an area that has often been of great concern to Christians who fear that psychotherapy will undermine their faith. He notes the limited goals and methods of psychotherapy. He concludes that a successful psychoanalysis can produce an integrated person but not necessarily a good person and that psychotherapy can teach us how and why we choose the value we do, but that psychotherapy cannot tell us which values we should choose.

13. *McKENZIE, J. G., *Guilt: Its Meaning and Significance,* ABP,

1963, 192 pp., $3.25; AU, 1962, 21s. A British psychologist and devout Christian, McKenzie presents a study of man's conscience in terms of both depth psychology and contemporary theology. He examines the legal, ethical, and religious concepts of guilt and shows how each must take into account the findings of the other. He points up the role of Christian faith in relation to forgiveness while psychological methods of treatment address themselves to neurotic aspects of guilt.

14. *BERTOCCI, P. A., *Religion as Creative Insecurity,* ASP, 1958, 128 pp., Pb $1.95; MAY, 20s. (OoP) A Roman Catholic professor of philosophy has provided us with a succinct, psychological-theological appraisal of the role of anxiety in human life and religion. Attacking the peace-of-mind cult in religion he asserts that to flee from insecurity is to miss the whole point of being human, the whole point of religion, and the Christian faith in particular . . . is catastrophic. Mature religion emerges as creative insecurity that brings not happiness but blessedness. Superb.

15. LINN, Louis, and L. W. Schwarz, *Psychiatry and Religious Experience,* RH, 1958, 305 pp., $4.95. Written by an eminent psychoanalyst and a chaplain, this book provides a broad overview of the many overlapping situations where mental health professionals and church professionals collaborate in the treatment of the mentally ill. Written like a textbook, it summarizes the domains of psychiatry and religion, religious development, principles of religious counseling, methods of psychiatric treatment, and the practical ways in which religion may help people face inevitable stresses and crises throughout life. No theological position is taken and religion is viewed as a useful psychological mechanism.

16. GASSERT, R. G., and B. H. Hall, *Psychiatry and Religious Faith,* VIP, 1964, 171 pp., $3.95. A priest and a psychiatrist, both Roman Catholic, address this book especially to Christian people to enhance their knowledge of psychiatric treatment and to demonstrate that there is no conflict between psychiatry and faith. In simple language they explain the nature of mental illness, what can be expected from psychiatric treatment, and relate the whole subject to the needs of the religious life. Although written within the Catholic structure, the authors show a sympathetic understanding for the concerns of all who experience emotional problems that may be related to their faith.

17. PATTISON, E. M., *Clinical Psychiatry and Religion,* LB, 1968, 250 pp., $4.50. A symposium of twenty-five chapters by leading psychiatrists who have had long experience in treating religious persons. Although written for the practicing clinician, the articles present summaries of the current thinking and research which take into account the particular needs and concerns of the religious person in treatment. Sections take up theoretical formulations of religion, the mental health and illness of persons in religious vocations, the role of religion in psychotherapy, research on religious phenomena, diagnosis and evaluation of religious candidates, and the function of churches and clergy in community mental health.

18. MENG, Heinrich, and E. L. Freud, ed., *Sigmund Freud: Psychoanalysis and Faith, Dialogues with the Reverend Oakar Pfister,* BB, 1963, 152 pp., $4.95; HO, 21s. Freud, the founder of modern psychotherapy, maintained that religion was the universal neurosis of mankind. Yet one of his closest associates was a Swiss pastor who be came

a psychoanalyst. This correspondence between them from 1909 to 1937 illuminates Freud's open interest and concern for religion and his defense of Pfister's faith although he often disagreed with him. The letters are warm, personal, frank, and revealing of the real sense of a dialogue that did not pit psychoanalysis against faith.

19. RIEFF, Philip, *Freud: The Mind of the Moralist,* VIP, 1959, 397 pp., Hb $6.00; DC, 1961, Pb $1.75; GOL, 1960, 416 pp., 30s. An eminent sociologist has provided a very significant understanding of Freud's thoughts and insights. Although Freud was often unjustly accused of being immoral or amoral, Rieff demonstrates that Freud handed down no final answers and no ethical imperatives, yet worked ceaselessly upon one of the most fundamental human problems, the problem of morality. Rieff concludes that moral implications run throughout the whole of Freud's work. An excellent summation that should redress many distortions of psychoanalytic theory. For the advanced reader.

20. OATES, W. E., *Religious Factors in Mental Illness,* Ri, ASP, 1966, 239 pp., $4.00; AU, 1957, 16s. A Southern Baptist minister and professor of psychology of religion and pastoral care, Oates has summarized here many studies. He notes that for the emotionally ill their religious convictions become symbols for which they are willing to lose everything. He discusses how to distinguish healthful from unhealthful religion and how to use religion in a positive, constructive manner with the mentally ill. He points out that religion does not make one ill, but that the way one uses religion certainly may aggravate illness. He explains the need for understanding between the mentally ill and the larger community of religious faith.

21. BOWERS, M. K., *Conflicts of the Clergy,* TNS, 1963, 252 pp., $4.95. A psychoanalyst with many years of experience treating clergymen has written a highly interesting series of actual case studies. The merit of the book lies in her demonstration of the way *religious* vocations play a role in neurotic conflict and how religious commitment can be strengthened through therapy. Her aim is to help a person realign his unconscious religious distortions so that he can act and feel in accord with his conscious religious convictions.

22. *ROKEACH, Milton, *The Three Christs of Ypsilanti,* AAK, 1964, 336 pp., Hb $5.95; VI, Pb $1.95. A leading social psychologist has given a narrative, almost verbatim account of an experiment in which he brought three men together for a period of two years for daily encounters with each other. All three were chronic psychotics in a state hospital and each claimed that he was Jesus Christ. This poignant, moving, bitter, real-life story describes how each man renounced his own identity and sought to adopt the name that symbolized the greatest and best of man. The use of religion to solve profound human deprivation and conflict is nowhere else better told.

23. LaBARRE, Weston, *They Shall Take Up Serpents, Psychology of the Southern Snake-Handling Cult,* UMP, 1961, 208 pp., $3.75. An anthropologist in a psychiatric department gives a detailed description of a curious example of cultic religion. He explores the symbolism involved and explains it psychologically in psychoanalytic terms. His explanations may explain too much away, but his descriptions of the sociology of culturally determined religion is apt and his psychological descriptions of the participants instructive. Photographs and detailed histories add to the veracity of the account.

24. *EDMUNDS, Vincent, and C. G. Scorer, *Ideals in Medicine. A Christian Approach to Medical Practice,* CMS, 1958, 192 pp., $3.00 (OoP); TP, 12s 6d. A symposium by thirteen English physicians, this small book covers a wide gamut of topics: ethical codes, a doctor's personal standards, doctor-patient relations, sexual problems, contraception, abortion, euthanasia, the dying, research ethics, behavioral problems, faith healing, and medical missions. The articles are crisp and thoughtful in the British style, yet highly applicable to American medicine. Medical practice as such is only touched upon, but rather the focus lies squarely on Christian perspectives as they influence one's practice.

25. BELGUM, David, *Religion and Medicine. Essays on Meaning, Values and Health,* ISUP, 1967, 345 pp., $4.95. This anthology of twenty-three research papers and theoretical essays focuses on the relationship between religion and psychosomatic medicine. It is intended to stimulate dialogue between ministers and physicians. It inquires into the nature of man, how his being as a person influences the function of his body, and how health or sickness must be viewed as a problem of the whole person. A wide variety of theological positions is taken and some of the psychological positions are just as disparate. An uneven book that contains both classic papers and some very speculative ones.

6H. PSYCHOLOGY AND COUNSELING

Harold I. Haas

Psychology is a broad field involving such diverse topics as learning, perception, motivation, psychophysiological functioning, human assessment, personality, and social behavior. It is a scientific discipline which stresses measurement, experimentation, and hypothesis testing, a point

often not understood by the layman. Like other sciences, psychology has both pure and applied science aspects. Counseling (and psychotherapy) fall into the latter category and at the point of application involve "art" as well as science.

The difficulties psychology presents for the devout Christian stem primarily from its fundamental assumptions, namely, that all things are purely natural (vs. the biblical view which assumes a supernatural order as well), its stress on determinism (vs. some measure of freedom and choice for man), its dependence on man's efforts as the only source of valid knowledge (vs. willingness to accept the Bible as divine revelation). Not all psychologists accept these assumptions in the same degree, of course.

The volumes selected cover, in the following order, personality development and mental health, the psychology of religion, counseling and psychotherapy, and issues involving psychology as a scientific discipline. Books primarily about pastoral counseling are not included.

1. *JABAY, Earl, *Search for Identity,* ZPH, 1967, 150 pp., $3.95. A thoroughly biblically oriented treatise, rich with illustrations from life, about one of the great problems of our day, the problem of finding meaning and identity. In this context many important questions are confronted: guilt, human worth, maturity, marriage, sex, child rearing.

2. MAVES, P. B., *Understanding Ourselves as Adults,* ABP, 1959, 217 pp., $2.50. A well-written examination of the nature of personality development, education, and change in the adult years. Social factors, family influences, developmental tasks of adulthood, and concepts of maturity are related to a Christian view of man.

3. AUGSBURGER, A. D., *Creating Christian Personality,* HE, 1966, 128 pp., $4.00. A pastor-educator examines, in a series of lectures, the development of human personality from an explicitly Christian viewpoint and with special references to the needs of adolescents. Topics include early emotional needs, importance of family life, the nature of faith and love, problems concerning doubt, hostility, sex, and the need for independence.

4. *OATES, W. E., *The Religious Dimensions of Personality,* ASP, 1957, 320 pp., $4.50. An unusual book— this is a scholarly treatment of personality and religion from an author who demonstrates competence both in psychology and theology while maintaining a well-articulated expression of the Christian gospel. Deals with the fundamental issues psychology presents for the Christian as well as specific topics like heredity, personality development, structure of personality, personality disorganization.

5. HILTNER, Seward, *Self-understanding Through Psychology and Religion,* CSS, 1951, 224 pp., $2.75; CSS, 15s. (OoP) The importance of self-understanding gained through scientific psychology and religion from a liberal religious viewpoint. Explores topics like physical and emotional reactions to crisis, social perception, conscience, sex, personal freedom, failure, and aging.

6. *HAAS, H. I., *Mental Illness,* CON, 1966, 111 pp., Pb $1.00; CON, 100 pp., Pb 7s. A brief treatment by a Christian psychologist which tries to answer for the layman basic questions about mental disorder: its nature, causes, and treatment. Chapters on how the need for help can be recognized, where help can be found, how to live with emotional problems, and the responsibility of the churches.

7. *BOISEN, A. T., *Out of the Depths,* HRP, 1960, 217 pp. (OoP) A deeply moving autobiographical account of the religious and emotional experiences of a man who suffered through an acute mental disorder, recovered, and became a vital force in the movement to relate religion and mental health. A "must" for anyone interested in this field, but out of print at present.

8. CLINEBELL, H. J., *Mental Health Through Christian Community,* ABP, 1965, 300 pp., $4.75. Mental health and social problems are examined in breadth and detail in this volume. Although the nature of Christian community is never really spelled out, the challenge to the churches to find a new vitality through social concern and action is clearly laid down. Religious, and in a broad sense Christian, but not specifically Christ-centered.

9. McCANN, R. V., *The Churches and Mental Health,* BB, 1962, 278 pp. (OoP) One of ten monographs published by the Joint Commission on Mental Health as part of a national study. A blunt, readable, and theologically impartial look at the churches and the clergy and their role in the national problem of mental health. Important background reading for anyone interested in this area, but out of print.

10. WITHERINGTON, H. C., *Psychology of Religion,* WBE, 1955, 344 pp., $3.50. Unlike most books on the psychology of religion, this one approaches the subject from an explicitly Christian point of view and without attempting to discuss non-Christian religions. Most of the topics are those one would expect: man's needs, conversion and spiritual growth, prayer, worship. A few are unusual: religion and semantics, prophetic concepts in religion, psychology and revivals. The author clearly asserts his own beliefs but discusses

alternate viewpoints and allows the reader to form his own judgment.

11. *WHITE, Ernest, *Christian Life and the Unconscious,* HS, 1955, 190 pp., 10s 6d. (OoP) The book shows that Christian life is not limited to the conscious area of the mind, which in fact is a unity. The redemptive process brings about changes in the whole personality. The relation of modern psychological theories to several Christian doctrines and practices has an important practical bearing on Christian thought and conduct.

12. ALLPORT, G. W., *The Individual and His Religion,* MC, 1951, 147 pp., $3.95, Pb $1.50; CM, 1950; Ri, CM, 1962, Pb 11s 6d. A noted psychologist explores the place of religious attitudes within the structure of normal personality. Written from a stance that is naturalistic but not hostile to religion, the author concludes that a religious outlook can reflect either an unhealthy or a mature personality. Examines the nature of religious sentiment, religion in youth and maturity, the nature of faith and doubt.

13. JOHNSON, P. E., *Psychology of Religion,* ABP, 1945, 288 pp., $5.00. A textbook-type approach to the phenomena of religion. Draws on diverse forms of religious practice from numerous cultures in discussing topics like religious growth, worship forms, belief and behavior. Takes a "psychological" rather than a biblical point of view toward its subject matter.

14. CLARK, W. H., *The Psychology of Religion,* MC, 1958, 485 pp., $6.95. A competent approach to the psychology of religion which is basically sympathetic to religion but not committed to a particular religious viewpoint. Covers methodological problems in the study of religion, the phenomena of religious growth and various aspects of religious life. Recommended especially for the serious student of this topic.

15. *JAMES, William, *The Varieties of Religious Experience,* UB, 629 pp., $10.00; ML, 1963, 526 pp., Pb $1.95; CO, 1960, 7s 7d. A series of lectures published in 1902 by one of America's great thinkers in philosophy and psychology. Subject: The psychology of religion, with special reference to conversion and deeply personal religious experience. Probably the best known book on this subject and one which every educated Christian should have read, even though the author does not commit himself to a specifically Christian point of view.

16. NARRAMORE, C. M., *The Psychology of Counseling,* ZPH, 1960, 303 pp., $3.95; OL, 1962, 304 pp., 40s. Written for a general audience interested in counseling and for ministers, this book will have strong appeal for some Christians, just as it will make those with a different religious background uncomfortable with its emphasis on the importance of a conscious conversion experience and its highly literalistic approach to the Bible. It will make professionally trained counselors uncomfortable with its rather too pat problems and solutions. Emphasis on spiritual backsliding, sexual problems, use of Scripture in counseling.

17. TWEEDIE, D. F., *The Christian and the Couch,* BBH, 1963, 240 pp., $3.95. A broad-ranging and free-wheeling book on psychotherapy which approaches within a basically Christian viewpoint such problems as anxiety, alternative models for understanding human behavior, Freudian theory, types of mental disorder, and treatment. Stimulating but certainly not to be read uncritically.

18. FROMM, Erich, *Psychoanalysis and Religion,* YUP, 1950, 119 pp., $4.00; YUP, 1959, Pb $1.25; YUP, 1950, Hb 22s 6d, Pb 8s 6d. A noted psychoanalyst and gifted writer, who is much concerned with human worth and potential, explores the relation between religious and psychological views of man. Discusses Freud's and Jung's controversial views of religion and presents a third alternative: the psychiatrist as physician of the soul. Essentially an ethico-humanist approach to religion but an approach with which the educated Christian should be acquainted.

19. DRAKEFORD, J. W., *Integrity Therapy,* BR, 1967, 154 pp., $3.95. An enthusiastic statement of the point of view in psychology and religion which holds that what the world needs is a return to moral responsibility. Stresses the reality of guilt and the importance of confession, restitution, and right living for mental health. Not a word about Christ as Lord and Savior, but a provocative analysis of the above topics.

20. ODEN, T. C., *Contemporary Theology and Psychotherapy,* WP, 1967, 158 pp., $4.95. A scholarly examination of several contemporary theological positions (Bonhoeffer, Teilhard de Chardin, Tillich, Bultmann, et al.) in an attempt to explore the relationship between theology and secular psychotherapy and between pastoral care and current theology. Not for the theological neophyte or the lazy reader, but an important book.

21. *LLOYD-JONES, D. M., *Conversions: Psychological and Spiritual,* IVP, 1957, 40 pp., 60¢; TP, 2s 6d. Written largely from a defensive stance, this little booklet attempts to refute one of the assaults on Christian faith from secular psychology, namely, the assertion that conversion is a type of "brain washing" or psychological "conditioning." Vigorous argumentation but it is questionable whether this kind of apologetic is desirable or necessary.

22. OUTLER, A. C., *Psychotherapy and the Christian Message,* HRP, 1954, 286 pp., Pb $1.75. Although the specific focus of this book is on the relationship between psychotherapy and Christian belief, it is also a bold examination of many of the fundamental issues which appear to divide psychology and biblical Christianity. The author contrasts secular and Christian approaches to man in terms of the human quandary, man's freedom and potential, the basis for morality, and the potential for an alliance between the two approaches.

23. DONIGER, Simon, *The Nature of Man in Theological and Psychological Perspective,* HRP, 1962, 264 pp. (OoP); *Nature of Man,* HRP, 45s. A most fortuitous collection of essays by noted theologians, psychologists, and psychiatrists covering man's nature, good and evil in man, and man's problems and potentialities, but unfortunately out of print at present. The theological spectrum represented is diverse.

24. *What, Then, Is Man?* CON, 1958, 356 pp., $3.50; CON, 358 pp., 25s. A symposium with contributions from theology, psychology, and psychiatry. Covers in detail the complex problems involved in scientific views of the nature of man, human motivation, personality, psychopathology, guilt, conversion, and pastoral counseling from an explicitly Christian point of view. Readable, but aimed at the serious reader.

6I. JOURNALISM
McCandlish Phillips
News affects the American culture. Hundreds of thousands of words are sent out daily on the news wires, and they flow into every city, town, and

hamlet in the nation. Let a riot or a student strike break out and reports of it, transmitted by the instantaneous word of the news media, spark outbreaks elsewhere. Bad news, riots, and rebellions are infectious social ills, and news reports spread them quickly. Good news, effective solutions, and revivals are infectious, too. But it is a sad and scandalous fact that there are almost no evangelical Christians working as reporters and editors on major newspapers in the United States.

The information media are therefore a monopoly conferred upon unbelievers—by the conspicuous default of believers. It does not have to be that way. The mass media today are wide open to bright, energetic, qualified, young Christians. By reading any two of the following books a believer will obtain quite a good picture of the rigors, rewards, and privileges of news reporting and what it is like to have a way-up-front view of history in the making. (Books with specifically Christian emphases are so identified in the annotations.)

1. BROWN, David, and W. R. Bruner, eds., *How I Got That Story*, EPD, 1967, 380 pp., $5.95. Thirty-five notable reporters recall, with considerable flair, how they got their biggest, or hardest, or most dangerous stories. The perils and adventures of covering the news are sometimes more exciting than the news itself.

2. *ADLER, R., ed., *The Working Press*, GPP, 1966, 287 pp., $5.95. Fifty *New York Times* reporters tell, with wit and vivid detail, what life is really like covering the news on every continent against sundry perils. A. M. Rosenthal tells "How it Felt to Be Kicked Out of Poland" and Homer Bigart recalls getting the "Heave Ho, Vietnamese Style." In "The Story Behind the Jewish Klansman," McCandlish Phillips tells how a news source repeatedly threatened to kill

him and how he responded by telling him of God's offer of salvation through Jesus Christ.

3. *PHILLIPS, McCandlish, *Christian Penetration of the Secular Mass Media*, a booklet obtainable from Mr. McCandlish Phillips, *New York Times*, Times Square, New York, 10036, 1968, 54 pp., 50¢. A call for Christian action in the nation's press and electronic news media. A Christian of evangelical persuasion who has been a reporter for *The New York Times* since 1955 challenges college-age evangelicals to get into the thick of news reporting; describes it from the inside, tells how to get started, where to seek work, what to expect, discusses schooling and the development of good writing style, describes how faith helps a newsman meet a daily deadline and obtain exclusives against the competition. With examples of sound news reporting from a Christian perspective.

4. BUSH, C. R., *Newswriting and Reporting Public Affairs*, CC, 1965, 576 pp., $11.75. A basic textbook on writing the news and reporting public affairs by a college professor, including chapters on "Organizing the Facts," "Making an Event Vivid," how to cover "City Hall."

5. JUERGENS, George, *Joseph Pulitzer and The New York World*, PUP, 1966, 391 pp., $10.00; OUP, 1967, 408 pp., 80s. Describes how Pulitzer—a great popularizer, crusader, iconoclast, and prodder of the social conscience—quickly "converted the *New York World* from a moribund sheet into one of the most prosperous and influential dailies" in the nation.

6. MOTT, F. L., *American Journalism. A History: 1690-1960*, MC, 1960, 901 pp., $9.95; CM, ED 3, 1962, 63s. A comprehensive history of the American newspaper, begin-

ning with "The First Newspaper in New England." A very broad overview, with concise glimpses of some of the great figures, characters, and rascals of the American press. Chronicles the rise of the penny press in the 1930's, the development of intense news competition, the rise of the chains and of mass circulation tabloids. Interesting note: *The New England Courant* was founded as a paper opposing smallpox innoculations at a time when Increase and Cotton Mather, the formidable clerics, strongly supported the much-reviled preventive innovation! Many illustrations. If you want it all, it's all here.

7. LYONS, L. M., ed., *Reporting the News: Selections from the Nieman Reports,* HUP, 1965, 443 pp. (OoP); HUP, 1966, 456 pp., 52s. Authoritative pieces by some of the best writers and editors in American journalism edited by Louis M. Lyons, for twenty-five years the Curator at Harvard of the Nieman Fellowships for newspaper men. Authors include Anthony Lewis, a two-time Pulitzer Prize winner; Clifton Daniel, managing editor of the *New York Times;* Mark Ethridge, Alfred Friendly, a 1968 Pulitzer Prize winner for coverage of the Arab-Israeli war, writes on "Attribution of News." Subjects include "How Best to Prepare for Newspaper Work," "Free Press and Fair Trial."

8. CRANE, Stephen, *The War Despatches of Stephen Crane,* NYUP, 1964, 343 pp., $7.00; OW, 1964, 45s. Stephen Crane, author of *The Red Badge of Courage,* was a brilliant writer of fiction and no less a brilliant correspondent in the Greco-Turkish and the Spanish-American wars. Crane, the son of a Methodist minister, died at thirty, leaving a small treasury of graceful and wonderfully descriptive prose. This book also includes four parodies on Crane as a war correspondent.

9. RESTON, James, *Sketches in the Sand,* AAK, 1967, 479 pp., $6.95. A collection of the best pieces of commentary and news analysis written by James Reston, who is among the most perceptive and renowned of American journalists. Most of the material appeared in Reston's "Washington" column in *The New York Times.* "A newspaper column, like a fish, should be consumed when fresh; otherwise it is not only undigestible but unspeakable," Reston admits in his introduction, but he goes on to disprove his own anathema. Still fresh.

10. MURPHY, R. D., *Reporting Public Problems,* CC, 1960, 370 pp. (OoP); CC, 372 pp., 58s. A journalism professor looks at the reporting of serious public affairs in government, education, population trends, the growth of great cities, law, finance, public health, and the courts.

11. *Books on Journalism, Catalogue Eleven,* AB, P. O. Box 1706, Oakland, California, 94 pp., 25¢. This is an amazing resource booklet. Nearly every book on journalism published in the last fifty years is recorded here. There are 1,482 old, new, and out-of-print titles, annotated, with prices, all available from Acme. Perfect for anyone who wants to build a bookshelf on journalism. Most of the books listed above are available here.

6J. POLITICAL SCIENCE
Samuel Richey Kamm

Political literature covers a broad spectrum of human experience. Originally couched in the epics of man's earliest mythological interpretations of life, it has now sought complete conformity to the latest insights of natural science. In between these two extremes lies a large body of literature which portrays the institutions and processes of government either as representative of a divinely ordained plan or a system inherent in the na-

ture of things. In either case the writings tend to be expository and didactic. They often convey a sense of individual and group obligation. Now the tone of political literature is explanatory and descriptive. Its moral thrust is nil. Political literature, consequently, tends to be impersonal in the sense that it invites no obligation for involvement.

The moral sterility inherent in this excessive emphasis upon the science of politics has led to a two-dimensional reaction. Modern ideologists have sought to overcome the amorality of political inquiry by the erection of ideologies which assign purpose to political existence through some dialectically sanctioned form of revolutionary utopia. The best known of these is the Marxist ideology with its communist utopia. The latest is the existentialist stress upon individual revolt leading ultimately to a visionary socialism.

In contradistinction there is a growing body of literature which seeks to revive the classical Christian perspective in politics. By-passing for the most part the apocalyptic vision of the Kingdom of God, so dramatically portrayed by Augustine in the fifth century, it generally seeks to win men to a realistic view of politics. Here man made in the image of God is challenged by the dictum that government is the "art of the possible." Traditional values of authority and justice are recognized as binding upon men in human society. They are to be applied within the limits of human finiteness. Out of this stress has come a new emphasis upon the validity of representative or constitutional democracy as the system of government most compatible with human nature.

The titles listed here are those which give expression to these current modes of thought. Systematic treatises, usually found in textbooks, will be passed over in favor of books which convey points of view on cur-

rent issues. Some will deal with the nature of political inquiry; most will be concerned with contemporary ideas and problems. Each title will provide an introduction to one phase of political science as it is now conceived. The initial entry will serve as an introduction to the study of politics.

1. *SORAUF, F. J., Political Science: An Informal Overview, Charles E. Merrill, 1965, 115 pp., Hb $3.95, Pb $1.75; PH, Hb 32s, Pb 14s. The best brief statement of the meaning and scope of political science as now taught in colleges and universities. Employs the concept of the political system as the unifying theme. Deals with the modern concept of things political, traces the development of the study of political science in America, describes the relation of the individual to political institutions and processes and traces the quest of man for an "ideals" political system. (Chapter VI of the Social Science Seminar edition contains a helpful chapter by Raymond H. Muessig and Vincent R. Rogers on the teaching of political science in the schools.)

Principles and Theory

Principles of human action derived from the disciplines of psychology, anthropology and sociology are drawn upon by contemporary political scientists in their definition of the principles and theory to be followed in the interpretation of political action. Discussions of theory tend to be governed by those formulations which can be tested through an organized study of empirical evidence. There are some writers, however, who have not abandoned the older canons of exposition in political science. And there are a few who, sensing the drift of political theory from its classical and Christian universals, are endeavoring to restore the theoretical foundations of politics to principles of universal meaning. This sec-

tion will include titles that are representative of the various schools of thought in the profession of political science today.

2. FRIEDRICH, C. J., *Constitutional Government and Democracy,* Blaisdell, RE, 1968, 687 pp., $9.50. Using the historical and legal concept of the state, the author describes the development of those "limiting" features of various Western governmental systems which have contributed to the growth of constitutional democracy. One of the best discussions of constitutional government in the West now available.

3. HALLOWELL, J. H., *Main Currents in Modern Political Thought,* Henry Holt, 1950, 695 pp., $9.95; HRW, 60s. The development of political thought in the Western world from the Greeks to the modern existentialist philosophers. Most valuable for its critique of modern political philosophy from Hobbes and Locke until the present from the perspective of the "classical Christian tradition." Concludes with a consideration of pronouncements on the prevailing social order by the major schools of thought in Christendom.

4. DEAN, H. E., *Judicial Review and Democracy,* PS, 1966, 206 pp., Hb $3.75; RH, Pb $1.95. A concise and informative statement of the role of the judiciary in a constitutional democracy. Rousseauean democracy and American democracy are contrasted in an effort to demonstrate the necessity of judicial review if a totalitarian democracy is to be avoided. The role of the Supreme Court in the development of the American political tradition is helpfully outlined. More readable than most books on the work of the Supreme Court.

5. DAHL, R. A., *Modern Political Analysis,* PH, 1963, 118 pp., Hb $4.50, Pb $1.95; PH, 16s. A very

readable introduction to the "political systems" method of studying politics. Uses a variety of diagrammatic representations and statistical distributions to illustrate the modern concepts of political analysis. The author is one of the recognized leaders in the "behavioral" study of politics in the United States.

6. *WILLIAMSON, Rene de Visme, *Independence and Involvement: A Christian Reorientation in Political Science,* LSUP, 1964, 269 pp., $7.50. A professor of political science proposes that we return to the Christian faith for spiritual and intellectual guidance in "rightly dividing" political issues. Such topics as the role of the church in government, the issue of civil rights, the nature of a constitutional system, the fundamental concepts underlying democratic and totalitarian political systems, and the problems of citizenship are brilliantly discussed. One layman after reading the book declared it to have outstanding ability to communicate a Christian view of political issues in a manner that does not offend those who may disagree. The critical definition of such terms as liberal and conservative is excellent.

American Political Institutions and Politics

The American political system is unique. The concept of a constitutional democracy by which it is governed was long entertained by theologians and philosophers of Western Europe as a possible reality. It was in America that this dream was given an opportunity to develop. The concept of equality in political life, the idea of individual participation in public policy formation, the ideal of the rule of law under a popularly approved constitution, the conviction that powers of government must be separated under a dual federal system, and the vision of social justice for all men in a political commu-

nity became the foundation stones of the American republic.

Today the political scientist is absorbed very often in the task of analytical description of the American political process. But there are some still who are concerned about the value system which provided an integrating mythos for the founders of the republic. The titles listed in this section will provide ample opportunity to become acquainted with both aspects of the study of American institutions and politics.

7. *de TOCQUEVILLE, Alexis, Democracy in America, Arlington, 1966, V. I, 431 pp., V. II, 382 pp., Hb $6.00 each; VI, 1954, V. I, 452 pp., V. II, 518 pp., Pb $1.45 each; BAIB, V. I, 522 pp., V. II, 432 pp., 11s each. A French visitor to America in the 1830's interprets the new democracy in the light of its Puritan cultural foundations. He is particularly intrigued by the concept of equality in American society and the relation of religion to the American political system. It is still the most helpful interpretation of American political institutions because of its recognition of the relationship between religion and politics in American culture. Volume I contains a description of the American federal system that has provided the conceptual apparatus for the study of American government for several generations.

8. McLAUGHLIN, A. C., The Foundations of American Constitutionalism, NYUP, 1961, 160 pp., Pb 60¢. Six brief but informative essays upon the basic concepts which underlie the American constitutional system. Deals with the English trading corporation, the Puritan idea of church covenant, the seventeenth-century concept of social compact, and their contribution to American political life. An attractive style of writing invites further inquiry into topics

which at first glance may be formidable in appearance.

9. *MITCHELL, Broadus and Louise, A Biography of the Constitution of the United States: Its Origins, Formation, Adoption, Interpretation, OUP, 1964, 384 pp., Hb $6.75, Pb $2.50. The title of this volume is indicative of what it provides—a very interesting and readable account of the origin, construction, and development of the Constitution. Teachers of history and of government have found this to be a stimulus to their own thought and a challenge to their best students whether in high school or in college. The lay reader will find that it provides insights and understandings that could be secured formerly only in reading volumes of more extended content and less interesting style.

10. WRIGHT, B. F., ed., The Federalist, HUP, 1961, 572 pp., $7.50; OUP, 60s. An excellent edition in modern literary style of the classic interpretation of the American federal system. The author's introduction to the essays of Hamilton, Jay, and Madison provides one of the most readable and comprehensive expositions of the papers now available. Professor Wright is most helpful in relating the political issues of the late eighteenth century to those of today.

11. CARTER, Douglass, Power in Washington, RH, 1964, 275 pp., Hb $4.95, Pb $1.65. The author, a journalist and now special assistant to the President, describes the American constitutional system as it now operates. Persons desiring to secure a more accurate understanding of the role of the presidency, the Congress, the political parties, and the so-called sub-governments of the administrative establishment will find this volume an excellent entree to the various works that have been written in recent years to describe the "reali-

ties" of government in the nation's capital.

12. ABRAHAM, H. J., *The Judicial Process,* OUP, 1962, 381 pp., $2.50; OUP, 394 pp., 20s. The role of the courts in the American constitutional system and the nature of their day-by-day operation has remained a mystery for many. Professor Abraham endeavors to dispel that mystery for Americans and to relate the operation and functions of their court system to that of England and France. Written in a very lucid style, it provides an excellent background for the study of constitutional law.

13. *BERMAN, D. M., *It Is Ordered: The Supreme Court Rules on School Segregation,* WWN, 1966, 161 pp., Hb $4.50, Pb $1.75. This little volume is designed to acquaint one with the manner in which a particular case—Brown v. Board of Education (1954)—originated in the lower courts, was tried, and then found its way to the Supreme Court of the United States for review. It is a case study in the judicial process involving both state and federal courts. Includes the text of opinions rendered at both levels.

14. FENTON, J. H., *Unofficial Makers of Public Policy: People and Parties in Politics,* Scott, Foresman Co., 1966, 147 pp., Hb $3.95, Pb $2.10. People who are puzzled about the role of political parties in the American constitutional system will find this to be one of the clearest expositions of the subject now in print. Professor Fenton's very interesting essay will prepare the reader for the more comprehensive studies recently authored by Professors Sorauf and Rossiter.

15. PRICE, D. K., *The Scientific Estate,* Belknap Press, 1965, 323 pp., $6.50; OUP, 336 pp., 48s. The author is the Dean of the Graduate School of Public Administration at Harvard University. An essay which endeavors to demonstrate that the rise of a scientific "estate" in American society has introduced a new order of institutional balance in the constitutional system. Dean Price is particularly sensitive to the influence of government-sponsored research programs on the civil liberties of the citizen. He concludes that the nation must maintain separate roles in the decision-making process for those who seek absolute truth through science and those who formulate public policy. A stimulating and readable book for both the layman and the expert.

16. *WALTER, James, *The Christian in Politics,* OUP, 1962, 216 pp., $7.00; OUP, 208 pp., 30s. A British journalist conducts an inquiry into the role of the Christian in politics. To illustrate his findings Mr. James draws upon the political experience of nineteenth-century British evangelicals who endeavored to maintain their own religious commitment in public life and, yet, to adjust to the changing demands of party loyalty. This is a book that should be read by every Christian who contemplates a career in politics and government.

17. *Report of the National Advisory Commission on Civil Disorders.* BAB, 1968, 608 pp., Pb $1.25. The controversial but very readable report of the Kerner Commission on recent disorders in American cities. Even though its findings are heavily biased toward an "environmentalist" interpretation of the race issue and related urban problems, it is a document that should be read by every American who desires to be prepared for the responsibilities of citizenship in the United States.

Ideologies and International Politics

International politics were once view-

ed as an imperialistic contest for raw materials and markets. Now the relations of states are conceived as absorbed in a contest for men's minds. Economics may be the basis of political power, but it is no longer the determinant of political systems. The question which confronts men everywhere is this: Shall government be built upon a pattern of revolutionary change, or shall it subscribe to the more orderly system of development guided by the traditions of constitutional democracy? This section of the reading list is designed to acquaint the reader with the leading antidemocratic ideologies of the twentieth century and their impact upon international politics.

18. GYORGY, Andrew, and G. D. Blackwood, *Ideologies in World Affairs,* Blaisdell, 1967, 262 pp., Pb $3.50. A series of lectures, simple in style and attractive in format, which discuss the nature and impact of modern political ideologies upon national and international politics in the twentieth century. Reading lists are well selected.

19. MAYO, H. B., *Introduction to Marxist Theory,* OUP, 1960, 334 pp., Pb $2.25; OUP, 344 pp., 18s. Published originally in 1955 under the title *Democracy and Marxism,* this book provides one of the best expositions of Marxian doctrine now available. The major doctrines of Marx and Engels are elucidated as well as those of their followers. Two fine chapters on "Marxism and Scientific Method" and "Marxism, Morality and Religion" help the beginning student to gain a clear perspective of Marxism as an ideology. The final chapter, "Democracy and Marxism," is an analysis of Marxist political concepts in the light of democratic theory. The author communicated clearly and meaningfully his critical evaluation of Marxian principles. An excellent bibliography, annotated,

provides a splendid guide to further study of Marxism.

20. *TUCKER, R. C., Philosophy and Myth in Karl Marx,* CAUP, 1961, 263 pp., Hb $5.50, Pb $1.75; CAUP, Hb 40s, Pb 12s 6d. The *Economic and Philosophic Manuscripts of 1844,* only recently published in English translation, have provoked a re-interpretation of Marx as a social thinker. Eric Fromm, the modern Freudian humanist, endeavors to identify Marx as a forerunner of existential humanism; Tucker seeks to show that Marx is strongly influenced by the German idealists, Kant and Hegel, who deify man and thus commit him to an ideology of self-salvation. Marx, according to Tucker, saw man as alienated from his primal creative self through the historical economic process—capitalism. Man's restoration to selfhood, argued Marx, must be by means of a revolution which destroys capitalism and liberates man to his original role as artist. Tucker's brilliant exposition lays a meaningful basis for an intelligent understanding of the implications of Marxism.

21. *DANIELS, R. V., The Nature of Communism,* RH, 1962, 398 pp., Hb $6.00; VI, Pb $1.95. An excellent historical and topical survey of the rise of communism as a revolutionary movement. The author deals with the relationship of communism to Marxian theory and to twentieth-century revolutionary movements in Russia and China. He describes in detail the intellectual and sociological aspects of communist ideology and criticizes its application in contemporary totalitarian societies. He concludes with a perceptive chapter on communism as a "faith" movement. Professor Daniels writes convincingly in support of the thesis that communism, as an ideology, is as divergent from its Marxian antecendents as the Christianity of the renaissance popes is from the twelve apostles. See also,

two books by Lester DeKoster, *Communism and Christian Faith*, WBE, $3.50; and *The Vocabulary of Communism*, WBE, $3.50.

22. WEBER, Eugen, *Varieties of Fascism: Doctrines of Revolution in the Twentieth Century*, D. Van Nostrand, 1964, 191 pp., Pb $1.45; D. Van Nostrand, Pb 12s 6d. The best brief historical survey of fascist political movements now available. Written in an interesting style by a leading authority in the field, it provides a sound basis for an understanding of political ideological movements of the right in the modern world. Short documentary selections supplement the text.

23. KENNAN, G. F., *American Diplomacy, 1900-1950.* UCP, 1951, 146 pp., Hb $3.95; NAL, 1952, Pb 75¢; NEL, 1965, Pb 5s. The Charles R. Walgreen lectures for 1950, plus two articles previously published, represent the opinions of a former American diplomat who established the trend toward "realism" in American foreign policy. Ambassador Kennan is best known for his early enunciation of the policy of "containment" in dealing with the Soviet Union. These lectures comprise one of the better analyses of the limits of political power in the conduct of relations among major states that are committed to radically different value systems.

24. *MORGENTHAU, Hans, *Politics among Nations: The Struggle for Power and Peace*, AAK, RE 3, 1966, 615 pp., $11.25. The author looks at world politics from the perspective of the balance of power theory. He discusses the role of political ideologies, the concept of political alliances, the problem of nuclear disarmament, and the effort to maintain world order through the United Nations and its related international services. The style is vigorous and trenchant. A

classic study because of its broad sweep of historical observation and its expressed confidence in the ability of man to maintain peace in spite of his acknowledged irrationality.

25. *THOMPSON, K. W., *Christian Ethics and the Dilemma of Foreign Policy*, DUP, 1959, 148 pp., $3.50. A series of lectures on the application of Christian ethical principles in the conduct of international relations. The author deals with the moral ambiguities of international politics as illustrated in the current diplomatic interchange over the problems of armament and colonialism. He tries to make plain the ethical tensions which arise when Christian principles governing interpersonal relations are applied to international issues. The lectures are very conversational in form and stimulating in content.

26. *RASKIN, M. G., and B. B. Fall, ed., *The Vietnam Reader: Articles and Documents on American Foreign Policy and the Vietnam Crisis*, RH, RE, 1967, Pb $2.95. The best collection of contemporary writing on American involvement in Vietnam. The editors endeavor to include representative opinions from journalists, diplomats, military leaders, and government officials on the issues as they see them. Co-editor, the late Bernard B. Fall was one of the most perceptive journalists covering Vietnam for the American and European press.

6K. ECONOMICS
David O. Moberg

No longer "the dismal science," economics has become one of the most glamorous and influential social sciences. Both the classical economics associated with Adam Smith and Keynesian economic theory are gradually being replaced with new perspectives, so the Christian who wishes to be in tune with the times must get beyond traditionally-oriented resources.

Because economics deals with the production, distribution, and consumption of goods and services, it is directly related to Christian stewardship. The Bible, therefore, presents many principles that are pertinent to it, even though it imposes no single economic system on all societies and presents no structural framework as ideal. The references that follow are all worthy of study even though neither this writer nor the readers will agree with every idea expressed in them.

1. *HEYNE, P. T., *The Christian Encounters the World of Economics,* CON, 1965, 117 pp., Pb $1.00; CON, 7s. Perhaps the best brief survey of economics from a Christian perspective, this book deals with order and the market, principles of economics, change and the featherbed, and the Christian encounter with economic affairs. It concludes that "Christianity has very little to say about the economic order," yet it indicates clearly that Christianity has much to say about behavior within any economic system.

2. *CATHERWOOD, H. F. R., *The Christian in Industrial Society,* IVP, 1966, 130 pp., $1.25; TP, Ed 2, 6s. This examination of implications of Christian faith and life in economics, politics, and industry by the Chief Industrial Advisor to the Ministry of Economic Affairs in England explores competition, wealth, attitudes to work, investment, accounts, trade unions, and other subjects in the light of Christian principles.

3. *SIMON, Paul, *The Christian Encounters a Hungry World,* CON, 1965, 101 pp., Pb $1.00; CON, 7s. The dilemma of full Christian stomachs in a world of empty stomachs is explored. Efforts to feed the hungry and to deal with poverty in the

U.S.A. and in "the world of nations" are explored in the light of Christ's "Inasmuch." This first-class book is a challenge to show the love of Christ in one's life both as a person and, through government, as a citizen.

4. POWELL, L. P., *Money and the Church,* AP, 1963, 236 pp., Pb $1.50. The way churches raise money is presented as just as much a spiritual matter as the purposes for which they spend it. Methods and purposes of money raising in the Apostolic Church, early Christianity, the Middle Ages, the Reformation Era, the American Colonies, and Contemporary America are surveyed and appraised.

5. *FULLER, R. H., and B. K. Rice, *Christianity and the Affluent Society,* WBE, 1967, 191 pp., Hb $3.95, Pb $2.45; HS, 1966, 192 pp., 30s. Looking at the world of the Bible and that of the twentieth century in the light of Christian responsibility, the authors analyze the biblical attitude toward wealth and its implications for modern society. They draw upon both British and American examples, include "the Laws of Life which our Saviour Christ declares unto us," and assert that "the affluent society can be redeemed by faith—and by our willingness to risk all for the gospel."

6. MUNBY, D. L., *God and the Rich Society,* OUP, 1961, 220 pp., $5.50; OUP, 25s. Munby holds that an economy of abundance is not evil in and of itself, so an intelligent Christian will accept its advantages while recognizing and correcting its faults. Quasi-economic pronouncements of ecclesiastic leaders and religious bodies are disparaged because they typically are based upon inadequate knowledge of the realities of the issues with which they grapple.

7. HEILBRONER, R. L., *The Great Ascent: The Struggle for Economic Development in our Time,* HRP, 1963, 160 pp., Pb 95¢; HRP, 30s. The explosive economic development of Asian, African, and Latin American nations in the world-wide struggle to escape from poverty and misery, the political, economic, and social challenges it poses for America, and the choice before the U.S.A. and the West are the chief topics of this thought-provoking book. It can serve as a basic resource for discussions of foreign aid and foreign trade.

8. SNIDER, D. A., *Economic Myth and Reality,* PH, 1965, 150 pp., $1.95; PH, 16s. Each of the sixteen chapters deals with a misconception about economics that is firmly entrenched and endlessly repeated in the mass media of communications and in private discussions. This "other side of the story" on the nature and value of money, government finance, progress, poverty, the economics of foreign relations, and free enterprise is upheld by most professional economists.

9. CHILDS, M. W., and Douglass Cater, *Ethics in a Business Society,* HRP, RE, 1966, 192 pp., Hb $3.50, Pb 50¢; HRP, 5s. A journalistic summary of six books resulting from a major project on religious and economic life in which theologians, philosophers, and ministers interacted with social scientists, this book's interpretations and opinions should be taken as a basis for reflection and discussion more than as a guide to action.

10. EARLE, Clifford, Margaret Kuhn, and H. B. Sissel, *The Camel and the Needle's Eye,* NCC, 1954, 40 pp., Pb 30¢. This study guide for *Ethics in a Business Society* by Childs and Cater (see above) includes discussion starters and suggestions, tips on discussion techniques, and informa-

tion resources dealing with "Christian Conscience and the American Economy."

11. MUNBY, D. L., *Christianity and Economic Problems,* SM, 1956, 290 pp., $5.00; MC, 25s. General principles, particular problems, and conclusions on the main Christian doctrines that have economic implications for society and daily life are the focus of attention in this book for laymen.

12. POPE, Liston, *Millhands and Preachers,* YUP, 1942, 369 pp., Hb $7.50, Pb $2.45; YUP, Pb 17s. The historical background and surrounding events of a cotton mill strike in 1929 are analyzed with special reference to the role of churches and the clergy and its impact upon them. The findings carry significant implications for all churches' relationships to economic institutions, social classes, and community problems.

13. OKUN, A. M., ed., *The Battle Against Unemployment: An Introduction to a Current Issue of Public Policy,* WWN, 1965, 204 pp., Hb $4.00, Pb $1.75. Twenty-seven papers on concepts, costs, and consequences of unemployment, the balance of employment and price stability, principles and instruments of fiscal policy, and monetary policy are brought together into an excellent survey of economic stability and employment. No single line of interpretation dominates, although maximum employment, production, and purchasing power is an implicit goal of all the authors.

14. *GALBRAITH, J. K., *The New Industrial State,* HM, 1967, 427 pp., $6.95. In great corporations people increasingly serve the conveniences of organizations which were meant to serve them. Traditional interpretations of motives, relationships between business and state, and the role of markets in the economy are large-

ly invalidated by the development of planned decisions serving the goals of large-scale organizations in a world in which the lines dividing state and industry are disappearing. This stimulating and controversial look at economics and the quality of modern life poses significant challenges to Christian thought and action.

15. VAN OYEN, Hendrik, *Affluence and the Christian,* FP, 1966, 37 pp., 85¢; SPCK, 1964, 20 pp., 1s 6d. This seven-chapter essay by a University of Basel theologian deals with luxury and the Christian. Biblical teachings are related to Christian attitudes, values, and actions. Superficial reading may give the incorrect impression that luxurious living is unconditionally sanctioned.

16. HELLER, W. W., *New Dimensions of Political Economy,* WWN, 1967, Hb $3.50, Pb $1.75; OUP, 28s. "The new economics" which arises "out of the swift and progressive weaving of modern economics into the fabric of national thinking and policy" involves new uses of the discipline more than new substance. Professor Heller, the former Chairman of the Council of Economic Advisors under Presidents Kennedy and Johnson, indicates the how and why of a flexible approach to national fiscal policy, including his plan for states to share federal revenues.

17. BOULDING, K. E., *The Organization Revolution: A Study in the Ethics of Economic Organization,* HRP, 1953, 286 pp., $4.00. The great increase in the number, size, and power of organizations and the silent revolution which occurs as a result is the focus of this book by a Quaker economist. Individuals are made willing to serve their organization's ends even at the cost of ethical and moral compromises. The penetrating moral insight of the Word of God is a necessary corrective.

18. MYRDAL, Gunnar, *Beyond the Welfare State,* YUP, 1960, 287 pp., Pb $1.95; ME, 1965, 214 pp., 16s. One of the world's leading economic theorists deals with the trend toward national planning in rich Western nations and its international implications. He throws light on social forces that contributed to this trend, the type of national community that is emerging, and the effects of such planning upon economic relations between nations, especially with underdeveloped countries.

19. *WEBER, Max, *The Protestant Ethic and the Spirit of Capitalism,* CSS, 1958, 292 pp., Hb $3.95, Pb $1.45; Ri, AU, 1965, 16s. This classic study of relationships between religion and economic life theorizes that the mentality associated with the Calvinistic worldly asceticism of Puritanism was a source of psychological sanctions and mental attitudes underlying modern Western capitalism.

20. CLARK, J. W., *Religion and the Moral Standards of American Businessmen,* SWP, 1966, 198 pp., $4.50. The first part of this study deals with Catholic, Jewish, and Protestant religious influence upon attitudes toward the problems of ethical behavior in business and includes results of a questionnaire survey. The second part attempts to indicate the parameters of the actual moral content of contemporary business and includes a "tentative statement of ethical guides."

6L. ROMAN CATHOLICISM
Herbert M. Carson

There has always been a gulf between Roman Catholic theory and practice which has made it difficult for the uninitiated to discover what Rome actually teaches. There is, for example, a vast difference between popular devotion and the precise statements of Roman theology. Then again, Catholi-

cism shows different faces in different lands—there is a marked divergence between say Dutch and Latin American Catholicism.

Today this problem appears in a different form as we confront the deep cleavage in Rome between the conservatives, holding fast to the traditional dogmas, and the progressives who are trying to produce formulations acceptable to the present age. It must, however, be remembered that whatever changes may have taken place, the essential dogmatic structure remains unaltered. Hence in the following list of books, while attention is paid to the new Catholicism, the traditional dogmatic formulations are still the issue of major concern.

1. *CARSON, H. M., Roman Catholicism Today*, WBE, 1965, 128 pp., Pb $1.45; TP, 1964, Pb 4s. Designed as a general introduction to a study of the subject. It covers the whole field of doctrine and assesses Roman Catholic beliefs from a biblical standpoint. It aims to be of service not only to Protestants who are beginning to study Roman Catholicism but also to thinking Roman Catholics. See also, Dreyer and Weller, *Roman Catholicism in the Light of Scripture*, PTS, 1958, 210 pp., 8s 6d. (OoP)

2. CARSON, H. M., *The New Catholicism*, BTT, 24 pp. Serves by way of a supplement to the previous entry in which the stress was on traditional Roman dogma. An attempt is made to avoid the extremes of dismissing the new Catholicism in a summary way and that of welcoming it uncritically. What are the progressives saying? What are their problems? This booklet suggests some answers to these questions.

3. *BOETTNER, Loraine, *Roman Catholicism*, PRPC, 1962, 466 pp., Hb $5.95; BTT, 1966, 559 pp., Pb 8s 6d. The author not only covers the usual field of Roman doctrine but

ranges very widely, dealing with such issues as Roman attitudes to marriage and divorce and to education. He is strongly oriented in his criticism towards a consideration of American Catholicism.

4. WILSON, Ewin, *Leading Roman Catholics to Christ*, Dublin, Christian Publications Centre, 1966, 112 pp., Pb 4s 6d. The author and the reviser have been working in two of the most Roman Catholic countries in the world—Quebec and Southern Ireland respectively. Hence this practical manual on reaching Roman Catholics commands respect, for it is not merely theoretical work but one born out of actual experience of such evangelism.

5. *SALMON, George, *Infallibility of the Church*, BBH, ED 3, 1959, 497 pp., $3.95; JM, 1953, 222 pp., 12s 6d. Originally delivered as a series of lectures in the Divinity School of the University of Dublin, it is a powerful refutation of the basic conception which underlies the whole Roman dogmatic structure. Here is scholarly polemic spiced with humor. Papal infallibility is weighed in the scales of Scripture and history and found wanting.

6. KIDD, B. J., *The Roman Primacy to A. D. 461*, SPCK, 1936, 159 pp., 5s. (OoP) A specialist in patristic studies exposes the fallacies of the papal claims by appealing to the history of the early Church. His own sympathy with a great deal of Roman Catholicism makes his rejection of papal primacy all the more telling.

7. KERR, W. S., *A Handbook on the Papacy*, MMS, ED 3, 1962, 322 pp., 18s. The papal claims to primacy, supremacy, and infallibility are examined and rejected. The appeal is to Scripture and to history. An invaluable companion to Salmon's work. In spite of the concessions to the bishops at Vatican II Papal infallibility

is still a major factor in Rome's system, hence the continuing importance of this book.

8. PARIS, Arnold, *The Vatican Against Europe*, PTS, ED 2, 1964, 311 pp., 25s. A well-documented account of Rome's political activities in Europe. The part played by the Catholic political parties and the papal diplomatic service in the rise of Nazism and Fascism is the main theme. Written from a secular standpoint it is a sober, balanced, and realistic appraisal of Catholic action in the political sphere.

9. MANHATTAN, Avro, *Vatican Imperialism in the Twentieth Century*, ZPH, 1965, 414 pp., $5.95. A devastating exposure of the outworking of Roman ambitions on a world scale. The Vatican is not only the center of a religious organization but also of a powerful political system whose agencies reach out to every country in the world. This critique is reinforced by thorough documentation.

10. RAHNER, Karl, *The Teaching of the Catholic Church*, ALBA, 461 pp., $6.95; MER, 1967, 30s. This is a Jesuit compilation of documents giving the essential doctrines of Rome. Each section has an introductory exposition of the doctrine indexed with reference to the documents which follow. It is very useful for those who want to find in Rome's own statements what she teaches.

11. OTT, Ludwig, *Fundamentals of Catholic Dogma*, HH, 1955, 519 pp., $7.50; MER, 1962, 544 pp., 30s. Invaluable as a book of reference. This work by a German Catholic theologian presents in systematic fashion the whole dogmatic system of Rome. It is particularly useful to the Protestant who wants a succinct statement from a Roman point of view of any aspect of Catholic dogma.

12. ABBOTT, W. M., ed., *Documents of Vatican II*, ASP, 1966, 792 pp., Hb $10.00, Pb 95¢; GC, 794 pp., Pb 10s 6d. This is a compilation of the sixteen official documents promulgated by the Council together with Council speeches of Pope John and Pope Paul. For those who do not wish to have the commentary which is included in this volume, the documents are also published separately by Catholic Truth Society. Of these the most significant are the Dogmatic Constitutions on the Church and on Divine Revelation, the Decrees on Ecumenism and the Bishops Pastoral Office and the Declaration on Religious Freedom.

13. *DAVIS, Charles, *A Question of Conscience*, HRP, 1967, 278 pp., $6.95; HS, 251 pp., 30s. A leading English theologian and a noted "progressive" whose defection and the reason he gives are a reply to those who naively think that Rome is changing—he saw no sign of any major reform. It is particularly significant and challenging in that it reveals the possibility of leaving Rome without finding the evangelical faith.

14. *MIEGGE, Giovanni, *The Virgin Mary*, WP, 1956, 196 pp., $3.50; LU, 1955, 21s. A notable feature of contemporary Roman Catholicism is the extraordinary growth of the cult of Mary. A professor of the Waldensian faculty of Theology in Rome is in a special position to assess both the dogmas and the practical outworking. The result is a massive demonstration of the unbiblical character of the cult and of the disastrous conclusions towards which its advocates are being led.

15. *BERKOUWER, G. C., *The Conflict with Rome*, PRPC, 1958, 319 pp., $5.95. The author has possibly an unrivaled knowledge of Roman theology both traditional and modern. He is very fair to his oppo-

nents—indeed he only seems to be roused by Mariological excess! This is a searching analysis of the underlying pre-suppositions of Rome, especially in the realms of sin, grace, and salvation. See also, G. C. Berkouwer, *Recent Developments in Roman Catholic Thought*, WBE, 1958, 82 pp., $1.50.

16. *BERKOUWER, G. C., *The Second Vatican Council and the New Catholicism*, WBE, 1964, 264 pp., $5.95. This is not simply a discussion of the debates and the conclusions of Vatican II. It goes far beyond this and in a brilliant survey of modern Catholic theological writings introduces us to the background to the present ferment in Rome. His ecumenical sympathies rather blunt the edge of his criticism, but for a grasp and understanding of the new Catholicism this book is invaluable.

17. SUBILIA, V., *The Problem of Catholicism*, WP, 1964, $4.50; SCMP, 190 pp., 30s. A brilliant and devastating critique of Rome. The heart of the Roman dogmatic system is her doctrine of the Church which leads not only to an authoritarian system but to one that is virtually impervious to biblical reform. Professor Subilia is a Waldensian who writes from first-hand experience as well as profound knowledge. See also, W. von Loewenich, *Modern Catholicism*, MC, 1959, 380 pp., 50s.

18. CARTER, C. S., and G. E. Weeks, ed., *The Protestant Dictionary*, HAS, 1933, 805 pp., 25s. Ranges over the whole field. Information on a multiplicity of topics is made available in an accessible form. Especially useful in such areas as Roman dogma, Papal history, and Roman ritual and practices.

6M. MODERN CULTS AND SECTS
Anthony A. Hoekema

No religious groups in America today are growing more rapidly than the cults. These groups do an amazing amount of propagandizing and proselytizing, both at home and on mission fields abroad. Hence, the evangelical Christian should be well-informed on the activities and teachings of the cults. He should know on what points the cults are to be distinguished from the Church, and should be prepared to deal with cultists in order that he may win them for Christ.

The following books will give guidance in this important area of study. The first seven titles are generally more popular and less thorough treatments, whereas the last six titles deal with the cults discussed more intensively and in greater detail. Except where specifically noted, each author mentioned writes from the standpoint of evangelical Christianity.

1. ADAIR, J. R., and Ted Miller, eds., *We Found Our Way Out*, BBH, 1964, 76 pp., Pb $1.00. Fifteen individuals explain how they were led to leave the cult to which they formerly belonged. Interesting and informative.

2. CLARK, E. T., *The Small Sects in America*, ABP, RE, 1949, 256 pp., Hb $3.00, Pb $1.25. Three hundred little-known religious groups are described under five headings in this book. Though many of these groups would be considered Christian denominations, a number of them should be classified as non-Christian cults. Includes a helpful chapter on the characteristics of the small sects.

3. DAVIES, Horton, *Christian Deviations*, WP, RE, 1965, 126 pp., Pb $1.45; SCMP, RE, 1964, 144 pp., 7s 6d. The views of eight groups considered to be deviations from Christian-

ity are briefly set forth. Interestingly written, though the standpoint is not consistently conservative.

4. MATHISON, R. R., *Faiths, Cults, and Sects of America,* BM, 1960, 384 pp., $5.00. A brief survey of various types of cults in America, including many lesser-known groups. Factually informative but weak on doctrinal analysis.

5. *SANDERS, J. O., *Cults and Isms, Ancient and Modern,* ZPH, RE 8, 1963, 167 pp., $2.50; *Heresies and Cults,* MMS, 1963, 168 pp., 12s 6d. Deals with several deviations, both ancient and modern. Includes discussions of Spiritism, Christadelphianism, British-Israelism, and faith healing.

6. SPITTLER, R. P., *Cults and Isms,* BBH, 1962, 143 pp., $2.95. "Twenty alternates to evangelical Christianity," including Zen Buddhism, Roman Catholicism, humanism, Unitarianism, liberalism, and neo-orthodoxy are briefly described. The main teachings of each group are stated and evaluated, with suggestions for further reading.

7. TANIS, E. J., *What the Sects Teach,* BBH, 1958, 88 pp., Pb $1.00. Discusses the main doctrinal teachings of Jehovah's Witnesses, Seventh-day Adventism, Christian Science, and Spiritism. Contains Scriptural refutations of cultic errors, and includes questions for discussion.

8. BRADEN, C. S., *These Also Believe,* MC, 1949, 491 pp., $7.50; CM, 55s. Thirteen religious groups are discussed in considerable detail, including some no longer active. An appendix gives brief descriptions of eighteen lesser religious movements. The author, a professor of the History of Religion, calls himself "an unrepentant liberal." The doctrinal evalua-

tion of these cults is unsatisfactory from the evangelical point of view.

9. GERSTNER, J. H., *The Theology of the Major Sects,* BBH, 1960, 206 pp., $2.95. A rather sketchy treatment of the doctrinal teachings of nine movements (including liberalism, New Thought, Spiritism, Theosophy, and faith healing) by a professor of church history. Includes a glossary of terms used by the sects, and tables setting forth brief abstracts of their doctrines.

10. HOEKEMA, A. A., *The Four Major Cults,* WBE, 1963, $5.95; PP, 1964, 447 pp., 30s. A thorough study, based on primary sources, of the doctrinal teachings of Mormonism, Seventh-day Adventism, Christian Science, and Jehovah's Witnesses, by a professor of systematic theology. Includes material on history and source of authority. Five appendices provide apologetic material. Has chapters on the distinctive traits of the cult and the approach to the cultist. Includes nineteen-page bibliography.

11. *LEWIS, G. R., *Confronting the Cults,* BBH, 1966, 198 pp., Pb $2.95. A discerning and warmly evangelical treatment of six cults by a Baptist professor of theology. Asks seven questions of each cult to determine its relation to historic Christianity. Purpose of the book is not primarily negative but positive: to win cultists to Christ. Includes suggestions for teachers.

12. MARTIN, W. R., *The Kingdom of the Cults,* ZPH, 1965, 443 pp., $5.95. A recent analysis by an evangelical Baptist of fifteen cult systems, including such groups as Spiritism, Father Divine, Zen Buddhism, Swedenborgianism, Black Muslim, Unity, Bahai, Herbert Armstrong, and Rosicrucianism. Considers Seventh-day Adventism a Christian denomination

rather than a cult. Each chapter contains a short history, brief quotations from cult authors under doctrinal topics, and refutations of cult teachings. Includes chapters on the psychology of cultism and methods of cult evangelism.

13. *VAN BAALEN, J. K., *The Chaos of Cults,* WBE, RE 4, 1962, 414 pp., $3.95; PI, 1957, 289 pp., 22s 6d. A well-known study, originally published in 1938. Examines thirteen cultic movements, including astrology, Spiritism, Anglo-Israelism, and Moral Rearmament. Each chapter contains a brief historical introduction, a summary and evaluation of the main doctrines, a series of direct quotations from cult authors, and some questions for discussion.

section 7

HUMANITIES & THE ARTS

7. HUMANITIES AND THE ARTS
Frank E. Gaebelein

The humanities and the arts, as subjects listed below are sometimes called, are intimately related to the nature and life of man and the use of his creative ability. They point like a barometer to his condition as he was in the past and as he is today. More than most fields of knowledge, the humanities and the arts are affected by the distortion that sin brought into the world. Yet, because the image of God in man, though grievously marred, was not effaced by the fall, man can still exercise his creative ability and produce works having some genuine measure of truth.

The prime criterion for the humanities and the arts, as for all other areas of human knowledge and endeavor, is truth. God is the God of truth. All truth is his and in him it all has unity. The outreach of Christianity is as wide as human life and the whole of creation. It goes beyond time to eternity and nothing true is alien to it. In Paul's charter for Christian thought (Philippians 4:8), the first category is "whatsoever things are true." And as Justin Martyr declared, "All that has been well-said belongs to us Christians." Thus, literature, whether in the factual domain of history or in the imaginative realm of fiction and poetry, that is committed to telling the truth has relevance for Christians, while literature that lacks integrity must be the object of their concern. Likewise with the arts, for not all truth-telling is verbal and truth may be expressed aesthetically through color, form, sound, or movement.

If Christians ignore or disparage the works of the creative faculty with which God, who gives talent as he wills, has endowed men, they do him no honor. Being the light of the world and the salt of the earth, they cannot stand aloof from the humanities and the arts, especially the as- *pects which so distinctively reflect the human condition. They are responsible to know what the humanities and the arts say, to express themselves through them if they have talent to do so, and to bring to bear upon them a criticism informed by criteria implicit in Scripture, the written Word of truth, and in Christ, the incarnate Word of truth.*

The following bibliography will assist the reader who wants to know and do the truth in the humanities and the arts.

7A. FICTION
Charles Huttar

Why read fiction? Paradoxically, because it often leads to truth. We are prone to self-deception by a hundred devices—preconceived categories for what we see, stereotypes of human behavior, universal doctrines that prepackage neat explanations for everything. Novelists have a passion for stripping away disguise and "telling it like it is." We need them to help keep our perceptions accurate. One reason: without the psychological exertion to truly know one's fellowman, Christian compassion cannot exist.

Truth, of course, is not limited to the seen. Accurate perception of life is an important first step, but beneath the surface appear patterns of meaning. The novelist naturally tries to unfold meaning according to his philosophy of life. Sometimes the result may seem utterly wrong—yet valuable for powerfully expressing a widespread belief. (If the Christian reader responds honestly to questions raised, even such a book can lead him, indirectly, to truth.) But frequently an author's effort to make sense of social injustices, growing up, love, temptation, or forgiveness, even if not avowedly Christian will show some debt to Christian ideas, helping us understand our own faith better.

The date of original publication, if before 1900, is added in parenthe-

ses. Other dates given are merely those of the selected edition, which in some cases is only one of many available.

1. AUSTEN, Jane, *Emma* (1816), HA, 1962, 367 pp., Hb $3.95; COL, 1965, Pb 95¢; PE, 480 pp., Pb 6s. Subtle, gently amused observation of a young woman's pretensions and self-discovery, combined with the author's deeply moral vision, has made this work a classic, and reading it a quietly exciting revelation.

2. *BALDWIN, James, *Go Tell It on the Mountain,* DI, 1963, 253 pp., Hb $3.50; DE, 1954, Pb 60¢; MJ, 256 pp., 25s. One of today's leading black spokesmen draws in this tale upon his own experience as an adolescent in the New York ghetto. Of especial interest is the religious orientation of the young protagonist's life and the way it complicates his struggle to find himself.

3. BERNANOS, George, *The Diary of a Country Priest,* MC, 1962, 255 pp., Pb $1.95; CO, Pb 3s 6d. His first parish proves a situation of severe spiritual testing for a young curé, as he is forced to deal with a variety of moral and economic problems. Most of all he tries to discover what he himself is: which of the various tendencies toward doubt, sanctity, love, and death is really his defining character.

4. BUNYAN, John, *The Pilgrim's Progress,* MP, 1964, 256 pp., Hb $3.95; REV, 1965, Pb 60¢; YUP, 1966, Hb 48s; JMD, 1962, Pb 5s 6d. This classic allegory of the Christian life combines great spiritual insight with an engaging narrative style. Even long passages of instruction come alive with Bunyan's power of presenting personality types.

5. *CAMUS, Albert, *The Stranger,* AAK, 1946, 154 pp., Hb $3.95; VIN,

1954, Pb $1.25; *The Outsider,* PE, Pb 3s 6d. Like all Camus' novels this offers much for meditation. Its existentialist "hero" determines to be absolutely true to himself—for he knows no other absolutes. He refuses all the stock responses society demands—love, loyalty, remorse, faith, even a sense of his own heroism. Still, he is a sort of secular Christ figure: society kills him to relieve its guilt.

6. CHESTERTON, G. K., *The Father Brown Omnibus,* DODD, 1933, 140 pp., Hb $6.00; CAS, 1959, Hb 30s, Pb 6s. These detective stories follow the classic formula of an improbable sleuth (in this case a dumpy Catholic priest) who by observation and reasoning solves baffling mysteries. Thanks to Chesterton's wit they are always entertaining and usually make a moral point as well, for Father Brown depends most on his amazing knowledge of human nature.

7. CONRAD, Joseph, *Heart of Darkness* (1899), WWN, 1963, 231 pp., Hb $3.27, Pb $1.55; *Youth, Heart of Darkness,* JMD, 1961, 178 pp., Pb 4s 6d. Civilization—the pride of mankind—is only the thinnest of veneers, says Conrad. Deep in the human heart something answers promptly to the bestial tom-tom of savagery; the heart of the Congo is only a symbol, for that is the world. So far as it goes (stopping short of God's work, that is) this story drives home a chilling truth.

8. *DOSTOEVSKY, Fyodor, *Crime and Punishment* (1866), DODD, 1963, 484 pp., Hb $4.95; BAB, 1962, 472 pp., Pb 60¢; PE, Pb 6s. Desperate for identity, a young man asserts himself by committing murder. At this point he discovers he has a conscience. In the depths of misery he goes on to learn—from someone who also is a suffering outcast—the

reality of love and the gospel of forgiveness.

9. DOSTOEVSKY, Fyodor, *The Grand Inquisitor on the Nature of Man* (1880), BM, 1956, Pb 45¢. What think ye of Christ? The question still fascinates many who reject a biblical answer. Dostoevsky's story, excerpted from his *The Brothers Karamazov* (well worth reading whole), is a classic instance. In it Christ, seeing that men he died to free are again enslaved, returns to earth but is again rejected—by the Church, in the name of Christian charity.

10. EDGREN, C. H., *Of Marble and Mud: Studies in Spiritual Values in Fiction,* Exposition Press, 1959, 127 pp., $3.00. (OoP) The range of this valuable work of criticism is indicated by the subtitle. A Christian scholar carefully scrutinizes the work of several contemporary authors.

11. *ELLIOT, Elisabeth, *No Graven Image,* HRP, 1966, 244 pp., Hb $3.95; Avon, 1967, Pb 60¢; HS, 18s. A young missionary learns painfully that works offered in service to God cannot substitute for himself. It seems obvious to us now that anything, even the most cherished evangelical pieties, can become idolatrous, but judging from the controversy stirred by the appearance of this novel, that is a truth hard to bear.

12. ELLISON, Ralph, *Invisible Man,* ML, 1963, 439 pp., Hb $2.45; NAL, Pb 95¢; PE, 470 pp., Pb 6s. For those who do not know what to make of recent Negro militancy (which is most of us), this novel provides understanding. But it rises beyond the race question to a universal theme, showing unforgettably how seldom a human being is genuinely "seen," being instead an object that fits someone's preconceived idea or that can be used for a certain purpose.

13. FAULKNER, William, *Intruder in the Dust,* RH, 1964, 274 pp., Pb $2.45; PE, Pb 3s 6d. Faulkner was a master of fictional art who respected the Christian tradition and owed an immense debt to it. A native Mississippian, he understood the Southern ethos with a sympathy which nevertheless did not detract from his prophet-like repudiation of its racism. This short novel sensitively explores aspects of race relations in the South.

14. FULLER, Edmund, *Man in Modern Fiction,* RH, 1958, 171 pp., Hb $3.95, Pb 95¢. To this critic the naturalists' dwelling on sordidness and the recent vogue for "compassion" in the novel are both dead-end streets. He sees the vaunted compassion as vacuous, devoid of moral content. A Christian view of human nature is required, if fiction is to tell the truth.

15. GOLDING, William, *Pincher Martin,* Berkley Publishing, 1956, Pb 75¢; FF, 208 pp., Pb 6s. Death at sea threatens a man who all his life has looked out for himself, and (at the expense of everyone else) succeeded very well. Desperately he struggles to survive, but his way of life proves to have been, all along, a denial of God, hence of life, and ultimately the hell he has forged for himself swallows him up.

16. *GOLDING, William, *The Spire,* HA, 1964, 215 pp., Hb $3.95, Pb $1.35; FF, Hb 18s, Pb 6s. As the grand project of erecting a medieval cathedral proceeds, we are given abundant evidence of how closely faith and carnality, love and aggressiveness, good and evil are interwoven in human affairs. As always, Golding's almost-Christian vision of reality is presented with a sure mastery of prose style.

17. GREENE, Graham, *The Power and the Glory,* VIP, 1958, 216 pp.,

Pb $1.65; HEE, 1963, 9s 6d. Again we are presented with the question of what constitutes sainthood. A Mexican priest, living in sin, seems an utter failure—in no eyes more than his own. Yet in the end, his life and death in the face of persecution are heroic, and others derive spiritual strength from them.

18. *HARTMAN, Olov, *Holy Masquerade*, WBE, 1964, 142 pp., Hb $3.00, Pb $1.95. A pastor's wife, fed up with the sham of living a faith she no longer possesses, tries to make a clean break with Christianity—but instead has a genuine encounter with God in a "passion week" of her own. This Christian author handles beautifully and honestly a theme many would have shied away from.

19. HAWTHORNE, Nathaniel, *The Scarlet Letter* (1859), WWN, 1966, 375 pp., Hb $4.10; HRP, 1965, 234 pp., Pb $1.50; CM, 1962, Pb 5s. Which sin is greater, too much love or too little? With great psychological and moral insight Hawthorne details the effects of passion, hate, concealment, and guilt on members of a New England Puritan community.

20. HAWTHORNE, Nathaniel, *Selected Tales and Sketches*, HRW, 1950, 410 pp., Pb $1.75; HRW, Pb 8s. One of the main recurrent themes of this collection is the tendency of sin and guilt to weaken human relationships, destroy love, and lead finally to death. Hawthorne sees this as all too frequently typical of life itself.

21. HEMINGWAY, Ernest, *A Farewell to Arms*, CSS, 1967, 358 pp., Hb $4.60, Pb $1.65; PE, Pb 4s 6d. Hemingway's novel of love and death in World War I is a classic of the atheistic neo-stoicism which has by now become silently absorbed into modern culture. The familiar Hemingway toughness may be read as a form of sentimentalism.

22. HUXLEY, Aldous, *Brave New World and Brave New World Revisited*, HRP, 1965, 296 pp., Hb $3.95, Pb $2.45; CW, 1959, 15s. Some see man's salvation in science's ultimate conquest of all evil. To psychologist B. G. Skinner (*Walden Two*) this is a benign vision. But quite apart from Christian reasoning, Huxley could realize that no men, even scientists, can be trusted with such power. *Brave New World* (1932) is his satiric exposure of the threatened "utopia."

23. JELLEMA, Roderick, ed., "Contemporary Writers in Christian Perspective: A Continuing Series," WBE, 1966, Pb 85¢ each. In this successful and continuing series of booklets various selected critics offer accounts of recent and current authors, many of them novelists, with analyses of their most important works and theologically oriented critiques.

24. JOYCE, James, *Dubliners*, VIP, 1958, 224 pp., Hb $3.50, Pb $1.45; PE, Pb 3s 6d. In a series of short stories Joyce's sharp eye chronicles the manners and mannerisms of his countrymen—who are, in the final analysis, not so much Irishmen as members of the human race, interdependent but forever trying to deny it.

25. JOYCE, James, *A Portrait of the Artist as a Young Man*, WAT, 1964, 253 pp., Hb $6.95; VIP, Pb $1.45; HEE, 300 pp., 10s 6d. Colored, of course, by the facts of Joyce's own upbringing and early career, this novel has also a broader significance as the general account of what may happen when an adolescent of high moral and aesthetic sensitivity feels the pressures of creed, cult, and code.

26. JOHNSON, Samuel, *Rasselas* (1759), Barron, 1962, 189 pp., Hb $2.95, Pb 75¢; OUP, 1927, 250 pp., 8s 6d. The great Christian humanist

has distilled into this book a lifetime of wisdom. Like Candide but free of Voltaire's cynicism, his young and in-experienced hero observes human na-ture and learns basic principles to live by.

27. *KAFKA, Franz, *The Trial,* AAK, RE, 1957, 340 pp., $4.95; SW, 1956, 304 pp., Hb 30s, PE, Pb 3s 6d. With highly suggestive vagueness Kafka depicts a nightmare world in which Everyman is existentially guil-ty but can never face his Accuser, gain a hearing, or even find out the charges. A forerunner of today's absurdists, Kafka eloquently de-scribes the predicament of fallen man.

28. KAZANTZAKIS, Nikos, *The Last Temptation of Christ,* SS, 1960, 506 pp., Hb $6.00; BAB, Pb $1.25; Cassirer, 1961, 520 pp., 25s. Though based on a view of Christ as mere man, this major work by a recent European novelist is a testimony to his position at the crossroads of hu-man thought. Working from his as-sumptions with honesty and respect, Kazantzakis demands from Christian readers a thoughtful response that will genuinely speak to contemporary attitudes.

29. *LEWIS, C. S., *Perelandra,* COL, 1962, Pb 95¢; BH, 1943, 256 pp., Hb 12s 6d. In this brilliantly imagined space novel, evil attempts to gain a foothold on Venus by a strategy closely resembling Satan's temptation of Eve. The attempt will surely suc-ceed unless a scholar named Ransom who "happens" to be there can find a way—and the strength—to block it. Lewis's striking insights into Chris-tian truth abound.

30. LEWIS, C. S., *That Hideous Strength,* MC, 1965, 362 pp., Pb $1.50; BH, 1945, 476 pp., 18s. The "hideous strength" of this novel (which is third of a series, following

Perelandra) is Satan's. Working now through two channels at once—super-natural powers plus the natural schemes of a corps of scientists who, well intentioned enough, seek to con-trol the world—evil almost destroys England. Its defeat depends on sim-ple things like love, obedience, and reason.

31. *LEWIS, C. S., *Till We Have Faces,* HA, 1957, 313 pp., Hb $4.75; WBE, 1964, Pb $1.95; BLES, 1956, 320 pp., 15s. Rationalism may deny it and even religion itself may by shallowness betray it, but the possi-bility of a human being's knowing God remains. In this his finest work of fiction a great Christian writer demonstrates the terribleness and the tenderness of that knowledge.

32. MALAMUD, Bernard, *The Assis-tant,* Signet, 1959, Pb 60¢; ES, 224 pp., 18s. One of America's postwar generation of talented Jewish novel-ists models his hero on the figure of Christ, as one who suffers on behalf even of enemies. This is only one ex-ample of contemporary novels on the theme of redemption; but the com-panion Christian doctrine of incarna-tion is much less widely appreciated.

33. MELVILLE, Herman, *Billy Budd, Sailor,* UCP, 1962, 431 pp., Hb $8.00; UCP, 219 pp., Pb $1.50; UCP, Pb 10s 6d. In this cunningly contrived confrontation of opposing principles of order and justice, it is decided expedient that one man should die for the people. Melville does not offer answers—despite his masterful use of the Christ symbol he does not believe that ultimately there are any—but he poses most compel-ling questions.

34. MELVILLE, Herman, *Moby Dick* (1851), Naylor, 1965, 172 pp., Hb $3.95; HRP, 1966, 516 pp., Pb 75¢; CM, 1962, Pb 7s 6d. A whale of a book, Melville's masterpiece depicts

the cosmic aloneness of man—by his own choice, yet a choice that seems an almost inevitable condition of self-respect. An answer to Melville's despair is possible—one is, in fact, implicit in the book—but no glib answer will stand up five minutes in the tidal wave of Melville's prose.

35. MOSELEY, E. M., *Pseudonyms of Christ in the Modern Novel,* University of Pittsburg Press, 1963, 231 pp., $4.95. Sometimes as redeemer, sometimes merely as a teacher, martyr, exemplar, or archetypal man, the figure of Christ has become a symbol used in various ways by modern novelists to help them express their ideas. Dean Moseley traces some of his appearances in American, British, and Continental works.

36. *O'CONNOR, Flannery, *Everything That Rises Must Converge,* FSG, 1965, 267 pp., Hb $4.95; Signet, 1967, Pb 75¢; FF, 269 pp., 25s. The twistedness of the human heart and the surprising presence and power of grace are the recurrent themes of this gifted Christian artist. This collection of short stories was her last—the conclusion of a short but remarkable career.

37. *PATON, Alan, *Cry, the Beloved Country,* WAT, 1967, 283 pp., Hb $7.95; CSS, 1948, 278 pp., Pb $1.45; PE, 277 pp., 3s 6d. In the explosive world of South Africa a simple, devout black pastor travels to the city seeking his wayward son, and a white man who has labored to relieve racial tensions is murdered by a black burglar. Paton's conclusion points to what may be the only possible solution to racial antagonism.

38. SALINGER, J. D., *Nine Stories,* LB, 1953, 302 pp., Hb $4.95; BAB, 1954, Pb 75¢. Like the author's *Franny and Zooey,* this collection displays the anguish of a world in which crucifixion (but not resurrec-

tion) is a basic principle. Salinger sees man as having nothing but his own efforts by which to live in tune with that principle.

39. SPARK, Muriel, *Memento Mori,* Avon, 1966, Pb 75¢; MC, 1959, 246 pp., Hb 21s; PE, Pb 3s 6d. Life—and the awareness of approaching death —among the aged serves to focus the bittersweet vision of this important Catholic novelist. The title reminds us that facing death is ultimately a religious question. Her other novels are also warmly recommended.

40. STEINBECK, John, *The Pearl,* WAT, 1966, 122 pp., Hb $6.95; BAB, 1962, Pb 50¢. A parable of the "Pearl of the World" and a man who finds it desirable enough to give up all for it: based directly on the New Testament "pearl of great price."

41. STEWART, Randall, *American Literature and Christian Doctrine,* LSUP, 1958, 154 pp., Hb $3.50. This critical study surveys the work of several major American writers old and recent (including some novelists), tracing a falling away from and then a return to basic Christian insights concerning the nature of man.

42. STYRON, William, *The Confessions of Nat Turner,* RH, 1967, 428 pp., $6.95. This exploration of the causes of racial violence in America is remarkable for its white author's sensitive grasp of a black viewpoint. The problem is convincingly reduced pretty much to terms of hatred versus love. Part of Styron's indictment is that the force of religion is usually felt on the side of the former.

43. *TOLKIEN, J. R. R., *The Lord of the Rings,* 3 V., HM, RE, 1967, Hb $6.00 each; Ballantine, Pb 95¢ each; AU, 1966, 423, 352, 411 pp., 25s each. A magnificent work of the "baptized imagination" for which the terms "epic," "fantasy," "romance,"

"adventure story," and "myth" are all appropriate, but none of them adequate. The trilogy's non-hero, Frodo the Hobbit, not only catches the contemporary taste for unpretentious achievement but acts out (unknowingly) some profound truths about the universe and its moral laws. Song and splendor abound.

44. TOLSTOY, Leo, *Anna Karenina* (1875-77), DODD, 1966, 897 pp., Hb $4.95; WSP, Pb 95¢; HEE, 904 pp., Hb 50s; OUP, 1939, Pb 12s 6d. Tolstoy weaves a rich tapestry of nineteenth-century Russian life, presenting in believable and gripping action those who have everything except happiness and those who have happiness and need nothing. His own experience of returning to childhood faith after years of self-sufficiency and doubt is powerfully reflected in the character of Levin.

45. TOLSTOY, Leo, *Resurrection* (1899), Heritage, 1963, 403 pp., Hb $6.95; WWN, 1966, 499 pp., Pb $1.95; OUP, 476 pp., Hb 9s 6d; PE, Pb 5s. A somewhat contrived but still powerfully written story of a Russian nobleman's sin, repentance, attempted restitution, and quest for a new life through following the ethical ideals of Tolstoy's own brand of liberal Christianity.

46. UPDIKE, John, *Pigeon Feathers and Other Stories*, AAK, 1962, 278 pp., Hb $4.00; FAW, Pb 50¢; PE, 192 pp., Pb 3s 6d. Short stories and sketches: keen observation of contemporary life and of boyhood in the recent past. In the title story a boy finds a satisfying answer to his anxiety about the existence of God and the meaning of the universe.

47. WEST, Morris, *The Devil's Advocate*, MOR, 1961, 134 pp., Hb $3.50; DE, 1960, Pb 60¢; HEE, 1959, 240 pp., Hb 25s; Pan Books, 288 pp., Pb 3s 6d. Popular enthusiasm for a mar-

tyred political leader in southern Italy has led to efforts to have him canonized. By some standards his life was anything but saintly—yet what are the ultimate criteria of judgment? The official investigation of claims brings the living to face themselves in the light of such questions, which perhaps means more than the canonization itself.

48. *WIEBE, Rudy, *First and Vital Candle*, WBE, 1966, 354 pp., $4.95. Mr. Wiebe possesses a talent which is outstanding among evangelical writers of fiction. In this novel, set in the Canadian arctic, a disillusioned idealist finds he cannot run away from God's claims—however strangely presented those claims may seem to be.

49. WILDER, Thornton, *The Bridge of San Luis Rey*, HRP, 1967, 148 pp., Hb $3.95; WSP, Pb 45¢; PE, Pb 3s 6d. FIVE DIE IN BRIDGE COLLAPSE—behind this event (in colonial Latin America) are the stories of five and more interwoven lives. Wilder, a master of story-telling, uses the catastrophe to focus the questions of the meaning of these lives, and of divine purpose in history.

50. *WILLIAMS, Charles, *All Hallow's Eve*, Noonday, 1963, 273 pp., Pb $1.75; FF, 1945, 240 pp., 21s. The final work of a unique Christian novelist, this book has been described as a "metaphysical thriller." Williams saw evil as having tremendous power —enough almost to overcome death and rule the world. Against it only love can prevail; happily for that too, death is no barrier.

51. WILLIAMS, Charles, *Descent into Hell*, WBE, 1965, 222 pp., Pb $1.95; FF, 1949, 15s. Here is a fully Christian treatment of two doctrines together. The heroine learns the place of suffering in discipleship, and even her "descent into hell" becomes creative. By it she can redeem someone

else, for it is not she but Christ in her. In contrast another character, totally immersed in self, descends therefore into a hell that is destructive.

7B1. NON-FICTION TWENTIETH CENTURY
S. Barton Babbage

It is useful to distinguish between works of the creative imagination (fiction, drama, and poetry) and other forms of literature (descriptive, narrative, biography, essays, and literary criticism). Each form of literature demands a certain combination of gifts, and each has its own distinctive excellence. Because of the exigencies of space, we limit ourselves to the work of the twentieth century and to three categories of non-fiction: essays, literary criticism, and theology and literature.

Christians can study, with real profit, the work of essayists and critics, not only for aesthetic pleasure, but also for intellectual insight and awareness.

Essays

1. ORWELL, George, *A Collection of Essays,* DC, 1954, Pb $1.45; MB, 1961, 320 pp., 42s. The celebrated author of *1984* and *Animal Farm* was also an accomplished essayist. This Anchor paperback contains some of the best of his descriptive writing (e.g., "Shooting an Elephant" and "England, your England"). "Writing a book," he confessed, "is an horrible, exhausting struggle, like a long bout of some painful illness. One would never undertake such a thing if one were not driven on by some demon whom one can neither resist nor understand."

2. QUILLER-COUCH, Sir Arthur, *Cambridge Lectures,* EPD, 1943, 312 pp. (OoP) This edition in the Everyman series contains selections from *On the Art of Living, On the Art of Reading,* and *Studies in Literature.*

These essays, on various facets of English literature, will delight those who enjoy both lucidity of thought and felicity of expression.

3. CHESTERTON, G. K., *Stories, Essays and Poems,* EVL, 1935, Pb $1.00; JMD, 1935; Ri, JMD, 1966, 3s. This collection, in the Everyman edition, illustrates Chesterton's amazing versatility as pamphleteer, literary commentator, Christian apologist, essayist, novelist, and poet. His outstanding characteristic was an extraordinary gift for paradox. See also, *The Man Who Was Chesterton: The Best Essays, Stories, Poems and Other Writings of G. K. Chesterton,* DC, 1960, 512 pp., Pb $1.45.

4. ELIOT, T. S., *The Idea of a Christian Society,* HA, 1949, 104 pp., $2.50; FF, 1939, 99 pp., 12s 6d. Eliot argues that "The Church must struggle for a condition of society which will give the maximum of opportunity for us to lead wholly Christian lives, and the maximum of opportunity for others to become Christians." Eliot once described himself as "a classicist, a royalist and an Anglo-Catholic."

5. MUNBY, D. L., *The Idea of a Secular Society and its Significance for Christians,* OUP, 1963, 91 pp., $3.00; OUP, 12s 6d. A vigorous rebuttal of Eliot's thesis that what we need is a "new Christian culture." The proper pattern of sanctity in this world of politics and people is not, Munby insists, withdrawal but permeation, not segregation but transformation.

6. *BALDWIN, James, *Notes of a Native Son,* DI, 1963, $4.50; BP, 1954, Pb $1.45; MJ, 1964, 165 pp., 21s; TW, 1965, Pb 5s. These essays, suffused with furious wrath, reveal something of the measure of Negro anger and frustration. No other Negro writer has the same gift for fierce, accusatory polemics. See also,

Nobody Knows My Name, DI, 1961, 241 pp., Hb $4.50, Pb 50¢; MJ, 1964, 196 pp., 21s; TW, 1965, 192 pp., 5s; and *The Fire Next Time,* DI, 1963, 120 pp., Hb $3.50, Pb 50¢; MJ, 112 pp., Hb 13s 6d, Pb 2s 6d.

7. CAMUS, Albert, *Resistance, Rebellion and Death,* AAK, 1961; ML, 1963, Hb $4.95, Pb $2.45; HHA, 1964, 272 pp., 12s 6d. On the occasion of the award of the Nobel Prize for literature, it was said that Camus had, in a unique way, illuminated "the problems of the human conscience in our time." These essays, ranging from political liberty to capital punishment, illustrate the truth of this tribute. Of particular topicality and significance is the address reprinted as "The Unbeliever and Christians."

8. *CAMUS, Albert, *The Myth of Sisyphus and Other Essays,* RH, 1955, 151 pp., Hb $4.50, Pb $1.25; HHA, 18s. According to Camus, "there are only two universes for a human spirit; that of the sacred (or, in Christian language, of grace) and that of revolt." In these essays, Camus, in passages of poignant and poetic beauty, explains why he was unable to accept the Christian alternative. For further reading, see *The Rebel,* AAK, 1954, Hb $4.50; VIN, 273 pp., Pb $1.65; AP, 7s 6d.

9. WEST, Paul, *The Wine of Absurdity: Essays on Literature and Consolation,* PSUP, 1965, 249 pp., $6.00; PSUP, 1966, 310 pp., 45s. A more technical discussion of the same theme. The author subscribes to Camus' belief that, in "this insane world," man "will find again the wine of absurdity and the bread of indifference which nourish his greatness."

10. *SAYERS, D. L., *Unpopular Opinions,* HA, 1947, 236 pp., $3.00. (OoP); Ri, GOL, 1951, 192 pp., 4s

6d. These essays are divided into three categories: theological, political, critical. Miss Sayers was an Anglo-Catholic who believed firmly in the truth of revealed religion. She had a vigorous argumentative style and her work can be read with profit by all Christians. She also wrote memorable Christian drama.

11. KNOX, R. A., *Essays in Satire,* DC, 1930, 287 pp., $2.50 (OoP); SHE, 1928, 7s 6d. (OoP) With devastating wit the Roman Catholic convert ridicules the scepticism of modernism and the vagaries of higher criticism by using their own weapons to their own discomfiture. A work that scintillates and delights.

12. *LEWIS, C. S., *Christian Reflections,* WBE, 1967, 176 pp., $3.95; BLES, 192 pp., 18s. C. S. Lewis was able to use, with extraordinary skill, the resources of wit and learning in the defense and service of the faith. A selection of articles dealing with various facets of Christianity in relation to the current debate with unbelief.

13. *SAYERS, D. L., *The Mind of the Maker,* HA, 1942, 229 pp., $2.00; ME, 1941, 198 pp., 12s 6d. In this important pioneer study of the creative process, Miss Sayers argues "that the Trinitarian structure which can be shown to exist in the mind of man and in all his works is . . . the integral structure of the universe and corresponds . . . with the nature of God."

14. KOESTLER, Arthur, *The Act of Creation,* MC, 1964, $8.95; Ri, DE, 1966, 751 pp., Pb $1.25; HU, 1964, 42s; PIS, RE, 1966, Pb 12s 6d. A major exploration of the process of creativity in a number of different fields—artistic, scientific, and comic. Koestler, a repentant communist, has a curious and restless intelligence. His philosophy is that of secular human-

ism. His political essays include *The Yogi and the Commissar and Other Essays,* MC, 1945, 256 pp., Hb $5.95, Pb 95¢; HU, 1965, Hb 30s, Pb 10s 6d, and *Reflections on Hanging,* GOL, 1956, 196 pp., 12s 6d.

15. *SCOTT, N. A., Sr., *The New Orpheus: Essay Toward a Christian Poetic,* SHE, 1964, 431 pp., Hb $7.50, Pb $3.95. A symposium of unusual quality and diversity on Christian aesthetics. Denis de Rougemont suggests that the criteria by which we ought to judge the quality of a work of art are (1) technical and (2) theological. Scott himself is one of the best scholars in the area of literature and theology.

16. ELIOT, T. S., *After Strange Gods: A Primer of Modern Heresy,* HA, 1934, 72 pp., 3s 6d (OoP); FF, 68 pp. Eliot trenchantly castigates the cult of self-expression. "Thomas Hardy," Eliot accuses, "seems to me to have written as nearly for the sake of 'self-expression' as a man well can; and the self which he had to express does not strike me as a particularly wholesome or edifying matter of communication." The personality generally expressed is unregenerate, "partly self-deceived and partly irresponsible." See also, *Essays: Ancient and Modern,* FF, 1936, 190 pp. (OoP), and *Selected Prose,* AP, 1953, 251 pp., 7s 6d.

17. HUXLEY, Aldous, *Ends and Means: An Enquiry into the Nature of Ideals and into the Methods Employed for their Realization,* HRP, 1937, 386 pp., $3.50 (OoP); CW, RE, 1960, 344 pp., 12s 6d. In these essays Aldous Huxley (who was not a believing Christian) discusses the way in which the means we use are related to the ends we serve. A discussion that must concern every Christian engaged in social and political action.

18. HUXLEY, Aldous, *Brave New World Revisited,* HRP, 1958, 164 pp., Hb $3.95, Pb $2.45; CW, 1959, 15s. Huxley's satire, *Brave New World,* was published in 1931. In these essays Huxley discusses, nearly thirty years later, the degree to which the imaginary horrors he portrayed have already become terrifying actualities.

Literary Criticism
19. *FULLER, Edmund, *Man in Modern Fiction: Some Minority Opinions on Contemporary American Writing,* Ri, RH, 1958, 171 pp., Hb $3.95, Pb 95¢. Fuller launches a powerful polemic against our preoccupation with "glandular" writing. "The loss of wonder, of awe, of the sense of the sublime," he charges, "is a condition leading to the death of the soul."

20. GROSS, S. L., and J. E. Hardy, *Images of the Negro in American Literature,* UCP, 1966, 321 pp., Hb $6.50, Pb $2.95; UCP, Hb 48s, Pb 21s. This symposium illustrates the truth of Richard Wright's profound saying that "the Negro is America's metaphor." For too long the Negro, from the point of view of the literary imagination, has been treated as a stereotype rather than a human being. This study substantiates this charge.

21. LEWIS, C. S., and E. M. W. Tillyard, *The Personal Heresy: A Controversy,* OUP, 1939, 156 pp., $3.50, RE, 1965, Pb $1.50; OUP, Pb 6s. He who enjoys the delights of the thrust and parry of hard-hitting debate will follow with lively interest this battle between the giants over the question whether poetry is the expression of subjective feeling or objective reality.

22. SEWALL, R. B., *The Vision of Tragedy,* YUP, 1959, 178 pp., Hb $5.00, RE, 1962, Pb $1.45; YUP, 9s 6d. Tragedy, the author affirms, "sees man as questioner, naked, un-

accomodated, alone, facing mysterious demonic forces in his own nature and outside and the irreducible facts of suffering and death." A moving discussion of the tragic vision. The author treats The Book of Job as a notable example of the category of the tragic.

23. BROOKS, Cleanth, ed., *Tragic Themes in Western Literature*, YUP, 1955, 178 pp., Hb $5.00, RE, 1960, Pb $1.25; YUP, 8s 6d. A learned symposium on great works of tragedy from Sophocles to Eliot. Each contribution is concerned with the role of the tragic hero and the meaning of suffering. A suggestive study by a critic with Christian sympathies.

24. WEISINGER, Herbert, *Tragedy and the Paradox of the Fortunate Fall*, MSCP, 1953, 300 pp., $5.00. A learned technical study of tragedy which takes as its theme Augustine's ecstatic exclamation "felix culpa!" The author finds the roots of tragedy in the myths and ritual of the ancient Near East.

25. HARPER, H. M., Jr., *Desperate Faith: A Study of Bellow, Salinger, Baldwin and Updike*, UNCP, 1967, 200 pp., $6.00. An illustration of the way in which contemporary literature enables us to explore the nature of our human condition. American fiction, he notes, is no longer concerned with social problems; it is concerned with the way in which "man, despite his inevitable and perhaps inexplicable suffering, can find salvation."

26. BAUMBACH, Jonathan, *The Landscape of Nightmare: Studies in the Contemporary American Novel*, NYUP, 173 pp., Hb $6.00, RE, 1966, Pb $1.95; OW, 1966, 27s 6d. Modern American writers (Negro, Jew, and Catholic), this critic suggests, are increasingly concerned with 'the heart of darkness'—"that nightmare land-

scape we all inhabit." They are all seeking, he believes, to delineate, in its various ways, the burden and ambivalence of personal responsibility in a world which is fallen.

Theology and Literature
27. SCOTT, N. A., Jr., *Modern Literature and the Religious Frontier*, HRP, 1958, 138 pp., $2.50. Nathan Scott claims that, in the literature of our times, we have "the richest mine of confessional experience and spiritual exploration . . . available since the Renaissance." This book seeks to substantiate this claim. For a further illustration of this theme, see *The Climate of Faith in Modern Literature*, SP, 1964, 257 pp., $5.95.

28. *SCOTT, N. A., Jr., *The Broken Center: Studies in the Theological Horizon of Modern Literature*, YUP, 1966, 237 pp., $5.00; YUP, 37s 6d. A collection of papers on facets of faith and literature written with Scott's characteristic verve and brilliance. The title is taken from Yeats' haunting poem, "The Second Coming": "Things fall apart; the center cannot hold; Mere anarchy is loosed upon the world. . . ."

29. WILDER, A. N., *Theology and Modern Literature*, HUP, 1958, 145 pp., $3.00; OUP, 28s. (OoP) An early pioneer work on the religious dimensions in modern literature. Amos Wilder, the brother of Thornton Wilder, the playwright, discusses, sympathetically and helpfully, the relation between theology and aesthetic judgment.

30. STEWART, Randall, *American Literature and Christian Doctrine*, LSUP, 1958, 155 pp., $3.50. "The influence of Puritanism in American life and letters," Randall Stewart affirms, "has been pervasive." What we are given in this study is a synoptic view of progressive changes in American life and thought, illustrated by

references to major works of literature. An illuminating survey.

31. *VAHANIAN, Gabriel, *Wait Without Idols,* GB, 1964, 256 pp., Hb $5.00, Pb $1.95. A Christian scholar brilliantly applies the insights of the faith to illumine the interpretation of literature. In this incisive work, Vahanian accuses that Christendom has too often substituted "the accommodating complacencies of religiosity for the exigent demands of faith in a transcendent God."

32. DAVIES, Horton, *A Mirror of the Ministry in Modern Novels,* OUP, 1959, 211 pp., $4.50; OUP, 224 pp., 26s. The Princeton Professor, an English-born Congregational minister, discusses some of the images of the minister in modern fiction "as a clue to the understanding of the inspirational and fructifying role that religion has played and still plays in the development of our Western civilization."

33. WOODHOUSE, A. S. P., *The Poet and His Faith: Religion and Poetry in England from Spencer to Eliot and Auden,* UCP, 1965, 304 pp., $6.95; UCP, 52s. A learned and engrossing account of the way in which the faith of an age is reflected in its poetry.

34. DILLISTONE, F. W., *The Novelist and the Passion Story,* SHE, 1961, 128 pp., $3.00; CO, 1960, 12s 6d; CO, RE, 1964, Pb 5s. "To attempt to represent the passion of Christ *directly* as a work of art is to invite failure. It can only be represented obliquely, indirectly, above all, paradoxically." An account of the way in which five novelists, Mauriac, Melville, Dostoevsky, Faulkner, and Kazantzakis, have attempted to do this.

35. MUELLER, W. R., *The Prophetic Voice in Modern Fiction,* ASP, 1959, 183 pp., Hb $3.50, Pb 95¢. By

reference to notable works of fiction, the writer illustrates some of the central doctrines of the Christian faith. A helpful demonstration of the way in which literature and theology can be related to their mutual enrichment.

36. *HOPPER, S. R., ed., *Spiritual Problems in Contemporary Literature,* HRP, 1952, 298 pp., Hb $3.00, Pb $1.95; HRP, 1957, 16s. A symposium devoted to a discussion of three themes: (1) Religion and the Artist's Situation, (2) Religion and the Artist's Means, and (3) Religion and the Artist's Beliefs. An attempt to wrestle with some of the basic issues involved in relation to being both a Christian and an artist.

37. *ZYLSTRA, Henry, *Testament of Vision,* WBE, 1961, 144 pp., Pb $1.45. A posthumous collection of essays and addresses by the late Professor of English at Calvin College on aspects of literature and the philosophy of education. The collection includes a devastating critique of so-called "religious fiction."

38. LEWIS, C. S., *They Asked for a Paper,* CO, 1962, 211 pp., $3.75; BLES, 216 pp., 16s. A stimulating selection of sermons and essays on subjects literary and theological. This collection contains the text of Lewis's celebrated Inaugural as Professor of Medieval and Renaissance Literature at Cambridge University.

39. HAMILTON, Kenneth, *In Search of Contemporary Man,* WBE, 1967, 48 pp., Pb 95¢. An introductory pamphlet to a continuing series entitled "Contemporary Writers in Christian Perspective." Each booklet gives an account of the work of a given writer and examines it both from the point of view of Christianity and of literary criticism. Authors discussed include William Golding, Graham Greene, and Ernest Heming-

way. An invaluable series for the Christian who desires to know who are the significant writers today.

40. FRYE, R. M., *Perspective on Man: Literature and the Christian Tradition,* WP, 1961, 207 pp., $4.50. The author agrees with Luther that "without knowledge of literature theology cannot at all endure." He illustrates this thesis by references to what he calls "the literature of clarification" and "the literature of redemption." A penetrating pioneer study.

41. TESELLE, S. M., *Literature and the Christian Life,* YUP, 1966, 238 pp., $6.50; YUP, 1967, 48s. A book for the advanced student with some competence in the fields of theology and literary criticism. The author is interested in art as a means of knowing, as a means by which one can be more deeply instructed in the complexities and subtleties of human life.

42. GRIFFITH, G. O., *Interpreters of Man: A Review of Secular and Religious Thought from Hegel to Barth,* LU, 1943, 242 pp., 15s. The present age marks, the author suggests, the last phase of Renaissance humanism. Here we have an arresting analysis of current interpretations of man in the light of the Christian faith.

43. NICHOLSON, Norman, *Man and Literature,* MC, 1944, 218 pp., $3.50 (OoP); SCMP, 1943, 10s 6d. (OoP) In this fascinating study, Norman Nicholson categorizes writers according to their doctrine of man. He discerns three main emphases which he describes as liberal man, natural man, and imperfect man. An original study of unusual suggestiveness.

44. *BABBAGE, S. B., *The Mark of Cain: Studies in Literature and Theology,* WBE, 1966, 157 pp., Pb $1.95. The main doctrines of the Christian faith are illustrated by references to writers, ancient and modern.

45. JONES, W. S. H., *The Priest and the Siren and other Literary Studies,* EP, 1953, 154 pp., 10s 6d. (OoP) An English Methodist writes perceptively on a number of writers from G. K. Chesterton to Aldous Huxley. A useful introductory study.

46. HANNA, Thomas, *The Thought and Art of Albert Camus,* HR, 1959, 264 pp., Pb $1.25. A helpful and sympathetic analysis, from the Christian point of view, of the French Nobel Prize winning author. Camus was passionately preoccupied with one "human condition." "Is it possible," he wondered, "to be a saint without God?"

47. RAMSEY, Paul, *Nine Modern Moralists,* PH, 1962, 271 pp., Hb $5.75, Pb $2.95; PH, 24s. An examination of the thought of nine thinkers (Jacques Maritain, Reinhold Niebuhr, Karl Marx, Jean-Paul Sartre, Fyodor Dostoevski, Edmond Cahn, Paul Tillich, Richard Niebuhr, Emil Brunner) and their contribution to Christian social ethics.

48. DETWEILER, Robert, *Four Spiritual Crises in Mid-Century American Fiction,* UFP, 1964, 53 pp., Pb $2.00. This monograph is an analysis in depth of four writers: William Styron, John Updike, Philip Roth and J. D. Salinger. "These talented artists . . . with demonstrated ability to compose good fiction, have taken the religious element seriously. . . ."

49. BROOKS, Cleanth, *The Hidden God: Studies in Hemingway, Faulkner, Yeats, Eliot and Warren,* YUP, 1963, 136 pp., Hb $5.00, Pb $1.45; YUP, Hb 35s 6d, Pb 9s 6d. "Every religion which does not affirm that God is hidden is not true," Pascal said. Brooks sensitively explores the

vision of life hidden in the work of five twentieth-century writers.

50. HUNT, J. W., *William Faulkner: Art in Theological Tension,* SUP, 1965, 184 pp., $5.00. This work illustrates the way in which the philosophy of a writer, as embodied in imaginative literature, can be subjected to theological scrutiny and examination. The author's conclusion is that Faulkner's "Christian humanism" is stoic rather than Christian.

51. AXTHELM, P. M., *The Modern Confessional Novel,* YUP, 1967, 189 pp., $5.75. The author examines the modern confessional novel in which a hero—afflicted and unbalanced—examines his past as well as his innermost thoughts in order to achieve some form of perception. The author provides a luminous account of the work of Dostoevsky, Gide, Sartre, Camus, Koestler, Golding, and Bellow. Augustine, he argues, was the pioneer of the modern confessional novel.

7B2. NON-FICTION (Early)
Daryl Adrian

Our contemporary evangelical Christian faith is, in part, the product of centuries of earnest preaching, writing, and thoughtful re-evaluation of the major religious doctrines and traditions by both clergymen and laymen. Just as they sought to relate their personal beliefs to their ages and their problems, so ought we to do today. Thus, perhaps a careful study of some of these early non-fictional writings might be helpful in better comprehending the relevance or irrelevance of our own religious doctrines, traditions, habits, and practices. A selected bibliography of significant non-fictional works and collections of works written before 1900 which currently are available (most in paperback) is listed below.

1. BAXTER, Richard, *Devotions and Prayers of Richard Baxter,* BBH, 1966, 119 pp., Pb $1.00. Excellent collection for learning about the private religious life of this important British non-conformist of the seventeenth century, whose sermons, prayers and writings did much to promote devout Puritanism during the Restoration Period. Well-written and inspiring to read.

2. JOHNSON, Samuel, *Diaries, Prayers, and Annals,* YUP, 1958, 461 pp., $10.00; YUP, 1960, 72s. This little-read but important book portrays the sincere, devout religious faith of this important British literary figure during the later eighteenth century. The selections help to substantiate and more fully develop the view of Johnson's religion as documented by James Boswell.

3. AQUINAS, Saint Thomas, *On the Truth of the Catholic Faith, Book One: God,* DC, 1955, 317 pp., Pb $1.25. This is an excellent, readable translation by an outstanding Thomist scholar which clearly presents St. Aquinas' perceptive comprehension of the various aspects of God and his work. It is the first volume of a five-volume set of the Latin text of *Summa Contra Gentiles,* which surely will become the definitive English edition of this masterpiece.

4. CALVIN, John, *On the Christian Faith: Selections from the Institutes, Commentaries, and Tracts,* Liberal Arts Press, 1958, 219 pp., Pb $1.00. These selections from the voluminous writings of this sixteenth-century reformer are invaluable for every evangelical reader who wishes to compare Calvin's doctrines and teaching with those of reformers such as Luther, Zwingli, and Erasmus. The selections from the *Institutes of the Christian Religion,* WP, 2 V., 1959, 849, 950-1734 pp., $12.50; JC, 2 V., 1957, 1314 pp., 42s; SCMP, 2 V.,

1961, 900 pp., 6s 6d set, intended as a manual for religious inquirers and a manifesto of new evangelical, scriptural doctrines, illustrate clearly the theology and doctrines of Calvin. Those from the Commentaries present typical examples of Calvin's verse-by-verse method of expounding the Scriptures. Though the style is more fluent and casual in the Commentaries, Calvin generally wrote in an enthusiastic, persuasive rhetoric which stressed simplicity, clarity, and brevity as his ruling principles.

5. FERRY, A. D., ed., *Religious Prose of 17th Century England*, AAK, 1967, 258 pp., Pb $2.95. This is an excellent, inexpensive collection of significant excerpts from the religious prose of John Donne, Sir Thomas Browne, Jeremy Taylor, John Milton, John Bunyan, Thomas Traherne, Augustine Baker, Lancelot Andrewes, Edward Lord Herbert, George Herbert, Isaac Barrow, Thomas Sprat, John Tillotson, Benjamin Whichcote, Richard Baxter, and George Fox. Bibliography and biographical data, unfortunately, are somewhat limited.

6. FOSDICK, H. E., *Great Voices of the Reformation: An Anthology*, RH, 1952, 546 pp., $5.00; ML, Pb $3.95. This anthology, which belongs in the library of every evangelical Christian, presents the gist of the historic writings of twenty early Protestant Reformers from John Wycliffe to John Wesley, from Europe to America. The focus is on the affirmative, vigorous "protestation" of positive religious principles by each of these individual Reformers.

7. *The Ancrene Riwle: A Rule for Religious Women*, UND, 1956, 196 pp., Pb $2.75. This medieval "Guide for Anchoresses" was written anonymously for the purpose of providing moral instruction for three young sisters who were preparing to live clois-

tered lives. Filled with wit, charm, warmth, and practical wisdom, it blends moral earnestness, compassion, and urbanity as it stresses the need for a strict inner religious discipline which will negate the need for burdensome outer forms.

8. EDWARDS, Jonathan, *Selections*, PS, 1962, 434 pp., $4.25; HWD, RE, Pb $2.25. This is a collection of sermons, theological and philosophical treatises, letters, and autobiographical selections which help the reader to understand more correctly the mind, theology, and philosophy of Jonathan Edwards, a major Puritan theologian of eighteenth-century America. A very useful, well-written, critical introduction also helps the reader to understand the man, his mind, and his subjective writings.

9. NYE, R. B., and N. S. Grabo, *American Thought and Writing*, 2 V., HM, 1965, 447, 456 pp., $3.00 each, Pb $1.95 each. These are excellent, inexpensive collections which are particularly useful in the reader's obtaining a quick, overall view of the primary concerns of seventeenth and eighteenth-century America. From the flesh-versus-spirit struggles in the New England Canaan to the more rational religious philosophy of the New Republic, the true temper of the age is reflected in these myriad selections.

10. WIGGLESWORTH, Michael, *The Diary of Michael Wigglesworth, 1653-1657: The Conscience of a Puritan*, PS, 1965, $3.25; HRP, 125 pp., Pb $1.25. The diary is a kind of running ledger of the assets and liabilities in the life of one of New England's most conscientious Puritans of the seventeenth century. Written in a readable, fluent style, it appropriately portrays Wigglesworth as an exceptional but intensely devout Puritan with a unique zeal for correcting the sins of himself and others.

11. DONNE, John, "Devotions Upon Emergent Occasions" and "Sermons," in *John Donne: Poetry and Prose,* RH, 1967, 437 pp., Pb $2.45; OUP, 1946, 184 pp., 9s 6d; John Sparrow, ed., *Devotions Upon Emergent Occasions,* CAUP, 1923. (OoP) The "Devotions" consist of twenty-three groups of essays, each composed of a meditation, an expostulation, and a prayer. Each group corresponds to a stage of Donne's illness in 1623-24, through which he felt God was speaking to him. The "Sermons" included are sensuous and vivid in style but serious in tone.

12. MILTON, John, *The Prose of John Milton,* DC, 1967, 675 pp., $7.50. These selections include antiprelatical tracts, divorce tracts, political and religious tracts, letters, and other treatises which help the reader to better comprehend the religious thought of this major Puritan writer of the seventeenth century. The summary of *De Doctrina Christiana* also is most useful in more fully understanding the unique religious philosophy of Milton.

13. NEWMAN, J. H., (Cardinal), *Apologia Pro Vita Sua,* OUP, 1964, 506 pp., Hb $3.00; Houghton, Pb $1.45; OUP, 440 pp., Hb 12s 6d; CO, 1959, 384 pp., Pb 5s. This is a biographical history of the religious uncertainty, turmoil, and opinions of this ardent British Anglican cleric who, daring to examine the dogmas and traditions of Roman Catholicism, became an even more ardent Catholic priest. This work graphically portrays not only the tumultuous years in Newman's life but also those turbulent years in the religious life of nineteenth-century England.

14. BROWNE, Sir Thomas, *The Prose of Sir Thomas Browne,* DC, 1967, 646 pp., $7.50. This collection reflects the intellectual attempt of a seventeenth-century Christian scientist to reconcile reason and faith (*Religio Medici*), to platonically comprehend God and heaven through external nature (*The Garden of Cyprus*), and to contrast pagan and Christian attitudes toward death (*Hydriotaphia: Urn Burial*). The tone generally is highly personal; and the style of the ornate baroque prose is rhythmic, lyrical, and fervent.

15. STEPHEN, Leslie, *History of English Thought in the Eighteenth Century,* 2 V., PS, $10.00; HA, 1963, RE 3, 396, 399 pp., Pb $2.95 each. This is a reprint of a well-written, important late nineteenth-century work which should interest anyone interested in religion and the humanities. Written by a sensitive Christian, it particularly focuses on the eighteenth-century problem of how to reconcile a traditional Christian view of the universe with the findings of scientists and philosophers.

16. JAMES, William, *The Varieties of Religious Experience,* University Books, 1963, 626 pp., $10.00; ML, 1963, 526 pp., Pb $1.95; CO, 1960, 508 pp., Pb 7s 6d. This classic of the psychology of religious impulses is one of the most brilliant works of one of America's greatest philosophical minds. Presenting his arguments boldly but sympathetically, James examines religious phenomena such as conversion, repentance, mysticism, saintliness, and the hopes and fears of the life after death.

17. PAINE, Thomas, *The Age of Reason,* MCL, 1968, 256 pp., $1.75. Written to attack revealed religion (Christianity) but not to attack religion as such, this work was intended to be a rational attempt to rescue the essentials of (deistic) religion, although many orthodox readers have considered it to be strongly atheistic. This controversial booklet requires careful reading in order to be understood properly.

18. MARX, Karl, *Communist Manifesto*, REG, 1954, 83 pp., Pb 30¢. Every evangelical Christian needs to read this controversial work and then discuss "Communism versus Christianity" with his pastor. The result of such a study would be a spiritual maturation which would prepare the Christian to live more dynamically and offensively in a society where Communism often seems to have better answers than Christianity does. Possomy's introduction also is very good.

19. DARWIN, Charles, *The Origin of Species by Means of Natural Selection,* Ri, OUP, 1956, 592 pp., $3.00; DC, 1960, Pb $1.25. This is a controversial book which every evangelical Christian should read, not just hear about. Darwin uses scientific data and logic to develop his theory of natural selection in the preservation of plants and animals and the emergence of new species. (His theory of man as a product of natural selection, possibly a scion of the anthropoid apes, was later presented in *The Descent of Man*).

7C. POETRY

Clyde S. Kilby

It is a remarkable fact not only that poetry precedes prose in the history of nations but that it has the best survival value. The Iliad *and the Odyssey are as alive today as they were almost three thousand years ago, and the Anglo-Saxon epic* Beowulf *not only reveals the fine poetical gifts of our own eighteenth-century ancestors but gives us the best possible evidence of their culture. At an earlier time the poet, like the builders of such structures as the superb medieval cathedrals, was close to the people. In most recent times he has tended for various reasons to become isolated and to speak a somewhat private language.*

Nevertheless poets in our time,

both Christian and secular, can often reach us more profoundly than preachers. These poets, however, require closer attention and will generally yield little to the person coming to them casually or simply for a versified illustration. The normal purpose of prose is to inform, but poetry goes deeper and may give us a participation in the very nature of things. A simple but readable introduction to the nature of poetry is Max Eastman's Enjoyment of Poetry, *CSS, 1951, 646 pp., $7.50.*

1. CECIL, L. D., ed., *The Oxford Book of Christian Verse,* OUP, 1940, 594 pp., $5.75; OUP, 25s. This has been a standard collection of poetry for nearly thirty years. It goes back to the Middle Ages and contains poems representative of the periods since then up to 1940.

2. NICHOLSON, D. H., and A. H. Lee, *The Oxford Book of English Mystical Verse,* OUP, 660 pp., $5.00; OUP, 21s. First published in 1917, this volume includes about 150 poets, with emphasis on the seventeenth-century metaphysical poets and the nineteenth-century romantic and Victorian poets such as Wordsworth, Tennyson, Browning, Whitman, and Francis Thompson. For an excellent short collection edited by A. W. Tozer, see *The Christian Book of Mystical Verse,* CHPU, 1963, 152 pp., $3.00.

3. HAZO, Samuel, *A Selection of Contemporary Religious Poetry,* PAUP, 95¢. As the title suggests, this volume, published in 1963, includes many contemporary poets, with emphasis on Roman Catholic ones. For the Protestant emphasis see, H. Martin, *A Treasury of Christian Verse,* FP, 1966, 126 pp., $2.00.

4. WALSH, Thomas, *The Catholic Anthology,* MC, RE, 1939, 584 pp. (OoP) Poems from the early Christian

Church to the present. A very good selection of poems of the centuries. As the title indicates, Catholic poems are emphasized.

5. *Devotional Poets of the XVII Century,* NE, $1.75; NE, 5s 9d. Contains poems by John Donne, George Herbert, Robert Herrick, Henry Vaughn, and Thomas Traherne. Though the conceit and other peculiarities may make some of these poems sound odd to modern ears, there is often in them great Christian profundity.

6. CLARKSON, E. M., *Clear Shining After Rain,* WBE, 1962, 80 pp., $2.50. In commending this book, A. W. Tozer writes, "... [the book] comes as something of a surprise and a relief to those who love good religious verse and who had almost given up the hope of finding any such verse written in this generation. A fine craftsmanship enables the poet to body forth the true poetic spirit with which she is so clearly possessed."

7. LEWIS, C. S., *Poems,* HA, 1965, 142 pp., $4.50; BLES, 1964, 16s. Lewis' poetry is a valuable complement to his other works. In this volume the many facets of Lewis' mind are shown by poems on angels, Adam, evolution, a unicorn that failed to get into Noah's ark, the shallowness of modern life, prayer, the glory of heaven, etc.

8. WALSH, Chad, *Psalm of Christ,* WP, 1964, 80 pp., $2.95. This is only one of several books of poetry by Dr. Walsh, professor at Beloit College and Episcopal priest. It deals with the twenty-second Psalm and contains forty poems.

9. AVISON, Margaret, *The Dumbfounding,* WWN, 1966, 99 pp., Hb $4.50, Pb $1.95. Among the leading Canadian poets, Miss Avison was awarded the Governor General's Medal for an earlier book of poems.

She has become a Christian only in recent years.

10. SCOTT, N. A., Jr., ed., *Four Ways of Modern Poetry,* JKP, 1965, 95 pp., Pb $1.00. Four essays on the works of Wallace Stevens, Robert Frost, Dylan Thomas, and W. H. Auden "to provide for a Christian response to some of the focal bodies of ... the rich diversity in the poetic art of our time."

11. HOPKINS, G. M., *Collected Poems,* OUP, 1967, 362 pp., $6.00. Do not go to one of Hopkins' poems unless you are prepared to read it several times and feel into its special sort of poetic structure. But when this is done it often results in ideas, images, and a poetic experience one will not easily forget.

12. ELIOT, T. S., *Complete Poems and Plays: 1909-1950,* HA, 1952, 329 pp., $6.95. Though the poetry of Eliot is not easy reading, it is greatly rewarding. His early poems, such as "The Waste Land," manifest a hopeless view of the world, but after his conversion he produced such great things as "Ash Wednesday," the "Four Quartets," and verse dramas like "Murder in the Cathedral." Clearly one of the great poets of our time. For recordings, see Caedmon 1045; *Four Quartets,* Angel 45012; *Wasteland,* London Argo 10.

13. AUDEN, W. H., *Collected Poems,* RH, $4.75; *Collected Poetry,* FF, 1940, 80 pp., 5s. At first quite proletarian in his political and social views, Auden later turned to Christianity. His views of man, nature, and God often bear the strongest spiritual implications. His *Age of Anxiety* is suggested—a poem in which the seven stages of man are represented by a barren plain, a tavern, a city, a house, a graveyard, a garden, and a forest. For the recordings, see Caedmon

1019, Spoken Arts 780, and London Argo 780.

14. MILTON, John, *Complete Poems*, ACC, $6.00; NOP, 1938, 892 pp., 35s. One of the great poets of the world. His "Paradise Lost" is an account of the celestial and earthly events leading to Adam and Eve's ejection from Eden. "Paradise Regained" is an account of Christ's death and the consequent victory over sin. "Samson Agonistes" recounts Samson's agony after his hair had been shorn and of his spiritual victory in death. "On the Morning of Christ's Nativity" describes the splendor and glory of this event. There are many other great poems by Milton. For recordings, see *Paradise Lost*, London Argo 431/32, 463/64 and 508/09; *Samson Agonistes*, Caedmon 92028 and London Argo 433.

15. DANTE, Alighieri, *Divine Comedy*, HUP, 1965, 795 pp., $8.95; HRW, 1954, 364 pp., Pb $1.75; SHP, 1965, 795 pp., 63s. Among the greatest of poets, Dante is best known for his *Divine Comedy*. Its three parts, "Hell," "Purgatory," and "Paradise," carry the reader down through the circles of punishment to the bottom of hell, then upwards to the dazzling glories of heaven. Dorothy Sayers' translation is particularly recommended because of her penetrating explanatory notes.

7D. HISTORY
C. Gregg Singer
The proper interpretation of history is fundamental and very necessary for a well-rounded biblical "weltanschauung." A mature Christian student should have both an appreciation for the relationship between God and history, and sufficient biblical insight to properly interpret the stream of history.

Unfortunately there are not many books which present a consistently coherent biblical view of history, and a bibliography, if limited to the orthodox approach, would be scanty indeed. Therefore, it is necessary to include some authors who have some valuable insights into the biblical meaning of history at some point even though their theology is deficient from an evangelical viewpoint. Some of these other authors are also included, in spite of their unacceptable doctrinal presuppositions, simply for the purpose of offering a contrast with the conservative biblical approach.

History
1. ST. AUGUSTINE, *The City of God*, DC, 428 pp., Pb $1.45; OUP, 1963, 452 pp., 30s. For a biblical understanding of history the student must begin with this great Christian classic.

2. VAN TIL, Cornelius, *The Defense of the Faith*, PRPC, 1955, 436 pp., $4.95; PRPC, 1967, RE 3, Pb $3.00. One of the best modern statements of the Augustinian position although it is not primarily written to discuss history as such. This superb presentation of the biblical world and life view and its basic postulates necessarily lays the foundation for a profound biblical interpretation of human history.

3. *CLARK, G. H., *A Christian View of Men and Things*, WBE, 1952, 325 pp., Hb $4.00, Pb $2.95. An excellent modernization of James Orr with a chapter devoted to basic problems involved in the interpretation of history from the biblical point of view.

4. ORR, James, *A Christian View of God and the World*, WBE, 1948, 480 pp., $3.50. (OoP) A classic statement of the biblical "weltanschauung" and presents the basic biblical doctrines for the proper understanding of the world in the light of biblical revelation.

5. WARFIELD, B. B., *Studies in Tertullian and Augustine,* BBH, 1930, 412 pp., $3.00 (OoP); OUP, 1931, 15s. (OoP) A study of Augustine by one of the greatest of the twentieth-century reformed theologians. He interprets the Augustinian doctrines of sin and grace and their basic relevance to a biblical view of history. For study of Calvin in the same manner, consult now out-of-print book, *Studies in Calvin and Calvinism.*

6. MACHEN, J. G., *The Christian View of Man,* MC, 1937, 302 pp., $2.50 (OoP); Ri, BTT, 1965, 254 pp., Pb 5s. Study of the biblical doctrine of man and its meaning for human history.

7. *HYMA, Albert, *Renaissance to Reformation,* WBE, 1950, 591 pp., $6.00. (OoP) This book evaluates the Renaissance from the biblical perspective and will give the student a much better insight into the differences between the Renaissance and the Reformation. It is not easy reading; however it is very rewarding. See also, Q. Breen, *Christianity and Humanism,* WBE, $6.95.

8. SCHAFF, Phillip, *History of the Christian Church,* 8 V., WBE, 1960, $49.50 set. This great work is both a history of the Christian Church and an interpretation of history as well. At many points in the text Schaff offers tremendous insights into the biblical view of history.

9. CALVIN, John, *Institutes of the Christian Religion,* 2 V., WBE, 1953, Hb $8.95, Pb $6.95; 2 V., CLA, 1314 pp., 42s set. A great work of the Reformation scholar. A thorough knowledge and appreciation of this Reformation classic is the best of all introductions to the biblical view of history.

10. *SINGER, C. G., *A Theological Interpretation of American History,* PRPC, 1964, 305 pp., $4.95. A study of liberalism in American history against the backdrop of its denial of biblical theism. See also, T. J. Campbell, *Central Themes of American Life,* WBE, $3.50.

11. SINGER, C. G., *John Calvin: His Roots and His Fruits,* PRPC, Pb $1.50. A brief presentation of Calvinism and its world and life view and of the ingredients of Calvin's view of history.

12. SINGER, C. G., *Arnold Toynbee,* PRPC, Pb $1.00. An evaluation of Toynbee's philosophy of history from the point of view of biblical theism, designed primarily for the university student.

13. SINGER, C. G., "The Meaning of History," *Christianity Today,* March 14, March 28, April 11, April 18, 1961. These four articles originally delivered for the Wheaton College Centennial present the basic answers which biblical theism gives to the perennial problems involved in the interpretation of secular history.

14. STOB, Ralph, *Christianity and Classical Civilization,* WBE, 1960, 198 pp. (OoP) Essentially the Calvinistic answer to the neo-orthodox position of Charles Norris Cochrane as set forth in his *Christianity and Classical Culture* (see below).

15. HYMA, Albert, *Christianity and Politics,* LC, 1938, 331 pp., $3.00 (OoP); LC, 1940, 15s. (OoP) Although this book deals primarily with the impact of the Reformation on political thought and practice, it presents valuable insights into the biblical view of history.

16. HOOGSTRA, Jacob, ed., *John Calvin, Contemporary Prophet,* BBH, 1959, 257 pp., $4.50. An excellent introduction to Calvin's view of his-.

tory of the state and social relations. It is biblical theism at its best.

17. ORR, John, *English Deism: Its Roots and Its Fruits*, WBE, 1934, 289 pp., $2.50. (OoP) A profound interpretation of the influence of English deism on English and American life. It is particularly good in that it presents deep insight into the real impact of deism on American history.

18. FULLER, D. P., *Easter Faith and History*, WBE, 1964, 288 pp., $4.95; TP, 1967, 15s. Traces the theological debate in Europe between history and faith since the Enlightenment. The author maintains that "redemptive history" is the norm by which all claims to Christian truth are to be controlled.

*   *   *

The following works are valuable if they are used properly by the discerning student. To various degrees they are less than orthodox in regard to one or more Christian doctrines. Nevertheless, some of them contain valuable insights and present a wealth of original material which can be of great benefit.

19. *COCHRANE, C. N., *Christianity and Classical Culture*, OUP, Ri, 1960, 534 pp., Hb $7.00, Pb $2.45; OUP, Hb 50s, Pb 15s. This work, brilliantly written, contains some very fine study material on Roman culture in general and the Augustinian view of history. But the author has a weak view of inspiration of the Scriptures and leans to neo-orthodoxy.

20. CASSERLEY, J. V., *Toward a Christian Theology of History*, HRW, 1965, 238 pp., $6.00; MO, 1965, 25s. The value of this book lies in the fact that it shows the impact on the understanding of history of a theology which is less than biblical.

21. *McINTYRE, John, *The Christian Doctrine of History*, WBE, 1958, 119 pp., $2.50; OB, 1957, 120 pp., Pb 12s 6d. One of the best books of this group and could be of great value if used carefully by the discerning student.

22. HALLOWELL, John, *Main Currents of Modern Political Thought*, HRW, 1950, 759 pp., $9.95; HRW, 60s. In many respects this is a very profound book and Professor Howell has done a magnificent job in tracing the relationship between liberalism and theology and the growth of the modern totalitarian state. It is regrettable that at certain points the author is guilty of some of the liberalism which he so vividly portrays as being an influential factor in American history.

23. BUTTERFIELD, Herbert, *Christianity and History*, CSS, 1950, 146 pp., Pb $1.25; CO, 1959, 192 pp., Pb 3s 6d. Although seriously defective at certain points of doctrine this book helps offset the claims of Marxian and other modern views.

24. LOWITH, Karl, *Meaning in History*, UCP, 1957, 257 pp., Pb $1.50; UCP, 1949, 10s 6d. An extensive neo-orthodox approach and must be used with great caution, but it may be of use to those students who are firmly grounded in biblical theism.

25. BUTTERFIELD, Herbert, *Christianity, Diplomacy and War*, ABP, 1953, 125 pp., $1.75 (OoP); EP, 1962, 128 pp., Pb 2s 6d; *Christianity in European History*, MC, 1953, 63 pp., $1.75 (OoP); CO, 1951, 64 pp., 7s 6d. These works give some valuable insight in regard to the influence of Christianity on the history of European culture. For the mature student it can be used with great profit provided he is aware of its weak view of inspiration and biblical authority.

26. BUTTERFIELD, Herbert, *International Conflict in the Twentieth-Century: A Christian View*, HRP, 1960, 123 pp., $3.00 (OoP); RO, 12s 6d. A core, mature reflection on one of Butterfield's basic ideas and should be used with care.

27. NIEBUHR, Reinhold, *Beyond Tragedy: Essays in the Christian Interpretation of History*, CSS, 1937, 306 pp., Hb $3.95, Pb $1.45; NI, 1938, 318 pp., 10s 6d; *Faith and History, A Comparison of Christianity and Modern Views*, CSS, 1949, 257 pp., $4.50 (OoP); NI, 16s. (OoP) The author was and is thoroughly existentialist in his approach and holds a much lower view of inspiration than Butterfield. He is at his best in his analysis of competing views.

28. NEIBUHR, Reinhold, *Pious and Secular America*, CSS, 1958, 150 pp., $3.00; *Self and the Drama of History*, CSS, 1955, 246 pp., $5.95; FF, 1956, 25s. An application of his basic view of history to the American past. Has value for the mature Christian student.

29. *LATOURETTE, K. S., *History of the Expansion of Christianity*, 7 V., HRP, 1937-1945, $22.50; ES, 1937-1945, 200s. Although this seven-volume work is basically a history of Christianity in its contact with pagan cultures, it presents a well-defined view of history from the Christian point of view. Latourette is well acquainted with the evangelical position and on the whole supports it. It is the best general work of its kind available in English.

7E. CULTURE
Gwyn Walters

"Culture" sometimes refers to the enhanced quality of life that follows or accompanies interest and involvement in the artistic facets of experience in such areas as art, architecture, drama, literature, music, poetry, and sculpture. Elsewhere its sense approaches that of "civilization," milieu, ethics and includes the sum total of practices, customs, and habits of a larger or smaller segment of humanity (e.g., Western, American, or Southern [U.S.] culture).

Further expansion of the term makes it coextensive with the whole human enterprise of constructing an artificial environment for man-at-large in society and state. This links up with the biblical mandate to man as husbandman to cultivate the earth, as husband to cohabit for the furnishing of family life, and as scientist to categorize the various materials at his disposal. Culture thus becomes the result and setting of man's labor, love, and learning.

The book selections reflect these three respective meanings.

1. *KIDNER, Derek, *The Christian and the Arts*, Ri, IVP, 1961, 32 pp., Pb 30¢; TP, 1959, 1s 6d. Are the arts a "By-path Meadow" for the Christian and should cultural pursuits be subordinated if not rejected? Is "Art for Art's sake" and the artist's integrity morally neutral or autonomous? How do moral standards apply? Balanced, biblically-based guidelines and an excerpt from Augustine's *Confessions* make this booklet a valuable introduction to the Christ-culture debate.

2. *KILBY, C. S., *Christianity and Aesthetics*, IVP, 1961, 43 pp., Pb 95¢. This appetizer for aesthetics derives the Christian's cultural enterprise from Genesis' creation account. Christianity provides subject matter and climate for art to flourish and opposes not art but artistic abuses. In expressing worship and experiencing identity in life, man is enhanced through artistic involvement. True vision in art and religion looks outward and upward to the Creator Artist.

3. *EVERSOLE, Finley, ed., *Christian Faith and the Contemporary Arts,* ABP, 1962, 318 pp., $5.00. A symposium of articles and illustrations by a galaxy of writers in theology and the arts shows that to receive modern art with its anguish and freedom is to receive "a mixture of blessing and pain." A theology of imagination and a spirit of humility will help art and faith to make contact and use traditional and contemporary media wisely.

4. GORDH, George, *Christian Faith and its Cultural Expression,* PH, 1962, 354 pp., $8.50. Scripture, historic Christianity, and current literature form this work on the tri-dimensional wholeness of Christian faith as a way of looking at the world and man, a set of attitudes in intra- and inter-personal relationships, a set of expressions through the arts and in action. Christianity's self-consistent character is described in relation to individuals, the Church, and Western culture.

5. *NIDA, E. A., *Customs, Culture and Christianity,* HRP, 1954, 306 pp., $4.00; TP, 1963, 320 pp., 15s. An entertainingly written, anthropological study based on extensive experiences in traveling and Scripture translation. Serious consideration of the relation of anthropology, culture, and Christian mission is not hindered by such humorous titles as "hoes and headaches," "fried or scrambled," "sour mush and sauerkraut." An appendix locates resource material on anthropological background especially useful for prospective missionaries and Christians living abroad.

6. LAW, H. W., *Winning a Hearing,* WBE, 1967, 160 pp., $3.95. Treating culture as non-verbal behavior, as language and communication, and as changing behavior, this introductory work on anthropology and linguistics aids theoretically and practically

Christian service amongst various ethnic groups on native and foreign soil. The dynamics of cultural development on material, social, and ideological levels are discussed. The book features useful elementary language exercises.

7. *McLUHAN, Marshall, *Understanding Media: The Extensions of Man,* MH, 1964, 359 pp., Hb $7.50; NAL, 1966, Pb 95¢; RO, 1964, 42s. An excursion into the complex world of mass media by the "philosopher of the electronic age" in which the founder of "McLuhanism" claims that culture is affected (in later writing "massaged") directly by the medium (especially the electrically conditioned) which is itself a message apart from the so-called message-content communicated through it. A controversial book for the Christian communicator.

8. DAWSON, Christopher, *The Historic Reality of Christian Culture,* HRP, 1960, 124 pp., $3.00; RO, 12s 6d. Against the backdrop of six cultural ages of the Christian Church vis-a-vis secular life, this Roman Catholic historian analyzes contemporary secularized society. Convinced of the moral ingredients of culture and that Christian culture transcends Western and Oriental differences, he urges the rediscovery by higher education of such a culture as the only hope for civilization and humanity itself.

9. VAN TIL, H. R., *The Calvinistic Concept of Culture,* PRPC, 1959, 245 pp. (OoP) The lineage of the Reformed definition of culture, traced through Calvin back to Augustine and on to Kuyper and Schilder, shows the prominence given to the authority of Scripture, faith, Christ's Mediatorial Kingship, vocation, and common grace. The dangers of indiscriminately relating the latter term to Christians and non-Christians alike in

culture are noted. Christ alone truly transforms culture.

10. NIEBUHR, H. R., *Christ and Culture,* HRP, 1956, 259 pp., Hb $2.65, Pb $1.25; FF, 1952, 156 pp., 21s. An "essay on the double wrestle of the Church with its Lord and with the cultural society with which it lives in symbiosis." After referring to traditional constructs of the Christ-Culture relation, he particularizes five: Christ against Culture, Christ of Culture, Christ above Culture, Christ and Culture in Paradox, and (his favorite?) Christ the Transformer of Culture.

11. CAILLIET, Emile, *The Christian Approach to Culture,* AC, 1952, 288 pp. (OoP) A Christian philosopher, jealous both for the Christian's enrichment and for the cultural order, urges a "conversation with culture," a viewing of "cultural manifestations with Christian eyes." The divorce of Christianity and culture involves impoverishment and decay for both; their mutuality under the hand of the Creator leads to the peace, not of the grave, but "of a great dawn."

12. PELIKAN, Jaroslav, *Human Culture and the Holy: Essays on the True, the Good and the Beautiful,* MUP, 1955, 172 pp., $3.00 (OoP); SCMP, 1959, 15s. (OoP) The category of the Holy is beyond the reach of the normally sane, cultural intellectuals, moralists, and aesthetes. Three "insane" writers—Kierkegaard, Dostoevsky, and Nietzsche are portrayed in tension between the Holy and the True, the Good and the Beautiful respectively. Three "fools," Paul, Luther, and Bach grasp Truth, Goodness, and Beauty in Christ, the Holy Transcender of cultural values.

13. COCHRANE, C. N., *Christianity and Classical Culture, A Study of Thought and Action from Augustus to Augustine,* Ri, OUP, 1960, 523

pp., Hb $7.00, Pb $2.45; OUP, Hb 50s, Pb 15s. Under "Reconstruction, Renovation, Regeneration" the author examines revolution in thought and action which came about through the impact of Christianity upon the Graeco-Roman world. He hints that the historically justified Christian criticism of that world's claims to produce permanent security, peace, and freedom through "creative politics" might well be updated from the fourth century to the twentieth.

14. BRUNNER, Emil, *Christianity and Civilization,* CSS, 1948, 172 pp. (OoP); NI, 1948, 180 pp., 10s. Written with prophetic constraint as civilization lay under a post-war pall, this work warns against the severing of civilization and culture from their transcendent roots in Christian faith. De-Christianized autonomies of "creative genius" in the arts or sciences or in political totalitarianism must yield to God, the source of justice, truth, and love to avoid annihilation of the truly human.

15. TILLICH, Paul, *Theology of Culture,* OUP, 1959, 213 pp., Hb $4.75, Pb $1.45; OUP, 1964, 224 pp., Hb 18s, Pb 8s. Fifteen essays chosen "to show the religious dimension in many spheres of man's cultural activity." Tillich's correlation of existential (secular?) questions and theological answers familiar to readers of his *Systematic Theology,* Ri, UCP, 1967, 791 pp., $12.50; NI, 1953-1957, 354, 228, 404 pp., 30s, 25s, 42s, is here applied to several facets of the current culture including language, artistic style, psychoanalysis, science, education, and morality. American, European, Russian, Protestant, and Jewish cultures are compared.

7F1. DRAMA
Nancy M. Tischler
Drama has traditionally grown out of the liturgy of religions; Greek tragedy

and comedy have both been traced to their origins in the worship of the Greek gods. Medieval drama was similarly an expansion of the worship service—based on Scripture, on saints' legends, or on patterns of the Christian life. In recent years, the dramatists have been concerned with a return to these roots of the drama, but have found the need to adjust their form to a more sophisticated and skeptical audience. The modern plays are consequently more oblique and difficult theologically, but rewarding aesthetically to the Christian reader striving to understand himself, his world, and his God.

1. HALVERSON, Marvin, ed., *Religious Drama,* 3 V., PS, 1959, V. 1, 410 pp.; V. 2, 317 pp., $3.50; V. 3, MEB, 314 pp., Pb $1.45; V. 3, May, 1960, Pb 12s. This excellent series, now available in paperback, is a collection of the best of medieval and modern religious, mystery, and morality plays. Both short and full-length plays are included, some quite suitable for production in the parish. Among the contemporary plays are those by W. H. Auden, Christopher Fry, D. H. Lawrence, Dorothy Sayers, and James Schevill. See also, J. W. Bachmann and E. M. Browne, eds., *Better Plays for Today's Churches,* ASP, 1964, 474 pp., $8.95, which includes the deservedly popular "Christ in the Concrete City." For a good annotated list of religious plays, see Harold Ehrensperger, *Religious Drama: Ends and Means,* ABP, 1962, 287 pp., $6.00.

2. *SAYERS, Dorothy, *The Man Born to Be King,* HRP, 1949, 344 pp., $4.50; GOL, RE, 1947, 12s 6d. In these plays, written for a British Broadcasting Company radio series presentation, Miss Sayers, an Anglican playwright-theologian-scholar, dramatizes the life of Christ, translating the gospel story into very human terms while concentrating on the divine purpose underlying each incident.

3. FRY, Christopher, *A Sleep of Prisoners: Play,* OUP, 1951, 60 pp., $3.50; OUP, 8s 6d. Set in a church, this tale of four prisoners of war includes a series of biblical dreams. Fry explores modern man's efforts to understand himself and to find some meaning in a confused and violent world.

4. *MacLEISH, Archibald, *JB,* HM, 1961. (On record, RCA Victor LD 6076) A delightful and fanciful interpretation of Job's archetypal plight. MacLeish chooses to picture his characters as modern, but in a theatrical rather than a realistic mode. Very effective in spots, but misses some of the point of biblical Job.

5. GREENE, Graham, *The Living Room,* VIP, 1954, 126 pp., $2.50; HEE, 1955, 88 pp., 6s. Greene explores the confusion and despair of human life in terms of the need for redemption and the recognition of God's grace. The play is written in the tradition of medieval passion dramas.

6. *GREENE, Graham, *The Potting Shed: Play,* VIP, 1957, 123 pp., $3.00; VIP, 1961, Pb 95¢; HEE, 1958, 76 pp., 10s 6d. A man whose life is a chronicle of disappointment finds that he was once restored to life physically but not spiritually as the result of his uncle's prayer. The miracle that revived him is an embarrassment to the family and to the uncle whose unfortunate prayer preserved his worthless life. The story of a man asking God to alter his plans only to discover that answered prayer can be cruel is an interesting study in human psychology, in the workings of God's will, in the nature of prayer, and in the reality of miracles.

7. *CANNON, Denis, and Pierre Bost, *The Power and the Glory,* VIP, 1946, 288 pp., Hb $5.00, Pb $1.65; HEE, 1963, 9s 6d; PE, Pb 3s 6d. Originally a novel and later a film, this startling representation of the Roman Catholic attitude toward the Church and the priesthood pictures a lecherous, degenerate "whiskey priest" who finds he cannot escape his role as God's servant and the Church's spokesman. He is obliged to continue his ministry to the poor people of revolutionary Mexico regardless of his own unworthiness.

8. *MILLER, Arthur, *The Crucible,* VIP, 1964, 145 pp., Hb $3.50, Pb $1.25; BAB, 95¢. (On record, Spoken Arts 704-1956) (VE) Although the play is not specifically religious, it shows the abuses available to the hypocritic, the demonic, and the vicious members of a religious society. Miller uses the Salem witch trials as the scene for this exploration of hysteria and evil. See also, *Collected Plays,* VIP, 1957, 439 pp., $6.00; CRE, 1958, 25s.

9. TOLSTOY, Leo, *The Power of Darkness* (in various collections including John Gassner's *A Treasury of the Theatre,* SS, 1960, 1275 pp.). This late nineteenth-century Russian play dramatizes the nature of evil and the progressive development of sin until man must repent or face damnation. It is a rare example of conservative attitudes toward good and evil, God and Satan, in the modern theater.

10. *SHAW, G. B., *St. Joan: Play,* LO, 1964, 271 pp., Pb $1.40; LO, 208 pp., Hb 7s, Pb 4s 3d. (On record, Caedman TR5-S311, 4 records.) (VE) A witty, whimsical study of the French saint and her role as heroine and martyr. Shaw has an opportunity to say many startling and several perceptive things about morality, faith, and life.

11. OSBORNE, John, *Luther,* CRIB, 1962, 102 pp., $2.95; NAL, 1964, Pb 60¢; FF, 1961, 12s 6d, FF, 1965, Pb 5s. Osborne interprets Luther as less heroic than human, but does credit his intense faith and the enormous impact of his teachings. The play is not historically accurate and does overemphasize Luther's disgestive difficulties, but is nevertheless a colorful and sympathetic portrait.

12. BOLT, Robert, *A Man for All Seasons: Play,* RH, 1962, 163 pp., Hb $4.50, Pb $1.45; HEE, 1960, 99 pp., 7s 6d; HEE, RE, 1967, Pb 6s. A study of the Renaissance courtier, Sir Thomas More, whose concern for his immortal soul transforms him into the Christian wayfarer, weighing the delights of this world against the hopes of the next.

13. ELIOT, T. S., *Murder in the Cathedral,* HA, 1964, 88 pp., Hb $2.75, Pb $1.25; FF, ED 4, 1938, 9s 6d; BRO, 1950, Pb 2s 6d. The chorus and the cathedral setting are part of Eliot's effort to convey a combination of Greek and Medieval liturgical drama in this saint's legend, but his presentation of Thomas Becket is clearly modern withal.

14. *ELIOT, T. S., *The Cocktail Party,* HA, 1964, 190 pp., Hb $4.00, Pb $1.65; FF, 1950, 167 pp., Pb 6s; FF, RE, 1962, 356 pp., 30s. (On record, Decca, DX-100, 2 records.) In this play, Eliot transforms a cocktail party into a mystic experience and a psychiatrist into a God-image. His parable of the paths available to man is difficult but entertaining and rewarding reading.

15. WILLIAMS, Tennessee, *The Night of the Iguana,* ND, 1962, 128 pp., $3.50; NAL, 1964, Pb 60¢; SW, 1963, 108 pp., 18s. (VE) This macabre presentation of the dark side of the religious mind focuses on a defrocked Episcopal minister who can-

not reconcile the role of God, the reality of suffering and evil, and the nature of human responsibility. It is a disturbing use of Christian symbolism in a perversely cannibalistic world.

16. BERRYHILL, Elizabeth, *The Cup of Trembling*, SP, 1958, Pb $1.50. The play is based on the life of Dietrich Bonhoeffer, the German theologian martyred by the Nazis. Despite some dramatic faults, the play has considerable impact in presenting the climactic events of the theologian's life and death.

17. BECKETT, Samuel, *Waiting for Godot: Play*, GP, 1965, Pb $1.75; FF, 1956, 94 pp., Hb 13s 6p, Pb 5s; DUC, 1966, 238 pp., 13s. (On record, Columbia 02L-238, 2 records.) (VE) Presents the modern wasteland scene in metaphoric and bleak terms. The play expresses the meaninglessness of those who see God as absent from the world and unwilling to communicate with frustrated and confused mankind. Other plays in this collection reflect the same tone of alienation and anguish.

18. RUTENBORN, Guenter, *The Sign of Jonah*, NE, 1960, $2.50. A play by a German author explores the question of collective guilt. For a witty and provocative one act play presenting the confrontation between God, Satan, and a Lover of God, see Stanley Solomon, "Armageddon" in *Motive,* 24 (Dec. 1963).

7F2. THEATER
George Ralph

The relationship—actual, historical, or potential—between the theater and religion has long fascinated critics dealing with the performing arts. Approaches to the subject have been quite varied and have included such types of writing as (a) discussions of religious theater per se as one specific form of dramatic art, including attempts to define the concept and

studies of its historical development, (b) analyses of the religious implications in "secular" drama, that is, looking at theater tradition and practice as a whole from a theological perspective, and (c) more or less personal statements by creative artists in the theater, reflecting the way in which one's understanding of the demands of the Christian life can affect one's vocation as playwright, director, etc. In addition to theologically orientated writings, general critical analyses of drama and interpretations of what the theater has been and where it is going are of value to the Christian who is serious about increasing his understanding and appreciation of the art form itself.

1. *EHRENSPERGER, Harold, *Religious Drama: Ends and Means,* ABP, 1962, 287 pp., $6.00. Of the various manuals for the production of religious drama, this is the most comprehensive, including discussions of dramatic form and content and the history of the contemporary religious drama movement. The sections devoted to practical problems of staging will be of less interest to the general reader.

2. *EVERSOLE, Finley, ed., *Christian Faith and the Contemporary Arts,* ABP, 1962, 318 pp., $5.00. In the three essays in this volume which deal with drama, E. Martin Browne succinctly explains "Contemporary Drama in the Catholic Tradition" (pp. 132-141); Tom F. Driver discusses criteria for a new and distinctively Protestant dramatic form in "Thesis for a Playwright Still in Hiding" (pp. 142-145); and Edward C. Hobbs presents an extreme position in "liberal" criticism as he seeks "The Gospel in So-Called Secular Drama" (pp. 146-151).

3. COGGIN, P. A., *The Uses of Drama,* GB, 1956, 327 pp., $5.00. This is an historical survey of soci-

ety's natural impulse toward dramatic expression and the relation between this impulse and changing concepts of education. The Church is seen as having been a factor in the relationship—or lack of it—between theater art and formal education.

4. MARSHALL, M. H., ed., "Aesthetic Values of the Liturgical Drama," in A. S. Downer, ed., *English Institute Essays: 1950*, AMSP, 1965, 236 pp., $7.50. This is the most readable account available of the drama which grew out of the liturgy of the Church in the Middle Ages. While written as an historical study, the article's implications have to do with the relationship in general between dramatic form and Christian worship.

5. *SPEAIGHT, Robert, *Christian Theatre*, HAW, 1960, 142 pp., $3.95; BO, 1966, 4s. This is the best work available which deals with the history of theater, from the standpoint of the effect of Christianity on the drama, from the Middle Ages to the present. As the actor who created the role of Becket in Eliot's *Murder in the Cathedral*, Speaight combines scholarship with an intimate practical knowledge of the theater. It is recommended that the reader be prepared to look into some of the plays mentioned in this study.

6. GHÉON, Henri, *The Art of the Theatre*, HWD, 1961, 100 pp., Hb $3.50, Pb $1.25; MAG, 12s 6d. Ghéon discusses his views of theater and his own development as a dramatist, culminating in his attempt to create a religious drama appealing to a widely popular contemporary audience.

7. *SCOTT, N. A., Jr., ed., *Man in the Modern Theatre*, JKP, 1965, 100 pp., Pb $1.00. Each of five essays on modern dramatists is intended to "express something of the Christian

reader's response." Of particular merit are Tom Driver's balanced introduction to Eugene O'Neill and Nathan Scott's illumination of the theological content of T. S. Eliot's drama.

8. VOS, Nelvin, *The Drama of Comedy: Victim and Victor*, JKP, 1966, 125 pp., Pb $1.95. Vos explores three types of comic drama and the degree to which they correspond to a Christian view of reality. The study is scholarly, and a reading of it will be enhanced by a knowledge of the work of playwrights Thorton Wilder, Eugene Ionesco, and Christopher Fry.

9. BAXTER, K. M., *Contemporary Theatre and the Christian Faith*, ABP, 1965, 112 pp., $2.75; *Speak What We Feel*, SCMP, 1964, 96 pp., 12s 6d. Mrs. Baxter looks at examples of drama written from the standpoint of Christian faith as well as drama which does not reflect a specifically Christian perspective, examining both in the light of contemporary theology. She concludes that the modern theater has not yet produced a drama which has *both* religious depth *and* stage vitality, but sees possibilities in current new trends.

10. MERCHANT, W. M., *Creed and Drama: An Essay in Religious Drama*, FP, 1966, 119 pp., Pb $1.95; SPCK, 1965, 138 pp., 16s. Each chapter of this book studies a separate historical period or major playwright in terms of the relation of the drama to Christian doctrine. Each is placed clearly within the theological context of the particular age, as well as related to a continuing tradition of religious drama. For a full appreciation of Merchant's view of the function of drama, the reader should refer also to his statement on the relation between playwright and religious belief, "The Church's Mission to the Artist," in F.

S. Cellier, ed., *Liturgy is Mission*, SP, 1964, 159 pp., $3.95.

11. *ESSLIN, Martin, *The Theatre of the Absurd*, PS, 1961, 364 pp., $3.50; DC, Pb $1.45; ES, 1962, 288 pp., 35s. Of a number of recent books on the subject, this is probably the best and most comprehensive introduction. Esslin discusses such dramatists as Beckett, Ionesco, Pinter, and Albee. He views contemporary trends in the theater as reflecting our age's loss of faith in permanent values.

12. BENTLEY, Eric, *The Life of the Drama*, ATH, 1964, 371 pp., $5.95; ME, 1965, 384 pp., 36s. This is a detailed study of what the drama is and how the playwright assembles his materials to reveal to us his vision of life. Bentley is not concerned with writing from a religious perspective; but at the same time he discusses some interesting instances of the relation between religious belief and dramatic form.

13. PEACOCK, Ronald, *The Poet in the Theatre*, ATH, 1964, 198 pp., Hb $5.95, Pb $2.95. Peacock analyzes major dramatists of the past century and a half, illustrating the way in which their view of man and society has affected the dramatic forms they have employed. The author is not concerned with theological questions *per se*; but the book offers real insight into the way in which the theater reflects and relates to the predominant values in society.

14. FRYE, R. M., *Shakespeare and Christian Doctrine*, PUP, 1963, 324 pp., Hb $6.00, Pb $2.95; OUP, 35s. This is a well-balanced study of Shakespeare's knowledge and use of Christian doctrine. While Frye takes issue with critics who regard Shakespeare as an *explicitly* Christian playwright, he demonstrates that Shakespeare does clearly reflect the kinds

of theological formulations which would have been most current in his day. The book is suitable for the general reader, but of particular value to one already conversant with Shakespeare's plays.

7F3. FILMS
J. Summers and
Harish D. Merchant
Our age is as much the age of the vacuum tube as of the printing press with the result that the image has come to supplant in large part the primacy of the written word. Film is of central importance amid this "graphic revolution" of our time. Capturing as it does the spirit and beat of our age, film has been termed "the characteristic art form of the twentieth-century."

Many of our young adult generation attend the cinema religiously and they find the works of Fellini, Antonioni, Bergman, Kurosawa, and Ray, for instance, of more vivid and arresting import than the more prosaic literary, religious, and political expressions generally acclaimed by the academic world.

In view of the fact that man has been so made that he must think in terms of pictures and images and of the further fact of man's intuitive attraction to the motion picture, it is understandable that so many thousands of churches have invested in motion picture projection equipment. However, in most situations this tool has not been put to wise use. Here are some films available in 16 mm sound versions as well as pertinent books related to the subject, to help the situation. The prices quoted are for rental.

FILMS:
What is Man?
1. *The Oxbow Incident*, BRAN, 72 mins., $22.50. A classic Western which points up such basic topics as motivation, law-justice, guilt, and

leads to the question "How is 'right' made effective in this world?"

2. *Death of a Salesman,* BRAN, 115 mins., $20.00. Illusion, self-identity, and family relationship are basic themes of this important American drama.

3. *La Strada,* BRAN, 107 mins., $50.00. The celebrated Fellini film about three souls who travel an Italian highway is a story of every man's loneliness in which the "strong man" must finally confront the state of his soul.

4. *Billy Budd,* AFIP, 123 mins., $35.00. The youthful Billy presents a refreshing image of innocence and goodness. From the classic Melville story of forgiveness and redemption.

5. *The Given Word,* BRAN, 98 mins., $50.00. A simple man makes a promise to the Madonna and seeks to carry it out despite hell, high water, or the powers of church and state. A Brazilian film which presents a vivid image of dedication in our time.

6. *Diary of a Country Priest,* BRAN, 95 mins., $60.00. A French film directed by Bresson and based on the Bernanos novel. A young priest in the midst of personal conflicts seeks to give himself to others.

7. *Woman of the Dunes,* CONT, 123 mins., $10.00. An important Japanese film which is a parable of man seeking his basic needs.

The Search for Identity
8. *David and Lisa,* COAL, 82 mins., $75.00. Two young people help each other toward health in an atmosphere of sympathy and understanding. An outstanding American film which suggests the amazing ways of grace.

9. *The Quiet One,* CONT, 70 mins., $25.00. A unique and highly ac-claimed American "documentary" which offers insight into the unlovely behavior of the unloved. In this film a young Harlem Negro boy makes the painful journey from being nobody toward finding love. An outstanding film in this area.

10. *Nobody Waved Goodbye,* BRAN, 90 mins., $50.00-$100.00. A Canadian film which shows two teen-agers rebelling against suburban mores and heading toward delinquency. Candid . . . Authentic.

No Man is an Island
11. *On the Waterfront,* BRAN, 108 mins., $22.50. The award-winning film starring Marlon Brando. A priest speaks out amidst labor strife.

12. *The Bicycle Thief,* BRAN, 87 mins., $45.00. The classic film by de Sica. The poignant and ironic story of a worker buffeted by an indifferent world.

13. *Day of Wrath,* CONT, 98 mins., $45.00-$75.00. Although a dramatic story about witchcraft in seventeenth-century Denmark, this film contains implications relating to the universal human condition. It is by the Danish film pioneer, Carl Dryer.

His Brother's Keeper?
14. *Breathless,* BRAN, 89 mins., $50.00-$100.00. French . . . "new wave" . . . TIME says it is on the theme that life is just one damn thing after another and death is the thing after that.

15. *Lord of the Flies,* COAL, 90 mins., $75.00. English schoolboys cast upon a deserted island repeat the history of the race. The guide examines both film and book in a depth examination of what they express regarding democracy, authoritarianism, and the role of the leader.

16. *Twelve Angry Men,* 95 mins., $125.00. The setting is a jury room. The goal is to get twelve men to reach an agreement. The film is a text on "human interaction."

17. *Question 7,* COUS, 107 mins., $50.00. An action-packed drama of courage by people unwilling to sacrifice ideals, this timely film from behind the Berlin wall has already won twenty-two international awards. A film for the person who must someday decide between what is easy and expedient and what is right and honorable.

Society
18. *It's About This Carpenter,* 15 mins., $15.00. A prize-winning student film about what happens to a beatnik carpenter who makes a cross and delivers it to a church up-town.

19. *On the Bowery,* 65 mins., $40.00. A searching picture of three men existing on New York's skid row. A prize-winning documentary which shows hope and hopelessness, desolation and humor.

20. *The Hangman,* CONT, MMM, 12 mins., $12.50. A morality tale through images and poetry of the fatal consequences of silence in the face of evil. Powerful.

21. *Scorpio Rising,* 30 mins., $40.00. Kenneth Anger's acclaimed film on the motorcycle cult in California and its Nazi-sadistic overtones.

22. *I Don't Want to Get Involved,* COUS, 30 mins., $15.00. This film documents apathy and the problems of growing impersonalism, particularly in metropolitan areas. Creates a climate for discussion on how churches and individual Christians can overcome attitudes of apathy.

23. *The Other Six Days,* COUS, 30 mins., $15.00. Religion and business—sanctuary and marketplace. Can a Christian live without conflict in both of these worlds at once? Ideal to provoke discussion on the problems of Christian living within the business world.

24. *Our Youth Culture,* COUS, 30 mins., $15.00. A serious study of our youth. Their struggle for maturity and identity challenges the church to make its message relevant to their needs. Youth are shown reacting to the social, commercial, political, and religious pressures.

25. *The Work Crisis,* COUS, 30 mins., $15.00. Film that probes basic questions: Are people necessary, when machines and computers can do the work? What is the biblical concept of work? How do you find meaning in meaningless work? What to do with leisure? What is the church's responsibility in answering these questions?

26. *Big Steve,* COUS, 30 mins., $13.50. One of an estimated six million Americans who gamble compulsively, Steve drags himself and his family through a private hell before asking help from Gamblers Anonymous.

Prejudice
27. *Portrait of Andrew Goodman,* COUS, 27 mins., $15.00. The story of a modern martyr, a young civil rights worker who was killed in the South in 1964.

28. *The Victims,* COUS, 50 mins., $20.00. Dr. Spock diagnoses the causes of prejudice in children. He sees parents as carriers (and curers) of the disease.

29. *Nothing But a Man,* BRAN, 90 mins., $50.00. A highly acclaimed low-budget film with an all-Negro cast which graphically suggests why the Negro is often the way he is.

War

30. *Eyewitness... North Vietnam,* COUS, 43 mins., $75.00. A documentary which shows the people of the North in the midst of war. Filmed by a British journalist.

31. *Sons and Daughters,* COUS, 98 mins., $125.00. Beginning with the peace demonstrations at Berkeley this film moves out into the wider world at war.

Health

32. *The Losers,* MMM, 31 mins., $15.00. The dangers of teenage drug addiction . . . the damage, mental and physical.

33. *Hooked,* COUS, 20 mins., $12.00. Experiences of addicts in their own words.

34. *Alcohol and Tobacco: What They Do to Our Bodies,* COUS, 10 mins., $5.00.

35. *Smoking and You,* CONT, 11 mins., $10.00. Produced in England for the Central Office of Information.

SCIENCE

36. *Signposts Aloft,* MIS, 28 mins., $17.50. Story of instrument flight and the relevance of faith in the age of science. *Signposts Aloft* gives a fresh, new understanding of why man needs a point of reference outside himself and what a commitment to God actually means.

37. *City of the Bees,* MIS, 45 mins., $25.00. Insect city boasts air conditioning, police and sanitation squads, nurseries, chemical processing plants, some remarkable structural engineers and a concise and effective language that man has learned to "read." Men everywhere are struggling with the problem of human behavior. This film reveals God's solution to this age-old problem.

38. *God of the Atom,* MIS, 28 mins., $15.00. Equipment used in atomic research, demonstrations of the tremendous energies within every tiny particle of matter. The theme of man's spiritual bankruptcy and his need for regeneration is stressed.

39. *God of Creation,* MIS, 28 mins., $15.00. Immensity of space and the teeming world of tiny creatures in a single drop of water. The power and beauty of growing things evidence God's infinite care in all his creation.

40. *Red River of Life,* MIS, 62 mins., $25.00. Story of the most efficient pump in the world, the human heart. Shows how life hangs by a very slender thread, the chemistry of the red blood cell. A positive Christian message, abundantly supported by scientific fact, biblical and secular history.

41. *Time and Eternity,* MIS, 28 mins., $15.00. Explains the meaning of time and space. The reality of eternity is seen as scientific fact. In *Time and Eternity* an infinite God of time, space, and eternity offers the solution to life's one absolute necessity— forgiveness.

Archaeology

42. *The Quest,* MIS, 33 mins., $12.50. The wreckage of mighty cities and empires of the past points up the futility of man's greatest and most ambitious efforts to build for eternity. *The Quest* shows some of man's age-old efforts to achieve eternal life and brings home the truth that only ". . . he that doeth the will of God abideth forever."

43. *The Stones Cry Out,* MIS, 45 mins., $12.50. Here is a pioneer exploration into the marvels of fulfilled prophecy. The crushing weight of archaeological evidence reveals an unfailing God who fulfills his judgments

upon sin—and his promises of eternal life.

Religions

44. *The Professor and the Prophets,* MIS, 30 mins., $12.50. Is the accuracy of Bible prophecy due merely to human guesswork or to divine inspiration? The prophecies of the Bible have not been produced by human invention, but by God speaking through his chosen servants.

45. *Mightier Than the Sword,* MIS, 45 mins., $10.00. Dramatizes the importance of gospel literature in mission work around the world. People are now learning to read and write at fully twice the rate of the world's increase in population. Their hunger for something to read presents the greatest missionary opportunity of our time.

46. *Martin Luther,* AFIP, 100 mins., $25.00. The story of the man who sparked the Reformation. A highly successful film produced by the Lutheran Church. It can be ordered in three parts or as a single film. The guide developed for its use offers excellent program possibilities.

47. *Gospel According to Matthew,* BRAN, 123 mins., $100.00. Is a director justified in attempting to image Jesus through the "high definition" of film? This is a valid theological question. Here is what many regard as the most "successful" attempt.

48. *The Third Devil,* COUS, 30 mins., $13.50. A fantasy concerning a business depression in hell and the efforts of Satan to find a more effective means of luring humans into Hades.

49. *Africa and Schweitzer,* COUS, 28 mins., $10.00. Filmed in Africa, this documentary shows one of the great mission accomplishments of modern times.

50. *To Every Creature,* MIS, 45 mins., $10.00. Some of the difficulties faced by frontier missionaries. It explains how the effectiveness of missionaries can be multiplied many times through modern marvels of transportation and communication, and through specialists trained to operate and maintain these marvels.

51. *The Paul Carlson Story,* CYC, 53 mins., $30.00. On November 24, 1964, the attention of the entire world was drawn to the name of Paul Carlson, who in the last weeks of his life became a twentieth-century symbol of strength and dedication. The facts of his life, his medicine, his love for God, his courage, and tragic death are told.

BOOKS:

52. EVERSOLE, Finley, ed., *Christian Faith and the Contemporary Arts,* ABP, 1962, 255 pp., $5.00. A good, general survey of the range of the arts . . . film, television, dance, comic strips, jazz, etc.

53. SCOTT, Nathan, ed., *The New Orpheus,* SHE, 1964, 431 pp., Hb $7.50, Pb $3.95. A more scholarly collection of essays covering the various areas of the arts.

54. ROSENBERG, Bernard and D. M. White, eds., *Mass Culture,* FRP, 1957, Pb $2.95; CM, 562 pp., 22s 6d. An excellent collection of essays on the popular arts with a "secular" orientation.

55. WHITTLE, D. C., *Christianity and the Arts,* FP, Pb $1.50; MO, 196 pp., Pb 12s 6d; MO, 170 pp., Hb 25s. A comparatively brief survey of the relationship between Christianity and the arts by a British Christian educator.

56. McLUHAN, Marshall, *Understanding Media,* MH, 1964, 359 pp., Hb $7.50; Signet, 1966, Pb 95¢; RO, 1964, 42s. A highly suggestive work on the modern media. The first section of the book is an exposition of its thesis and is the most important.

57. WHANNEL, Paddy, and Stuart Hall, *The Popular Arts,* PAB, 1965, $7.95; BHP, Pb $2.95; HU, 1964, 485 pp., 45s. A valuable work which gives application to theory in the areas of the popular arts. It concludes with curriculum units in six topical areas which draw on the materials of the various media.

58. *LYNCH, William, *The Image Industries,* SHE, 1959, $3.50; SHE, 1960, 176 pp., 12s 6d. A most valuable delineation of criteria with respect to the content criticism of films by a modern Jesuit scholar.

59. JACOBS, Lewis, ed., *The Movies,* Noonday, Pb $1.95. An anthology of articles on the nature of the film art.

60. *JONES, William, *Sunday Night at the Movies,* JKP, Pb $1.95. A minister and film specialist has written this book especially for the film-using church. Its theological contention is that a film, as all of existence, is to be measured according to the norm of the "Christ-event." A listing of valuable film information is appended.

61. KUHNS, William, *Short Films in Religious Education,* George Pflaum, 1957, $7.50. Prefatory material concerns the use of the film in religious education. There follow page guides to over eighty selected short films.

62. ROBINSON, W. R., ed., *Man and the Movies,* LSUP, 1967, 371 pp., $7.95. An outstanding new collection of essays on film theory and practice.

63. *A Cinematic "Care" Package,*

Fordham Film Study Center, Fordham University, Bronx, New York 10558, $10.00. This has been prepared by the film study movement at Fordham University. It consists of important paperback books in the field as well as reprints of articles.

7F4. TELEVISION
Haddon W. Robinson

For the last decade and a half, television has been at, or near, the center of attention in America. The people have been watching television a good part of every day, and the critics, commentators, and educators have been studying the people staring at television. The man in front of his set regards television as a blessing in a box; but the social scientists and educators are not quite so sure.

Christians need to take a hard look at television in our society. Whether we view it with alarm or see it as an asset will depend on knowing its place in our society. In most of the literature, there is a great deal of opinion. Unfortunately, solid fact is more difficult to come by. Television cannot be ignored. It will not go away. Ninety percent of our homes average over one-third of each waking day with the television set on. In that statistic lies its problem and its potential.

1. *STEINER, G. A., *The People Look at Television,* AAK, 1963, 425 pp., $7.95. This is the first comprehensive effort to provide factual and objective information on how Americans think about TV. It is based on a thorough national survey using the most advanced techniques of modern social research. It is easy to read and quite startling.

2. SKORNIA, H. J., *Television and Society,* MH, 1965, 268 pp., Hb $7.50, Pb $2.45. Skornia, a former director of national educational television and a lecturer at the University of Illinois, takes a critical look at the

place of television in American society. He is especially concerned with the forces that control what is broadcast in the United States. If you don't like television, this man gives you the facts to support your view.

3. SIMONSON, Solomon, *Crisis in Television,* Living Books, 1966, 229 pp., $5.95. Here is another writer who feels that something is radically wrong with television in American life. He not only curses the flickering picture, but he suggests means by which we can change the channels. If enough people analyze what is taking place, Simonson maintains things can be changed.

4. *Public Television: A Program for Action,* HRP, $4.95; HRP, 40s. One solution is to change the idiot box into an information box. This book is a report of the Carnegie Commission on Educational Television. It advances the proposition that a well financed, well directed educational television system, larger and more effective than that which exists in the United States now, must be brought into being. This is an important book for serious students of television in our society.

5. *McLUHAN, Marshall, *The Medium is the Message,* RH, 1967, 157 pp., $10.95. Right or wrong, McLuhan is the man of the hour in communications. He believes that societies have always been shaped more by the media through which men communicate than by the content of the communication. McLuhan doesn't win any ribbons for easy reading. To understand him, it is best to read his last book first, and work backwards. In that way, you move from illustration to concept. See also, *Understanding Media,* MH, 1964, 359 pp., Hb $7.50; NAL, 1966, Pb 95¢; RO, 1964, 42s.

6. *BOYD, Malcolm, *Crisis in Com-

munication: A Christian Examination of the Mass Media,* DC, 1957, 128 pp., $2.95 (OoP); SPCK, 10s 6d. From a liberal perspective, Boyd wrestles with the theological implications of using television and other mass media to communicate the Gospel. He recognizes the dangers that exist in working with media that exploit in order to communicate Christian love. This is an important book for people interested in communicating the Christian message through a secular medium.

7. BACHMAN, J. W., *The Church in the World of Radio-Television,* ASP, 1960, 191 pp., $3.50. (OoP) Again from a theologically liberal viewpoint, Bachman tackles in specific terms how Christians should react to the advent of an electronic culture. He presents some thought-provoking material on the Christian use of drama on TV as well as examining four possible purposes for the Christian communicator on the medium.

8. PARKER, E. C., D. W. Barry, and D. W. Smythe, *The Television Radio Audience and Religion,* HRP, 1955, 464 pp., $6.00. (OoP) Theories can be spun in ivy-covered towers. This is the first comprehensive study done on the impact of religious radio and television programs on the residents of a New England community. It is a basic work in the field of religious broadcasting, and although somewhat out-of-date, it has not been replaced.

9. *PARKER, E. C., *Religious Television: What to Do and How,* HRP, 1961, 244 pp., $4.00 (OoP); HRP, 1961, 30s. A practical, down-to-earth handbook of what church groups can do to make creative use of television time. Especially helpful for people with no professional experience.

7F5. DANCE
Katherine Iverson
Man has been dancing as long as he

has been walking, and he has used his dance for worship, fellowship, therapy, and performance. Yet, it has been only in this century that men have set down guidelines for the choreography—the creating—of dances. The books recommended here offer a general background in dance, with particular focus on the modern dance as it has developed in America in the twentieth century. The books are verbal attempts at communicating the power and beauty of a non-verbal art form. Dance expresses man's whole being; his mind, emotions, body and soul pour forth as he gives himself to dance.

1. CAGE, John, *Silence*, M.I.T. Press, Cambridge, Massachusetts, 1967, 55 pp., Pb $2.95. John Cage presents his lectures and thoughts on contemporary music and dance, and provides background for an understanding of the avant-garde in electronic and serial music.

2. COHEN, Selma, *The Modern Dance: Seven Statements of Belief*, Wesleyan University Press, 1966, 106 pp., $6.50. Seven leading American dancers discuss how they would put the story of the prodigal son into dance. Their varied approaches to modern dance make this book a significant exploration of contemporary dance theories in America.

3. FISK, Margaret (Palmer), *The Art of the Rhythmic Choir*, HRP, 1950, 205 pp., $2.50. (OoP) Along with a discussion of the expressive potential of movement, this book presents a history of dance-drama and rhythmic choir work within the church, and offers suggestions for organizing such work. The author gives examples of themes and diagrams of rhythmic choirs to help illustrate possible movement interpretations of Christian themes.

4. *Focus on Dance*, National Education Association, 1201 Sixteenth Street, N.W., Washington, D.C. 20006, $4.00 per issue. An annual publication. Each *Focus* issue offers a well-written journal on dance. *Focus on Dance I*, was edited by Gertrude Lippincott and gave an "exploitation of general ideas" (1961). *Focus on Dance II*, edited by Bettie Jane Wooten, presents "an inter-disciplinary search for meaning in movement" (1962). Two more issues were published in 1963 and 1964.

5. HORST, Louis, and Carrol Russell, *Modern Dance Forms in Relation to Other Modern Arts*, Impulse Publications, 1961, 149 pp., $5.00 (OoP); Dance Horizons, Pb $2.95. This book, written by the important composer, accompanist and critic for Martha Graham, includes a definition of the modern dance, a description of the elements of dance, and a discussion of the backgrounds of modern dance, e.g., primitivism, medievalism, expressionism. Recommended for readers who have, or want, a good background in contemporary trends in art.

6. HUMPHREY, Doris, *The Art of Making Dances*, GP, 1959, 189 pp., Pb $1.95; HRW, 52s. In this book, one of the pioneers of American modern dance describes the basic elements and considerations of choreography. It is important both for an understanding of modern dance as an art form in our culture, and for a practical understanding of the elements of composition. The first chapters are an excellent general introduction; the rest of the book is written for the person who wants to dance with understanding.

7. *Impulse*, Impulse Publications, Inc., 160 Palo Alto Avenue, San Francisco, California. *Impulse* magazine is an annual publication. Each year the articles focus on one particu-

lar aspect of dance. For example, *Impulse 1968: Dance, a Projection for the Future* covers the Developmental Conference on Dance held at the University of California, Los Angeles, and includes dance philosophy, music and dance, and four statements on the function of dance in education.

8. *Language of Dance,* Audio-Visual Center, Indiana University, Bloomington, Indiana, 29 minutes, $5.25 rental. José Limón in this film discusses the elements of dance with narrator Martha Myers of Smith College before he and his company present exerpts from his dance, "There is a Time," based on Ecclesiastes 3:1-8. The narrative is informative, although rather pedestrian; the dance and music are superb.

9. *Learning Through Movement,* S-L Film Productions, 5126 Hartwick Street, Los Angeles, California, 90041, 32 minutes, purchase price $165.00, rental price $20.00. This excellent film should be seen by every teacher concerned with the creative education of children. Through numerous creative and ingenious movement explorations, the children in the film found increased self-awareness and joy.

10. MARTIN, J. J., *The Book of the Dance,* TUD, 1963, 192 pp., $7.95. John Martin, *New York Times* dance critic of long standing, writes a general introduction to folk and social dancing, ballet, and modern dance, and describes the significant contributions of such famous dancers as Uday Shankar, Michael Fokine, Antony Tudor, Jerome Robbins, Isadora Duncan, Mary Wigman, Martha Graham, and José Limón. He gives a good over-view of dance.

11. NIEBUHR, Reinhold, "Christianity, Arts, and Mass Media," *Christianity and Crisis,* February 6, 1956. Niebuhr challenges the Christian art-

ist to bring integrity and wholeness of vision to his work. His demand for maturity in the arts needs to be faced if a dancer claims to be working with an art form. An equally powerful article is Paul Tillich's rebuttal in the May 5, 1956, issue of *Christianity and Crisis.*

12. *Nine Variations on a Dance Theme,* University of California Berkeley Media Center, 13 minutes, $7.50 rental. These nine film variations on a single dance sequence present without words the texture and refinement of the dancer's movements. The study is danced by Betty de Jong of the Paul Taylor Company.

13. *Procession: Contemporary Direction in American Dance,* University of California Media Center, 19 minutes, $8.00 rental. Ann Halprin and Company challenge traditional perspectives on dance and art by presenting a "dance-theater" experience. The film shows one aspect of the avant-garde in contemporary art, and is both informative and thought-provoking.

14. PROKSH, Rev. George, "The Sacred Dance." *Jubilee,* November, 1964. Rev. Proksh finds that Indian dance originates within the dancer: "This close relation between the dance and religion in Hindu thought should inspire Christians. One wonders if dance might not be a vehicle of conveying Christian thought."

15. SORELL, Walter, *The Dance Has Many Faces,* COLP, 1967, 276 pp., 59s. This compilation of essays by dancers and dance critics includes articles on religious dance, organizing a dance class, and principles of belief about dance. It helps clarify these several artists' opinions on the place of dance in contemporary society.

16. TAYLOR, Margaret Fisk, *A Time to Dance,* United Church Press,

Philadelphia and Boston, 1967, 180 pp., Pb $2.95. This is a very complete book, with a good use of quotes from modern dance leaders as well as graphic suggestions telling how to organize and develop a rhythmic choir. This unique book would enrich both the rhythmic choir director and dance teacher.

17. TAYLOR, Margaret Fisk, *Time for Discovery,* United Church Press, 1964, 76 pp., $3.25. This book links creative movement for children with religious education. Included are general instructions for the beginning teacher and a few proposed projects for children eight to eleven years old.

18. TAYLOR, Margaret Fisk, *Time for Wonder,* Christian Education Press, 1961, 70 pp., Pb $2.95. This book is a primer for creative dramatic movement in the program of Christian education for five to seven year olds. It is a companion book to *Time for Discovery* by the same author.

19. WIGMAN, Mary, *The Language of Dance,* MACD, 1966, 118 pp., 84s. This book, recently translated from German, is written by one of the most outstanding dancers of our century. It is a beautifully written book that shares much of the sensitivity and depth of its author. She captures verbally some of the grandeur of this non-verbal art form— dance. Recommended for all.

7F6. CARTOONS
Robert L. Short

In recent years comic strip artists around the world have begun taking their work more and more seriously. For they have increasingly come to appreciate the fact that the comics not only serve to provide the public with amusement and light entertainment, but that "the funnies" also are an extremely effective medium for unobtrusively communicating impor-

tant truths, as well as shaping attitudes and opinions. This more significant role of the comics is especially impressive in view of their popularity. In the United States alone the comics are "religiously" followed each day by more than half the population. These factors have caused the church to take a more appreciative and critical look at the comics, and at the same time to use them more frequently and creatively in the communication of its own message. In addition to the many published collections *of the more popular comic strips—such as* Peanuts, Pogo, Miss Peach, Andy Capp, Feiffer's Fables, B.C., Beetle Bailey, *and others—there is the following material of interest:*

1. *SHORT, R. L., *The Gospel According to Peanuts,* JKP, 1965, 127 pp., Hb $2.50, Pb $1.50; FO, 1966, Pb 3s 6d. Charles Schulz, the creator of *Peanuts* and a devout Christian, has admitted he "preaches" in his phenomenally popular strip. This book, containing eighty-eight cartoons, is an examination of some of the preaching Schulz has subtly woven into the fabric of *Peanuts.* The book has been called "a modern-day handbook of the Christian faith." For while examining *Peanuts,* it also serves as an introduction to basic Christian doctrine. The book's doctrinal stance is "classical Protestantism," and its light style has helped to make it popular reading for a wide variety of readers—from high school to older.

2. SCHREIVOGEL, P. A., *The World of Art—The World of Youth,* APH, 1968, 69 pp., $2.50. This well-illustrated book, which calls itself "a primer on the use of arts in youth ministry," contains an excellent chapter on the use of the comics by youth in their local church situations. Mr. Schreivogel is an associate of the Office of Youth Ministries of the Lutheran Church—Missouri Synod.

3. *SHORT, R. L., *The Parables of Peanuts,* HRP, 1968, 320 pp., Pb $1.95. This book, by the author of *The Gospel According to Peanuts,* attempts to make a clear and explicit statement of the actual content of the Christian message—again using illustrations, or modern "parables," from *Peanuts* every step of the way. Over two hundred fifty *Peanuts* cartoons are coupled with the thoughts of theologians such as Bonhoeffer, Barth, Luther, and Kierkegaard. For sophisticated high-schoolers and older.

4. "Good Grief," *Time,* April 9, 1965, V. 85, No. 15. Although this feature-length article centers around Schulz's *Peanuts,* it also provides an excellent discussion of the more important roles played by current comic strips in general. The article examines many of the more popular strips and sees them as providing valuable commentaries on today's world.

5. ELLER, Vernard, "The 'Mad' Morality: An Expose," *The Christian Century,* V. 84, No. 52, December 27, 1967. Mr. Eller, a Church of the Brethren college professor, is unimpressed by either the "new morality" or the old moralisms. But he *is* impressed with the strong moralistic bent he finds in *Mad Magazine,* an ever-popular favorite with young people. Eller sees the "Mad morality" as an indication of the need of today's youth for a more honest appraisal of human nature than provided for them in current liberalism's "new morality."

6. EVERSOLE, Finley, ed., *Christian Faith and the Contemporary Arts,* ABP, 1962, 318 pp., $5.00. In a section entitled "Cartoon and Comic Strip," two articles in this book deal primarily with the theological implications behind the humor of Charles Schulz and Jim Crane. Crane, author

of one of the articles, also examines the work of cartoonists William Steig, Robert Osborn, Jules Feiffer, et al. Many of Crane's cartoons have subsequently been published in two collections of his work, *Inside Out,* HRP; 1967, Pb $1.95, and *On Edge,* JKP, 1965, Pb $1.25.

7. SHORT, R. L., "Sick, Sick, Sick? Then Give, Give, Give—Or Die!" *Motive,* V. 25, No. 1, October, 1964. Examining the cartoons of Jules Feiffer from a Christian perspective, this article finds Feiffer to be a close relative of the Old Testament prophets and of modern religious existentialists such as Kierkegaard. Several of Feiffer's more representative cartoons are reproduced in this article, which was reprinted in the Reorganized Church of Jesus Christ of Latter Day Saints' *University Bulletin.* V. 20, Winter, 1968.

8. WHITE, D. M., and R. H. Abel, eds., *The Funnies: An American Idiom,* Free Press of Glencoe, 1963, 303 pp., $7.50; CM, 55s. An anthology of articles by eminent sociologists, psychologists, educators, and writers (but—alas—no theologians), this book is a fairly well-balanced and systematic examination of the role of comic strips in American culture. Of special interest are three articles written by working cartoonists—the creators of *Pogo* (Walt Kelly), *Li'l Abner* (Al Capp), and *Mary Worth* (Allen Saunders). The book also contains an excellent bibliography on the comics.

9. COUPERIE, Pierre, and H. C. Horn, et al., *A History of the Comic Strip,* Crown Publishers, 1968, 256 pp., $4.95. This generously illustrated and interesting book was prepared in conjunction with the first international exhibition of comic art held at the Louvre in Paris. The authors are a group of scholars who consider the comic strip an art form

and are rightly impressed with the cultural influence exerted by the comics.

7G1. CHRISTIANITY IN THE ARTS: PAINTING AND RELATED MEDIA

Ellen Clinkenbeard
Harish D. Merchant

Approaching the arts in reference to Christianity raises problems of definition and delineation. Therefore, for the purpose of this reading list, Christian art will be defined as painting and the related media (sculpture, mosaics, stained glass, and tapestries) on biblical themes or for the purpose of devotion or communication of faith.

The Church needed art for worship and teaching; thus, a large body of sacred work, representing all periods and media, created in juxtaposition with secular and pagan themes, grew from the time of Christ through the post-Renaissance. Since the Reformation, the influences of humanism, of Asian art, of depth psychology, of textual criticism (lessening the impact of scriptural themes), and the growth of science and technology are a few of the contributing factors to the struggles of artists seeking to express their faith.

In studying the art of Christianity, first, Christians must be aware of the milieu of each artist: the technical limitations, the society, the theological climate, and the contemporary thought and art. Secondly, just as all aspects of our existence should be viewed from the perspective of a Christ-centered life, specifically art, so studied, sometimes will speak of man's sinfulness, degradation, and alienation, and sometimes will open new vistas of worship, but always will make Christians more aware of our Lord.

The increasing availability of fine books and prints and the growing excellence of many museum collections present exciting opportunities for learning. Overcoming prejudices, it is necessary to study and to learn. Not expecting only the pretty and pleasant, Christians must be open to what has been, and is being said about man, the world, and our Creator. It must be pointed out, however, that the value of an art book depends upon the number and quality of its color reproductions, as well as upon the integrity of the text. Such books by necessity are very expensive. For beginners, in addition to the expensive volumes, a number of inexpensive paperbacks are also mentioned below. They will serve the purpose of whetting the appetite.

1. *LEVY, Mervyn, ed., *The Pocket Dictionary of Art Terms*, GRS, 1961, 121 pp., Pb 95¢. The succinct entries for over five hundred techniques, styles, terms, schools, and movements of painting, sculpture, and architecture, make this a valuable aid for study. Page fifty-two covering fret, frottage, fugative pigments, and futurism, or pages sixty-two and sixty-three covering ikonostasis, illumination, illusionism, impasto, imperial, impressionism, and imprimatura indicate the scope of this handy volume of the vocabulary of the visual arts. See also, C. E. Kaltenbach, *Dictionary of Pronunciation of Artists' Names*, Ri, AIC, 1965, 75 pp., Pb $1.00.

2. *CANADAY, John, *Keep to Art*, TUD, 1963, 182 pp., $12.50. Not a history of art, but a book calculated to open doors to perception, this book with its lucid text, superb selection, and quality of plates and excellent format is most helpful to the fledgling and a joy to the serious student. Though not directly related to Christianity in art, this book is valuable, for here one can learn to see, to compare, and to discover the artists' messages and motivations and to communicate with all forms of the visual arts. See also, Kenneth Clark,

Looking at Pictures, HRW, 1960, 199 pp., 75 Illus., 6 C.P., $10.00; JM, 42s.

3. JANSON, H. W., *Key Monuments of the History of Art, A Visual Survey,* HAI, ED 5, 1964, 1000 pp., $12.50; PH, 1959, 1068 pp., 72s. The contents of this volume of over one thousand plates was decided upon after Professor Janson of New York University had consulted with many other art historians. This book is designed for student use. It is invaluable as a survey of the whole panorama of visual art forms and particularly useful for seeing the wide diversity and impact of Christianity in art. See also, Jakob Rosenberg, *Great Draughtsmen From Pisanello to Picasso,* HUP, 1959, 142 pp., 256 Illus., $12.50.

4. *NEWTON, Eric, and William Neil, *The Christian Faith in Art,* HS, 1966, 318 pp., 227 Illus., 16 C.P., 50s. The interaction between the Church and secular society and the conditioning of artistic expression by the theological climate are well-documented in this collaboration by an outstanding theologian and an art historian. Selected impeccably and reproduced superbly, the plates enrich this scholarly and worthwhile volume. If one can purchase only one book on this subject, this would be a fine choice. See also, *Christianity in Modern Art,* BRUP, 1965, $4.50; and W. Wilson, *Christian Art Since the Romantic Movement,* 2 V., BO, 1965, 175 pp., 19s.

5. *The Bible in Art,* 2 V., PHAP, over 250 Illus. (OoP) Wonderfully illustrating the diversity of iconography, expression, and media, from the third through the seventeenth centuries, the plates in these books are drawn from a wide spectrum of schools, and represent much of the finest art inspired by biblical themes.

6. *APPLETON, LeRoy, and Steph-

en Bridges, *Symbolism in Liturgical Art,* CSS, 1959, 120 pp., $3.95. This small volume is an aid to understanding much seen in manuscripts, gothic painting, and in contemporary works. Though primarily a Roman Catholic book, it has much useful information for any student.

7. FLEMING, D. J., *Each With His Own Brush,* FR, 1952, 85 pp., 65 P., Hb $2.75, Pb $2.00. Indigenous Christian art from Asia and Africa, reproduced in the sixty-five plates of this book are an interesting reminder of the universality of the gospel. Dr. Fleming has also written another book on this vein, *Christian Symbols in a World Community,* FR, 1940, 150 pp., Hb $2.75, Pb $2.00.

8. EVERSOLE, Finley, *Christian Faith and the Contemporary Arts,* ABP, 1962, 318 pp., $5.00. A symposium that covers "The Contemporary Situation of the Artist" and "The Contemporary Scene in the Arts," this book has much to say about the relevance of contemporary art to Christianity. The twenty-eight contributors include Sir Herbert Read, Malcolm Boyd, Pamela Ilott (Director of Religious Broadcasting for Columbia Broadcasting Company), and E. Martin Browne (director of all of T. S. Eliot's plays). See also, J. W. Dixon, Jr., *Nature and Grace in Art,* UNCP, 1964, 220 pp., $7.50; UNCP, 1967, 236 pp., 60s.

9. VAN DER LEEUW, Gerardus, *Sacred and Profane Beauty, The Holy in Art,* HRW, 1963, 357 pp., $6.50; WN, 384 pp., 42s. A well-organized study of the dance, drama, rhetoric, the fine arts, architecture, and music, this book by the late Professor of the History of Religion at the University of Groningen in the Netherlands, is of value to the serious student in a search for a theological aesthetic. For a source book of writings by artists, critics, and philosophers, see S. K.

Langer, *Reflections on Art*, JH, 1958, 356 pp., $6.50; OUP, 384 pp., 52s; GALX, 1961, Pb 12s 6d.

10. *GRABAR, André, *Early Christian Art*, ODP, 1968, 440 pp., 298 B.W.P., 107 C.P., $25.00. From the catacombs through the church architecture of Constantine, from Syria, Antioch, Sicily, and Rome, from Hellenistic and from Roman roots, a foremost scholar writes of four centuries of growth of both Eastern and Western Christian art. The period from 200-395 A.D. has been covered. For a less expensive version which is considerably limited in scope, see Pierre du Bourguet, *Early Christian Paintings*, VIP, 1965, 176 pp., Pb $2.25; WN, Hb 21s, Pb 12s 6d; and J. P. Natanson, *Early Christian Ivories*, TRA, 1953, 34 pp., 51 P., $2.75; ALTA, 9s.

11. *RICE, D. T., *Art of Byzantine Era*, PRA, 1963, 286 pp., Hb $7.50, Pb $3.95; TH, Hb 35s, Pb 21s. A great book and inexpensive for a well-written survey. It has fine color photographs and covers the period from the fifth to the fifteenth centuries.

12. *GRABAR, André, *The Golden Age of Justinian*, ODP, 1967, 440 pp., 246 B.W.P., 128 C.P., $25.00. Always mindful of the continuing influences of antiquity and of classical procedures, Grabar gives insights into the fifth- and sixth-century sculpture, painting and sumptuary arts. The period from the death of Theodosius to the rise of Islam has been covered. For a less expensive but somewhat limited treatment, see Manolis Chatzidakis and André Grabar, *Byzantine and Medieval Painting*, VIP, 1965, 176 pp., Pb $2.25; WN, 1966, Hb 21s, Pb 12s 6d.

13. TOESCA, Pietro, and Ferdinand Forlati, *Mosaics of St. Mark's*, NYGS, 1958, 32 B.W.P., 41 C.P., $22.50.

From the earliest Byzantine mosaic, circa 1071, through the fourteenth century, many anonymous and some famous masters contributed to the rich store of mosaic art in the Venetian Church. This volume is a fine index to the art.

14. *ONASCH, Konrad, *Icons*, BN, 1963, 28 B.W.P., 151 C.P., $50.00; FF, 423 pp., 252s. The subject of Byzantine icons is a confused one. There are so many icons scattered in remote monasteries that the work of sorting and classifying has begun only in recent years. Of excellent quality, full color plates of over one hundred and fifty Russian icons, each with notes, this volume displays the wealth of art in the Eastern Church, and especially in the paintings for individual devotion. For icons from Sinai, Greece, Bulgaria, and Yugoslavia, see another excellent study, Karl Weitzmann, et al., *Treasury of Icons*, HAI, 1967, 328 pp., 116 B.W.P., 58 C.P., $35.00.

15. STROBUCHA, Heinz, *Icons*, DUF, 1965, 125 pp., 45 C.P., $5.95; OB, 1963, 124 pp., 25s. Less expensive and detailed than the above volumes, they give a brief overall view which is useful. For authoritative essays, see Herbert Read, *Icon and Idea*, HUP, 1965, 161 pp., Hb $7.50; SCH, Pb $2.45; FF, 1955, 103 Illus., 42s.

16. *PLUMMER, John, ed., *The Hours of Catherine of Cleves*, GB, 1966, 358 pp., 160 C.P., $20.00; BAR, 359 pp., 105s. Manuscripts from c. 1000 to c. 1500 from all of Western Europe convey deep devotion in refreshing and excellent artistry. This volume, painted c. 1440-1445 by an anonymous master, is an exciting and fine example of the private devotionals of the Middle Ages. A beautiful reproduction of the imaginative Dutch original, done for the Duchess of Guelders. For a fuller

review of the fascinating art form, see also, Franz Unterkircher, *European Illuminated Manuscripts,* TH, 60 C.P., 252s (OoP); Mario Salmi, *Italian Miniatures,* HAI, 176 Illus., 77 C.P., $30.00; CO, 1957, 218 pp., 105s; L. A. Dournovo, *Armenian Miniatures,* HAI, 192 pp., 99 Illus., 97 C.P., $25.00; TH, 1962, 181 pp., 168s; Jean Porcher, *Medieval French Miniatures,* HAI, 282 pp., 184 Illus., 94 C.P., $25.00; CO, 1960, 126s; L. M. J. Delaisse, *Medieval Miniatures,* HAI, 1964, 272 pp., 50 C.P., Hb $25.00; OB, Pb $3.50; TH, 1965, 216 pp., Hb 168s.

17. MITCHELL, Sabrina, *Medieval Manuscript Painting,* VIP, 1965, 45 pp., 176 B.W.P., 64 C.P., Pb $2.25; WN, Hb 21s, Pb 12s 6d. This volume in the Compass History of Art Series makes the field of manuscript painting available at a reasonable price. See also, L. M. Delaisse, *Medieval Miniatures,* HAI, 1964, 272 pp., 50 C.P., $25.00; OB, Pb $3.50; TH, 1965, 216 pp., 50 C.P., 168s.

18. FREMANTLE, Anne, *The Age of Faith,* TIME, 1965, 129 pp., $3.95; SEYP, 1967, 200 pp., 36s. This is a popular readable treatment of the Middle Ages. The format is attractive and the selection and quality of plates what we expect from Time-Life publications. See for a more in-depth paperback format, Ernest Kitzinger, *Early Medieval Art,* PS, 114 pp., $4.00; IND, ED 2, 1964, 114 pp., Pb $1.95; TH, 1965, Hb 35s, Pb 21s.

19. NATANSON, J. P., *Gothic Ivories,* TRA, 1951, 40 pp., 64 P., $2.75; ALTA, 9s. The subjects were borrowed from the vast iconography of illuminated paintings, and yet true inspiration was derived from the Gothic architecture and sculpture. Abstract and symbolic are absent from this art, and there is no psychological probing of the characters. It was anecdotic art intent on pleasing the spectator. This aesthetic purpose it accomplishes easily in the quiet beauty of the carved ivories.

20. AINAUD, Juan, *Romanesque Painting,* VIP, 1963, 36 pp., 176 Illus., 64 C.P., Pb $2.25; WN, 224 pp., Hb 21s, Pb 12s 6d. Influenced by the Byzantine art forms and yet characterized by originality and vigor, the Romanesque Art flourished during the eleventh and twelfth centuries in most of Europe, especially in France, Italy, and Spain. This paperback is excellent treatment. For more detailed studies, see Jacques Lassaigne, *Spanish Painting,* V. 1, SKI, 1952, 138 pp., 71 C.P., $22.50; SKI, 155s; Hans Decker, *Romanesque Art in Italy,* HAI, 1959, 338 pp., 263 Illus., $15.00.

21. AMIRANASHVILI, Shalva, *Medieval Georgian Enamels of Russia,* HAI, 1964, 132 pp., 76 C.P., $30.00. The art of enameling never flourished again as it did in Eastern Europe during the later Medieval times. The volume is sumptuously illustrated and is stunning.

22. *LASSAIGNE, Jacques, *Flemish Painting,* V. 1, SKI, 1957, 181 pp., 112 C.P., $29.50; SKI, 168s. The volume deals with the fifteenth-century Flemish masters, specifically Van Eyck and his followers. Rich colors, quiet tones, deep spirituality, and technical beauty characterize this brilliant period of creativity. This is the very period when Italy was swept by the humanism of the Renaissance, whereas Belgium, Southern Netherlands, and Northern France remained attached to the Medieval art forms. See also the second volume in this series for the Flemish contribution to the Renaissance of the sixteenth and seventeenth centuries as seen in the art of Bosch, Bruegel, Rubens, and others; Jacques Lassaigne and R. L. Delevoy, *Flemish Painting,* V. 2, SKI,

1958, 202 pp., 112 C.P., $27.50; SKI, 220 pp., 168s.

23. SOUCHAL, Genevieve, Enzo Carli, and Jose Gudiol, *Gothic Painting,* VIP, 1965, 157 pp., 113 B.W.P., 63 C.P., Pb $2.25; WN, 192 pp., Pb 12s 6d. France, Italy, Northern and Central Europe, and Spain are each treated separately in this excellent and inexpensive book in the Compass History of Art Series. For a more detailed treatment, see Enzo Carli, *Italian Primitives,* HAI, 1965, 126 pp., 89 Illus., 44 C.P., $25.00. For the survey of the Sienese School, from the thirteenth to the sixteenth centuries, yet steeped in the Medieval tradition, see Enzo Carli, *Sienese Painting,* NYGS, 1957, 77 pp., 75 Illus., 62 C.P., $25.00; RAIN, 80 pp., 168s. (OoP)

24. *EIMERL, Sarel, *The World of Giotto C. 1267-1337,* TIME, 1967, 199 pp., $7.95. Time-Life, placing the artist in his contemporary world, has shown his contributions. Giotto, humanizing the human figure and reviving the art of painting, is interestingly presented. He forecast the coming of the Renaissance and made deep impact on the artists for many generations to follow. A commendable volume. The Giotto's work is placed with that of Duccio, Simone Martini, Pietro, and Ambrogio Lorenzetti in exceptionally fine color plates in another volume: Enzo Carli, *Giotto and His Contemporaries,* CRO, 1958, 98 pp., 64 C.P., $7.95. (OoP)

25. ARGAN, G. C., *Fra Angelico,* SKI, 1955, 123 pp., 56 C.P., $7.50; SKI, 127 pp., 60s. Planned by Skira and with biographical and critical study done by Argan, this is a little book, with excellent plates on an artist who was one of the outstanding monk-masters. One of the fathers of the Renaissance, he brought a new spiritual dimension into the Florentine art world with his gentle characters and revolutionary color schemes.

26. HALE, J. R., *Renaissance,* TIME, 1965, 192 pp., $4.95; TIME, 1967, 200 pp., 36s. The problem with this Great Ages of Man series by the publishers of *Life* magazine is that the text, although easy reading, is sketchy, racy, and journalistic in style. However, the book is helpful for beginners and the illustrations and color plates are well-chosen and well-reproduced.

27. *CHASTEL, André, *The Flowering of the Italian Renaissance,* ODP, 1965, 384 pp., 312 B.W.P., 100 C.P., $25.00. This superb volume presents each development of Renaissance art as a human activity within an historic setting. André Chastel is Director of Studies of Renaissance History at the École Pratique des Hautes Études, and Professor of the History of Modern Art at the Sorbonne. A continuation of this volume is equally good: André Chastel, *Studies and Styles of the Italian Renaissance,* ODP, 1966, 384 pp., 312 Illus., 100 C.P., $25.00.

28. PLUMB, J. H., *The Horizon Book of the Renaissance,* AHPC, 1961, 431 pp., 410 B.W.P., 125 C.P., $17.50. A worthy "coffee table issue," this is much more so because of the excellence of the text. For an inexpensive guide to the painting of this period, see Franco Russoli, *Renaissance Painting,* VIP, 1963, 40 pp., 176 C.P., Pb $2.25; WN, 1965, 224 pp., 64 C.P., 21s. Three specially helpful volumes by Linda and Peter Murray in the inexpensive format are, *Art of the Renaissance, The High Renaissance, The Late Renaissance and Mannerism in Europe,* PRA, 1963, 286 pp., 250 C.P., Hb $7.50, Pb $3.95; TH, 40 C.P., Hb 35s, Pb 21s.

29. *COUGHLAN, Robert, *The World of Michelangelo,* TIME, 1966,

202 pp., $5.95. This volume in a visually exciting format is a moderately priced edition. The excellent color photographs of sculpture and the wide scope of the other illustrations make this a captivating book. The text, however, is not uniformly satisfying. For a paperback format with superior text written in a biographical form, see Rolf Schott, *Michelangelo*, HAI, 1964, 130 Illus., 15 C.P., Pb $3.95; TH, 1963, 254 pp., Hb 35s, Pb 21s.

30. GOLDSCHEIDER, Ludwig, *Michelangelo: Paintings, Sculpture, Architecture and Drawings,* 2 V., PHAP, ED 4, 1962, 262 pp., 400 P., $12.50 each; PHAP, 59s 6d. A complete edition of all of his known work, with especially fine detail plates, this book's value is enhanced by a succinct and knowledgeable text. For another more recent set, yet in preparation, see *Michelangelo, Paintings, Sculpture and Drawings,* 3 V., HAI, 1965, $15.00 each.

31. *CLEMENTS, R. J., *Michelangelo, a Self Portrait,* PHI, 1963, 183 pp.; PHI, 190 pp., 18s. The master artist's letters and poetry, arranged ideologically, in translations by men such as Emerson and Santayana, offer deep insights into the man, his art and his faith. See also, *Poetry of Michelangelo,* NYUP, 1965, 368 pp., Hb $10.00, Pb $3.95; OW, 1966, 65s. For a highly recommended modern novel, see Irving Stone, *Agony and Ecstacy,* DC, 1961, 664 pp., Hb $6.95; NAL, Pb $1.25; CO, 1961, Hb 25s; FO, 1963, Pb 6s. It is easy reading, factual, and although somewhat romanticized, it provides splendid insights into the life and times of Michelangelo.

32. *WALLACE, Robert, *The World of Leonardo,* TIME, 1966, 192 pp., $5.95. Again, Time-Life Library of Art gives us an interesting book, placing the artist among his contemporaries and showing us the influences of his environment. Especially fine reproductions in inexpensive paperback format are to be found in Monti Raffaele, *Leonardo da Vinci,* GRO, 1967, 120 pp., 80 C.P., Pb $1.25.

33. PHILIPSON, Morris, ed., *Leonardo da Vinci, Aspects of the Renaissance Genius,* GB, 1966, 436 pp., 93 P., $7.95. B. Berenson, Kenneth Clark, Arnold Hauser, Sir Herbert Read, G. Santillana, Roger Shattuck, and others write of the social status of the Renaissance artist, the relation between his science and art and the psychoanalytic and philosophical dimensions of the enigmatic Leonardo. See also, Kenneth Clark, *Leonardo da Vinci,* PE, Pb $1.45; PE, Pb 6s.

34. GOLDSCHEIDER, Ludwig, *Leonardo da Vinci: Paintings and Drawings,* PHAP, ED 7, 1964, 192 pp., 42 C.P., $12.50; PHAP, 59s 6d. Leonardo, Michelangelo, and Rembrandt are the three greatest artists of all time. They were original creators of superb art which was beyond imitation. This book reproduces all the paintings of Leonardo with notes on each of the eighty plates. For a complete collection of Leonardo's drawings, see A. E. Popham, *The Drawings of Leonardo da Vinci,* HA, 1963, 320 Illus., 172 pp., Pb $2.95; CAPE, 1964, Pb 18s.

35. *RUSSELL, Francis, *The World of Dürer,* TIME, 1967, 183 pp., $7.95. An excellent volume. It gives good overview of the emergence of Renaissance in Germany. Charcoal and brush drawings, watercolor and oil paintings, wood-cuts and engravings, on subjects ranging from animal and human portraits, landscapes and geometrical constructions, private exercises and commissioned works for Maximilian I, and biblical studies, all attest to the spectrum of this fine artist so often known only for *Praying*

Hands. For an inexpensive bio-graphical work, see Marcel Brion, *Dürer,* TUD, 1960, 320 pp., 145 Illus., 59 C.P., $5.95; TH, Hb 35s, Pb 21s.

36. *GOLDSCHEIDER, Ludwig, *Rembrandt,* PHAP, 1960, 206 pp., 113 Illus., 35 C.P., $12.50; PHAP, 59s 6d. This volume is interesting principally for the excellent plates which are well-chosen and of fine quality. See also, for superb color reproductions, Ludwig Munz and B. Haak, eds., *Rembrandt,* HAI, RE, 1967, 164 pp., 100 Illus., 50 C.P., $15.00; TH, 188 pp., Pb 6s 6d.

37. *BOON, K. G., ed., *Rembrandt, the Complete Etchings,* HAI, 1963, 236 pp., 307 C.P., $18.50; TH, 258 pp., 90s. One never appreciates the spiritual and psychological depth of Rembrandt without exploring his graphic work. These etchings speak of his intensity and skill. For an excellent and inexpensive collection of Rembrandt's complete drawings, see Seymour Slive, *Drawings of Rembrandt,* 2 V., DO, 1965, 550 Illus., Hb $6.25 each, Pb $3.00 each. The etchings and drawings show breath-taking subtlety of expression with their light effects and abstraction. They are a source of delight for they contain the freshest and strongest statements of this great Christian artist. Recommended.

38. ROSENBERG, Jakob, *Rembrandt, Life and Work,* PHAP, 1964, 386 pp., 282 P., $8.50; PHAP, RE, 360 pp., 40s. A readable yet scholarly treatment that the *Art Bulletin* calls "one of the outstanding monographs of our time." This is another fine volume on the artist. For an outstanding commentary on the cultural climate of the artist's times and for beautiful reproductions, see Robert Wallace, *The World of Rembrandt,* TIME, 1968, 188 pp., $7.95.

39. *VISSER, 'T Hooft, W. A., *Rembrandt and the Gospel,* WP, 1958, 192 pp., 32 P., Hb $4.50; MEB, 1960, Pb $1.45; SPCK, 1957, 25s. The thesis of this inexpensive book makes it most valuable. Rembrandt, "a Protestant because he was absorbed in the Biblical testimony . . . which leads to the Cross . . . seeks to express a faith exclusively rooted in the Gospel."

40. BRONSTEIN, Leo, *El Greco, Domenicos Theotocopoulos,* HAI, 1950, 126 pp., 51 C.P., $15.00. This book is to be prized for the excellence of the color plates. Here is a mystical faith glowing from canvases of capitating chiaroscuro.

41. *KELEMEN, Pal, *El Greco Revisited, Candia, Venice, Toledo,* MC, 1961, 290 pp., 112 P., $7.50; CM, 95s. From his birthplace, Candia on Crete, through his travels to his final home in Toledo, the background of El Greco's Christian art is shown. The Byzantine influences, as well as the environmental influences and the visual images he had absorbed, and later reproduced are all traced in a fascinating book.

42. PUPPI, Lionello, *El Greco,* GRO, 1967, 118 pp., 80 C.P., Pb $1.25. The life of "the Greek" from 1541 on Crete through his time in Venice as a pupil of Titian and his visit in Rome and then on until he was established in Toledo about 1575, is well-documented in this inexpensive book. His work as painter, architect, and sculptor is covered.

43. *GRAETZ, H. R., *The Symbolic Language of Vincent Van Gogh,* MH, 1963, 315 pp., 68 B.W.P., 47 C.P., $9.95; TH, 1964, 122 Illus., 50 C.P., 63s. Using original letters, and sketches and paintings, Graetz has skillfully woven a story of the motivations, milieu, and intentions of this man who struggled with himself and

with his concept of God. Plates of unusual veracity, some of previously unpublished paintings and some of better known works, enhance this fascinating book. For an excellent short biographical portrait of the artist which reveals his fantastic life, see Peter Bura, *Van Gogh*, Ri, COL, 1962, 127 pp., Pb 95¢.

44. BLUNT, Anthony, *The Art of William Blake*, COLP, 1959, 122 pp., 64 P., $7.50; OUP, 1959, 134 pp., 42s. The English visionary, who frequently based his etchings and watercolors on biblical themes is introduced in the volume. Though far from evangelical Christianity, his mystical art is intriguing and thought-provoking.

45. *COURTHION, Pierre, *Georges Rouault*, HAI, 1962, 490 pp., 832 P., 49 C.P., $35.00; TH, 210s. This volume, superb in understanding of the man and his work and in the abundance and excellence of the plates, is well worth the cost. Whether Rouault's subjects are clowns, kings, or prostitutes, the utter degradation of man or the sins of society, they all ... "lead to the Face ... to the Cross, where are intertwined our unworthiness and the promise of our salvation through redemption."

46. HAFTMANN, Werner, *Emil Nolde*, HAI, 1959, 140 pp., 55 C.P., $15.00; Ri, TH, 1965, 126s. This is a fine collection of the work of a man whose lifetime, 1867-1953, encompassed the development of modern painting. A man of faith, who based much of his work on biblical themes, he developed independently into an early German expressionist. No doubt much of his Christian art is more meaningful today than that of the Renaissance.

47. *LEYMARIE, Jean, and Marc Chagall, *The Jerusalem Windows*, Ri, GB, 1967, 212 pp., 41 B.W.P., 66

C.P., $5.95. Each of these stained glass windows done for the synagogue at the Hadassah-Hebrew University Medical Center depicts one of the twelve tribes by using various biblical and semitic symbols. The format of the book shows the development from the first sketch through color, gouache, and collage to the finished window. Though obviously not Christian, these merit study because of their biblical basis.

48. *CLARK, Kenneth, *The Nude, a Study in Ideal Form*, PUP, 1956, 458 pp., 293 Illus., Hb $10.00; DC, 575 pp., Pb $2.45; Ri, JM, 1967, 432 pp., 30s. a scholarly and dignified treatment, this book deals with the tradition of the nude from the early Greek to contemporary sculpture and painting. The chapters on energy and pathos are useful in understanding the use of the nude to accentuate drama and expression in the art of Christianity.

49. VERLET, P., M. Florisoone, A. Hoffmeister, and F. Tabard, *Great Tapestries, the Web of History from the 12th to 20th Century*, NYGS, 1965, 278 pp., 100 B.W.P., 55 C.P., $30.00. This is an interesting art form, important during the Gothic period and of growing importance to today's artists. Graham Sutherland is a contemporary using this medium to speak of Christianity in art. This book thoroughly explains the craft and history of the art.

50. BEYER, Victor, *Stained Glass Windows*, DUF, 1965, 192 pp., 60 C.P., $5.95; OB, 1964, 140 pp., 30s. From 1050 to 1954, the finest of European stained glass is succinctly noted and wonderfully reproduced. This fine book explains the technique and history of the art. See also, Heribert Hutter, *Medieval Stained Glass*, CRO, 1964, 24 C.P., 95¢; ME, 7s 6d; and John Baker, *English Stained*

Glass, HAI, 1960, 248 pp., 137 Illus., 34 C.P., $25.00; TH, 126s.

51. *KOEPF, Hans, *Masterpieces of Sculpture,* PUT, 1966, 108 pp., 43 C.P., $25.00; MACD, Pb 6s 6d. The sculpture presents special difficulties in appreciation, mainly due to its third dimension. The two dimensional representation of sculpture in the printed form is often misleading and unsatisfactory. This explains the inadequate documentation and marginal interest in the sculptural art. For other volumes consult, H. D. Molesworth, *European Sculpture,* PRA, 1965, 288 pp., 277 Illus., 39 C.P., Hb $7.50, Pb $3.95; TH, Hb 35s, Pb 21s; John Beckwith, *Coptic Sculpture,* TRA, 1963, 56 pp., 147 Illus., $9.00; ALTA, 30s; Roberto Salvini, *Medieval Sculpture,* NYGS, 1968, 8 C.P., $12.50; J. P. Hennessy, *Italian Gothic Sculpture,* PHAP, $6.00 (OoP); Zeller, *Approach to Christian Sculpture,* SHE, 1959, 192 pp., $1.85 (OoP); SHE, 16s.

7G2. CHRISTIANITY IN THE ARTS: ARCHITECTURE
Donald J. Bruggink

Art and architecture are among the gifts of a good God as he gave to man the task of gaining dominion over the earth. In the development of those gifts, the aesthetics of architecture are for our enjoyment, but as man has exercised his dominion, he has, in his architecture, left an indelible imprint as to his concept of himself and his relationship to God.

Architecture provides a useful lens, if handled rightly, for understanding how Christians of other ages interpreted and translated their faith into creative projects. The pre-Gothic periods were preoccupied with God, with soaring basilicas and churches, anonymous artists, and bland attempts toward spiritualization of the arts.

The Renaissance found man discovering himself. The glories and de-

lights of being a man are found both in the buildings of the Renaissance and of the Baroque, despite the latter's ecclesiastical insistance upon the glory of God.

1. *PEVSNER, Nikolaus, *An Outline of European Architecture,* PE, 1960, 496 pp., Hb $35.00, Pb $2.25; PE, 1963, Hb 147s, Pb 12s 6d. An excellent survey for the beginner (especially if on a European tour), lavishly illustrated, but in a low cost paperback format. The emphasis is upon the aesthetic, but with enough history to keep the architecture in context. See also, John Flemming, Hugh Honour, and Nikolaus Pevsner, *The Penguin Dictionary of Architecture,* PE, 1966, 248 pp., Pb $1.95; PE, Pb 8s 6d.

2. FLETCHER, Banister, *A History of Architecture on the Comparative Method,* CSS, ED 17, 1961, 1366 pp., $17.95; CSS, 84s. A single volume guide to all architecture at all times complete with a multitude of illustrations and diagrams. Each style of architecture is considered in terms of geographical, climatic, social, geological, religious, and historical influences, architectural character, examples, comparative analysis and further reference books. A wealth of information but inadequate at the point of asking penetrating questions as to man's self-understanding.

3. *The Great Ages of World Architecture,* GB, 128 pp. each, PHI, with separate authors and titles as follows: William MacDonald, *Early Christian Byzantine,* PE, 1962, 416 pp., 5s 5d; Bates Lowry, *Renaissance Architecture,* GB, 1962, 128 pp., Hb $4.95, Pb $2.95; PH, 120 pp., 30s; H. S. Millon, *Baroque and Roccoco Architecture,* GB, 1962, 128 pp., Hb $4.95, Pb $2.95; PH, 120 pp., 30s; Robert Branner, *Gothic Architecture,* GB, 128 pp., Hb $4.95, Pb $2.95; H. Saalman, *Medieval Architecture,* GB,

1962, 128 pp., $4.95, Pb $2.95; PH, 120 pp., 30s; Vincent Scully Jr., *Modern Architecture*, GB, 1961, 128 pp., $4.95, Pb $2.95; PH, 1962, 120 pp., 30s. This series is extremely readable and well-illustrated. While lacking the plethora of interesting detail found in Banister Fletcher, these volumes are far more discerning in their appreciation of architecture within its total historical context—especially the philosophical and religious. This is the series with which to start one's journey into architecture as intellectual history.

4. *PEVSNER, Nikolaus, ed., *The Pelican History of Art*, PE. This series is the newest (1956 ff.), the largest, the most lavishly illustrated, and most important, the richest beneficiary of twentieth-century developments in historiography, all of which make this series by far the most reliable as a guide to understanding the interaction of man's architecture and his self-perception. Individual titles are listed in the appropriate sections. Only those volumes dealing with the architecture of Western Christendom not discussed elsewhere in this subsection are here cited. Geoffrey Webb, *Architecture in Britain in the Middle Ages*, PE, 1956, 234 pp., $20.00; George Kubler and Martin Soria, *Art and Architecture in Spain and Portugal and Their American Dominions, 1500-1800*, PE, 1959, 445 pp., $18.50; John Summerson, *Architecture in Britain: 1530-1830*, PE, 1963, 391 pp., $25.00; PE, 1953, 70s; Jakob Rosenberg, Seymour Slive, and E. H. ter Kuile, *Dutch Art and Architecture: 1600-1800*, PE, 1966, 329 pp., $20.00; PE, 330 pp., 105s; H. Gerson and E. H. ter Kuile, *Art and Architecture in Belgium 1600-1800*, PE, 1960, 236 pp., $16.50; PE, 1966, 330 pp., 105s; Eberhard Hempel, *Baroque Art and Architecture in Central Europe*, PE, 1965, 370 pp., $20.00; PE, 105s.

5. *Treasures of Christian Art—100 Churches in Europe*, Officine grafiche Poligrafici il Resto del Carline, Bologne, Italy, 100 booklets, 28 pp. each, 50¢ each. Each booklet deals with a church, discussing its history, architecture, and artistic treasures. Although meant as a guide to visit the churches, the writing is scholarly, and the numerous color reproductions are excellent. Divided into five volumes, each volume covering twenty churches. The five volumes are: Early Christian, Romanesque, Gothic, Renaissance, and Manneristic and Baroque. Inexpensive and satisfying survey of Christian churches in Europe.

6. *BIÉLER, André, *Architecture in Worship*, WP, 1965, 96 pp., $3.75; OB, 15s. A brief but lucid account of the relationship between theology and architecture from the pagan temples, Jewish temple and synagogues, the early churches, and on to the present. A basic primer in the field. The perspective of the author is Reformed.

7. MINCHIN, Basil, *Outward and Visible*, DLT, 1961, 388 pp., 21s. While primarily a history of worship from the early Church to the present, the author is extremely perceptive concerning the role of architecture. More extensive than Biéler and seen from the perspective of an Anglican scholar.

8. VAN DER MEER, F., and Christine Mohramann, *Atlas of the Early Christian World*, NE, 1958, 216 pp., 105s. These Dutch scholars have given not only the necessary maps to an understanding of the development of the early Church, but they have filled their atlas with pictures and lucid text to assist in a thorough understanding of architecture as well.

9. *KRAUTHEIMER, Richard, *Early Christian and Byzantine Architec-*

222

ture, PE, 1965, 390 pp., $20.00; PE, 416 pp., 105s. One of the *Pelican History of Art* series, this volume contains a detailed and reliable account of the architecture and the thought behind it. This book constitutes a superior historical analysis.

10. *CONANT, K. J., *Carolingian and Romanesque Architecture: 800-1200*, PE, 1959, 343 pp., $20.00; PE, 1958, 70s. Conant's work offers by far the best available insight into both the architecture and the piety of medieval monasticism. See also, I. Richards, *Abbeys of Europe*, PAH, 18s.

11. *PANOFSKY, Erwin, *Gothic Architecture and Scholasticism*, ARP, 1951, 156 pp., Pb $1.65. Within brief compass, Panofsky relates Gothic architecture to the intellectual structures of its age. While to us scholasticism often carries connotations of complex, interminable, intellectual conundrums, for its day it represented the exciting culmination of a way of thought which had been slowly emerging since the barbarian invasions had devastated the antiquity of the West. Panofsky puts the soaring pillars and ribs of the Gothic together with the soaring articulation of the thought of scholasticism and helps us to a greater appreciation of both. See also, for a photographic survey, Jean Bony, *French Cathedrals*, TH, 241 pp., 70s.

12. VON SIMSON, Otto, *The Gothic Cathedral, Origins of Gothic Architecture and the Medieval Concept of Order*, PAB, 1956, 278 pp. (OoP); RO, RE, 1962, 332 pp., 55s. A superb book which should be read following Panofsky for a larger and more detailed vision of the relation of architecture, ideas, and faith. Von Simson summarizes his work thus: "Gothic, perhaps the most creative achievement in the history of Western architecture, can only be under-

stood, as this book sets out to show, as the singularly sensitive response of artistic form to the theological vision of the twelfth-century." See also, for a photographic survey, Martin Hurlimann, *English Cathedrals*, VIP, 1962, 166 pp., $12.00; TH, 1950, 166 pp., 57s 6d; and *Cathedrals of England*, TH, 1967, Hb 35s, Pb 21s.

13. FRANKL, Paul, *The Gothic, Literary Sources and Interpretation Through Eight Centuries*, PUP, 1960, 916 pp., $17.50; *Gothic Architecture*, PE, 1962, 315 pp., $18.50; PE, 84s. These are two very different works. In the first Frankl cites the literary sources from the Gothic period through contemporary interpretations. In the second he examines Gothic architecture, religious and secular, in minute detail. A wealth of information, but less helpful in relating Gothic architecture to man's understanding of God and the world than Von Simson or Panofsky. For a photographic survey, see also, George Duby, *The Europe of the Cathedrals: 1140-1280*, SKI, 1968, $20.00; ZW, 1966, 220 pp., 170s.

14. LESSER, George, *Gothic Cathedrals and Sacred Geometry*, 3 V., TRA, 166 pp., V. 1 & 2, $18.00, V. 3, $9.00; ALTA, 1957-64, V. 1 & 2, 63s, V. 3, 30s. For the scholar who is by this time completely infatuated with Gothic architecture and the thought forms of the Middle Ages, these volumes, dealing with the lore of sacred numbers as applied to the building of cathedrals, will constitute an esoteric joy.

15. FITCHEN, John, *The Construction of Gothic Cathedrals, A Study of Medieval Vault Erection*, OUP, 1961, 366 pp., $12.00; OUP, 75s. A superb volume for those pragmatic souls who want to know how these ideas in stone were pushed hundreds of feet into the air.

16. *WITTKOWER, Rudolf, Architectural Principles in the Age of Humanism*, RH, 1965, 173 pp., Hb $4.95, Pb $2.95; ALTA, RE, 1962, Hb 25s, Pb 12s 6d. The old, purely aesthetic theory of Renaissance architecture is rejected, and instead it is integrated with Renaissance man's total view of himself, God, and the world—but mostly, himself. Wittkower does not neglect to relate architecture to philosophy, music, science, and religion. The book with which to start.

17. TAPIÉ, V. L., *The Age of Grandeur, Baroque Art and Architecture*, PRA, 1966, 294 pp., Hb $9.95, Pb $4.95. Helpful. Baroque is seen as an appeal to grandeur through architecture in a religious, but even more in a political, perspective.

18. WITTKOWER, Rudolf, *Art and Architecture in Italy, 1600-1750*, PE, 1958, 462 pp., $20.00. Wittkower again brings his massive learning to bear to relate architecture and art to ideas and emotions of the age. Any overly neat summary of this architecture as an appeal to the emotions in an age fast losing confidence in the viability of the old intellectual structures would be a disservice to the breadth of Wittkower's scholarship.

19. KAUFMANN, Emil, *Architecture in the Age of Reason, Baroque and Post-Baroque in England, Italy and France*, SHOE, 1955, 239 pp., $12.50; ARCH, RE, 1966, 90s. Even as the age of reason signaled the breakdown of old and established forms of thought, so too architecture changed with men's changing perception of reality. The book considers separately developments in England, Italy, and France.

20. HITCHCOCK, Henry-Russell, *Architecture, Nineteenth and Twentieth Centuries*, PE, ED 2, 1963, 510 pp., $20.00. Unlike the period of the Gothic or the Renaissance, when the ideas of an age produced an architecture, the two modern centuries witness an uneasy and often superficial relationship between ideas and forms. In these two centuries there was and is no universal perspective of life. Men are not very well agreed about man, let alone about God. Architecture is often hopelessly Romantic as it reacts to the formalism of reason, or else it is honestly commercial (and in that honesty often aesthetically superior to the products of the romanticists). We are undoubtedly too close to this age to see it clearly, but compared to the age of the Gothic, it would appear that civilization and culture have lost their clarity of perception—certainly about God, and about man as well.

7H. CHURCH ARCHITECTURE
Donald J. Bruggink and
Stephen S. Smalley
Up to the sixteenth century, the story of the architecture of Western Christendom was the story of Christianity and the Church. With the Reformation, the unity of Christendom was broken, so the story is no longer a unified while. As the fragmentation of Christendom continues, the story becomes more and more complex. At first there is a clear perception that building and faith have a relationship—at least in building churches if nowhere else.

But by the nineteenth century, one has moved so far from the period of the Gothic that not only is the Church no longer influencing culture in its architecture, but secular culture has largely come to dominate the building of churches. Because of the complexity of this story in the post-Reformation period, it will be necessary to consider in separation from general architecture those practices involved in the building of churches.
The Liturgical Movement in Europe and America has produced a

new desire to make the liturgy (or form) of Christian worship relevant as well as biblical. This has led in turn to a recovery of the scriptural emphasis on the Church as a community, which gathers round the places where the Word is preached and the sacraments are administered, sharing and not (as in the past) watching the liturgy.

The current "new look" in church architecture seeks to express this emphasis and relate the design and arrangement of church buildings to their immediate situation and purpose. It is becoming widely recognized in all parts of the Christian Church, in fact, that the shape of our buildings, as of any buildings, must be functional and not merely traditional. This is a concern with important spiritual implications and one to which every Christian should be sensitive.

1. ABBOTT, W. M., ed., "Constitution on the Sacred Liturgy," The Documents of Vatican II, ASP, 1966, 794 pp., Hb $10.00, Pb 95¢, GC, 1966, 794 pp., Pb 10s 6d. One should not presume to comment upon the worship of the Roman Church without having studied this document, which is resulting in architectural upheaval in Catholic parishes throughout the world. This Constitution ends the millenial reign of Latin in the Mass. Christology is central; the altar for sacrifice is also a table for the supper; the participation of the laity has increased; and there is an emphasis upon the "paramount importance" of Scripture in the celebration of the liturgy. A forceful example for Protestants that unless our worship is tested by the Scriptures we may soon appear to the world as those whose liturgy and architecture most need reformation.

2. ADDLESHAW, G. W., and Frederick Etchells, The Architectural Setting of Anglican Worship, FF, 1948, 288 pp., 36s. An excellent volume which tells how the Church of England moved from two hundred years of Reformed architecture to the Romantic Gothic of the nineteenth century which today passes as Anglican architecture, and which in turn has influenced aesthetics and status-seekers in other denominations as well. This volume gives a clear and detailed account as to the origins of the "split-chancel" altar-against-the-east-wall church so familiar to Americans and Englishmen alike.

3. BIELER, André, Architecture in Worship, WP, 1965, 96 pp., $3.75; OB, ET, 15s. This Swiss contribution, translated from the original French, is a brief but useful survey of the connection between "worship and sanctuary" from Judaism to the current period of liturgical renewal. It is definitely Protestant and written from within the Reformed tradition. The illustrations, however, are poor.

4. *BRUGGINK, D. J., and C. H. Droppers, Christ and Architecture: Building Presbyterian Reformed Churches, WBE, 1965, 708 pp., $20.00. A superbly produced and beautifully illustrated treatment, by a conservative theologian and an architect, of the influence which the doctrinal emphases of the Reformed tradition (Word, Sacraments, and Church) should exert on the shape of churches built for Presbyterian/Reformed worship. The second part deals comprehensively with practical issues. This volume will be invaluable for anyone concerned with building new churches.

5. *COPE, Gilbert, ed., Christianity and the Visual Arts, TFP, 1964, 107 pp., 42s. A collection of ten interesting essays on the problem of "sacred" art, its history and contemporary application. There are three useful (but not easy) contributions by Cope himself on the tension between

function and symbolism in church buildings.

6. COPE, Gilbert, ed., *Making the Building Serve the Liturgy: Studies in the Re-ordering of Churches,* MO, 1962, 71 pp., 15s. How can churches suited to medieval, unreformed worship, be adapted to a worship which stresses the importance of the Church as a body? These studies provide an important and readable answer, in terms of theology as well as architecture and suggest as examples the re-ordering of actual church buildings. The standpoint is English and Anglican, but it has wider application.

7. DAVIES, J. G., *The Origin and Development of Early Christian Church Architecture,* SCMP, 1952, 152 pp., 21s. (OoP) This technical study, from Birmingham, is the first of its kind in English and will be invaluable to the student of architecture as well as to anyone seriously interested in the origins of church buildings. It is a well-illustrated treatment of the shape and furniture of primitive churches, in the light of their geographical and historical background.

8. DRUMMOND, A. L., *The Church Architecture of Protestantism,* TTC, 1934, 342 pp. (OoP) Long the only survey work in English in this field, it remains useful for information, but lacking in the depth of its theological analysis.

9. FREY, E. S., *This Before Architecture,* FOB, 1963, 127 pp., $3.50. The author, the Executive Director of the Commission on Church Architecture of the Lutheran Church in America, combines a concern for correct and lucid theological expression for the glory of God with a wealth of practical experience in programming church architecture.

10. GERMANN, Georg, *Der Protes-*

tantische Kirchenbau in der Schweiz, von der Reformation bis zur Romantik, Zurich, Orell Fussli Verlag, 1963, 212 pp. Just what the title says it is. Again, a helpful antidote for a rationalistic type of worship that passes for Protestantism. The architecture gives evidence of a full New Testament worship of Word and Sacraments.

11. *HAMBERG, Gustaf, *Templebygge for Protestanter,* Stockholm, Svenska Kyrkans Diakonistyrelses Bokforlag, 1955, 255 pp. A superb study of Protestant church building in the sixteenth and seventeenth centuries. Replete with an abundance of illustrations.

12. HAY, George, *The Architecture of Scottish Post-Reformation Churches, 1560-1843,* OUP, 1957, 299 pp., $11.20; CLP, 70s. An excellent study which should be especially helpful to Presbyterians in understanding the richness of their architectural and liturgical past.

13. *HAMMOND, Peter, *Liturgy and Architecture,* BAR, 1960, 191 pp., 42s. Although the author's standpoint is not conservative, this seminally important treatment of functional church architecture deserves to be widely read. It is one of the fullest and most influential statements of the issue and takes the theological implications seriously. The scope is wide, even if the particular concern is Church of England buildings. Excellently illustrated.

14. HAMMOND, Peter, ed., *Towards a Church Architecture,* COLP, 1962, 262 pp., $6.00; TAP, 30s. The second important volume associated with the name of Peter Hammond is a collection of essays by theologians and architects arising from discussions within the New Churches Research Group. The traditions represented are diverse, but together the

writers plead convincingly for a "radical" approach to building for worship, which means taking seriously its spiritual and social basis. Illustrated.

15. LOCKETT, W. E., ed., *The Modern Architectural Setting of the Liturgy*, SPCK, 1964, 92 pp., 17s 6d. Seven leaders in the contemporary program of English functional church building deal here with some underlying principles. Their widely relevant approach is radical, but constructive and practical; and it represents a diversity of tradition and theological outlook. There is a fascinating description by Frederick Gibberd of the circular design of the new Roman Catholic Cathedral at Liverpool.

16. *MAGUIRE, Robert, and Keith Murray, *Modern Churches of the World*, EPD, 1964, 160 pp., Pb $1.75; SV, 1965, Pb 8s 6d. An extensively illustrated paperback by two church architects, with a brief but informative text. The authors show clearly that the architectural quality of contemporary church building depends not on predetermined "style," but on aptness at all levels for the activity being housed.

17. NYE, T. M., *An Introduction to Parish Church Architecture A.D. 600-1965*, HAS, 1965, 112 pp., $3.75; BAT, 13s 6d. The parish church has always been an important social as well as architectural feature of the English scene. This short introduction, clearly written and pleasingly illustrated, provides a comprehensive survey of the subject, arranged according to architectural styles. It forms a useful background to the total issue of contemporary church building.

18. PETTER, H. M., *Churches and Public Buildings*, OUP, 1963, 95 pp., $2.20; OUP, 13s 6d. This is a straightforward history of architectural styles in England from Stone-henge to the present day, showing the influence of function on buildings of all kinds. Its scope is wider than Miss Nye's book but it is equally readable and clearly illustrated. It will provide a useful introduction to the subject of architecture in general and church architecture in particular for the uninitiated.

19. ROSE, H. W., *The Colonial Houses of Worship in America*, HAS, 1963, 574 pp., $22.50. An extended consideration of the historical setting and architectural detail of America's still-remaining Colonial houses of worship. Again, one could wish for greater depth in analyzing intellectual and theological relationships to the architecture.

20. SCHWARTZ, Rudolph, *The Church Incarnate, the Sacred Function of Christian Architecture*, HR, 1958, 231 pp., $10.00. The movement of liturgical historiography and subsequent liturgical renewal within Continental Catholicism found its foremost architectural exponent in the late Rudolf Schwartz. If one understands the buildings of Schwartz, then one is not too surprised by the "Constitution on the Sacred Liturgy" promulgated at Vatican II.

21. *SHANDS, A. R., *The Liturgical Movement and the Local Church*, MG, 1965, 159 pp., Pb $2.50; SCMP, ED 2, 8s 6d. The liturgical movement has provided the incentive for the current trends in functional building for worship. The Anglican author of this lively book is not a conservative, but his deep and practical involvement in the movement enables him to assess accurately and for all of us its real basis and contribution. There is an excellent bibliography.

22. SINNOTT, E. W., *Meeting House and Church in Early New England*,

MH, 1963, 243 pp., $5.95; MH, 80s. A delightful and profusely illustrated book which sets the Colonial churches in their historical, albeit not theological, milieu.

23. *SMALLEY, S. S., *Building for Worship: Biblical Principles in Church Design,* HS, 1967, 95 pp., Pb 3s 6d. Number 17 in the "Christian Foundations" series, this paperback takes as its starting point what the Bible has to say about worship and then examines the relation between church architecture and worship in history and in the present. On this basis some principles are drawn out for evangelical Anglicans (and others), to guide them in providing reformed architecture for reformed worship. Illustrated.

24. *SMITH, G. E. K., *The New Churches of Europe,* HRW, 316 pp., $17.50; Edizioni di Communita, Milan, 1964, 73s 6d. Magnificently illustrated with lavish photographs and plans. It describes sixty modern churches in Europe and illustrates admirably (although only from one continent) the new horizons in church building and the variety of design possible. The text is non-technical and easy to read.

25. WEYRES, Willy, and Otto Bartning, *Kirchen, Handbuch fur den Kirchenbau,* Munich, Callwey, 1959, 448 pp. Many drawings and plates in historical and contemporary sections for both Protestant and Roman Catholic church building.

26. *WHITE, J. F., *Protestant Worship and Church Architecture,* OUP, 1964, 236 pp., $6.00; OUP, 42s. Is worship a matter of "feeling" or "service"? With this question Dr. White addresses himself to the problem of principles for liturgical architecture. This in turn is built on a historical study of early and medieval patterns, Reformation experiments, the impact of Romanticism, as well as that of nineteenth century American revivalism. It is this last factor that is essential to any understanding of American church building and is far more determinative of most of our church interiors than is anything found in a genuine Colonial church. The impact of revivalism remains to be defined in detail, and until some scholar performs this work, Dr. White's fifth chapter will remain the best compact analysis available.

7I. MUSIC

J. Buchanan MacMillan

By its nature, music can be of itself neither secular nor sacred. Music history attests the important place that music has had in Christian worship from early times. Indeed, the notation and theory of western music until the beginning of modern times was almost wholly developed by members of the clergy. The study of art music until the later Renaissance is overwhelmingly that of religious music and only in the seventeenth century —the age of the Baroque—does secular music outstrip that associated with religion. Today music is almost wholly secular, and there is much confused thinking about the place of music in life on the part of Christians.

The following selection of titles consists first of books on music of religious intent. Then follow several that try to clarify religious and philosophical problems attending music. The latter books deal simply with various aspects of music as an art. A formidable array of books on almost every aspect of music is now available, and much excellent material is now issued in paperback. The reader is directed especially to the catalogues of Dover, Norton, and Pelican.

1. *STEERE, Dwight, *Music in Protestant Worship,* JKP, 1960, 256 pp., $4.50. Every layman, no matter whether worshipper, choir member,

or church worker, ought to read this book thoughtfully. It is directed to the minister by a church musician of wide experience. It is sane, devoutly oriented, practical.

2. HALTER, Carl, *The Practice of Sacred Music*, CON, 1955, 96 pp., $1.50; CON, RE, 1963, 10s 6d. Although directed in particular to the practicing Lutheran church musician, Dr. Halter's observations on the place of music in worship are for anyone seeking a viable philosophy of church music.

3. APPLEBY, D. P., *History of Church Music*, MP, 1965, 192 pp., Hb $3.50, Pb $1.95. There is much here for the beginner in the field. Each chapter has a well-selected list of recommended reading. A basic glossary of terms is included and fifteen pages of bibliography, which is happily not restricted to works in English. Unfortunately too much is attempted in so small a compass, with the result that the coverage is a little unequal.

4. DOUGLAS, C. W., *Church Music in History and Practice*, CSS, RE, 1962, 263 pp., $5.95, FF, 1962, 266 pp., 35s. The introductory chapter on worship is particularly fine. This concise book approaches the subject from a high Episcopal viewpoint and is particularly helpful in understanding the music of the liturgical churches.

5. *WIENANDT, Elwyn, *Choral Music of the Church*, FRP, 1965, 494 pp., $8.95; CM, 63s. This is the only book of its kind at present. It distinguishes between *church* and *religious* music and discusses only functional choral music for the church service from early times to the present. It is scholarly and meticulously documented. It is both concise and readable. An extensive bibliography is included.

6. *STEVENS, Denis, *Tudor Church Music*, WWN, RE, 1967, 97 pp., Hb $10.00, Pb $1.35; FF, RE 2, 1966, 15s. An excellent short account of the English Church music of a brilliant era.

7. FELLOWES, E. H., *English Cathedral Music from Edward VI to Edward VII*, BBC, 288 pp. (OoP); ME, 1945, 268 pp., 18s. Canon Fellowes, the great authority on Elizabethan music, has provided the best available account of the rich British tradition of choral composition for the Church from the Reformation to the first decade of the present century. Only the Church of England tradition is considered.

8. *ELLINWOOD, Leonard, *The History of American Church Music*, MG, 1953, 274 pp., $6.00. (OoP) It is to be hoped that this important book will be revised and reprinted. A fine American scholar has given the most complete account of church music in this country thus far published. The book is remarkably concise. Details of the repertory performed in various periods are of especial interest.

9. *STEVENSON, Robert, *Protestant Church Music in America*, WWN, 1966, 168 pp., $7.50. As the author admits, this book is little more than an introductory survey; but it is an excellent one. It contains a number of interesting plates, is very painstakingly documented and has an extensive and up-to-date bibliography. It is highly recommended to both the serious student and the more general reader.

10. ROUTLEY, Erik, *Twentieth Century Church Music*, OUP, 1964, 244 pp., $5.75; JEN, 30s. The title might well be revised to read, "Twentieth Century *English* Church Music." While it is a needed addition to the available critical literature, it is a bit

partisan and distinctly inadequate for both the American and European music of recent years.

11. LOWENS, Irving, *Music and Musicians in Early America,* WWN, 1964, 328 pp., $7.50. Here is another important book in the remarkable Norton library of books on music. It is a collection of articles and deals with American music of all kinds. Since so much early American music was sacred in intent, the reader will find much in it that is relative to the psalmody, hymnody, and other types of church music before the middle of the nineteenth century.

12. CHASE, Gilbert, *America's Music, from the Pilgrims to the Present,* MH, RE, 1964, 733 pp., $8.50, text $6.95; MH, RE, 1967, 759 pp., 56s. An excellent and attractively written full-scale history of American music that devotes much space to early psalmody, folk hymns, white and Negro spirituals, and the more pretentious forms of religious music.

13. *ROUTLEY, Erik, *The Church and Music,* DUC, RE, 1967, 269 pp., 21s. The subtitle adequately sets forth the author's aims: "an enquiry into the history, the nature and the scope of Christian judgment on music." This is not an easy book to read, but it appeals to the reviewer as one of the author's best. Beginning with a discussion and interpretation of the views of Augustine and other great figures of church history, Dr. Routley tries to reach some solid conclusions in a very difficult and controversial area.

14. *ALLEN, W. D., *Philosophies of Music History,* PS, 1960, 382 pp., Hb $4.00; DO, RE, 1962, Pb $2.25; CS, 1963, 416 pp., 16s. A very significant book and a "must" for anyone searching for an insight into the true place of music in western culture. Thoughtfully written and well-documented, this is a good point from which to begin a study of the philosophical outlook of music historians from the Renaissance to the present.

15. MYERS, R. M., *Handel's Messiah: A Touchstone of Taste,* MC, 1948, 338 pp., $5.00 (OoP); MC, 25s. (OoP) The author traces the ways in which *Messiah* has been interpreted through the years, often sadly distorting its style. He points the way toward a more authentic interpretation of the great masterpiece. The serious reader will find more pertinent material in two other more detailed works: J. P. Larsen, *Handel's Messiah,* WWN, 1957, 336 pp., $6.00 (OoP); BK, 45s; and Winton Deane, *Handel's Dramatic Oratorios and Masques,* OUP, $26.90.

16. SCHOLES, Percy, *Puritans and Music in England and New England: A Contribution to the Cultural History of Two Nations,* RR, RE, 1962, 428 pp., $10.00; OUP, 1934, 21s. (OoP) This important study discloses that the Puritan antipathy to elaborate church music did not necessarily extend to other applications of the art. It is the only important monograph on the subject.

17. MORGENSTERN, Sam, *Composers on Music, An Anthology of Composers' Writings from Palestrina to Copland,* HHP, 1958, 584 pp., $6.50. Of a number of such books that are available today, this is perhaps the one of widest appeal to the general reader.

18. *HARMAN, Alec, et al., *Man and His Music, The Story of Musical Experience in the West,* OUP, 1962, 1172 pp., $10.50; BAR, 1220 pp., 55s. Originally published in four separate volumes, this comprehensive history of music is the work of several specialists designed for the serious reader who is not deeply versed in music. It is highly recommended.

19. *ROBERTSON, Alec, and Denis Stevens, eds., *The Pelican History of Music,* V. I, *Ancient Forms and Polyphony,* BN, 1962, 335 pp., $5.00; V. II, *Renaissance and Baroque,* BN, 1965, $7.50; PE, 1965-6, 7s 6d each. It is to be hoped that this fine, inexpensive history will be extended to cover the more recent periods. Like the work mentioned above, it is the result of the work of a number of specialists.

20. *SEAY, Albert, *Music in the Medieval World,* PH, 1965, 182 pp., Hb $5.95, Pb $2.45; PH, Hb 48s, Pb 17s 6d. Prentice-Hall is currently bringing out a series of fine paperbacks on the various periods of music history, each by an authority and incorporating recent scholarship. The reader interested in a scholarly approach will find this concise volume excellent.

21. REESE, Gustave, *Music in the Middle Ages,* WWN, 1940, 502 pp., $7.95; JMD, 1941, 500 pp., 55s. Although in need of being brought up to date, this is still the most comprehensive book on the music of the Middle Ages. The reader is directed to the Norton catalogue, *Books that Live in Music,* for the most extensive listing of significant works on many aspects of music available from any single publisher.

22. *REESE, Gustave, *Music in the Renaissance,* WWN, RE, 1959, 1022 pp., $10.95; JMD, 1954, 946 pp., 80s. This is not a book to select for easy continuous reading, although it is written with an excellent sense of style. Its coverage of every aspect of the music of the period is extraordinarily comprehensive, extending from the rich flowering of music at the fifteenth century Burgundian court to the widespread musical culture extending from England to the Balkans at the opening of the seventeenth century. It is an exceedingly convenient reference work with over sixty pages of bibliography, provided with symbols that appear in the footnotes.

23. BUKOFZER, Manfred, *Music in the Baroque Era from Monteverdi to Bach,* WWN, 1947, 489 pp., $7.95; JMD, 1948, 490 pp., 60s. This work is a little out of date, but still is the most comprehensive treatment of the period in English. After the Baroque, religious music occupies a place less and less important in the mainstream of music history. There are excellent summaries of the leading composers.

24. GROUT, D. J., *A History of Western Music,* WWN, RE, 742 pp., 1964, $8.50; JMD, 1962, 756 pp., 70s. This is widely considered to be the most significant general history of music currently available in English. It is exceedingly well written and was abreast of the latest scholarship at the time of publication.

25. BURNERY, Charles, *A General History of Music,* 4 V., DO, 1958, 817, 1098 pp., $12.50 set; HA, 1935, 31s 6d. Not only is this a remarkable source of information about the music of the author's time, and the many historic figures he knew or met, but it is a work of outstanding literary value from a great period in western history, by a pioneer in the field of music history.

26. *MELLERS, Wilfrid, *Music in the Making,* DO, 1952, 63 pp., Pb 75¢; DOB, ED 2, 1952, 64 pp., 7s 6d. Whether the reader is a mere novice in musical lore or considers himself knowledgeable, he should find this approach stimulating. It tries to get behind the purpose for creating music in times past and today. While it is addressed specifically to modern Englishmen and potential listeners of the British Broadcasting Company, it has something to say to all music lovers.

27. *DORIAN, Frederick, *The History of Music in Performance,* Ri, WWN, 1966, 387 pp., Pb $1.95. A very practical contribution of musicology has been clearer insight into *how* the music of the past ought to be performed. Of a growing number of books dealing with performance practice, this is one of the most suitable for the general reader.

28. SIMPSON, Robert, ed., *The Symphony,* V. I, *Haydn to Dvorak,* V. II, *Elgar to the Present,* PEL, 1964, 816, 716 pp., Pb $1.65 each; PE, 7s 6d each. This set replaces the book edited by Ralph Hill. It is more extensive and more up-to-date in its approach. Articles on the symphonies of the different composers are by specialists. Among the more recent composers, the selection is rather different than would have been made by an American editor.

29. EWEN, David, *The Complete Book of Classical Music,* PH, 1965, 946 pp., $14.95; HALE, 1966, 968 pp., 126s. This is an excellent book which discusses in some detail an extraordinary number of musical works in the standard repertoire. It is a useful reference work for the discophile and concert-goer who is really interested in what he listens to.

30. ABRAHAM, Gerald, *A Hundred Years of Music,* Ri, ALP, 1964, 325 pp., $6.95. For the person who finds contemporary music difficult, this relatively short work may prove a good first step toward comprehension. Maehlis's *Introduction to Contemporary Music* (section 7-J) might well be the next step.

31. SACHS, Curt, *The History of Musical Instruments,* WWN, 1940, 505 pp., $10.00; JMD, 1942, 70s. The late Dr. Sachs, a musicologist of extraordinary versatility, was one of the pioneers in the systematic study of instruments. Though not the most

recent, this book in the Norton series is one of the best on the subject.

32. *APEL, Willi, and R. T. Daniel, *The Harvard Brief Dictionary of Music,* HUP, 1960, 341 pp., Hb $3.95; WSP, 1961, Pb 60¢. This is not an abridgement of the celebrated *Harvard Dictionary of Music,* HUP, 1944, 836 pp., $10.00; HEE, 50s, which may well prove forbidding to the non-specialist. It is an excellent, completely new work designed for "people with a lively interest in music."

33. WESTRUP, J. A., and F. L. Harrison, *The New College Encyclopedia of Music,* WWN, 1960, 739 pp., Hb $8.50, Pb $3.25; CO, 1959, 768 pp., 25s. Originally published in 1959 as the *Collins Encyclopedia of Music* in England and compiled by two distinguished Oxford scholars, this is an extremely practical work for the non-specialist. Many articles are cross-referenced for ease of finding.

7J. COMPOSERS
J. Buchanan MacMillan
In compiling this bibliography about composers of great music, an attempt has been made to avoid the popular type of biography and to present books of solid worth. It was manifestly impossible to list books on all the great names of the centuries. Some important figures have no biography—at least, not in English. Others have called forth a large number of biographical volumes. A number of the better recent works grouping together the lives of a number of great composers have been given first. Then follow in chronological order some of the better works on individual composers. Some preference has been given to those who composed great religious music, but most of the foremost masters of each era since the Renaissance have been included.

The greatest problem was to decide which to leave out. No apology need be made for including four works on Sebastian Bach! Many of the books in the list contain comprehensive bibliographies that may prove useful to the reader. The standard reference work on musicians and composers in English is Baker's Biographical Dictionary of Musicians, *GS, RE 5, 1965, $25.00;* Grove's Dictionary of Music and Musicians, *9 V., SM, ED 5, 1954, is the most extensive work on every aspect of music in the language.*

1. *EWEN, David, ed., *The World of Great Composers,* PH, 1962, 576 pp., $15.00. A collection of essays may be what more readers are looking for than a complete book on one composer. Each essay in the present volume consists of four parts: an introductory biographical sketch by the editor, a short article on "the man" by a specialist, a brief article on his works, and an extract from the composer's own prose—a letter, preface, or other written statement. Over thirty composers are represented.

2. EWEN, David, *The New Book of Modern Composers,* AAK, 1962, 586 pp., $7.95. A work similar to the last, but dealing with composers whose work falls mostly or entirely in the twentieth century.

3. SCHOLES, P. A., *Complete Book of Great Musicians,* OUP, 1931, 362 pp., $7.00; Ri, OUP, 1958, Pb $1.25; OUP, Hb 35s, Pb 12s 6d. Although written primarily for younger readers, this book by the author of *The Oxford Companion To Music* and many other important works on music may prove very acceptable to some readers.

4. *BROCKWAY, Wallace, and Herbert Weinstock, *Men of Music,* SS, RE, 1962, 649 pp., Hb $6.95, Pb $1.95. A useful and inexpensive work

covering many of the outstanding composers from Palestrina (1525-1594) to Stravinsky (b. 1882). The book is well written with a touch of the rhetorical, but here and there is not above criticism. His treatment of Debussy and Stravinsky is somewhat less than sympathetic.

5. MACHLIS, Joseph, *Introduction to Contemporary Music,* WWN, 1961, 714 pp., $8.50; JMD, 1963, 736 pp., 25s. This book might well have been included in the previous section on music. The writer, however, gives much attention to the composers as well as to their music. In each case two or three important works are discussed in detail. This is an excellent book and is highly recommended.

6. COATES, Henry, *Palestrina,* FSG, 1949, 243 pp., $2.50; JMD, 1948, 224 pp., 12s 6d. This biography is a re-issue of a book published by Dent in 1938. It is so far the standard work in English. It is to be hoped that a new, up-to-date work on this great religious composer will become available.

7. *FELLOWES, E. H., *William Byrd,* OUP, ED 2, 1948, 283 pp., $4.80; OUP, 30s. Byrd was probably the greatest composer England has ever produced. He remained a Catholic in a Protestant country and wrote for both Roman and Anglican rites. This is a good and informative book by the editor of the modern edition of Byrd's complete works.

8. *SCHRADE, Leo, *Monteverdi: Creator of Modern Music,* WWN, 1950, 384 pp., $6.00 (OoP); GOL, 1951, 35s. The great Venetian innovator, who wrote the first great opera and established a new trend in madrigal and church music is presented for the first time in an adequate account in English by a noted authority.

9. MOSER, H. J., *Heinrich Schuetz:*

His Life and Work, Ri, CON, 1959, 740 pp., $16.00; CON, 105s. Schuetz was born a century before Bach. The greatest German composer of his time, he devoted most of his life to writing music for the Lutheran tradition. The book deals in detail both with his life and works, from simple Psalm tunes to the oratorios of his old age. A short account has just been published by Faber in London. It is by the same author and might appeal to one who finds the large work too detailed.

10. WESTRUP, J. A., *Purcell,* COL, 1962, 323 pp., Pb $1.50; JMD, RE, 1965, 336 pp., 18s. This volume is a reprint of the book originally published by Dent. The author is professor of music at Oxford. A good book for the general reader. More detailed recent works have appeared by the American, Franklin Zimmerman, *Henry Purcell, 1654-1695: An Analytical Catalogue of His Music,* SM, 1963, $39.50; and *Henry Purcell, His Life and Times,* SM, 1967, $15.00. Henry Purcell was the greatest native English composer of the Baroque era.

11. PINCHERLE, Marc, *Vivaldi, Genius of the Baroque,* WWN, 1962, 278 pp., Pb $1.65; GOL, 1958, 280 pp., 21s. From extraordinary popularity in his own day, this Venetian priest slipped into complete obscurity, not to be brought to light until the present day. He is now emerging not only as a master of the concerto, but a creator of great choral music.

12. GEIRINGER, Karl, *The Bach Family, Seven Generations of Creative Genius,* OUP, 1954, 528 pp., $12.50; AU, 530 pp., 50s. Not surprisingly a large part of the volume is devoted to Johann Sebastian. Until recent musicological research rejected a number of works long accepted as genius and necessitated a considerable revision of the chronology of many others, this was the most satis-

factory account in English. In the main, it is still valuable and most readable.

13. *GEIRINGER, Karl, *Johann Sebastian Bach, The Culmination of an Era,* OUP, 1966, 382 pp., $9.50. This is the only up-to-date scholarly book at present in English. It is certainly good, but seems a little disappointing after Geiringer's earlier books. There is still room for a new popularly priced book incorporating the fruits of recent German Bach scholarship.

14. *DAVID, H. T., and A. Mendel, eds., *The Bach Reader,* WWN, RE, 1966, 431 pp., Pb $2.45; JMD, 1967, 474 pp., 50s. This book contains letters and documents from the life of the great composer and contemporary opinions of him. It contains a number of illustrations. It does much to bring the great master to life.

15. SCHWEITZER, Albert, *Johann Sebastian Bach,* 2 V., HUM, ET, 1962, 498 pp., $4.95 each; BK, 1962, 428, 498 pp., 60s set. While much in this great work must now be regarded with caution, Schweitzer was one of the pioneers in the new approach to Bach's music that gave a great impetus to the modern appreciation of the composer.

16. ABRAHAM, Gerald, ed., *Handel: A Symposium,* OUP, 1954, 328 pp., $8.76; OUP, 336 pp., 35s. The number of books on Handel, as on Bach, is very considerable. As with the latter, the careful and scientific modes of research now in vogue have required much to be rewritten. This symposium brings together a series of articles on various aspects of the composer's life and work in a concise manner.

17. *LANG, P. H., *George Frideric Handel,* WWN, 1966, 731 pp., $12.00; FF, 1967, 105s. The title

uses the anglicized form of the composer's name actually used by him. This recent study, beautifully written and abounding with enthusiasm, disposes of much of the fiction that has grown up around Handel's image through the years. He emerges as a vital and life-like figure. This is the book to read—if you have time.

18. *GEIRINGER, Karl, *Haydn, A Creative Life in Music*, ANB, 1963, 430 pp., Pb $1.65; AU, 399 pp., 18s. This is by far the best biography in English. It is very attractively written and contains a very fine treatment of all phases of his immense creative output.

19. *BLOM, Eric, *Mozart*, COL, 1962, 348 pp., Pb $1.50. It is hard to choose one book on Mozart, for there are many with varying merits. This is a good one. It contains appendices with a calendar of the composer's life and a catalogue of his works, grouped by categories and using the Koechel numbers.

20. *ROBBINS, Landon, and Donald & H. C. Mitchell, eds., *The Mozart Companion*, OUP, 1956, 414 pp., $4.80 (OoP); FF, 401 pp., 15s. The two-hundredth anniversary of Mozart's birth brought forth a number of fine books, of which this is one. It contains sections on all phases of his remarkable output, each by a distinguished musicologist.

21. *BURK, J. N., *The Life and Works of Beethoven*, RH, 1943, 487 pp.; Ri, ML, Pb $2.45. About half of the pages are devoted to biography, the rest of the volume to a discussion of his works, beginning with the symphonies. This is an excellent book for the general reader. As with Mozart, there are many books to choose from.

22. BROWN, Maurice, *Schubert, A Critical Biography*, SM, 1958, 486 pp., $8.50; CS, 574 pp., 18s. This study largely supercedes existent biographies of the first great romantic composer. Brown gives a very different picture of the man than has been usually accepted and provides fine insights into his phenomenal output.

23. SCHAUFFLER, Robert, and R. H. Florestan, *The Life and Works of Robert Schumann*, PS, 1963, 574 pp., $4.25; DO, 1963, Pb $2.25. A somewhat popularizing presentation of a composer who also left his mark in musical journalism. The book is conveniently divided between biography and discussion of his music.

24. WERNER, Eric, *Felix Mendelssohn*, FRP, 1963, 545 pp., $12.96; CM, 75s. As with Schubert and Schumann, there are a number of readily available studies. This one is the latest, written by a distinguished Jewish musicologist. If the book is a trifle controversial in part, it is fresh and stimulating and avoids the romanticized fictions about the man.

25. NEWMAN, Ernest, *Wagner as Man and Artist*, GC, 1941, 399 pp., $3.75; VI, Pb $1.95; GOL, 1963, 488 pp., 30s. A whole literature exists about the incredibly egotistical genius who shook the musical world of the nineteenth century. Newman, whose writings on opera in general are widely known and read, wrote three works on Wagner, of which this is the third and most concise. The four-volume work is published by Knopf and is in all adequate libraries. See, *Wagner Opera*, AAK, 1949, 724 pp., $8.95.

26. GEIRINGER, Karl, *Brahms, His Life and Work*, DC, 1961, 344 pp., Pb $1.45; OUP, RE 2, 1947, 344 pp., Pb $1.45; AU, ED 2, 1948, 352 pp., 35s. There are many lives of Brahms available. This is recent, scholarly, and attractively written. While it soft-pedals the less desirable aspects

of his character, it gives an excellent account of his music and its importance.

27. NEWLIN, Dika, *Bruckner, Mahler, Schoenberg,* KCP, 1947, 238 pp. (OoP) This is considered one of the best works on three important composers of three succeeding generations in the Viennese tradition. Perhaps somewhat difficult reading, it does relate them to forces that eventuated in one of the most important aspects of twentieth-century music, the "serialism" of Schoenberg.

28. LOCKSPEISER, Edward, *Debussy,* FSG, ED 3, 1952, 304 pp., C1 $4.95; Ri, COL, 1962, Pb $1.50; JMD, 1963, 320 pp., 18s. This is the account of the extremely important composer recommended for the general reader. Those desirous of a more detailed study will find it in Lockspeiser's new two-volume work, *Debussy: His Life and Mind,* V. 1 & 2, MC, V. 1, 1962, $8.00; COL, V. 2, 1965, 337 pp., Hb $8.00, Pb $1.50; CAS, 1962-65, 42s each.

29. VAUGHAN WILLIAMS, Ursula, *R. V. W.: A biography of Ralph Vaughan Williams,* OUP, 1964, 464 pp., $11.50. A very interesting biography of one of the greatest forces in twentieth-century British music by his widow, a gifted literary woman. It seems appropriate here to call attention to Michael Kennedy's *The Works of Ralph Vaughan Williams,* OUP, 1964, 736 pp., $14.40; OUP, 84s, which serves as an almost indispensable companion volume.

30. WHITE, E. W., *Stravinsky: The Composer and His Works,* UOCP, 1966, 608 pp., $18.50; FF, 121s. This is a rather costly volume, but is the most complete and up-to-date work on this extremely important and forceful contemporary. Stravinsky has, like Schoenberg and Hindemith, done some important writing

about his music and ideals. The virtually complete bibliography in this work is worth consulting. Its biographical section is excellent.

7K. JAZZ AND POP
William Robert Miller

Since the emergence of the Beatles, and especially since their remarkable film, A Hard Day's Night, *the pop music scene has become one of the most vital and exciting sectors of popular culture, to some extent overshadowing jazz. Both jazz and rock-and-roll have strong and deep-going roots in Negro life, mediated in an important way through the Negro church and its distinctive music. One of the earliest jazzmen, the legendary trumpeter Buddy Bolden, was a lifelong member of a blues-shouting congregation in New Orleans, and it was religious tunes like "When the Saints Go Marching In" which formed the matrix of the jazz heritage. The musicians "preached the blues" in church, at picnics, in secular dance halls.*

The blues styles of Bob Dylan, the Beatles, the Blues Project, Richie Havens, and many other current pop stars in America and abroad, owe less to jazz than to other parts of the Negro musical heritage—first to the honky-tonk rhythm-and-blues as it developed in the 1940's, then to the old country blues band and the great migratory blues singers and shouters and the black gospel soloists and ensembles. To young moderns such as the Beatles, the names of Leadbelly, Big Bill Broonzy, John Lee Hooker, Lighting Hopkins, and Muddy Waters shine like beacons of tradition. At the same time, the new groups are crafting their own traditions and absorbing others.

The songs of Beatle Paul McCartney accord well with old English balladry if you remove the beat and the electrified instrumentation. And they are good enough to endure and transcend their use by the group. The

Rolling Stones, the Doors, the Jefferson Airplane, the Fifth Dimension, the Sopwith Camel—the names themselves bespeak a style that dares to be absurd, different. There are plain names, too: Simon and Garfunkel, Leonard Cohen, Phil Ochs, Joan Baez, Judy Collins. And ranging through them all is a tremendous talent, a seemingly inexhaustible resource—and a depth of seriousness such as the world of pop music barely touched, by comparison, before the sixties.

Songs of protest, commitment, social comment—for a start, think of "Eleanor Rigby," "Richard Cory," "A Day in the Life," "Handsome Johnny," "When the Music's Over." And interspersed among them are enough explicitly religious songs to start a new hymnal—Paul Simon's "Blessed" and "The Sounds of Silence," Richie Havens' "No Opportunity Necessary": I know your cross is gettin' heavier . . . but I know a Man who walked miles for you . . . Stop! Stay where you are! Take a look at yourself!
—or John Lennon's "The Word," which is straight out of the Gospel according to John. Often there is a directness and urgency which contrasts sharply with the lore of monarchs and diadems we have inherited from our pious Victorian forebears. There is no soggy sentimentality, no polite trimmings in these new songs, but a devastating earnestness, an immediacy of confrontation that is toughly evangelical despite (or because of?) its non-churchly origins.

To compile even a rudimentary listing of such songs would be a formidable task. The discography that follows has another purpose—to list the best and most representative of those LP recordings which are entirely or predominantly religious in an explicit way, within the jazz-pop spectrum. This, too, is a growing enterprise. There does not yet exist a 12" recording of the splendid pop hymns of Sydney Carter, but one can predict that there will be and that he will become as well known in America as he already is in Britain, where songs like "The Devil Wore a Crucifix" and "Jesus and Martha" are widely known in the churches.

There is probably only one book which takes any account of religious jazz; and it was published before there were pop songs like the ones which are mentioned here. In fact, adequate books on jazz are fairly recent and there is no adequate post-Beatles book on pop music. Hence the following bibliography is a bare and sparse listing. Annotation is of greater value for the list of recordings which follows. Except where noted, catalog numbers refer to stereo recordings, most of which are also available in monaural pressings.

Books

1. DACHS, David, Anything Goes: The World of Popular Music, BM, 1964, 328 pp., $5.00.

2. HODÉIR, André, Jazz: Its Evolution and Essence, GP, 1957, 259 pp., Pb $1.25.

3. JONES, LeRoi, Blues People, MOR, 1963, 244 pp., Hb., $5.00, Pb $1.65; MAG, 1965, 256 pp., 30s.

4. JONES, LeRoi, Black Music, MOR, 1968, $5.00.

5. LEONARD, Neil, Jazz and the White Americans, UCP, 1962, 215 pp., $4.50; UCP, 216 pp., 33s 6d.

6. *MILLER, W. R., The World of Pop Music and Jazz, CON, 1965, 112 pp., Pb $1.00; CON, 110 pp., Pb 7s.

7. SPELLMAN, A. B., Four Lives in the Bebop Business, PAB, 1966, 241 pp., $4.95; MAG, 1967, 36s.

8. WILLIAMS, Martin, The Jazz Tradition, GP, 1965.

Recordings

9. *AXELROD, David, *Mass in F Minor,* The Electric Prunes. Reprise 6275. There is a hokey "cop-out" in the use of bland organ interludes and of pious restraint in the vocal lines, but when the electronic twang comes to the fore, it begins to suggest energetic faith. The traditional Latin text is the one used here.

10. BOYD, Malcom, *Are You Running With Me, Jesus?* Columbia CS 9348. Also, *Happening: Prayers For Now.* Columbia CS 9457. These two disks encompass the prayers from the best-selling book. Father Boyd reads with earnest feeling, backed up with well-wrought pop-jazz compositions by the talented guitarist.

11. BRAESEL, H. G., *Rejoice!* Students of General Theological Seminary. Mace 10030. Pleasant but rather bland tunes for male choir accompanied unobtrusively by Appalachian-style guitar and banjo. The idiom is pop-folk, guts neatly removed and soul rather bleached, using traditional texts of the Mass in English and interpolating the Nicene Creed and the Lord's Prayer. Five ballads overside are livelier and catchier but hardly justify the exclamation mark either.

12. *COLTRANE, John, *A Love Supreme,* Impulse A-77. Of several recordings in which the late, great sax player voiced his faith through the jazz idiom, this is the most straightforward. Predominant style here is blues, by turns lyrical and percussive, with superb solos.

13. ELLINGTON, Duke, *Concert of Sacred Music,* RCA Victor 35832; *My People,* Contact 1. The "sacred" concert features some excellent religious songs from Ellington's musical, *My People,* adding little but pious padding. Compare the two; my vote

goes to the less-touted "original cast" version on the Contact label.

14. GUARALDI, Vince, *Vince Guaraldi at Grace Cathedral,* 68-voice choir of Eucharist at the Episcopal Cathedral, San Francisco. Fantasy 8367. A 68-voice choir sings the liturgy of the Eucharist at the Episcopal Cathedral in San Francisco, and pianist Guaraldi and his trio embellish the plain chant with amiable, unexciting improvisation. Bishop James A. Pike introduced the performance in 1965 and continues to do so each time you play this recording.

15. HUGHES, Langston, *Black Nativity,* The Stars of Faith and the Bradford Singers, Columbia (to be issued). A Christmas play in authentic Negro gospel style, performed by singers from an ethnically black church.

16. *HUGHES, Langston, *The Weary Blues,* Jazz ensembles led by Leonard Feather and Charles Mingus. Verve VSP 36. Remember "a raisin in the sun?" No, not the play but the metaphor—it occurs in the poetry of Langston Hughes, and this is where Lorraine Hansberry found it. Much else is to be found here, too, as read by the late poet and interpreted by two different groups of outstanding jazzmen. Religion is part of it, and all of it is about the joys and sorrows of Negro life.

17. LEWIS, George, *Jazz at Vespers,* George Lewis and his band. Riverside 230. (mono only) The performance dates from the mid-fifties. This is one of the first examples of jazz in church. The style is Dixieland, the playing is creditable, the tunes range from classic blues to ragtime versions of spirituals.

18. *MARVIN, Ernest, *A Man Dies.* Capitol Imports SX 1600. (mono only) First performed in 1960, this

"modern mystery play" features songs that have both bite and beat— not far-out by today's standards, but durably good throughout, with memorable tunes and words that "grab" you, confront you with the gospel. Outstanding!

19. MASTERS, Joe, *The Jazz Mass*, Loulie Jean Norman, Clark Burroughs, with jazz septet. Columbia CS 9398. A lightweight, tinkly-tunesy version of the Mass in English, blending hokey religiosity with an outdated swing style—neither good jazz nor good sacred music. Listen at your own risk.

20. *Praise the Lord in Many Voices*. Avant Garde. (to be issued) These three LPs, available singly, include something for everyone. The Medical Mission Sisters join forces with the Paulist Folk Singers in a groovy *Mass of a Pilgrim People*. Paul Quinlan, S. J., swings with trio in folk-rock *Psalms for the Young in Spirit*. One of the best sides is jazz pianist Mary Lou Williams' *Praise the Lord*, featuring soprano Honey Gordon. Lutheran Pastor John Ylvisaker's *Mass for the Secular City* is disappointing. Robert Edwin's chief talent seems to be to conscript book titles—one of his six songs, "Are You Running With Me, Jesus?" is more reminiscent of Sankey than of Boyd. Father Bruno Markaitis rounds out the ecumenical picture with a rather conventional *Community Mass*. There's gold in these disks—seek and find.

21. *RIVERS, Clarence, *An American Mass Program*. Queen's Men Drama Guild. A free adaptation, mostly of biblical texts, in easy, reverent, refreshingly tuneful style, blending Gregorian chant with the forms of the Negro spiritual. The composer-conductor-cantor is a Catholic priest and a Negro.

22. *SCHIFRIN, Lalo, *Jazz Suite on the Mass Texts*, Paul Horn, clarinet, also sax and flute, with jazz quintet, chorus and orchestra, RCA Victor 3414. Eclectic, polished, by turns serenely lyrical and jarringly experimental, the pyrotechnics sometimes obscure the authorized English-language texts. But there is undeniable talent here—a worthy effort.

23. SUMMERLIN, Edgar, *Liturgical Jazz*. Ecclesia ER 101. (mono only) Dating from 1959, this is the first recorded jazz liturgy, an attractive but episodic work with some fine solos by members of the jazz nonet, with Roger Ortmayer reading the text of John Wesley's order of morning prayer.

24. *SUMMERLIN, Edgar, *Liturgy of the Holy Spirit*, soloists, choir, with the Summerlin-Heckman Improvisational Ensemble. Avant Garde. (to be issued) When premiered, TIME likened the liturgy's four hymns to Kurt Weill songs—other sections tend to greater complexity of jazz "new thing" style. Rosemary Unutmaz' soprano solo on another piece, *Gift of Joy: A Paean for Pentecost*, is superb. Also featured: an Advent cantata, *The Coming of Christ.*

25. WINTER, Sister Miriam Therese, *I Know the Secret*. Avant Garde 105. Spirited, folk-like songs on traditional Christian themes, enlivened with relaxed lyrics, splendid tunes, and fluent voices over a guitar-based beat.

26. *WINTER, Sister Miriam Therese, *Joy is Like the Rain*, Medical Mission Sisters. Avant Garde AVS 101. Thirteen originals, most in easy ballad form, some with a catchy Latin-American beat, with the guitarist-composer leading ten singing, swinging nuns. On some of the tunes, Sister Rachel Poirot adds Indian spice with a deft *tabla* beat.

27. JONATHAN and Charles, *Another Week to Go,* Inter-Varsity Records, LPS-02. Christian folk-rock by two young men whom *Billboard* called a "religious-but-hip Simon and Garfunkel." This record catches the mood of college students today.

28. RICH, Linda, *There's More to Living than I Know So Far,* Inter-Varsity Records, LPS-03. Linda Rich's lyrical alto voice carries a profound Christian message in simple songs of personal devotion, social commentary and delight in nature. These songs are her own, born of a sensitivity and a creative urge to express both the frustrations and the joys of life in God's world.

author index

Aalders	1BA-16, 1BA-88	Allen, W.D.	7I-14
Abel	7F6-8	Allis	1BA-34, 1BA-72
Abbott	6L-12, 7H-1	Allport	6H-12
Abraham, G.	7I-30, 7J-16	Alonso-Schokel	1D-8
Abraham, H.	6J-12	Alou	8-80
Adair	6M-1	Althaus	5B-24
Adams	7G1-52	Altizer	6C-36
Addleshaw	7H-2	Amiranashvili	7G1-21
Adeney	3D-20, 3D-21,	Anderson, B.W.	1BA-6
	6J-27	Anderson, J.D.C.	4-1
Adler	6I-2	Anderson, J.N.D.	2D-37, 2D-38,
Adolf	3D-1		3E-2
Aharoni	1BA-49, 1EA-1	Anderson, S.E.	1BA-60
Ahn	3D-22	Anderson, W.J.	4B-23
Ainaud	7G1-20, 7G1-53	Andrew	8-110
Aland	1A-3, 1A-4	Andrewes	4C-1
Albright	1A-7, 1BA-8,	Andrews, D.	8-111
	1EA-2, 1EB-1	Andrews, S.J.	1BB-39
Alcott	8-18	Apel	7I-32
Aldis	6G-26	Appasamy	4A-38
Alexander, E.	3C-1	Appleby	7I-3
Alexander, J.A.	1BA-63, 1BA-70	Appleton	7G1-6
Allen, H.C.	1BA-28	Aquinas	7B2-3
Allen, R.	2F-15, 3D-23,	Archer	1BA-12
	3D-24, 3D-25,	Archibald	1C-8
	5B-23	Argan	7G1-25

*This list indexes books annotated in the present bibliography and books listed in the supplement (*Bibliography on Booklets, Paperbacks and Records*). See p. xxv. For example, all references to section 8 and all references to sections 3C and 7L are found in the supplement, as are all references to material in section 2D-37 to 63, 3A-30 to 47, 4B-32 to 46, etc.

Argyle	2B-17
Armstrong	3D-26
Arndt	1BB-13
Athanasius	2A-1
Atiya	3A-12
Atkinson	3A-20, 6L-19
Atwater, F.	8-28
Atwater, R.	8-28
Auden	7C-13, 7G1-54
Audu	3C-2
Augsburger	6H-3
Augustine	2A-2, 4A-24, 4C-2, 4C-3, 7D-1
Austen	7A-1
Avison	7C-9
Axelrod	7K-9
Axthelm	7B1-51
Babbage	2C-5, 5A-1, 5A-2, 7B1-44
Bach	7L-20, 7L-21, 7L-22, 7L-23
Bachman	7F1-1, 7F4-7
Bailey, A.	4D-5
Bailey, D.S.	4B-14
Bailey, S.	5A-21
Baillie, D.M.	2D-24
Baillie, J.	2B-18, 4-2, 6A-30, 6A-31, 6A-32
Bainton	3A-16, 3A-30, 4A-1, 5A-3, 5E-1
Baker, F.	4D-12
Baker, J.	7G1-50
Baker, T.G.A.	6C-21
Baldwin	7A-2, 7B-6, 7B1-6
Bales	5F-10
Balleine	3A-24
Baly	1EB-2
Bangster	4C-4
Bannerman	2G-1
Barbour	6D-8, 6E-3
Barbridge	3C-3
Barclay, O.R.	5A-4, 6H-25
Barclay, W.	3C-4
Barlow	3D-2
Barnes	5B-10
Barnette	5A-10, 6C-15
Baron	1BA-96
Barr, D.L.	6F-24
Barr, J.	1BB-130, 1D-24
Barrett, C.K.	1BB-17
Barrett, E.E.	6A-25
Barrett, E.	8-98
Barry, D.W.	7F4-8
Barry, F.R.	2D-39
Barth	2A-33, 2C-12, 4-3, 4B-12, 4B-32, 6C-12, 6C-35, 1F-24
Bartning	7H-25
Basham	3E-17
Batt	3C-5, 3C-6, 4-4, 4B-33
Baughen	2G-23
Baumbach	7B1-26
Bavinck, H.	2A-22, 2B-1
Bavinck, J.H.	3E-24, 3E-25
Baxter, K.M.	7F2-9
Baxter, R.	2A-12, 2H-8, 4C-5, 4C-43, 4C-44, 7B2-1
Bayly	3C-7, 8-88, 8-91
Beaver	3D-14, 3D-27, 6F-1
Beck	1A-8
Beckett	7F1-17
Beckwith, I.T.	1BB-121
Beckwith, J.	7G1-51
Bede	3A-31
Beecher	1BA-23
Beegle	1A-30, 1F-2
Beethoven	7L-32
Belgum, D.	6G-25
Belgum, H.J.	5D-2
Bell	4-5
Bemelmans	8-12
Bendall	6B-19
Bennett	3D-19, 5B-16, 5E-20, 6F-2
Benson	4D-21, 4D-22
Bentley, D.	3C-8
Bentley, E.	7F2-12
Berkhof	1D-3, 2A-27, 2A-34, 2H-26
Berkouwer	2B-2, 2C-4, 2D-35, 2E-1, 6L-15, 6L-16
Berlioz	7L-33, 7L-34
Berman, D.M.	6J-13
Bernanos	7A-3
Berryhill	7F1-16
Berstein	3E-12
Bertocci	5A-11, 6G-14
Berton	2G-24
Bertram	7G1-55
Best	2G-2
Bettenson	3A-2

Beyer	7G1-50	Brahms	7L-36
Beyerhaus	3D-28	Brandt	5A-34, 5B-27,
Bieler	7G2-6, 7H-3		6G-28
Billing	5B-25	Branner	7G2-3
Bindley	3B-1	Bratcher	1A-10
Birdsall	1BB-132	Bratt	6J-29
Blackburn	8-67, 8-77	Braybrooke	7B1-52
Blackman	1D-9	Breen	7D-7
Blackstone	2H-3	Bridges, C.	1BA-67
Blackwood, A.W.Jr.	1BA-61	Bridges, S.	7G1-6
Blackwood, G.D.	6J-18	Bright	1BA-8, 1BA-74
Blaiklock	1BB-18, 1BB-58,	Brink	8-17
	1BB-122, 1BB-132,	Brion	7G1-35
	3A-32, 4-6	Britt	4D-18
Blair	6G-27	Britten	7L-48
Blindheim	7G1-56	Brockway	7J-4
Bloch	7L-42	Bromiley	2G-65
Blom	7J-19	Bronstein	7G1-40
Blood	4B-9	Brooks	7B1-23, 7B1-49
Bloom	7J-31	Broomall	2F-16
Blunt	7G1-44	Broomhall	3C-9
Boer	3D-29	Brow	3D-3, 3E-6
Boettner	2H-14, 2H-16, 6L-3	Brown, C.	6C-40
Bohm	6D-16	Brown, D.A.	1BB-34
Boisen	6H-7	Brown, D.	6I-1
Bolt, D.	2H-29	Brown, D.M.	6C-34
Bolt, R.	7F1-12	Brown, M.	7J-22
Bonar	4A-39	Brown, S.C.	3C-10
Bonhoeffer	1BA-101, 2C-15,	Browne, E.M.	7F1-1
	4A-30, 4A-40,	Browne, L.E.	3A-14
	4C-6, 4C-7, 4C-8,	Browne, L.	3E-22
	5B-26, 6C-25	Browne, T. Sir	7B2-14
Bony	7G2-11	Bruce, F.F.	1A-31, 1A-32,
Boon	7G1-37		1BA-102, 1BB-6,
Borgatta	5F-10		1BB-19, 1BB-20,
Borgstrom	5D-11		1BB-59, 1BB-60,
Bornkamm	6J-28		1BB-68, 1BB-81,
Bosc	2G-3		1BB-85, 1BB-104,
Bost	7F1-7		1BB-133, 1BB-134,
Boswell	5E		1BB-135, 1EB-3,
Bouguet	3E-26		1EB-18, 2D-40,
Boulding	6K-17		2G-4, 3A-10, 6A
Bovet	4B-1	Bruce, M.	6C-19
Bowden	6C-37	Bruggink	7H-4
Bower	6F-29	Bruner, W.R.	6I-1
Bowers	6G-21	Brunner, E.	2A-29, 2D-27,
Bowman, A.	6A-6		2H-25, 5B-22,
Bowman, H.A.	4B-10		7E-14
Boyd, M.	7F4-6, 7K-10	Brunner, H.E.	1F-3
Boyd, R.L.F.	6E-15	Brush	3A-33
Braaten	1D-12	Bryson	6F-3
Braden	3E-1, 6M-8	Bube	6E-2
Braesel	7K-11	Buchanan	2E-2

Buis	2H-19
Bukofzer	7I-23
Bulgakov	7A-52
Bull	3D-30, 3D-31
Bullough	6L-21
Bultmann	1D-19, 1F-4
Bunyan	2H-30, 4-7, 4C-9,
	4C-10, 4C-45,
	4C-46, 7A-4
Bura	7G1-43
Burbridge	2C-16
Burk	7J-21
Burnery	7I-25
Burroughs	4C-47
Burrowes	1BA-68
Burrows	1A-33
Burtnes	2G-5
Burton	8-5
Burtt	3E-27
Bush	6I-4
Busignani	7G1-58
Bussagli	7G1-57
Buswell	2A-28, 2C-2,
	6A-26
Butterfield	7D-23, 7D-25,
	7D-26
Buttrick	1BA-3, 1BA-31,
	1BB-7
Buxtehude	7L-15
Bye	4B-34
Cadlier	4A-5
Cadoux	5E-2
Cage	7F5-1
Cailliet	4A-25, 4A-41,
	7E-11
Cairns	5B-6
Callahan	6C-29
Calvin	1BA-70, 1BA-84,
	2A-6, 4C-11,
	4C-48, 6J-30,
	7B2-4, 7D-9
Campbell, T.J.	7D-10
Campbell, W.D.	5E-21
Campigneulle	7G1-59
Campion	4A-42
Camus	7A-5, 7B1-7,
	7B1-8, 7B-8
Canaday	7G1-2
Candlish	2B-19
Cannon	7F1-7
Capenerhurst	3C-11
Capon, A.	4B-35

Capon, E.	4B-35
Capper	5A-5
Carli	7G1-23, 7G1-24
Carmichael	4C-49
Carnell	6A-15, 6A-16,
	6A-17, 6A-18,
	6B-6, 6C-41, 6D-3
Carpenter, H.J.	2A-35
Carpenter, S.C.	3A-25
Carr	4-8
Carissimi	7L-16
Carleson	1BA-91
Carson	1BB-86, 1C-2,
	6J-31, 6L-1
Carter, C.S.	6L-18
Carter, D.	6J-11
Cartwright, C.	7F6-10
Cartwright, D.	5F-9
Casserley	6B-2, 7D-20
Cassou	7G1-60
Cater	6K-9
Cather	8-51
Catherwood	6K-2
Cauthen	6G-11
Cecil	7C-1
Cellier	7F2-10
Chadwick, H.	3A-34, 3A-35
Chadwick, O.	3A-19
Chafer	2F-1, 2F-2, 3C-12
Chamberlain	2E-3
Chamberlayne	7G1-61
Chambers	4C-12
Champion	3E-23
Charpentier	7L-18
Chapman	6H-26
Chase	7I-12
Chastel	7G1-27
Chatzidakis	7G1-12
Chesterton	4A-2, 7A-6,
	7B1-3
Childs	6K-9
Clark, E.T.	6M-2
Clark, G.F.	6D-7
Clark, G.H.	6A-9, 6A-21,
	6B-7, 6B-8, 6B-34,
	6B-35, 6D-7, 7D-3
Clark, K.B.	5E-12
Clark, J.W.	6K-20
Clark, K.W.	1A-26, 7G1-2,
	7G1-33, 7G1-48
Clark, R.E.D.	6E-10, 6E-17
Clark, W.H.	6H-14
Clarkson	7C-6, 8-71

Cleary	8-23	Crawford	2D-23
Clements	7G1-31	Crockett	1BA-56
Clinebell	6H-8	Cross	3A-7
Close	6A-8	Crossley	6A-33
Clowney	2G-26, 4-9	Cruden	1BB-1
Coates	7J-6	Cullmann	2D-26, 2G-4,
Cobb	1D-20		2H-24, 2H-31,
Cochrane, C.N.	7D-19, 7E-13		6J-32
Cochrane, R.G.	6G-29	Cully	6F-5, 6F-6
Cockerton	4-10	Culpepper	2D-43
Coggin	7F2-3	Culver	1BA-78
Cogley	6F-4	Cundall	1BA-52
Cohen	7F5-2	Cunningham	2A-17
Cohon	3E-13	Curtis	4A-44
Cole, A.	1BB-46, 1BB-77,		
	1BB-136, 2F-27	Daane	5E-22
Cole, R.A.	2G-6	Dachs	7K-1
Cole, W.G.	5A-24	Dahl, M.E.	2C-17
Collier	6E-18	Dahl, R.A.	6J-5
Collins	6B-32	Dahlberg	7A-54
Colquhoun	2D-41, 2D-42,	Daniel	7I-32
	2E-24, 2G-28, 4-11	Daniels	6J-21
Coltrane	7K-12	Dante	7C-15
Come	2F-17	Darwin	7B2-19
Conant	7G2-10	Davey	4A-45
Condor	8-78	David	7J-14
Conrad	7A-7	Davidson, A.B.	1BB-105
Conybeare	1BB-63	Davidson, F.	1BA-27, 1BB-32,
Cooley	3E-14		2C-18
Coombs	2B-20	Davidson, R.	1BA-103
Cooper	3D-4	Davies, G.C.B.	4A-46
Copass, B.	1BA-71, 1BA-91	Davies, H.	6M-3, 7B1-32
Cope	7H-5, 7H-6	Davies, J.G.	7H-7
Coray	4A-43, 7A-53	Davies, R.E.	1F-5, 6F-7
Cotton	2B-4	Davies, W.D.	1BB-137
Coughlan	7G1-29	Davis	3D-5, 6L-13
Coulson	6D-13	Dawson	6F-8, 7E-8
Couperie	7F6-9	Day	5C-7
Couperin	7L-19	Dean	6J-4
Courthion	7G1-45	Deane	7I-15
Cousins	2D-1	deAngeli	8-57
Cowan	3D-32	Deansley	3A-13
Cox, H.	5C-1, 6C-28	Dearmer	4D-20
Cox, J.W.	2G-29	deBerry	6A-36
Cox, S.	1BA-55	DeBoer	6A-23
Coxhill	3B-2	deBroglie	6D-16
Crabtree	2E-4	Decker	7G1-20
Cragg, C.	3A-36	deFenelon	4C-13
Cragg, K.	3E-14	Defoe	7A-55, 8-45
Crane, J.	7F6-6	DeGraaf	6F-30
Crane, S.	6I-8	Deissman	1BB-14, 1EB-4
Cranfield	1BB-111	Deissmann	4A-47
Cranmer	2A-9	DeKoster	6J-21, 6J-33

De La Bedoyre	6L-20	Duvall	4B-21, 8-106
Delaisse	7G1-16, 7G1-17	Dye	6D-9, 6E-6
Delitzsch	1BA-32		
Demant	5A-12, 5B-28	Earle	6K-10
Demaray	2B-3	Eckel	2G-30
Dennett	1A-34	Eddington	6D-11
Denney	2A-24, 2D-20	Edersheim	1BB-40
Denton	4B-27	Edgren	7A-10
Denzinger	3B-3	Edmunds	6G-24, 6G-32,
dePres	7L-6		6G-33
Derek	6A-34	Edwards, J.	2A-14, 4C-15,
Derham	1C-4, 2H-2,		7B2-8
	5A-35, 6A-35	Edwards, Q.	5B-30
de Tocqueville	6J-7	Egermeiers	8-113
Detweiler	7B1-48, 7B1-53	Ehlert	7A-57
deVaux	1BA-9, 1EA-5	Ehrensperger	7F2-1
Dewbow	6L-22	Eimerl	7G1-24
DeWit	1BA-104	Eissefeldt	1BA-13
DeWolf	6C-8	Ekvall	3E-20
Dickens	8-44	Elbrecht	6J-34
Dillery	6B-30	Elgar	7G1-63
Dillistone	6A-37, 7B1-34	Eliade	3E-21
Dittes	6G-7	Eliot	6F-10, 7B1-4,
Dixon, J.W. Jr.	7G1-8		7B-16, 7B1-16,
Dixon, M.	2C-19, 6E-19		7C-12, 7E-16,
Dodd	1BA-105, 5B-29,		7F1-14
	6G-30, 7D-30	Eller	7F6-5
Dodge	8-14	Ellington	7K-13
Dolphin	6G-31	Ellinwood	7I-8
Doniger	2C-11, 6H-23	Elliot, E.	3D-33, 4A-3,
Donne	4C-14, 7B2-11		4A-4, 7A-11, 8-92
Dooyeweerd	2C-8, 6B-5	Elliot, P.	2D-45
Dorian	7I-27	Ellis, E.E.	1BB-64, 1BB-138
Dostoevsky	7A-8, 7A-9,	Ellis, W.T.	4A-49
	7A-56	Ellison, J.L.	1BA-22, 1BA-24,
Douglas, C.W.	7I-4		1BA-62, 1BA-75,
Douglas, J.D.	1BA-1, 3A-21		1BB-139
Dournovo	7G1-16	Ellison, J.W.	1BB-2
Drake	7B1-54	Ellison, R.	7A-12
Drakeford	6H-19	Ellzey	4B-24
Dreikurs	4B-18	Elmen	7B1-55
Dru	4A-48	Empie	3B-4
Drummond, A.L.	7H-8	Epp	4-13
Drummond, H.	4C-51	Epstein	3E-28
duBourguet	7G1-10	Erb	1C-14
Duby	7G2-13	Esslin	7F2-11
Dufay	7L-5	Estes	8-22
DuMont	7L-17	Eversole	7E-3, 7F2-2,
Dumont	7G1-62		7F3-52, 7F6-6,
Duncan	4-12		7G1-8
Dunn	6F-9	Ewen	7J-1, 7J-2, 7I-29
Dunne	5D-7		
Dunstone	2D-44	Faber	2B-5

Fager	5E-23	Foster, J.	3A-9, 3A-37
Fairbairn	1BA-76	Foster, M.B.	6B-14, 6B-26
Fairchild	4B-15, 4B-31	Foulkes	1BB-82, 1D-27
Fall	6J-25	Fox	4C-16
Farrer	6A-38, 6B-12	Frank	4A-31
Faulkner	7A-13	Frankl	7G2-13
Faure	7L-39	Franklin	5E-3
Faussett	1BB-34	Franks	2D-33
Fay	1EB-21	Frazee-Bower	7I-34
Feinberg	1BA-83, 1BA-85,	Fread	3A-38
	1BA-90, 1BA-94,	Freedman	1A-7, 1EB-20
	1BA-97	Freeman	6A-27, 6B-9,
Fellowes	7I-7, 7J-7		6C-42
Fenton	6J-14	Fremantle	3A-39, 3A-40,
Ferm	3E-5		7G1-18
Ferre, F.	6B-19, 6B-24	Freud	6G-18
Ferre, N.F.	6F-11	Frey	7H-9
Ferry	7B2-5	Friedrich, C.J.	6J-2
Feucht	4B-31	Friedrich, G.	1BB-11
Field	8-60, 8-107	Fromm	4B-5, 5A-37,
Fife	3D-6, 3D-34		6H-18
Filson	1EB-17	Frost	8-64
Finbert	1EB-5	Fry	7F1-3
Findlay	1BB-112	Frye	7B1-40, 7F2-14
Finegan	1EA-6, 1EB-6	Fuller, D.P.	2D-32, 7D-18
Finlayson	2A-37, 2D-6	Fuller, E.	6F-12, 7A-14,
Finney	5A-36		7B1-19
Fisher, A.	4B-36	Fuller, R.H.	5D-6, 6K-5
Fisher, F.L.	1D-3	Funk	1D-21
Fisk	7F5-3	Furness	1F-25
Fitch	2B-21, 4-14		
Fitcher	7G2-15	Gabrieli, F.	3E-29
Flack, E.E.	1BB-21	Gabrieli, G.	7L-10
Flack, E.F.	1BA-28	Gaebelein	1F-26, 6A-39,
Flack, M.	8-1		6F-13, 6F-14
Flavel	4C-52	Galbraith	6K-14
Fleming, D.J.	7G1-7	Gandhi	4A-50
Fleming, J.	7G2-1	Garland	1BA-86
Fletcher, B.A.	1BB-140	Garst	5D-4
Fletcher, B.	7G2-2	Garstand	1BA-51
Fletcher, J.	5A-25, 5A-26	Garstang	1BA-51
Flew, R.V.	2E-5, 2G-7	Garston	4A-51
Florisoone	7G1-49	Gasque	1EB-19
Foote	4D-17	Gassert	6G-16
Forbes	8-46	Gates	4A-52
Forlati	7G1-13	Gaussen	1F-7
Forsberg	3D-7	Geden	1BB-4
Forsyth	1F-6, 2A-24,	Geiringer	7J-12, 7J-13,
	2D-13, 2D-25,		7J-18, 7J-26
	2D-46, 2G-20,	Geisler	1BA-10
	4-15	Geldenhuys	1BB-49, 1F-8
Fosdick	6C-2, 6H-27,	Gelzer	4A-5
	7B2-6	Genne, E.	5A-27

Genne, W.	5A-27	Green, M.	1BB-113, 2D-4,
Germann	7H-10		2G-12
Gerrish	3B-5	Green, R.W.	6J-35
Gerson	7G2-4	Green, V.H.	4A-1
Gerstner	1F-27, 2C-20,	Greenaway	8-62
	2D-47, 6A-13,	Greene	7A-17, 7F1-5,
	6M-9		7F1-6
Gessweir	6H-28	Greenstone	1BA-44
Gettys	1BA-48	Griffith	7B1-42
Gheon	7F2-6	Griffiths	3D-35, 4-16,
Gill	4A-6		4-17, 4-18, 4-19,
Gilles	7L-17		5F-13
Gilson	6B-3, 6B-15	Grillmeier	2D-29
Gingrich	1BB-13	Grimley	3D-37
Ginott	4B-20	Grimm, H.	3A-18
Glass	8-100	Grimm, R.	5A-7
Glasser	3D-6	Grollenberg	1EB-7
Glasson	1BB-141	Grosheide	1BB-73
Golding	5F-6, 7A-16	Gross	7B1-20
Goldscheider	7G1-30, 7G1-34,	Grosse	4A-26
	7G1-36	Grounds	6A-3
Gollwitzer	2B-6	Grout	7I-24
Gooding	1BA-41	Grubb, K.G.	3B-2
Goodman, Paul	5C-2	Grubb, N.P.	4A-54
Goodman, Percival	5C-2	Grundler	3B-7
Goodspeed	1A-12, 1A-35,	Guaraldi	7K-14
	1A-46	Guillaume	3E-30
Gordh	7E-4	Guillebaud	2D-7, 6A-12
Gordis	1BA-67, 1BA-69	Guiness	3C-16, 3C-17,
Gordon, C.H.	1BA-7, 1EA-7		3C-18, 4-20
Gordon, E.	8-95	Gustafson	3D-38
Gordon, M.S.	5D-9	Guthrie, D.	1BB-22, 1BB-23,
Gordon, T.	5F-7		1BB-65, 1BB-100,
Gottwald	1BA-106		1BB-143
Goudge	2D-48, 4A-53,	Guthrie, W.	4C-41
	4C-20	Gyorgy	6J-18
Goyder	2G-31		
Grabar	7G1-10, 7G1-12,	Haak	7G1-36
	7G1-64	Haas	6H-6
Grabo	7B2-9	Hackett	6A-28
Graetz	7G1-43	Haeussler	4D-7
Graf	3C-13	Haftmann	7G1-46
Graham, B.	3C-14	Hagen	3D-39
Graham, K.	8-13	Hale, J.R.	7G1-26
Grant, F.B.	5B-7	Hale, L.P.	8-33
Grant, F.C.	1A-36	Hall, B.H.	6G-16
Grant, R.M.	1EB-20	Hall, P.	3B-8
Gray, A.H.	4B-37	Hall, S.	7F3-57
Gray, R.M.	2G-41	Hallesby	2C-21, 2E-6,
Green, B.	3B-6		2G-32, 4-21,
Green, B.S.	3C-15		6H-29
Green, E.M.	1BB-142, 2D-14	Hallowell	6J-3, 7D-22

Halter	7I-2
Halverson	7F1-1
Hamberg	7H-11
Hamburger	7J-32
Hamilton, F.E.	2B-7, 6A-14
Hamilton, K.	6C-44, 6C-45, 7B1-39, 7B1-56, 7B1-57
Hamilton, M.	5E-4
Hamilton, R.W.	1EB-10
Hamilton, W.	6C-26
Hammarskjold	4A-32
Hammond, P.	7H-13, 7H-14
Hammond, T.C.	2A-32, 2A-38, 6A-15
Handel	7L-24, 7L-25
Handy	3A-27
Hanna	7B1-46
Hanson	2G-17, 6A-40
Happold	3C-31
Harbison	3A-17
Hardy	7B1-20
Hare	5F-10
Harman	7I-18
Harnack	2A-40, 6C-1
Harper, A.F.	1BA-30
Harper, H.M. Jr.	7B1-25
Harrington, J.T.	5B-8
Harrington, M.	5D-10
Harris	1BA-17
Harrison, E.	1BB-24
Harrison, F.L.	7I-33
Harrison, F.M.	4A-55
Harrison, R.K.	1BA-5
Hart, G.	2G-33, 4A-56
Hartman	7A-18
Hartmann	6G-12
Hartog	7I-35
Haselden	5E-5
Hastings	1BB-8
Havermann	4B-6
Hawthorne, J.N.	6E-20
Hawthorne, N.	7A-19, 7A-20
Hay	7H-12
Haydn	7L-26, 7L-27
Hazo	7C-3
Heaton	1BA-107
Herbert, G.	2G-34
Heidel	1BA-35
Heilbroner	6K-7
Heim	6D-12, 6D-21
Heinisch	1BA-9
Heller	6K-16
Hemingway	7A-21
Hempel	7G2-4
Henderson	6C-46
Hendricksen	1BB-53, 1BB-87, 1BB-88, 1BB-97, 1BB-101, 1BB-123
Hendry	2B-8
Hengstenberg	1BA-20, 1BA-64
Hennessy	7G1-51
Henry, C.	1F-9, 2A-31, 2A-41, 2B-9, 2B-10, 2D-28
Henry, M.	8-31
Henry, Matthew	1BB-33, 4C-17
Herbert	4C-18
Hercus	1BA-108, 1BA-109, 4A-7
Herdern	6B-25
Herman	4C-19
Hershberger	5E-6
Herzog	1D-23
Hewitt	1BB-106
Heyerdahl	8-43
Heyne	6K-1
Hick	6B-23
Hill, E.	7G1-65
Hill, J.R.	1C-6
Hiltner	5A-14, 6H-5
Hilton	8-42
Hitchcock, H.R.	7G2-20
Hitchcock, H.W.	7I-36
Hitt	4A-8, 4A-9
Hodeir	7K-2
Hodge	1BB-69, 2A-18
Hodgson	2B-11, 2B-23
Hoekema	6M-10
Hoffmeister	7G1-49
Hollingsworth	1C-21, 1C-24
Holmes	6B-1
Honour	7G2-1
Hoogstra	7D-16
Hooke	1A-13
Hooker	2A-11
Hooykaas	6D-5, 6E-22, 6E-23
Hopkins, G.M.	7C-11
Hopkins, H.A.E.	2C-22, 3C-19, 3C-20
Hopkins, T.K.	5F-11
Hopkinson	4C-26

Hopper	7B1-36	Jabay	6H-1
Horden	6C-24	Jackmann	7A-61
Horn	7F6-9	Jackson, D.M.	2C-23
Horst	7F5-5	Jackson, G.P.	4D-15, 4D-16
Hort	2G-8	Jacobs	7F3-59
Horton	5B-18	Jahsmann	8-120
Hough	5E-24	James, E.O.	3E-3, 3E-33,
Houghton, A.T.	2G-36, 3D-40		3E-34
Houghton, F.	2G-35, 4A-10,	James, R.	6C-37
	4-22	James, William	6H-15, 7B2-16
Howe	5A-38	James, Will	8-35
Howie	1BA-77	Jamieson	1BB-34
Howley	1BA-19	Janacek	7L-40
Howson	1BB-63	Janson	7G1-3
Huddleston	5E-25	Jeeves	6H-31
Hudson	3D-41	Jellema	7A-23, 7B1-58
Huegel	3D-45	Jenkins, D.	2B-13, 2G-9
Hughes, A.	2H-13	Jenkins, D.E.	6C-23, 6C-33
Hughes, L.	7K-15, 7K-16	Jensen	1BA-45, 1BA-53
Hughes, P.	1BB-74, 2A-7,	Jeremias	1BB-144
	2A-30, 2B-24,	Jewett	6C-47
	2E-8, 3A-5	Joad	6B-10
Hughes, R.	7J-33	Johnson, C.	8-101
Huisjen	3C-21	Johnson, D.	1F-28, 3A-41,
Huizimga	4A-57		3D-42, 5F-15
Hulme	2E-7, 4B-3	Johnson, J.L.	7A-62
Hulsbosch	2B-12	Johnson, M.S.	7H-27
Hummel, C.E.	1C-22, 3C-22	Johnson, P.E.	6H-13
Hummel, C.T.	6H-30	Johnson, R.C.	1F-10
Humphrey	7F5-6	Johnson, S.	4C-20, 7A-26,
Humphreys	3E-32		7B2-2
Hunt, E.	4-23	Jonathan and	
Hunt, G.	4A-58, 5A-39	Charles	7K-27
Hunt, K.	5A-39	Jones, A.	1A-14
Hunt, J.W.	7B1-50	Jones, E.S.	4C-21
Hunt, M.	4B-8	Jones, F.P.	2G-37
Hunter, A.M.	1D-10	Jones, H.K.	5A-20
Hunter, D.	6F-15	Jones, L.	7K-3, 7K-4
Hurlburt	8-112	Jones, O.R.	2E-9
Hurlimann	7G2-12	Jones, W.	7F3-60
Hussey	3A-14	Jones, W.S.	7B1-45
Hutter	7G1-50	Joppie	2B-25
Huxley	7A-22, 7B1-17,	Jose	7G1-23
	7B1-18	Josephus	1BB-145,
Hyma	3A-18, 7D-7,		1BB-146
	7D-15	Joy	1BB-3
		Joyce	7A-24, 7A-25
Irwin	7A-58, 7A-59,	Judge	1BB-147
	7A-60	Juergens	6I-15
Isais	3D-8	Julian, J.	4D-23
Isherwood	3E-38	Julian of Norwich	4C-22
		Jung	6H-32
Jaarsma	6F-16	Jurgensen	8-127

Kac	2H-20
Kafka	7A-27
Kaltenbach	7G1-1
Kaufman, J.	1BA-54
Kaufmann, E.	7G2-19
Kazantzakis	7A-28
Keats	8-3
Kee	5B-31
Keech	6K-22
Keen	6C-48
Keil	1BA-32
Keith-Lucas, A.	5B-1
Kelemen	7G1-41
Keller	4A-58
Kellett	3E-35
Kelley	8-40
Kellogg	1BA-43
Kelly, H.W.	5F-12
Kelly, J.N.D.	3B-9
Kelly, T.	4C-23
Kelsey	5E-7
Kempis, T.á	4C-24
Kennan	6J-23
Kennedy, M.	7-J
Kennedy, W.B.	6F-17
Kenrick	5C-3
Kenyon	1A-37, 1A-38, 1EB-8
Kephart	4B-29
Kerr, H.T.	6A-41
Kerr, W.S.	6L-7
Kevan	1BA-27, 1BB-32, 2E-10, 2E-11
Kidd	6L-6
Kidner, D.	1BA-37, 1BA-66, 4D-9, 5B-32, 7E-1
Kidner, F.D.	1BA-110
Kierkegaard	1F-11, 4C-53, 6A-42
Kik	6J-36
Kilby	4A-34, 7E-2
Kildahl	2G-5
Kilpatrick	1A-5
King	5E-8
Kinper	3C-23
Kipling	8-29, 8-38
Kirk	2B-26
Kirkpatrick	4B-30
Kittel, G.	1BB-11
Kittel, R.	1A-1
Kitzinger	7G1-18, 7G1-66
Klassen	1D-22
Klausler	5A-40
Klausner	6G-8
Klinck	1BB-148
Klooster	2C-1
Knox, J.	1BB-149
Knox, R.A.	1A-15, 1A-39, 7B1-11
Koberle	2E-12
Koehler	7G1-67
Koepf	7G1-51
Koestler	7B-14, 7B1-14
Krabill	6G-34
Kraemer	3D-9, 5B-13
Kraus, H.J.	1BA-6
Krauss	8-10
Krautheimer	7G2-9
Krentel	8-119
Kromminga	4C-25
Kroner	6B-16
Krummacher	4C-54
Kubler	7G2-4
Kuhn, I.	4A-27, 8-86
Kuhn, M.	6K-10
Kuhns	7F3-61
Kung	2G-10
Kunz	1C-13, 1C-16, 1C-20
Kurzweg	6A-43
Kuyper, A.	1F-12, 2A-21, 2E-13, 2F-3
Kuyper, R.B.	2G-11
Kvet	7G1-68
LaBarre	6G-23
Lack	6E-9
Lackmann	3B-10
Ladd	2H-10, 2H-12, 2H-27, 6C-49, 7D-31
Laetoch	1BA-73, 1BA-81
Landon, R.	7J-20
Lalande	7L-17
Lane	1BB-47
Lang	7J-17
Lange	1BB-35
Langer,	7G1-9, 7G1-69, 7G1-70
Lankester	1EB-9
Lasareff	7G1-71
LaSor	1EA-14
Lassaigne	7G1-20, 7G1-22
Lasso	7L-8
Latham	7J-34

Latimer	2A-10
Latourette	3A-1, 3A-4, 3D-10, 4A-25, 7D-29
Laurenti	5E-9
Law, Henry	1BA-111
Law, H.W.	7E-6
Law, W.	4C-26
Lawes	5A-43
Leaf	8-11
Lear	8-56
LeBar	8-108, 8-124
Lecerf	2A-28
Lee, A.H.	7C-2
Lee, H.R.	4B-38
Lee, H.	8-54
Lee, R.	5C-4, 5C-5
Lee, R.A.	8-81
Leeuw	7G1-9
LeFevre	2C-24, 3D-28
Leiffer	5C-6
Legge	6G-35
Leith	3B-11
Lemarie	7G1-47
L'Engle	8-41
Lenski	8-4
Leonard	7K-5
Leslie	5B-18
Lesser	7G2-14
LeTourneau	4A-28
Leuphold	1BA-39, 1BA-65
Lever	2B-14
Levie	1D-14
Levy	7G1-1
Lewis, C.S.	1A-47, 1BA-112, 4A-29, 4A-33, 4A-34, 5A-18, 6A-11, 6A-44, 6A-45, 6D-5, 6F-18, 7A-30, 7A-31, 7A-63, 7B1-12, 7B1-21, 7B1-38, 7B1-59, 7C-7, 7C-16, 8-73, 8-82
Lewis, G.	7K-17
Lewis, G.R.	6M-11
Lewis, J.P.	1BA-82
Liddon	1BB-70, 2D-10
Lifton	5F-8
Lightfoot	1BB-78, 1BB-89, 1BB-90
Lind	6G-34
Lindgren	8-26
Lindsell	3D-11
Lines	8-63
Linn	6G-15
Linnemann	1D-11
Little, P.E.	6A-1
Little, S.	5F-1
Litton	2A-20
Lloyd-Jones	1BA-93, 1F-29, 2C-3, 2E-14, 2G-38, 6A-46, 6E-24, 6H-21
Loane	2A-32, 4A-11
Lockett	7H-15
Lockspeiser	7J-28
Lockyer	2B-27
Loetscher	3A-27
Lofting	8-19
Logsdon	1BA-100
Long	5E-10
Longyear	7I-37
Lovelace	4D-12
Lowens	7I-11
Lowith	7D-24
Lowrie	4A-59, 7G1-72
Lowry	7G2-3
Ludwigson	2H-4
Luther	1BB-150, 2A-3, 2A-4, 2A-5, 2C-14, 4A-60, 4C-27
Lyall	2G-39, 3D-12, 3D-43, 3D-44
Lynch	7F3-58
Lynn	6F-19
Lyons	6I-7
McCann	6H-9
McCloskey	8-6, 8-25
McCluskey, N.G.	6F-21
McCluskey, S.J.	6F-21
McCord	3B-4
McCormack	5D-8
McCutchan	4D-13
McDonald	1F-15, 6B-21
McGavren	3D-13, 3D-14, 3D-45
McIntyre	7D-21
McKenzie	6G-13
McLaughlin	6J-8
McLuhan	7E-7, 7F3-56, 7F4-5
McNeil	3D-46

MacDonald, G.	7A-64, 8-16	Mathison	6M-4
MacDonald, W.	7G2-3	Mauser	1BB-152
MacGregor	1A-40	Maves	6G-6, 6H-2
Machaut	7L-4	Mawson	3C-24
Machen	1BB-15, 1BB-66,	May, E.	5D-5
	1F-13, 2A-26,	May, E.G.	1EB-10
	2B-28, 2C-5,	Mayer	3A-28, 3B-12
	2D-31, 2E-15,	Mayo	6J-19
	6A-10, 6A-47,	Mayor	1BB-108, 1BB-114
	6A-48, 6C-3,	Mead	3B-13
	7D-6	Mehl	2C-25, 4B-25
Machlis	7J-5	Mehta	6C-22
Macintosh	2D-23	Meiss	7G1-76
Mackay	6C-50, 6D-1,	Meissner	6G-1
	6E-25	Mellers	7I-26
MacKinnon	5A-41	Melville	7A-33, 7A-34,
Mackintosh	6C-10		8-50
MacLeish	7F1-4	Mendel	7J-14
Macmillan	4D-3	Mendelssohn	7L-35
MacNeice	7C-17	Meng	6G-18
MacQuarrie	6C-14	Menotti	7L-46
Magurie	7H-16	Merchant	7F2-10
Mahler	7L-41	Messenger	4D-1
Maier	1BA-92	Metzger	1BA-10, 1BB-26
Malamud	7A-32	Meyer	1BA-42
Male	7G1-73	Mickelsen	1D-5, 6F-22
Manhattan	6L-9	Miegge	6L-14
Manley	1BA-11, 1BA-46,	Mikolaski	2B-29
	1BB-25, 1F-14,	Miles, O.T.	4-27
	2G-15, 2H-1	Miles, R.H.	7J-35
Manning	4D-11	Miller, Alexander	2E-17
Manson	2A-42	Miller, Arthur	7F1-8
Manwarning	4-25	Miller, H.M.	5B-14
March	2G-40	Miller, W.L.	6J-37
Margenau	6D-14	Miller, W.R.	7K-6
Maritain	4A-61, 6F-20,	Milligan	1EB-11
	7G1-74	Millin	7G2-3
Marle	1D-7	Mills	7B1-60
Marsh	2F-4	Milne	8-59
Marshall, C.	4-26, 4A-12,	Milton	7B2-12, 7C-14
	8-84, 8-104	Minchin	7G2-7
Marshall, I.H.	2E-16, 2H-32	Minear	1D-6, 2H-28
Marshall, M.H.	7F2-4	M'Intyre	4C-28
Marshall, P.	4A-62	Mitchell, Basil	6B-27
Martin, H.	1BA-89, 7C-3	Mitchell, Broadus	6J-9
Martin, J.J.	7F5-10	Mitchell, D.	7J-20
Martin, R.P.	1BB-91, 1BB-151	Mitchell, L.	6J-9
Martin, W.R.	6M-12	Mitchell, S.	7G1-17
Marvin	7K-18	Mixter	2B-15, 6E-13
Marx	7B2-18	Moberg, D.O.	2G-40, 5B-2
Mascall	6C-32, 6D-2	Moberg, W.	5A-42
Masini	7G1-75	Moffatt	1A-16
Masters	7K-19	Mohrmann	1EB-15, 7G2-8

Molesworth	7G1-51	Murray, A.	2F-7, 4-30,
Montagu	5E-11, 6E-28		4C-29, 4C-55
Montefiore	1BB-153	Murray, I.	4A-64
Monteverdi	7L-11	Murray, J.	1BA-113, 1BB-72,
Montgomery	3A-8		1F-31, 2B-30,
Monti	7G1-77		2C-7, 2D-11,
Moore	5C-7		2D-51, 2E-18,
Moreau	1D-18		2E-19, 2G-13,
Morey	7G1-78		4B-13, 5A-16
Morgan, G.C.	1BB-154, 2D-9	Murray, K.	7H-16
Morgan, K.W.	3E-15	Murray, L.	7G1-28
Morgenthau	6J-24	Murray, P.	7G1-28
Morgenstern	7I-17	Myers	7I-15
Morris, H.M.	1BA-40	Myrdal	6K-18
Morris, L.	1BA-52, 1BB-42,		
	1BB-54, 1BB-75,	Narramore	4B-41, 4B-42,
	1BB-98, 1BB-99,		4B-43, 6H-16,
	1BB-124, 1BB-155,		6H-33
	2D-3, 2D-8,	Nash, D.F.E.	5F-15
	2D-14, 2D-15,	Nash, E.J.H.	4-31
	2D-21, 2F-5,	Natanson	7G1-10, 7G1-19
	2G-12, 2H-21,	Nathan	7F-2
	4-28, 6C-51	Naylor	5B-20
Morrison, F.	2D-5	Nedoncelle	6B-4
Morrison, J.M.	6C-20	Nee	4C-56, 4C-57
Moseley	7A-35, 7B1-61	Neil	2D-52, 7G1-4
Moser	7J-9	Neill	1D-2, 2E-20,
Mott	6I-6		3D-15, 6A-13
Motyer	1BB-92, 1F-30,	Nettl	7I-38
	2H-33	Neufeld	3B-14
Moule, C.F.	1BB-16, 2C-26,	Newbigin	2G-14, 2G-39
	2C-27, 2D-49	Newlin	7J-27
Moule, H.C.	1BB-71, 1BB-83,	Newman, E.	7J-25
	1BB-93, 1BB-94,	Newman, J.	7I-39
	2D-50, 2F-6,	Newman, J.H.	4C-30, 7B2-13
	4A-13	Newman, W.	7I-40
Moulton	1BB-4	Newton, E.	7G1-4
Mounce	1BB-125	Newton, F.	7I-41
Mow	4B-19	Newton, J.	4A-65, 4C-41
Mozart	7L-28, 7L-29,	Nicholas of Cusa	4C-58
	7L-30	Nichols, J.H.	3A-23
Muelder	5A-28	Nichols, S.	5F-16
Mueller	7B1-35	Nicholson, D.H.	7C-2
Muller	1BB-95	Nicholson, N.	7B1-43
Mullins, D.	4B-40	Nicoll	1BB-36
Mullins, M.	4B-40	Nida	1D-16, 1D-17,
Munby	6K-6, 6K-11,		3E-11, 7E-5
	7B1-5	Niebuhr	2C-13, 5B-15,
Munger	4-29		5B-19, 6C-7,
Munz	7G1-36		6C-9, 7D-27,
Murch	6F-23		7D-28, 7E-10,
Murphy, R.	8-36		7F5-11
Murphy, R.D.	6I-10	Nikhilananda	3E-36

Niles	6C-52	Paine	7B2-17
Nix	1BA-10	Palestrina	7L-7
Nixon	1BB-156	Palisca	7I-42
Norden	6K-23	Palmer	4-32
Norman, J.	7G1-79	Panoch	6F-24
Norman, T.	7G1-79	Panofsky	7G2-11
Norton, M.	8-24	Pardington	2A-44
Norton, P.L.	5C-8	Paris	6L-8
Noss, J.B.	3E-7	Parker, E.C.	7F4-8, 7F4-9
Noss, L.	4D-9	Parker, G.H.	3A-15
Nye, R.B.	7B2-9	Parker, T.H.	2D-30, 4A-5
Nye, T.M.	7H-17	Parry	1BB-102
Nygren	2G-15, 2G-16	Parson	3C-27
Nyquist	1C-12	Parsons, M.	4B-43
		Parsons, T.	5E-12
Oates	6G-20, 6H-4	Pascal	4C-31
Obrecht	7L-5	Paterson	4-33
Ockegem	7L-5	Paton	7A-37
O'Connor	7A-36	Patrick	4D-19
Oden	6H-20	Pattison	6G-17
Oehler	1BA-19	Pauk	2A-45
Oetting	3A-42	Paul	3D-47, 6J-39
Ogletree	6C-16	Pauly	7I-43
Okun	6K-13	Payne, D.F.	2B-33
Oldham	1C-9	Payne, J.B.	2H-23
Olford	5A-43	Peerman	6C-30
Olmstead	3A-26	Peers	4C-32
Onasch	7G1-14	Pelikan	6L-23, 7E-12
Oraison	6G-11	Pemberton	5A-29
Orr, James	1BA-4, 1BB-9,	Penderecki	7L-49
	1F-16, 2A-17,	Pentecost	2F-10
	2C-5, 2D-31,	Perone	6J-40
	6A-22, 7D-4	Perotin	7L-4
Orr, J.E.	2B-31	Pepys	4A-35
Orr, John	7D-17	Perry	3E-3
Orr, W.W.	2H-34, 3C-25,	Peterson	4A-14
	4B-44, 5A-44,	Petter	7H-18
	5A-45, 6H-34	Pevsner	7G2-1, 7G2-4
Orwell	7B1-1	Pfatteicher	4D-1, 4D-2
Osborne	7F1-11	Pfeiffer	1BA-29, 1BA-36,
Osment	6J-38		1BA-57, 1EA-9
Ott	6L-11	Phenix	6F-25
Otto	3E-37	Philip	2E-25
Outler	2A-15, 4A-37,	Philipson	7G1-33
	6H-22	Phillip	2D-53
Owen	2A-13, 2D-36,	Phillips, J.B.	1A-18, 1A-19,
	2F-8		6A-2, 6A-51
		Phillips, McC.	6I-3
Pache	2F-9	Phipps	2G-42
Packer	1F-17, 1F-32,	Pierce	2C-28
	2A-43, 2B-32,	Pierson	4A-15
	3C-26	Pieters	1BA-38
Padwick	4A-66	Pike	6A-5

Pincherle	7J-11
Pink	1BA-50, 1BA-114, 2B-34, 2E-21
Pinnock	1F-33, 6A-7
Piper	4B-12, 5A-19
Plantinga	6B-20
Plumb	7G1-28
Plummer, A.	1BB-50
Plummer, J.	7G1-16
Pollard	6E-5, 6E-12
Pollock	3D-48, 4A-16, 4A-17
Polman	6C-53
Pope, H.	1A-41
Pope, L.	6K-12
Popham	7G1-34
Porcher	7G1-16
Potter	8-2
Poulenc	7L-44, 7L-45
Powell	6K-4
Prabhavananda	3E-38
Preus	2C-6
Price, D.K.	6J-15
Price, E.	8-103
Prime	4-34, 5F-17, 8-125
Prior	2E-26, 3C-28, 6K-24
Pritchared	1EA-10, 1EA-11
Proksh	7F5-14
Pruyser	6G-3
Puppi	7G1-42
Quiller-Couch	7B1-2
Quoist	4C-33
Rackham	1BB-61
Radcliffe	7J-36
Radhakrishan	3E-17, 3E-39
Raffaele	7G1-32
Rahner	6L-10
Rahtjen	5B-9
Raines	3C-29
Ramm	1D-4, 1F-18, 2A-45, 2H-17, 6A-19, 6A-20, 6D-4, 6E-7
Ramsey, D.	8-126
Ramsey, I.T.	6B-22, 6B-28, 6B-31
Ramsey, P.	5A-30, 5E-13, 7B1-47
Ramsey, W.	1BB-51, 1BB-62, 1BB-67, 1BB-79, 1BB-126, 1EB-12, 3A-9
Raskin	6J-26
Rasmussen	5B-17
Rattenbury	4D-11
Rauschenbusch	5B-4, 6C-6
Rawlings	8-48
Read	3D-49, 7G1-15
Redpath	6H-35
Reed	6H-36
Rees, J.	2G-43
Rees, T.	3C-30
Reese	7I-21, 7I-22
Reid, A.	1C-24
Reid, J.C.	8-68
Reider	1BA-47
Reimers	5E-14
Renwick	3A-43, 3A-44
Reston	6I-9
Reu	1D-28
Reumann	1A-42
Reynolds	4D-8
Rhodes, F.H.T.	6E-27
Rhodes, J.	2A-46
Rice, B.K.	5D-6, 6K-5
Rice, D.T.	7G1-11, 7G1-80
Rich, L.	7K-28
Richards	7G2-10
Richardson	6C-31
Richmond	6B-36
Ridderbos	1BB-43, 1BB-80, 1BB-157, 6C-54, 6E-28
Ridenour	8-96, 8-97
Ridout	2F-11
Rieff	6G-19
Rieu, C.H.	1A-22
Rieu, E.V.	1A-23
Rinker	3C-31, 4-36, 4-37, 4-38, 8-102
Risenfeld	1BB-158
Rivers	7K-21
Rizk	4D-26
Roberts	3D-16, 6B-33, 6G-4
Robertson, A.	7I-19, 7I-44, 7J-37
Robertson, A.T.	1BB-37, 1BB-96
Robertson, E.	6C-55
Robinson, C.	5A-46
Robinson, D.	2H-35
Robinson, G.	4-39
Robinson, G.E.	3D-37

Robinson, H.	1A-43, 1BA-115
Robinson, J.A.	1BB-84, 2C-29, 5A-31, 5A-32, 6C-17, 6C-18, 6C-56
Robinson, J.M.	1D-20
Robinson, W.R.	7F3-62
Rodgers	1F-19
Rodman	7C-18
Rokeach	6G-22
Rooy	3D-50
Rose	7H-19
Rosenber	7F3-54
Rosenberg	7G1-3, 7G1-38, 7G2-4
Roseveare	3D-51
Ross, A.	1BB-109
Ross, K.N.	5A-47, 6M-14, 6M-15
Routley	3B-15, 4D-4, 4D-10, 4D-14, 4D-20, 7I-10, 7I-13
Rowell	3C-32
Runia	1F-20
Ruoff	3C-33
Rushdoony	6B-37, 6C-57, 6D-17
Russell, Carol	7F5-5
Russell, Cazzie	8-83
Russell, F.	7G1-35
Russell, S.	6G-36
Russoli	7G1-28
Rutenborn	7F1-18
Rutherford	4C-34
Ryden	4D-6
Ryle	1BA-116, 2A-19, 2E-22, 4A-67
Ryrie	6C-58
Saalman	7G2-3
Sachs	7I-31
St. John	8-75
Salinger	7A-38, 7A-65
Salmi	7G1-16
Salmon	6L-5
Salten	8-34
Salvina	7G1-51
Salzman	7I-45
Samuel	3C-34
Sandburg	8-65
Sanders	3C-35, 4-40, 6M-5, 6M-16
Sangster	4-41, 4-42, 4-43, 6K-25
Santoyana	7G1-81
Sargent	3D-52
Sauer	1BA-20, 2C-9, 2H-5, 2H-6, 2H-7, 4-44
Saunders	3D-53
Savage	4-45
Sayers	7B1-10, 7B1-13, 7F1-2
Scanzoni	8-99
Schaeffer	6A-29
Schaff	3A-6, 3B-16, 7D-8
Schaller	5C-9
Scharlemann	2C-10
Scharpff	3C-36
Schauffler	7J-23
Schein	7L-12
Schell	1C-13, 1C-16
Schep	2H-18
Schifrin	7K-22
Schilling	6E-11
Schlatter	2G-17
Schleiermacher	6C-5
Schlemmer	6G-37
Schmemann	3A-11
Scholes	7I-16, 7J-3
Schonfield	1A-24
Schoolland	8-69, 8-123
Schoonhoven	2H-36
Schott	7G1-29
Schrade	7J-8
Schreivogel	7F6-2
Schuller	5C-10
Schulz	7F6-11, 7F6-12, 7F6-13, 7F6-14
Schultz	1BA-5, 1BA-21
Schutz	7L-13, 7L-14
Schwantes	1BA-7
Schwartz	7H-20
Schwarz	6G-15
Schweitzer	7J-15
Schweizer	2G-18
Schwiekert	3A-20
Scorer	5A-8, 6G-24, 6G-32, 6G-33
Scott, L.G.	4B-45
Scott, N.A.	2H-37, 7A-66, 7B-27, 7B1-15, 7B1-27, 7B1-28, 7B1-62, 7C-10,

	7F2-7, 7F3-53	Slive	7G1-37, 7G2-4
Scougal	4C-59	Small	4B-4, 4B-11
Scudder	4B-16	Smalley, B.	1D-1
Scully	7G2-3	Smalley, S.S.	7H-23
Seamands	3C-37	Smalley, W.A.	3D-17, 3E-11
Seay	7I-20	Smart, J.D.	1D-15, 6F-29
Selwyn	1BB-115	Smart, N.	3E-41
Semenzata	7G1-82	Smeaton	2F-12
Sen	3E-40	Smethurst	6D-12
Sendak	8-8, 8-9	Smith, G.A.	1EB-13
Seredy	8-30	Smith, G.E.	7H-24
Sessions	7I-46	Smith, H.S.	3A-27
Seuss	8-7	Smith, H.W.	4C-50
Sewall	7B1-22	Smith, R.G.	6C-59
Shands	7H-21	Smith, T.L.	5B-5
Shannon	8-32	Smith, W.M.	2H-22
Shaw	7F1-10	Smith, W.S.	2D-18
Shawn	7F4-8	Smits	2C-6
Shearer	3D-54	Smythe	7F4-8
Shedd	2G-44	Snaith	1A-2
Sheldon	8-85	Snider	6K-8
Shelly	1F-34, 3A-29	Synder	1D-22
Sherrill	6F-27, 6M-17	Solomon	7F1-18
Shideler	7B1-63, 7B1-64	Soper	2B-16
Shippey	3C-38, 5C-11	Sorauf	6J-1
Shoemaker	3C-39	Sorell	7F5-15
Short, A.H.	1EB-22	Soria	7G2-4
Short, A.R.	6A-4, 6D-10,	Souchal	7G1-23
	6E-29	Souter	1BB-27
Short, R.L.	7F6-1, 7F6-3,	Southard	3C-40
	7F6-7	Spanner	6E-30
Silberman	5E-16	Spark	7A-39
Simeon	4C-35	Sparrow	7B2-11
Simmon	8-120	Speaight	7F2-5
Simms	4-46	Speare	8-47
Simon, A.	5D-3	Spellman	7K-7
Simon, P.	5D-1, 6K-3	Speshock	7A-67
Simonson	7F4-3	Spittler	6M-6
Simpson, E.K.	1BB-85	Spurgeon	3C-41
Simpson, G.E.	5E-17	Spryi	8-15
Simpson, J.A.	2D-54	Stackhouse	6J-41
Simpson, P.C.	2D-3	Stahlin	2G-19
Simpson, R.	7I-28	Stainer	7L-38
Singer	6B-38, 7D-10,	Stalker	2D-2, 4A-69
	7D-11, 7D-12,	Stanley	2G-20
	7D-13	Stauffer	3A-9
Sinnott	7H-22	Steele	2C-30
Sissel	6K-10	Steere	7I-1
Sizer	6F-28	Steeves	1C-18
Skilton	1BB-116	Steinbeck	7A-40, 8-52,
Skornia	7F4-2		8-53
Slater	3E-8	Steiner	7F4-1
Slaughter	4A-68	Stendahl	1D-13, 2G-45

Stephen	7B2-15	Tasker	1BB-45, 1BB-55,
Stevens	7I-6, 7I-19,		1BB-76, 1BB-110,
	7I-44		1BB-161,
Stevenson, R.	7I-9		1BB-162, 2B-36
Stevenson, R.L.	8-49, 8-61	Tawney	6K-26
Stewart, C.W.	6G-4	Taylor, Mrs. H.	4A-19, 8-87
Stewart, J.S.	2D-55, 2E-22	Taylor, H.	4A-19, 5B-33,
Stewart, R.	7A-41, 7B1-30		8-72
Stewart, R.A.	1BB-159	Taylor, J.	3D-45, 4C-36
Stibbs	1BA-27, 1BA-117,	Taylor, J.C.	7G1-84
	1BB-32, 1BB-117,	Taylor, J.R.S.	2A-47
	1C-7, 1C-9,	Taylor, J.V.	3D-55
	2D-12, 2D-56,	Taylor, John B.	1BA-118
	2D-57, 2D-58,	Taylor, K.	8-121, 8-122
	2D-59, 2D-60,	Taylor, K.N.	3C-47
	2D-61, 2F-18,	Taylor, M.F.	7F5-16, 7F5-17,
	2G-20, 2G-46,		7F5-18
	2G-47, 2G-48,	Taylor, M.G.	4A-20
	4-47	Taylor, M.J.	6F-30
Stob	7D-14	Taylor, V.	2D-19, 2D-22
Stoeffler	3A-24	Teasdale	8-58
Stone, I.	7G1-31	Teilhard de Chardin	6E-14
Stone, N.	8-76	Temple	6B-17
Stone, N.J.	2B-35	Tennant	6B-18
Stonehouse	1BB-28, 1BB-41,	Tenney	1BA-2, 1BB-10,
	1BB-44, 1F-21,		1BB-30, 1BB-31,
	4A-18		1BB-56, 1BB-128,
Stott	1BB-29, 1BB-118,		2D-17, 2H-15
	1BB-127, 1BB-160,	ter Kuile	7G2-4
	2A-32, 2C-31,	Terry, C.D.	7J-38
	2F-19, 2G-49,	Terry, M.S.	1D-2
	3C-42, 3C-43,	Teselle	7B1-41
	3C-44, 4-48,	Thass-Thienemann	1D-26
	4-49, 4-50, 6A-52	Thelen	5F-5
Strachan	3C-45, 3D-18	Theobald	5D-12
Stravinsky	7L-47	Thibaut	5F-12
Stringfellow	5C-12	Thiele	1BA-58
Strobucha	7G1-15	Thielicke	2A-48, 4B-12,
Strunk	6G-2		4C-37, 5A-33
Styron	7A-42	Thomas, C.C.	2C-30
Subilia	6L-17	Thomas, D.W.	1EA-12
Summerlin	7K-23, 7K-24	Thomas, I.	4-57
Summers, J.	8-117	Thomas, J.G.	8-109
Summerson	7G2-4	Thomas, J.H.	6C-60
Sundkler	3D-17	Thomas, W.H.G.	2A-27, 2D-62,
Suzuki	3E-18		2F-13
Sweazley	3C-46	Thompson, F.	7C-19
Sweeney	7G1-83	Thompson, J.A.	1BA-119
Swete	1BB-48	Thompson, J.G.S.S.	1BA-120, 2D-16
		Thompson, K.W.	6J-25
Tabard	7G1-49	Thomsen	3E-19
Tanis	6M-7	Thuyen	3C-48
Tapie	7G2-17	Tilak	3E-42

Tillich	6C-13, 6C-35, 6C-61, 6J-42, 7E-15
Tilson	5E-18
Toesca	7G1-13
Tolkien	7A-43, 7A-68, 8-55
Tolstoy	7A-44, 7A-45, 7F1-9
Torrance, J.B.	6E-31
Torrance, T.F.	2G-3, 2H-38
Toulmin	6B-29
Tournier	4B-7, 6G-10, 6H-37, 6H-38, 6H-39, 6H-40, 6H-41, 6H-42, 6H-43, 6H-44
Towers, B.	6C-62
Towns	2G-50
Townsend	4A-70
Tozer	2C-32, 4C-38, 4-52, 4-53, 7C-2
Traina	1C-5
Travers	8-27
Trecker, A.R.	5F-2
Trecker, H.B.	5F-2
Treece	8-79
Trench	1BB-12, 1BB-163, 1BB-164
Tresmontant	6B-13
Trobisch	4A-36, 8-105
Troeltsch	5B-21
Tucker	6J-20
Turnell	7B1-65
Turner	1BB-153
Twain	8-37
Tweedie	6H-17
Tyndale	2A-8
Unger	1BA-14, 1BA-35, 1BA-98, 1EB-14
Unterkircher	7G1-16
Unwin	8-118
Updike	7A-46
Utterback	5F-3
Vahanian	7B1-31
Valsecchi	7G1-86
Van Baalen	6M-13
Van Buren	6C-27
Van der Heuvel	2G-21
van der Meer	1EB-15, 7G2-8
Van der Ziel	6E-1, 6E-4
Van Dusen	6C-4
Van Elderen	1BB-103
Van Oyen	6K-15
Van Riessen	6B-39
van Ruler	5A-48
Van Til, C.	6A-24, 6C-63, 7D-2
Van Til, H.R.	7E-9
Varah	2C-33
Vassaday	2G-51
Vaughan	1A-44
Vaughan Williams, R.	7L-43
Vaughan Williams, U.	7J-29
Verdi	7L-37
Verhoeven	3E-16
Vermes	1EA-15
Viarda	7G1-85
Vicedom	3E-9
Victoria	7L-9
Vidler	3A-45
Vincent	1BB-38
Vischer	6K-27
Visser,'t Hooft	3E-10, 7G1-39
Von Campenhausen	3A-35
Von Loewenich	6L-17
Von Simson	7G2-12
Von Weissacker	6D-15
Vos, C.F.	8-114, 8-115
Vos, G.	2A-25, 2H-39
Vos, H.F.	3E-4
Vos, J.G.	6A-53
Vos, N.	7F2-8
Waddams	5B-34
Wagner	7J-25
Walker, G.S.M.	3A-13
Walker, H.B.	6G-10
Walker, W.	3A-3
Wallace, Robert	7G1-32, 7G1-38
Wallace, R.S.	1BA-58
Wallis	3D-19, 8-93, 8-94
Walls	1BB-52, 1BB-119
Walsh, C.	7C-8
Walsh, T.	7C-4
Walter	6J-16
Walvoord	1BB-129, 1F-22, 2F-14, 2H-11
Ward	2H-40
Ware	6L-24
Warfield	1F-23, 1F-35, 2A-6, 2A-23, 2B-37, 2D-34, 2E-23, 6A-54, 7D-5

Warner	8-70	Wiebe	7A-48, 7A-69
Warns	2G-22	Wienandt	7I-5
Washington	5E-19	Wigglesworth	7B2-10
Waterink	6F-31	Wigman	7F5-19
Watkins	4C-39	Wilder, A.N.	5B-35, 7B1-29
Watson, D.	2C-34	Wilder, L.I.	8-21
Watson, D.C.K.	1C-12	Wilder, T.	7A-49
Watson, T.	4C-40	Wiles	2A-49
Watts	1A-48, 1BA-87	Wilkerson	8-89
Weatherhead	5A-9, 6H-45	Williams, C.	7A-50, 7A-51,
Webb, G.	7G2-4		7A-70, 7A-71,
Webb, J.F.	4C-61		7A-72
Webb, M.S.	5B-8	Williams, C.B.	1A-28
Webb, P.C.	8-66	Williams, C.K.	1A-29
Webber	3C-49, 5C-13	Williams, E.	3C-50
Weber, E.	6J-22	Williams, G.H.	3A-22
Weber, M.	6J-43, 6J-44,	Williams, H.M.	5A-5
	6K-19	Williams, M.	7K-8
Webster	2D-63	Williams, N.P.	2B-39
Weeks	6L-18	Williams, T.	7F1-15
Wegener	1A-45	Williamson, M.	3D-56, 5B-12
Weinstock	7J-4	Williamson, R.C.	4B-28
Weisinger	7B1-24	Williamson, R.deV.	6J-6
Weiss	3A-46	Wilson, D.C.	4A-21, 4A-22
Weitzmann	7G1-14	Wilson, E.	6L-4
Weller	6G-38	Wilson, W.	7G1-4
Wenham	1BA-121	Winslow	2F-20
Werner	7J-24	Winter, D.	2G-53, 6K-28
Wescott	1BB-57	Winter, G.	3C-51, 4B-22,
Wesley	4A-37, 4C-41,		5C-14
	4C-42	Winter, Sister M.T.	7K-25, 7K-26
West, M.	7A-47	Wirt	5B-3
West, P.	7B1-9	Wiseman	1BA-122
Westcott	1BB-107, 1BB-120	Witherington	6F-32, 6H-10
Westermann	1D-25, 2B-38	Wittkower	7F2-16, 7F2-18
Westrup	7I-33, 7J-10	Wold	3D-57
Weymouth	1A-27	Wolff	1BA-95, 5E-26,
Weyres	7H-25		6G-39
Whannel	7F3-57	Wolters	4C-62
Whitcomb	1BA-40, 1BA-80,	Wollerstorff	6F-20, 6J-45
	6D-18	Wood, A.S.	1D-29, 2H-9,
White, A.D.	6E-32		3A-25
White, D.M.	7F6-8	Wood, D.	1D-1
White, E.	4B-2, 6G-9, 6H-11	Wood, F.P.	3C-52
White, E.B.	8-20	Wood, J.	2G-54
White, E.W.	7J-30	Wood, M.A.P.	3C-53, 6H-46
White, J.F.	7H-26	Wood, S.	1C-6
White, P.H.	8-74	Woodhouse	7B1-33
White, T.H.	8-39	Woods	6A-55
Whitefield	2A-16	Workman	3A-47
Whittemore	2G-52, 4D-3	Wouk	8-90
Whittle	7F3-55	Wren-Lewis	6A-56
Whyte	5F-4	Wright, B.F.	6J-10

Wright, G.E.	1BA-18, 1BA-25, 1EA-13, 1EB-16, 1EB-17
Wright, J.S.	1BA-59, 1BB-165, 1D-30, 1F-36
Wunderlich, L.	2F-21
Wunderlich, R.E.	7G1-87
Wurth	6C-64
Wynbeck	4A-23
Wynn	4B-17, 4B-26, 4B-31
Yarnold	6E-8
Yates	7B1-66
Yinger	5E-17
Young, E.J.	1BA-15, 1BA-26, 1BA-72, 1BA-79, 1BA-123, 1BA-124, 1BA-125, 1BA-126, 1BA-127, 1F-37
Young, J.M.L.	2B-40
Young, R.	1BB-5
Young, W.C.	6B-11
Younger	5C-15
Zander	5F-9
Zeller	7G1-51
Zimmer	3E-43
Zimmerman	7J-10
Zuidema	6B-40, 6B-41
Zylstra	6F-33, 7B1-37